COURTROOM GLADIATOR

Albert J. Mestemaker is co-author of *Anderson's Ohio Criminal Practice and Procedure* (1978, 4th ed., 2000) and author of the *Ohio Search Warrant Manual* (1997, 4th ed., 2000), also by Anderson Publishing Company.

Judge Albert J. Mestemaker, 1981

ALBERT J. MESTEMAKER

COURTROOM GLADIATOR

*Best Wishes
Judge Mike Mestemaker
Buffalo, Wyoming 2001*

Brandenburg Publications, Ltd.
Cincinnati, Ohio

Published by Brandenburg Publications, Ltd.
Cincinnati, Ohio

Cover design: Mark Eberhard
Cover portrait of author: Dave Warren
Manuscript preparation: Elizabeth Siegert
Book design: Eberhard + Eberhard
Production and marketing: PSA Consulting, Inc.
Printing: John S. Swift Co., Inc.

This book is printed on acid-free paper in the United States of America.
August 2000
First Edition

ISBN: 0-9703579-0-7
ISBN: 0-9703579-1-5 limited edition

For purchasing information, see www.courtroomgladiator.com.

Mail orders to Courtroom Gladiator, Brandenburg Publications, Ltd., PO Box 41, North Bend OH 45052.

This work is dedicated to three of the most important women in my life:

To my mother, Jean Frances, who besides being the world's greatest mom in my eyes, provided the moral training that has formed the life-long habits of her three children.

To my wife, Judy, my partner in every endeavor, who in addition to being my wonderful wife has always stood by me without question or judgment.

Finally to my great grandmother, Maria Catherina grafin von Spaunhorst, for being so brave in 1855 as to leave her native land in western Prussia and journey to America to marry my great grandfather. She was the glue that held the family together during the early years in Cincinnati. It is from her own writings that I learned of the phrase coined by the Reverend Martin Luther while he was in residence at Wartburg Castle.

"There I stood, what else could I do."

Albert J. Mestemaker
Former Judge
Cincinnati, Ohio
2000

INTRODUCTION

In the later days of the Roman Empire, the most popular spectator sport involved bloody battles fought in a public arena between two or more armed combatants known as gladiators. It was a popular belief among Romans that such contests, which were often fought to the death, promoted Roman ideals of discipline and courage.

Although many gladiators came from the ranks of captive slaves and the conquered of the empire, the profession did attract a limited number from the highest social classes — including one Roman emperor, Commodus. Probably the most famous of all of the gladiators was Spartacus, an ex-slave who led a nearly successful revolt against Roman authority, finally dying in battle in 71 B.C.

Today, Spartacus may well choose to train to be a trial lawyer, where he could perform and perfect his skills in almost daily combat. He would do well in the arena of the modern courtroom — where discipline, mental toughness, a quick mind, and aggressiveness are considered the highest of virtues.

Gladiators were trained in imperial academies where the curriculum was demanding and the failure rates high. Similarly, today's American law schools, especially the few remaining evening institutions, can be successfully navigated only by those whose desire to succeed is reminiscent of the gladiatorial qualities of dedication, discipline, and desire.

Most gladiator contests were one-to-one matches in the same manner observed in modern courtrooms — where two lawyers square off with each other to do mental combat, seeking victory on behalf of their clients.

Today, the trial judge serves much in the same capacity as the emperor did at the games — by overseeing the tournament and enforcing the rules of the contest. Likewise, jurors serve in a capacity similar to the Roman spectators — indicating their preference through the written verdict in place of the ancient thumbs up or thumbs down but, nevertheless, choosing one side over the other.

I did not come from a family of lawyers. I came from a family of businessmen and women who possessed a keen German-American work ethic, religious beliefs and a sense of fairness and justice that saw most decisions in black or white with very little gray area in between. Ambivalence didn't have much of a chance where I grew up.

My period of training to become a courtroom gladiator commenced in the fall of 1962 at the old YMCA evening law school named for Salmon P. Chase, secretary of the Treasury under Abraham Lincoln, chief justice of the United States (1864-1873), and Cincinnati native. This training program required attendance at evening classes three nights each week, 48 weeks a year, for four years — supplemented by an equal amount of out-of-class preparation — all after a full day of work as a Treasury agent.

By June 1966, the four years of classroom training were finally completed. In July of that year, the Ohio bar examination was conquered. My swearing-in ceremony was held in October. It was followed shortly by the most welcome break of all, an appointment as an assistant criminal trial lawyer in what was then the most prestigious law office in existence, the Hamilton County prosecutor's staff under the leadership of Prosecutor Melvin G. Rueger.

The next 30 years my life was devoted to daily combat in the arena of this public edifice, first as a lawyer and assistant prosecutor (1967-1981) and later as a judge (1981-1996). For those 30 years, I traversed the halls of the Hamilton County Courthouse in the belief that there was much more there in the way of good than there could ever be in the way of bad. I still believe that, despite all that has been rendered archaic by the gradual changes that have strained our concept of idealism and honor.

During those 30 years, I have witnessed the end of the old common law days and the adoption of the rules and social engineering that provoke many lawyers and judges to lament the passing of the old times. I witnessed the coming of new civil and criminal rules, domestic relations rules, juvenile rules, rules of professional conduct, gender rules, civil rights, tort reform, contract safeguards, product liability issues, elderly care issues, gender bias issues, harassment issues, and women's reproductive health issues — just to name a few of the many changes designed, as we have been told, to make our society more caring and more in tune with today's value systems.

Simultaneously, we witnessed a wildly fluctuating adult crime rate and an escalating juvenile rate. We have presided over the near destruction of the American family, the banishment of God from our public institutions, and a general lack of respect for each other and for ourselves.

I started out in an era when a young, over-zealous lawyer could be locked up by an irate and exasperated senior judge and ended up in an era where a judge can be removed from office for telling an unmarried couple with a child to quit fighting and either get married or stop seeing each other altogether.

When I started in this profession, it was cause for suspension if a lawyer dropped his or her card at an accident site. Today, an auto accident victim may receive a dozen or more solicitation letters from local practitioners before being released from the hospital. Much of what society dislikes today about lawyers actually has its beginning in 1977, when the United States Supreme Court ruled in the landmark Arizona lawsuit of John Bates and Van O'Steen, two young Phoenix lawyers who sued the Arizona State Bar Association. The court ruled that lawyers do have a First Amendment freedom of speech right to advertise their services — the same as the local used car lot or furnace repair company.

Once legal advertising became acceptable and protected, legal clinics sprang up all over the country, spending as much as 15 percent of their income on advertising. All one has to do is check the telephone directory to see which lawyer claims to be the best and the least expensive in any given legal specialty.

In Abraham Lincoln's time, lawyers believed that their role was to serve the legal needs of society. In short, lawyers helped people. They acted as society's problem-solvers. Profit was not the main goal, but was rather a by-product of legal services offered to the public. Helping to amicably settle a dispute between neighbors, easing a client's concern about the future with a well-drafted will or trust agreement, or calming the fears of someone who has been sued, has traditionally been what the practice of law was about.

Today, sadly, the practice of law has become a business more than a profession. Large law firms have become shops where the more important considerations are time cards, computer billings, paralegals performing legal services right up to the courtroom door, and outright theft of other law firms' clients.

In 1966, there were 370,000 lawyers. Today, the number is 800,000. In 1966, there was one lawyer for every 640 people. Today, that number has increased so that there is one lawyer for every 305 persons. Today, there are more than 300 law firms nationally that employ 100 or more lawyers, doing an estimated $119 billion a year in billable fees. These are the law firms that annually recruit the cream of the big-name law schools' senior crop with six-figure starting salaries.

In these 30 years, plying my trade first as a trial lawyer and finally as a judge, like any human being, I made mistakes. Unfortunately, the mistakes that I paid the steepest price for were those made as a judge. By January 1996, I had been labeled as "soft" on domestic violence by some and racist by others.

In a span of less than two years, my world collapsed. I had suffered a major heart attack, been defeated for re-election by an unknown lawyer, had open heart surgery, and was reprimanded by the Ohio Supreme Court.

But as time is capable of healing all setbacks, I have refused to give in or to give up. First of all, I made mistakes. Secondly, I said things that should not have been said. Thirdly, I am responsible for my own actions and words.

As General Robert E. Lee, commander of the Confederate army, said after Major General George E. Pickett's failed charge at Gettysburg, the turning point of the Civil War: "This is my fault. It's all my fault."

Perhaps we, as individuals and as a society, need to return to those days when we took full responsibility for our misdeeds and mistakes. If we were to do this, I believe that we would see a tremendous improvement in our attitudes toward life and toward each other. This book represents an effort on my part to set the record straight and to make amends as circumstances dictate.

My research for this work commenced in May 1996. It took me just short of four years to put this story together and to verify its accuracy.

I am a collector and saver, with an appreciation for the raw materials of history and literature. I collect trial transcripts, newspaper articles, photographs, records of exhibits and notes. I save these items and store them wherever I find room. My wife, Judy, has tried to clean our basement storage area numerous times — to no avail, and to her great frustration. My files, mildewed as they may be, are still there. Perhaps, as she believes, full of paper mites that will ultimately fell both of us with fatal respiratory attacks.

But if not for these musty old transcripts and records, it would have been impossible for me to complete this story. Each case, each trial and each incident — funny or sad, good or bad — has as its foundation in the transcript record of who said and did what, who testified, and who was hurt. The newspaper articles have been compared to actual court transcripts, especially in those instances where the media's versions were at odds with my recollection of what was said or ordered.

The milestones of my legal career are all here. The story is not embellished or perfumed. My earnest wish is that it has integrity and will be of general interest. For the student of law, I hope that it will be educational and enlightening.

This work starts with my first experience in our criminal justice system, the trial of Posteal Laskey Jr., accused of being "The Cincinnati Strangler." The story continues with several memorable cases from my days in the prosecutor's office; my experiences as a defense attorney in private practice; and, finally, my service as a judge. In a few instances — in fact, very few — names have been changed out of respect for the privacy of those individuals concerned.

Now, as this part of my journey ends and a new challenge presents itself, I recall two of the more significant days in my life being: January 2, 1967, the day that I walked into the Hamilton County Courthouse as a prosecutor; and January 3, 1996, the day I left — 29 years and one day later.

PART ONE

PROSECUTOR AND DEFENSE COUNSEL

CHAPTER 1

THE CINCINNATI STRANGLER

She was 31 years old and pretty, with black hair and hazel eyes. She was 5-feet, 7-inches tall and weighed 120 pounds. She had long, shapely legs and a small waist. She was a sweater girl, with a natural bathing-suit figure. She had lived in Cincinnati for four years, having moved from Indianapolis, Indiana, in 1962. She was a secretary for Kelly Girl Services, and a member of Saints Peter & Paul United Church of Christ.

She was single and lived alone at 2909 Warsaw Avenue in the Price Hill neighborhood. She lived only three blocks from Cincinnati Police District 3.

It was 2:30 a.m. on a humid Sunday, the 14th of August, 1966. It was dark and moonless and raining hard. She had spent the evening at the Lark Cafe at 3001 Vine Street, near the University of Cincinnati campus. She had called for a cab to take her to her apartment.

Now, she was a mere half-city block from where she lived. She was lying on her back on a storm sewer grate on Ring Place. She was slowly bleeding to death from the five ripping, jagged knife wounds inflicted to the right side of her throat. Her life's blood was mixing with the rain and running into the storm sewer. She and the storm sewer grate were exactly 29 feet from the corner of Ring Place and Grand Avenue. Three feet from her outstretched left arm was a yellow Checker cab, headlights on, driver door open, left front bumper and fender caved in from the force of striking her in the legs and back as she ran desperately up Grand Avenue toward the safety of her apartment. She had been brutally run down by the cab, which bore the number 870 on its sides and trunk. She had fled up Grand Avenue, running out of her blue high-heeled shoes. And as she ran along the sidewalk at the intersection of Grand and Ring Place, she glanced over her shoulder as the taxicab bore down on her from the rear. She ran to the left to escape the oncoming front bumper. She could not out-distance the bulky, box-like vehicle as it slammed into her legs, throwing her to the street and crushing her right ankle and foot.

Now, as she lay bleeding to death, her apartment keys and a $5 bill intended to be used to pay her fare lying next to her, the driver of this cab was running as fast as possible down the wooded hillside that separated Ring Place from Glenway Avenue. He had done something that necessitated a rapid departure. So hurried had been his efforts to get away, he had left the driver's door of the cab open to the rain, which soaked the interior. It obliterated any fingerprints that he may have left behind. As he ran along Ring Place, he had first thrown away his victim's black clutch purse. Then, several doors farther east, he tossed her billfold. He had taken all the money from the billfold except a folded and hidden $1 bill intended by its owner to be used in case of an emergency.

The name of the young woman — who Hamilton County's coroner, Dr. Frank Cleveland, would describe as having been "slaughtered" — was Barbara Bowman. The name of the 29-year-old man who was fleeing the scene of this grizzly incident was Posteal Laskey Jr.

Was Posteal Laskey, in fact, the "Cincinnati Strangler?" Was he the sole perpetrator of 12 assaults on woman in Cincinnati in which seven of the victims had been either strangled or stabbed to death during a 14-month period commencing October 12, 1965, and ending December 9, 1966, when he was arrested at his place of employment? Was Barbara Bowman his only victim — or one of his many victims?

Posteal Laskey not only denied any knowledge or responsibility for any of the attacks, his defense to the Bowman case was that he had an alibi, that he was at home with his mother that Sunday morning in August, 1966, when Barbara Bowman was "slaughtered." In fact, the evidence linking Laskey with all but the murder of Barbara Bowman and the assaults and robberies of Virginia Hinners and Della S. Ernst was so meager that no indictments were sought against him to bring him to trial in those cases. Nevertheless, to this date, 30 years later, the survivors of the slain women remain convinced that Posteal Laskey was their murderer.

Without an admission by Laskey, who remains in prison — having been saved from Ohio's electric chair in 1972 by the United States Supreme Court — it can never be determined beyond a reasonable doubt that he was the Cincinnati Strangler. There will always be those who maintain that he was, and those who argue that he did not kill Lois Dant of Price Hill, Jeanette Messer of Clifton, or Rose Winstel of Vine Street Hill. Regardless of the answer, the assaults, rapes and strangulations ceased after Laskey's arrest. The 14 months of terror (some compared the fear that gripped Cincinnati then with the terror experienced by London in 1888 during the reign of Jack the Ripper or Boston in the early 1960s, when Albert DeSalvo, the "Boston Strangler," stalked women) did not abate until Posteal Laskey was in the custody of Cincinnati police.

If, in fact, Posteal Laskey was the strangler, he was not a serial killer – but, rather, a spree killer, or a killer of opportunity. The Cincinnati Strangler killed when he felt inclined to kill and rape. His perverted sexual appetite achieved complete gratification if he believed his victim was dead. Barbara Bowman was not raped because she refused to die in the rear seat of the Checker cab being driven by Laskey. Once overwhelmed and mortally injured, but still alive, Bowman was at least spared the insult of a sexual assault or rape simply because her throat was slashed and she was lying on a storm sewer grate in pouring rain bleeding to death. But she was not yet dead, and the time for her killer to satisfy his sexual appetite had run out.

Cincinnati's nightmare began at noon on Tuesday, October 12, 1965, when Elizabeth Kreco, a 65-year-old Caucasian woman, was leaving her residence at the Verona Apartments, 2356 Park Avenue in the Walnut Hills neighborhood of Cincinnati. As Kreco, a widow, walked through the courtyard toward the street, she was approached by a slender black man between 25 and 30 years old, about 5-feet, 6-inches tall. He had dark skin and a thin mustache. He was presentably dressed and very polite. The young man calmly asked Ms. Kreco where he might find the building's caretaker. He told her that he had an appointment for a job interview as a janitor for the complex. He asked the unsuspecting woman if she would show him to the caretaker's office. Being a kind, trusting lady, Kreco led this young man into the basement area of the complex via the outside steps.

Once the basement level was reached and it appeared that they were alone, Elizabeth Kreco was punched in the jaw with such force that she nearly lost consciousness. A piece of nylon cord was knotted around her neck, and she was dragged backward into a small bathroom. While lying on the floor, unable to scream or even breathe, her clothing was pushed up.

Her underclothing was then ripped open, and she was raped. To her attacker, she appeared to be dead. Her purse and its contents were strewn on the floor of the bathroom stall, and her money removed from her billfold. It was just past noon when the caretaker entered the building's basement and saw a pair of legs sticking out of the bathroom stall. His call for help, and an ambulance crew saved Elizabeth Kreco's life. She was revived by life squad personnel after removal of the rope ligature from around her neck and administered oxygen. She would remain in the hospital for over a week. She was alive, but her life was permanently changed.

Thirteen days later, on Monday, October 25, 1965, at 7:00 p.m., Margie Helton, a 39-year-old wife and mother left her job in Walnut Hills, exactly four blocks from the Verona Apartments. Just as she began to enter her parked automobile, a young, slender black man with a thin, short goatee approached her and asked for directions to the Alms Hotel. As she started to answer his question, he grabbed her, shoved her into her automobile, and jumped into the rear seat behind her. He whipped a knotted piece of rope over her head and around her throat. As he began to strangle her, he demanded her money. She fumbled in her purse and handed a $10 bill over her shoulder. As the rope tightened around her neck, her assailant reached over the seat back with his left hand and started to fondle her breasts. She leaned forward, jamming her elbows into the steering wheel ring, setting off the horn of her automobile in a loud and constant din. Her assailant screamed at her, "You bitch" and vaulted from the rear seat of her vehicle, leaving the knotted rope around her neck. He ran with tremendous speed and agility a half block before turning into a walkway between two apartment buildings. As in the assault on Elizabeth Kreco, there were no witnesses, just a victim and a piece of knotted rope. The police were not yet of a mind to link these assaults, but that was about to change.

Just before 1:00 p.m. on a crisp, sunny, early winter day, December 2, 1965, 56-year-old Emogene Harrington, the wife of a university professor, parked her station wagon in front of the Clermont Apartments at 1404-1406 East McMillan Street. She had been grocery shopping and wanted the building caretaker to help her carry her groceries to her apartment.

Harrington unlocked the security door to the lobby of the building with her tenant's passkey. She pushed the electric buzzer that was supposed to alert the caretaker, whose work area was directly below the lobby. She tried several times to arouse the elderly man by this method. Finally, becoming impatient and concluding that he might be napping, she abandoned her often vocalized fear of the building's basement and walked to the far end of the hall. She pushed open the door with the words "Caretaker Lower Level" painted on its center panel. She slowly descended the stair case, calling out to the caretaker as she proceeded down into the dimly lighted cellar. She never saw the dark fist that shot out of the shadows, colliding with the right side of her face. She was so stunned by this first blow that she barely felt the blows to her head, face and stomach that quickly followed. She would have no reason after this moment to be concerned about the groceries in her automobile.

About 1:20 p.m., the janitor returned from the errand that he had been assigned to by another tenant. As he walked toward the small bathroom located near his basement work area, he saw what looked like a pair of legs sticking out of the toilet room doorway. As he drew closer, he feared what he might find. He called out, "Who's there?" No one responded. When he was in a position to peer directly into the stall, he was struck with fear and horror. He recognized the badly battered body as Mrs. Harrington. She was lying there on her back, her bruised and bloody face turned to the right. She had been severely beaten. There was a length of plastic rope around her neck pulled so tight that her skin protruded around it. Her body was still warm.

There was a stench present that announced that her assailant had left only moments or even seconds earlier. Her blouse was ripped open. Her breasts were exposed. Her legs were spread apart, and her underwear was pulled down around her knees. The contents of her purse were strewn around her. Her wallet, empty of all currency, was 10 feet from her body, where it had been thrown by a fleeing killer. The police report, in its matter-of-fact language, recorded Emogene Harrington's death as "Homicide by strangulation incident to a rape and robbery."

The Harrington case prompted investigators to conclude they were dealing with one criminal. Two dozen Cincinnati police officers, including 18 members of the Crime Bureau, were assigned to canvass Walnut Hills. The only potential witness in the Harrington case was a young truck driver, who told investigators that he had noticed a nervous-acting, thin black man near the Clermont Apartments around 1:00 p.m. the day Mrs. Harrington was murdered. He described this person as being dark-skinned, about 5-foot-6 to 5-foot-8 and between 150 and 170 pounds. He could not recall if the man had any facial hair. "He just looked out of place and very nervous."

Thirty-seven known sex offenders, including 28-year-old Posteal

Laskey Jr. of 1820 Freeman Avenue, were questioned concerning the death of Emogene Harrington and the assaults on other women. Laskey, who had been arrested on October 9, 1965, for assaulting a young girl in the Clifton area less than 4 miles from the scene of the Harrington murder, was well known to former Police Detective Lytle Young, now a property custodian for the Hamilton County prosecutor's office. "Beanie," as Young was known to his close friends, had arrested Laskey in 1958 for an assault on a woman in the West End. The detective believed that of all the men brought in for questioning in the Harrington slaying, Laskey was the most likely suspect. As Beanie would later tell me, "I told Jackson that Laskey was probably the strangler. They needed to lean on that rotten, little jerk harder than they did." Russell Jackson, who was the chief of homicide for the Cincinnati PD, probably wished later than he had heeded Beanie's advice.

Without eye witnesses, fingerprints or other tangible evidence, all that the investigators could do was continue to canvass the area and warn women to take precautions, especially those who lived alone or those who had to enter hallways or basement areas. Local hardware stores sold out of all types of door and window locks. Local locksmiths and alarm distributors saw a sudden and sizable increase in their business.

Posteal Laskey had been questioned. He was aware that he was on the police list as a possible suspect. He was also aware that East Walnut Hills was being carefully watched and that the residents of that neighborhood were on guard. Perhaps it was time to lay low for a while. Thus, for the next four months, the "strangler" would become the "phantom." But in the late winter of 1966, the strangler struck again. Or did he?

1210 Rutledge Avenue, the location of the Rutledge Apartments, is one door east of Glenway Avenue in Price Hill. Rutledge is a narrow street of apartment buildings and single-family homes that runs downhill from Glenway Avenue to Rapid Run Pike. On Monday, April 4, 1966, about 10:30 a.m., 58-year-old Lois Dant was alone in her first-floor apartment at 1210 Rutledge. Her husband, Frank, was at their church. Lois Dant had been talking on the telephone when a young man knocked on her apartment door looking for the caretaker. Her body was discovered less than 20 minutes later by her husband, who literally fell over her as he entered their apartment. She had been beaten, raped and strangled. One of her nylon stockings was knotted tightly around her neck. She had been punched unconscious, stripped, strangled, and like the others, raped either in her death throes or after death. Beneath her body, homicide investigators found five pieces of mail. Had she been attacked as she returned to her first floor apartment from the hallway mailboxes? An upstairs neighbor told detectives that she had heard loud voices in the hall, a muffled scream and then, a door slam. She said that she thought the slam had come from the Dants' front door. Then, she recalled, there was silence. The next thing that this neighbor heard was Frank Dant screaming, "Oh no, oh no! Please someone help me. This is my wife."

The media drew the connection between Lois Dant's death and the East Walnut Hills cases. All women, white or black, now lived in terror. The West Side of Cincinnati was now believed to be involved with the thirst for murder by the "Cincinnati Strangler."

There were, however, a number of detectives and reporters who questioned the connection between the East Walnut Hills cases and the murder of Lois Dant. East Walnut Hills was a racially mixed area of town. In 1966, Rutledge Avenue was a 100 percent white neighborhood. Lois Dant's murder had occurred before noon near a busy thoroughfare. Yet, no sightings of a black man in the area had been reported. A black man may pass unnoticed in East Walnut Hills, but in 1966, he would have drawn more than a casual glance on Rutledge Avenue in Price Hill.

Throughout April and May, few women traveled Cincinnati's streets alone. Few women shopped alone, and even fewer did laundry alone. There was an eerie silence in the air. Most citizens of Cincinnati believed it would happen again. They just didn't know where or when.

Where was Burnet Woods just north of the University of Cincinnati's Corryville campus. When was Friday morning, June 10, 1966. James Wagner was walking his dog in Burnet Woods just off Jefferson Avenue. He was on a trail when his dog barked at a small wire-haired terrier tied to a tree limb about 12 feet into the woods. When Wagner went to investigate, he almost stumbled and fell backward in shock and fright at the sight of 56-year-old Jeanette Messer lying on her back naked, her clothes scattered all around her. Her face had been caved in by vicious blows. She had been raped and sexually brutalized. There was a necktie with two knots around her neck. The only witness to the slaying was her dog. There were no clues as to her attacker, other than the report of a lone black man who had been observed cruising in and near the park in a cream or white over brown, two-door automobile. Jacob "Jake" Schott, chief of detectives and acting police chief, told reporters that he personally believed that the same man was responsible for all of these crimes. He was not alone in this belief, but there were others who, like Sgt. Russell Jackson and Detectives Gene Moore and Bernard Kersker, suspected that the Dant and Messer cases were copycat killings. There was definitely not universal agreement. There was a universal lack of solid evidence. There was not, however, a lack of universal fear. The city of Cincinnati was awash with reports of suspicious-looking young black men staring or even attempting contact with women, white and black. That summer, the fastest way to end up being interrogated by a police officer was to be black, male, slender and young and unable to explain why you happened to be in an area of the city in which you did not live or work.

The month of July 1966 was hot and humid. There were several reports of assaults on women by young men, both black and white. But there were no homicides and no evidence to link these random incidents to the strangler. August rolled around. Again, it was hot and steamy. The air seemed to hang over the city in a motionless vacuum. It had not rained for weeks. It was quiet — too quiet. Something was going to happen. The clock ticked away on the wall at the Crime Bureau. Finally, it was Saturday, August 13. Rain was forecast for late that evening and for Sunday. The rain was needed, and it would be welcome. This might not be only a reprieve from the heat, it might also mean a quiet, crimeless weekend as well. Weather influences criminals bent on murder, as well as other outdoor activities.

Barbara Bowman arrived at the Lark Cafe on Vine Street in the Clifton area near the University of Cincinnati's campus just after 9:30 p.m. She was driven there by a friend, Betty Beckman, who was, like Bowman, a secretary. The Lark Cafe was a friendly neighborhood tavern owned by Clyde and Margaret Vollmer. Clyde was a former professional baseball player. He and his wife had owned this bar for more than 15 years. The only entertainment was a juke box, but there was a small dance floor for the patrons. Barbara Bowman, dressed in an aqua blue dress and blue high-heels, enjoyed dancing. She was a Friday and Saturday night regular at the Lark. Her favorite alcoholic beverage was Hudepohl draft beer. Nevertheless, she was not a heavy drinker.

An hour before Barbara Bowman arrived at the Lark Cafe, a 1962 Checker cab owned by Taxicabs of Cincinnati, doing business as Yellow Cabs, was stolen from the Yellow Cab Company's storage lot on Kenner Street in the city's West End. The number painted on the doors and trunk of this particular cab was 870. That evening and into the morning hours of Saturday, August 14, 1966, this stolen cab would become cab Number 186 for dispatch call purposes. Number 870 was a spare vehicle. It had not been in use since June 1 9, 1966. Cab No. 186 was not on the street that evening. It was parked in the same lot at 1110 Kenner Street, the same lot from which cab No. 870 had been stolen. Number 186 was the number of the cab that Posteal Laskey Jr. had been assigned to drive when he was a cabby for Yellow Cab Co. from July 13, 1962, until December 13, 1962, when he was fired for refusing to operate that cab. By 1966, Number 186 was no longer a Checker Cab vehicle. It was a 1965 Plymouth. But Number 870 was a Checker Cab, and the ignition keys for all Checker Cabs were the same. Any current or former employee of Yellow Cab who had been assigned to drive a Checker Cab and who had a spare ignition key made could start the ignition of any Checker-made cab vehicle.

Posteal Laskey knew the cab driver jargon. He knew how to take pick-up orders from the dispatcher and how to call in his pickups and deliveries. He also knew the city and its neighborhoods. And he knew that sooner or later this night, he would receive a call to pick up a lone woman. In the meantime, he would cruise the city, waiting and watching.

Leroy Smith and his lady friend, Debbie Gray, were cab No. 870's first fares that Saturday evening. Forty-five minutes before Barbara Bowman and Betty Beckman arrived at the Lark Cafe, this couple flagged the cab down on Central Avenue. They told the driver that they wanted to go to the Katanga Lounge at 12th and Pendleton. It seemed odd to Smith that the driver did not turn the cab's fare meter on until they had traveled over a mile and Smith had called this to the driver's attention. It was as if the driver didn't care about the fare. The driver was a slender black man, maybe 25 to 30 years old. He had the hint of chin whiskers, really only visible from a profile view. He was wearing a dark, knit beret that seemed to disappear into his black hair when shoved back on his head.

Despite the fact that Smith was with a lady friend, the cabby asked him if he wanted help to find a woman to have a good time with. Smith finally told the driver that he didn't appreciate this subject being discussed while Debbie Gray was present.

When they arrived at the Katanga Lounge, Smith's strange feeling about this cabby was compounded. Smith had to go inside the lounge, at the driver's request, to obtain the exact amount of the $1.30 fare because the driver did not have change for $2.

When Leroy Smith read about Barbara Bowman the next day, he telephoned Cincinnati police and related his strange cab ride to homicide detectives. He was logged in as a potential witness. On December 9, 1966, Leroy Smith would pick Posteal Laskey Jr. out of a police lineup as the driver of the cab that delivered himself and Debbie Gray to the Katanga Lounge.

Cab Number 870 would respond to five more calls between 8:30 p.m. and 2:09 a.m. On August 14, around 1:15 a.m., it began to rain. At first it was a light, steady, cooling rain. After a while, it became a heavy rain that filled gutters and storm sewers with a steady flow of water, accompanied by the rumbling artillery-like sound of thunder punctuated with shafts of lightning.

At 1:30 a.m. Barbara Bowman, who had been dancing with Raymond Holstein, another regular patron of the Lark, told Betty Beckman that she was going to call for a cab to take her home. After using the pay phone to call for a cab, Bowman walked outside and purchased a Sunday newspaper from a vending machine. She returned to the bar and sat down on a bar stool next to the waitress station, to the left of Raymond Holstein. She folded her newspaper in half and finished a draft beer that had been served to her earlier by Margaret Vollmer.

At exactly 2:09 a.m., the door of the Lark Cafe opened, exposing the interior of the bar for a brief period to the blowing rain that had commenced shortly after Bowman came back inside with her newspaper. A slender black man wearing what appeared to Clyde Vollmer to be a dark plaid shirt, cautiously entered the bar. He had very dark skin. He may have been 5-foot-7 or so and might have weighed 150 to 160 lbs.

Raymond Holstein would later testify that he saw the man enter the bar, that he "kind of glided in" and stood by the cigarette machine — from the light of which Holstein could see that he had some "short, stubby chin whiskers, that appeared to be the beginning of a goatee." Holstein also recalled that the man wore a short-billed tam on his head.

Carl Steigleiter, another patron and friend of Barbara Bowman, described this man as appearing very nervous as he stood by the cigarette machine, "as though he may rob the place or something."

Margaret Vollmer described the man as being about 5-foot-7, with very broad shoulders. "He was very, very black. He was spooky appearing."

This man took two steps toward the U-shaped bar and said one word, "Cab." Barbara Bowman responded immediately, "That's my cab." With these words, she picked up the morning newspaper and folded it in half. She took a final sip of her beer and picked up her black leather clutch purse. She stood up, straightened her blue dress and took a step toward the cabby. He turned and pushed the cafe's front door open and walked out into the rainy night. Barbara Bowman followed him, saying "good-night" to the

Vollmers and her fellow patrons of the Lark Cafe. She may well have said "goodbye," for no one at the Lark that night would ever see Barbara Bowman alive again. Her time of terror was about to begin.

Yellow Cab Number 870, bearing Barbara Bowman, proceeded down Vine Street to McMillan, down the hill and across the Western Hills Viaduct. The driver drove west on Westwood Avenue until he reached Grand Avenue, which he turned onto in order to deliver his fare to her apartment at 2909 Warsaw Avenue, only two doors east of the intersection of Grand and Warsaw avenues. When the driver crossed the intersection of Grand and Glenway, Barbara Bowman had been in the cab for nine minutes. She was one block from her apartment. There had been no conversation between her and the driver. She opened her purse and removed a $5 bill from her wallet. She knew from prior cab rides between her apartment and the Lark Cafe that the fare would be approximately $2.50. She folded the $5 bill in half. She also removed her apartment keys from her purse.

After the cab crossed Glenway and started up the incline on Grand Avenue toward Warsaw and the two-family apartment building where Bowman lived, the driver abruptly pulled over to the curb. He turned around in the cab's driver seat and stared at his startled passenger. She asked the driver the obvious question, "What's wrong?" He just stared at her and then vaulted his body over the seat back, knocking Bowman back so that she was almost reclining on the rear seat. He cupped his right hand over her mouth and with his left hand pulled a 30-inch piece of packaging rope from his jacket pocket. He looped the rope around the terrified young secretary's neck twice and began to pull the ends tight. As the rope dug into the glass-bead necklace that his victim was wearing, the force of the ligature caused several of the beads to become embedded in the loose rope fibers. Barbara Bowman choked and gagged. She could not scream. She could barely struggle. She tried to ward her assailant off with her flailing arms as he reached down and pulled her blue dress up, exposing her garter belt and underpants. He started to pull her underpants down but paused as he realized that an automobile had pulled up alongside the idling cab. Could it be a police cruiser? No, he felt a surge of relief. It was two women in a Plymouth looking for directions to the Summit Apartments.

Charlotte Barnhardt was driving. Eileen Aultz was her front-seat passenger. The two women had been to a birthday party. Now they were looking for the Summit Apartments, to which they had been invited for breakfast. Instead, they were near the Grandview Apartments and were in need of new directions. When she spotted the Yellow Cab pulled over to the curb on Grand Avenue, 275 feet north of Ring Place, Eileen told Charlotte to stop her vehicle so that Eileen could ask the driver for directions. Momentarily, Eileen was puzzled because she could not see anyone in the cab. She yelled, "Is anyone there?" Both women were startled to see a young, dark-skinned, black man raise his head up from the back seat and stare at them. Eileen asked him where the Summit Apartments were. The man just stared at her and said nothing. Eileen repeated her question and again received no answer. Suddenly, this man jumped back into the driver seat and put the cab into reverse gear. He started to back down Grand Avenue, staring at Eileen as he backed away. At the same instant, a white woman sat up in the rear seat of the cab for a mere four or five seconds, but then fell back again out of sight. It appeared to Eileen as though the white woman did not want to be seen by anyone. She would later testify at the murder trial that the woman laid back down as if she wanted to hide. Neither Charlotte Barnhardt or Eileen Aultz realized at the time that the white woman they saw was a semi-conscious Barbara Bowman unable to scream for help but who was desperate to attract attention. She was so traumatized that she could at that moment merely sit up for a few seconds, praying that someone would recognize her plight and save her.

As the cab backed away, Charlotte said to Eileen, "Well, that's a white woman in the back seat. What are they doing? We shouldn't stay here." With this final assessment of the situation, Charlotte and Eileen drove away. Barbara Bowman's last opportunity for rescue by an outsider vanished.

As the vehicle carrying Barnhardt and Aultz disappeared over the crest of Grand Avenue as it intersects with Ring Place, the darkened cab stopped backing up. Now, it was only 40 feet from Glenway Avenue. The rain continued hard and steady. As the cabby put the gear shift into park, the right rear door of the cab flew open. Barbara Bowman, choking and gagging, crawled out onto the sidewalk. She struggled to her feet, trying to tear the rope from her throat. Glass beads covered the floor of the cab. Her necklace was disintegrating. Her Sunday morning newspaper lay on the floor of the cab amid glass necklace beads. As she stumbled forward to escape the killer, she lost her left blue high-heeled shoe. Six feet later, she lost her right shoe. Now in her stocking feet, she ran in front of the cab, which the driver was frantically trying to start up. As she crossed Grand to the east side, she ran in an uphill direction toward her apartment. Sixty-three feet up the east side of Grand, police would later discover her black scrolled, horn-rimmed glasses. Suddenly, the cab sprang to life. It careened up Grand Avenue after the fleeing woman. She ran, soaking wet, as fast as she could in the dark, unrelenting night. She stumbled over the curb at the corner of Ring Place as it meets Grand Avenue. She could hear the engine and the slapping windshield wiper blades of the Checker cab that bore down on her from behind. Suddenly, the headlights were on. In an instant, the cab came over the sidewalk and crashed into the rear of Bowman's right leg, breaking her ankle and slamming her to the wet pavement. The cab came to a halt after striking the opposite curb of Ring Place. The driver tried to back up and turn the steering wheel to the left. He wanted to finish off the woman, who was now on her hands and knees trying to crawl along Ring Place, dragging a smashed right ankle and foot behind her. The steering was gone. The wheels wouldn't turn. The left front tie rod had been broken into two pieces. There was no chance of finishing the woman off with the cab. But finish her off was something that he had to do before someone else came along. The cabby also kept in mind that he was only two-and-a-half blocks from Cincinnati District 3 Police Headquarters and that police cars normally used Grand Avenue driving to and from the station house. In fact, he was surprised that a police cruiser had not been through this area already. He was surprised, but grateful.

As he leaped from the cab, the agile black man pulled a 5-inch paring knife from the same left jacket pocket from which he had obtained the binding cord, now lying in the center of Ring Place with several glass beads entwined in its fibers. As Barbara Bowman continued to crawl to get away, she dropped the folded $5 bill and her apartment keys. The man grabbed her from behind, pulling her head back by her hair. "You fucking whore. I should have slit your throat in the cab. Now you made me bust the steering. You're dead, bitch." The paring knife was raised up and flashed downward once, then again and again. Five times the knife ripped into the right side of her throat. Her right carotid artery was severed. Her right vocal cord was severed. Her jugular vein was nearly completely severed. She collapsed onto her back from the force of the knife thrusts to her throat. Her eyes were wide open in eternal terror. She would lie on the storm sewer grate on Ring Place, 29 feet from Grand Avenue while six pints of her life's blood would run out of her throat and, once mixed with rain water, would flow down into the storm sewer system. She could no longer scream or speak. She could only lie in the street and convulse. She could utter no sound except a low, wailful moan.

Grabbing her black purse, the killer threw the paring knife toward

Grand Avenue, where police officers would later find it, 25 feet from Barbara Bowman's body. He ran east along Ring Place, first dropping the black clutch purse on the sidewalk in front of 2611 and, finally, her brown billfold in front of 2601. The wallet was empty except for the $1 bill folded and secured inside a pocket of the billfold as emergency money. The trail of the purse and billfold would enable investigating detectives to conclude that Barbara Bowman's killer had run from the scene east along a dark and deserted Ring Place, continuing after the street's dead end down the wooded hillside to Glenway Avenue at its confluence with lower State Avenue to Bowman Street and Mistletoe.

About 2:40 a.m., Raymond Walker and Ruth Bailey turned onto Grand Avenue from Warsaw. As they proceeded past the first three houses, they observed a Yellow cab blocking the street on Ring Place. The cab's headlights were on, the wiper blades were operating and the driver's door was wide open. Ruth Bailey told Raymond Walker to stop his automobile. She told him that she thought that she saw someone lying in the street next to the cab. Bailey and Walker got out of his auto and walked around the cab. As Bailey would testify on April 4, 1967:

"The Yellow cab was blocking the street. I saw a woman lying on the curb bleeding very badly. She had on a blue dress. I could see her slip and her hose and her garter belt and panties. Her shoes were gone. Her right foot was muddy and twisted. There was a lot of blood around her head and neck. She was alive, but all she did was move her hands a little and moan."

Bailey and Walker thought that there had been some kind of an accident and that the cab driver may have gone for help. Walker said that they better go for help or the woman was going to bleed to death. So they returned to Walker's auto and drove the two-and-a-half blocks to Police District 3, where they reported their gruesome discovery to Officer Frank Sefton, who immediately left the district to respond to Ring Place and Warsaw Avenue. It was now 2:55 a.m.

Sol Thompson and his Parkway cab were on Denver Street off Glenway Avenue about eight-tenths of a mile from Ring Place and Grand Avenue. He had just delivered a fare to the 1400 block of Denver. It was pitch black and raining sheets. Earlier, he had passed a wrecked Yellow cab on Ring Place at Grand. Officer Frank Sefton had flagged him down and asked him whether he knew who might be operating the Yellow cab, and if he could radio Yellow cab to send a supervisor out to the scene. He had gotten out of his cab to see whether he could locate a trip sheet in the vehicle. On the way around to the open driver's door, he walked past the spot where Barbara Bowman had been lying before the life squad hurried her away to St. Mary's Hospital in a futile effort to save her. Thompson looked around the interior of the cab but could not find a trip sheet. He had then gone back to his cab and called to his dispatcher requesting on behalf of the police that a Yellow Cab Company supervisor be called and asked to come to Ring and Grand to identify one of the company's cabs and to try to locate the driver.

Now it was between 3:10 and 3:15 a.m. Sol Thompson was just about to pull away from the stop sign at Bowman Street and Mistletoe when he thought he heard someone whistle. He hit the brake pedal but couldn't see anyone. Just as he started to pull away again, a "male Negro" jerked the right rear door of his cab open and slid into the back seat. He was breathing very heavily and was soaking wet. Thompson would describe this man to police as about 5-foot-8, 140 to 150 pounds, thin, and 25 to 30 years old. He also told police that the man was wearing a black, leather-like, hip-length jacket, dark pants and a navy blue watch cap. "He had a rough voice as if he had a cold. It looked to me like he had been running out in the rain for a long time."

This strange passenger told Thompson to take him to Brighton. He laid two very wet $1 bills on the top of the front seat back, to the right of the driver and stated "This should cover it."

As Thompson drove north on State Avenue, he glanced in his rear vision mirror. His passenger had slid over in the rear seat so that he was directly behind Thompson and out of his view in the rear view mirror. Twice, Sol Thompson told the young man to slide back over to the middle or the right side of the back seat, where Thompson could see him in his mirror. Thompson was already suspicious of this man. The only thing that his passenger did in response to these instructions was to move to his right and snicker. Thompson kept his right eye on his passenger, who stared straight ahead with a glare. His eyes frightened Thompson, who had been robbed twice before. The windows were all up in the cab. The air inside was stale. It was not long before Thompson caught the strong odor of male sweat. His passenger was perspiring heavily, as if he had just run a foot race. Thompson became jittery with each tick of the cab's meter. He fully expected at any minute that he was going to be robbed.

After traveling east over the Western Hills Viaduct and Central Parkway to Central Avenue, Thompson's passenger told him to turn onto Baymiller. Just before the Parkway cab reached Bank Street, Thompson passed a Cincinnati police cruiser that was moving very slowly, as if the cop was looking for someone or something. Thompson was immediately told to pull over at the stop sign. Before the cab came to a complete stop, the rear door opened and his fare "vaulted" out of the cab, ran across the street and disappeared into an ancient tenement building. Later, after hearing on the radio that a woman had been hurt in a cab on Ring Place, Thompson stopped a police cruiser and told the officer about his strange passenger. He noted which building on Baymiller Street he had seen the man enter. Exactly one block west of that building on Baymiller Street was 1820 Freeman Avenue, the residence at that time of Nancy Laskey, the mother of Posteal Laskey.

At 3:30 a.m., 31-year-old Barbara Bowman was pronounced dead at St. Mary's Hospital, located in the city's West End, a little more than 3 miles from the scene of the attack on her, and less than a half-mile from 1820 Freeman Avenue, where a still wet, sinister-looking young man had just turned out his bedroom light, lying in bed, hands behind his head. In the quiet of the pitch-black room, he cursed the woman who had refused to submit to him.

On Monday, August 15, Lytle Young learned that a young woman had been stabbed to death by a black man who had stolen a Yellow cab. He immediately picked up the telephone to call the Homicide Squad to accuse Posteal Laskey Jr. The man who had previously arrested Laskey was told that all present and former cab drivers who fit the description given by potential witnesses from the Lark Cafe, as well as the cab driver who had picked a suspect up at Bowman and Mistletoe shortly after 3:00 a.m., were going to be questioned about the murder of Barbara Bowman. Young kept insisting that his intuition told him that Laskey was the probable killer. He was told that there was a problem with the descriptions given by the patrons of the Lark Cafe, but he continued to request that Laskey be picked up and put in a lineup where the people who saw the "cab driver" the night of Bowman's murder could view him.

On Wednesday, September 21, 1966, 53-year-old Virginia Hinners was in her office at the New Thought Unity Center, located at 1401 East McMillan Street in the Walnut Hills area of Cincinnati. The center happened to be directly across the street from the Clermont Apartments, the scene of the murder and rape of Emogene Harrington on December 2, 1965. Ever since the Harrington homicide, Virginia Hinners had been very careful to avoid being alone — both in the office and when arriving or leaving the center. She resided in the Mount Washington area with her husband and four children. Her family had pleaded with her continually to be

extremely careful while at work. These warnings and her fear had continued now for nine months.

The New Thought Unity Center is a place of religious worship and fel-
lowship. Virginia Hinners was employed at this time as a teacher and
counselor. It was 8:00 p.m., and a guest speaker was ready to address members at a service then being conducted in the large sanctuary, which
adjoined the office where Mrs. Hinners was working. Her office was separated from the stage by a small outer room, which contained the controls
for the microphone to the speaker's podium and a tape recorder, all of
which were operated by Hinners as part of her duties.

It was already dark outside as Virginia Hinners prepared to turn on
the tape recorder in order to record that evening's speaker when a young,
thin black man entered her office and asked her whether "he could have a
job." She advised the man that he would have to talk to Ernest Reams, the
building's custodian, whose apartment was in the basement area directly
below her office. She also explained to this visitor that she could not take
him downstairs because she was alone in the office and had to remain
there to operate the tape recorder.

The young man left her office and disappeared down the steps that
led to the basement. Within three minutes he was back and told her that
he couldn't locate the custodian and that he would appreciate it if she
would go down to the basement with him and show him where the custodian's apartment was located. Again, Hinners advised him that she could
not leave her office. In order to accommodate this persistent and somewhat frightening young man, Virginia Hinners walked out of her office and
pointed over the stair railing to the area where she believed that he could
find the custodian. Once again, the young man started down the basement steps and she returned to her office.

Within three minutes, Virginia Hinners realized that the young man
had returned a second time. On this occasion, he told her that he had seen
a man enter the basement from the other side of the building but he was
not sure if that man was the custodian. At this point he said, "Well, won't
you go down with me? I'm a little bit afraid, and maybe you could talk to
this man for me."

Hinners reminded her visitor that she had already told him that she
was alone in the office and that she could not leave. Once again the man
left her office and walked toward the staircase leading to the basement.
Hinners walked into the anteroom next to her office and turned the tape
recorder on. The guest speaker had just commenced his address. After

turning the tape recorder on, Hinners returned to her desk and sat down to type a label for the tape being used to record the speech. As she began typing, she sensed that someone had entered the room behind her, as her back was turned toward the entrance to the office. She swung around in her swivel chair just in time to see the visitor standing behind her with his forearms and hands cupped about 10 inches apart and on either side of her head. She screamed and jumped up, and her would-be assailant moved toward the window, which blocked her from leaving the office. He leaned forward and placed both of his hands on top of the window air conditioner and said, "You know, I used to work on these."

Suddenly, Virginia Hinners realized that he was not interested in securing a job. She backed away from him and around the front of her desk so that her typewriter separated her from this man who had by now become a source of fear to her. She would later testify at Laskey's trial that: "His attitude changed completely. Before this, he had been quiet and very respectful and refined, very soft-spoken. But then he got bold and started for me."

At this point, Laskey grabbed Hinners by her arms and drew her against his body. He pulled her hard into his body. She could feel that he had an erection. He nuzzled her with his chin His chin whiskers burned her cheeks. He tried to kiss her. She pushed him away and said emphatically, "Don't do that."

Now Laskey got rough. "He took my arm and bent it way up behind my back and began to shove me the length of the office and out the door. As he got me almost to the door, I caught my foot on the door and shoved it so that I ended up behind the door and he couldn't push me through without pulling me around the door."

Continuing on, Hinners related that "he began at first to talk very quietly and very fast, but he got louder. And he said over and over again, 'Do you want what the others got? Do you want what the others got? Do you want what the others got? Don't scream. Don't scream. Don't scream. I'll slit your throat like the others. I'll slit your throat. Don't scream!' And he kept saying this to me."

Laskey pulled and pulled on the struggling woman until he finally managed to yank her from her position on the other side of the half-closed office door. Just as she was about to be pulled sliding around the door, Hinners made a desperate move and tried to slam the office door on Laskey's arms.

"And then his entire attitude changed. This made him very angry.

He came rushing back into the office and he said, 'Now you're going to get it, bitch. I'll slit your goddamn throat just like hers.' He bare-fisted hit me very hard in the temple and threw me against the desk. Before I could get myself composed, he hit me again — very hard in the chin — and knocked me down to the floor.

"And I remember as I was getting up, I just kept saying, 'Please don't hurt me. Please don't hurt me.' And he got behind me. He had on a red-and-black checked, rough, woolen hunting shirt, and he got the crook of his arm around my neck and was pressing it and leaning over me, and I think that I lost a shoe at that time and was beginning to black out."

As if sent by Virginia Hinners' guardian angel, she could see the bald head of the elderly custodian, Ernest Reams, coming up the steps from the basement. Apparently, he had re-entered the rear of the basement from the outside door and had heard the sounds of the scuffle above his head. Now, totally unaware of the danger, he was climbing the stairs to investigate these sounds.

Virginia Hinners recalled saying to herself, "Thank God."

"But as soon as he got to the opening of the office door, this man threw me aside and went after him, and brutally pounded on him and knocked him out against the closed door of the minister's office, and he slumped to the floor unconscious and was lying there," Hinners said.

"And then this man, instead of running out, came very calmly back into the office again and I said, 'What do you want?' If you want money, I'll give you $10. And then he glanced over and saw my bag on a chair, and he grabbed it and he said, 'What's in here?' And he shook it out and took the cosmetic bag and asked me what was in there. And then he threw that on the floor when I told him, 'Nothing,' and he got my wallet and very calmly went through it and took only the bills and threw everything else aside.

"And then he grabbed me again and threw me very hard down on my face on the floor and I lost my earrings and my other shoe, and he left me lying there and ran out and leaped down the steps and went out the same door that he had entered. It was at that time that Mr. Reams was coming to and saw him run out, and then the custodian called the police."

This very quiet, mannerly young man — who was so agile that he could leap down a set of steps the same as he could leap in and out of automobiles and from front seat to back seat, and who told Virginia Hinners that if she screamed he would slit her throat "just like the others" — was once again running through the back yards and side streets of East Walnut

Hills. There was no doubt in the minds of the homicide and robbery squad detectives that the murderer of Emogene Harrington in the basement of the Clermont Apartments across the street from the New Thought Unity Center had also robbed Virginia Hinners of $28 in United States currency. The questions that remained unanswered were: Who was he? Where was he? And when would he strike again? The last was answered first.

Victim Number 8 was Della Ernst. It was Tuesday, October 4, 1966, 13 days after the robbery and assault of Virginia Hinners. The location was a posh apartment complex overlooking the Ohio River at 2012 Edgecliff Point, less than 2 miles from the New Thought Unity Center and the Clermont Apartments. Ernst was a 70-year-old widow. She lived alone. She had spent the evening having dinner with her married daughter. Around 9:00 p.m., she drove her automobile into the garage connected to her apartment building.

As she approached the lobby door, she had a strange feeling that she was being watched. As she turned to pass through the outer door to cover the 10 feet between the outer door and the inner locked door that led to the building's elevators, she became convinced that someone or something was behind her. As she unlocked the inner lobby door, she thought that she heard something pant like a dog. She caught a scent of sweat and soiled clothes. As she let the inner door go with her right hand so that it could close behind her, she heard a thump as the door came to a stop, short of closing, a thump caused by the door striking a shoe. She wheeled around in terror. The thin, young black man hissed at her, "Come here, I want to talk to you." She froze in total horror. She could not speak. She could not move. She had been reading the newspapers. She had been watching television news. She had observed numerous police cruisers traveling back and forth in front of her apartment building. In fact, her daughter and her son-in-law had suggested to her this very evening that she spend the night at their home rather than take the chance of being the Cincinnati Strangler's next victim by returning to her apartment alone after dark.

Now, here she was, faced with the prospect that she was about to become a victim. How could this be, she thought. "Oh, dear God, why me? Please not me. I don't want to die."

While she stared and her mind flashed multiple horrible pictures of her death at the hands of this hissing animal, the man reached around the partially open door with his left arm and struck Della Ernst in the jaw in much the same manner that Virginia Hinners had been punched. He quickly grabbed her purse, which contained $130. He continued to push against the door, cursing the elderly woman for her perseverance against his desire to murder her, and if there were time, to defile her.

From some unknown corner of her voice box, a scream started swelling and rising so that by the time it passed her lips, it was a shrill shriek that reverberated around the apartment lobby and halls like a gun shot.

Mattie Jones, the live-in manager, in Apartment 101, heard this scream. She was watching the *Carol Burnett Show*. She ran from her apartment toward the lobby as if an unseen hand were guiding her. She arrived in the lobby just in time to see the thin black man grab Della Ernst's purse. She hollered, "Stop," as loud as she could. The man looked at her, then evaporated into the night as though he was possessed of special powers of locomotion. Again, all the police could do was take a report and tell Della Ernst that she was lucky to be alive.

Now the pace of unspeakable terror began to pick up. As if he were frustrated by the Hinners and Ernst failures, there appeared to be an urgency to find another victim as quickly as possible. At long last, the spree killer crossed over the line and became a serial killer, a night stalker.

One week to the day after the close call experienced by Della Ernst, Alice K. Hockhausler, the attractive 51-year-old wife of the chief of surgery at Cincinnati's Good Samaritan Hospital, left her home to pick up her daughter, Beth, who was a night nurse. The Hockhauslers had been concerned about their daughter's safety ever since the body of Jeanette Messer was found on June 10 in Burnet Woods, the large city park across Clifton Avenue from the hospital that employed Mrs. Hockhausler's husband and their daughter.

Beth's parents had tried to get her to move back home until these gruesome murders could be solved and a suspect apprehended. However, like many young adults in their 20s, Beth insisted that she could take care of herself. Nevertheless, since she did not drive to work, she had consented to letting one of her parents pick her up at the end of her nursing shift to drive her to her Clifton apartment. It was less than three blocks from her parents' spacious residence located at 3480 Cornell Place, a tree-shaded, gas-lighted street of expensive older homes, many occupied by physicians and University of Cincinnati professors.

On Tuesday evening, October 11, 1966, Alice Hockhausler told her husband to stay home and go to bed since he had early surgery the next morning. She had already slipped into her pajamas. When the time arrived to leave to drive the short distance to pick up Beth, she put on her bathrobe and slippers and backed her Cadillac out of the separate two-car garage located behind the semi-Tudor home, leaving her husband, their other children, and the family German shepherd, which she had thought for a moment about taking with her to pick up Beth. However, the dog was already in the basement for the evening. "Let her stay there," Alice thought to herself. "I'm just being silly."

It took Alice Hockhausler about five minutes to drive to the hospital, where Beth was waiting for her. As the two women drove north on Clifton Avenue and then west on Ludlow toward Cornell Place, they became alarmed that they might be being followed by another automobile, which appeared to be tail-gating them. Beth's mother pulled over to the curb to see what might happen. Both were relieved when the automobile passed them and continued slowly down Ludlow Avenue. The driver was a young, slender black man. The vehicle that he was operating was cream over brown, Oldsmobile Delta 88, two-door, hard top. The man was alone. He didn't even look at the two women as he drove by. There was no need to write down the license number (1966 Ohio white on red plate 3097AA) because the driver looked so young and innocent. Nor did either Alice or Beth Hockhausler know that a similar cream over brown Oldsmobile had been seen cruising Clifton the night that Jeanette Messer was murdered while walking her dog in nearby Burnet Woods.

Once the Oldsmobile passed by, Alice Hockhausler remarked to her daughter that the whole city was living on the edge of panic. The two women talked about how dangerous society had become, and then Beth climbed out of her mother's car and headed up the walk to her apartment. Alice Hockhausler waited until she saw her daughter's apartment lights come on before pulling away from the curb. Now, home and to bed. It was a beautiful fall evening Crisp, clear — kind of like Halloween. No reason to be frightened. Just a few blocks and she would be home. She pulled the Cadillac into the driveway on Cornell Place. No reason to pull into the garage. It was such a clear evening that it wouldn't hurt to leave the car sit out. Besides, that stone garage was so dark inside.

Alice Hockhausler never saw the slender, 5-foot, 7-inch black man standing in the shadow of the side of her house. She never saw the fist that smashed into the side of her head. Before she could scream, a powerful hand clamped over her mouth like a vise. She felt herself being pulled backward. Before being dragged 5 feet, she had lost both of her slippers. She went numb with terror, which her eyes recorded for all time to come.

At 6:30 a.m., October 12, Carl J. Hockhausler, M.D., found his wife's body in their garage. She had been raped and strangled with the cord from her bathrobe. Panic in both Clifton and on the nearby University of Cincinnati campus was universal. Not one hardware store had a deadbolt lock left in stock. At UC, an escort service was started for all co-eds. Something — anything — had to be done to stop this carnage. Alice Hockhausler had become victim Number 9. Where would it end?

Was 81-year-old Rose Winstel of 2289 Vine Street near Inwood Park victim Number 10, or was she someone else's victim? The body of the frail old lady was found on the morning of Thursday, October 20, 1966, by her nephew, who had called police to meet him at her home. The deadbolt and night latches were broken on the front door of her small, ancient, frame home. Her body had been shoved under her bed. One arm and a leg stuck out. She had been partially wrapped in a bedspread. It looked as though her killer had felt bad about her death and wanted to hide her body. She had been severely beaten, raped and strangled with an electric cord. She was by far the oldest victim.

"My God," growled Colonel Jake Schott. "This poor little lady was 81 and damn near blind. What kind of goddamn animal derives satisfaction out of raping and strangling an old lady?"

Miss Winstel had never married. She had been retired for years. She had always lived alone, a semi-recluse. There had been rumors for a long time in the neighborhood that she was a "loaded old lady with lots of cash in the house." There was the belief among several homicide detectives and police brass that Miss Winstel's death was not the work of the Cincinnati Strangler. They pointed to the fact that she was 81 years old and that force had been used to gain entry to her home. This indicated that her murderer knew her and that he knew that she lived alone. Nevertheless, Rose Winstel was the 10th woman to be assaulted in this fashion since October 12, 1965, and she was the sixth woman to be murdered during this time of community terror.

On December 5, 1966, after meeting with Municipal Court Judge William S. Mathews, Posteal Laskey's probation officer issued a warrant for Laskey's arrest for violating the conditions of his probation. The main basis for this violation was Laskey's failure to report to his probation officer as required, and his having taken an apartment on Reading Road in Avondale without advising his probation officer that he was moving out of his mother's residence at 1820 Freeman Avenue in the city's West End. Laskey was on probation to Judge Mathews as the result of his conviction for assaulting a Clifton woman in the fall of 1965. Even at this time, there was no direct connection between Posteal Laskey and the murders of six women.

Thursday night, December 8, 1966, was a clear evening in Cincinnati. The temperature was in the 30s as 22-year-old Sandra Chapas left her job at the Kenner Toy Factory at midnight. Chapas was an attractive brunette, 5-feet, 4-inches tall, 115 pounds. She lived at 14 West Court Street, two floors above the Formosa Chinese restaurant, the one with the front painted "Chinese Red." The entrance to the second- and third-floor apartments above the restaurant was at the west end of the narrow brick building, 6 feet from the entrance to the restaurant.

Just after midnight, Friday, December 9, as Chapas headed west on Court Street, she became aware that an automobile was cruising slowly behind her as she walked on the south side of the street. She glanced over her right shoulder and saw by the light of the bright downtown street lamps a cream over brown Oldsmobile about 20 feet behind her. The vehicle's headlights were off. As the Oldsmobile passed under a street lamp, she could see that the driver was a young black man. She would later say that he was staring at her and that his eyes were quite large.

As she crossed Vine Street, one block from her building, she began to run. She ran across West Court Street toward the front door to Number 14. The Oldsmobile behind her suddenly sped up. The driver peeled rubber as he attempted to cut her off in the middle of the street. As she opened the exterior door, her pursuer pulled the cream over brown, two-door, hardtop convertible over to the curb and came after her. As she entered the narrow hallway, with mailboxes on the left wall, he yelled at her, "Come here, I want to talk to you." Chapas ran as fast as her slender legs would carry her up the stairs, past the second-floor hall, continuing to her third-floor apartment, and, luckily, her apartment key slipped into the lock on the first try. There was no time for fumbling with a key. As she ran into her small living room, she slammed the door shut. She threw on the safety latch just as a hand hit her door.

"Open the door. I want to talk to you."

"Go away. I am calling the police right now," replied Chapas, her knees trembling with fear.

Ethel Hall, who lived across from Chapas, opened her door just wide enough to peek out. She had been aroused from watching the *Tonight Show* by the sounds of the running footsteps and the slamming of the door. What she saw disturbed her greatly. A young black man was standing in front of Sandra Chapas' apartment door. His head was bowed. His right arm was extended, his hand on the door itself. With his left hand, he was clutching his crotch. And as Hall later told detectives, he was doing something that she had never seen before.

"He was grabbing at his crotch as if he were masturbating, and he was panting like a dog does. It was horrible."

Ethel Hall yelled. The intruder looked up, turned to his right and literally vaulted down the staircase. As he neared the ground level, he was met by Lawrence Hall, who was returning home and whom he knocked aside to make good his escape. Hall yelled at the man, and turned to follow him. Ethel Hall, who had now started down the steps, yelled after her husband that he should be careful. "He may have a gun," she shouted.

Lawrence Hall hit the sidewalk just as the young man jumped into a cream over brown two-door sedan. As the Oldsmobile sped away, Lawrence Hall got the license number and repeated it silently to himself until he was able to write it down after reaching his third-floor apartment The license number was "Ohio 1966, 3097AA" as written down on a piece of note paper by Lawrence Hall.

Three cruisers from Police District 1 arrived at 14 West Court Street within minutes after Sandra Chapas' near-death experience. For the first time in 14 months, there was, in addition to a description of the suspect, a license plate number. In the days before computers, it required several hours, especially at night or on weekends, to obtain the name of the individual to whom a license plate was registered. In this case, police learned at 8:20 a.m. December 9 that Number 3097AA was registered to one Posteal Laskey Jr. of 1820 Freeman Avenue, Cincinnati, Hamilton County, Ohio, Zone 3. At the same time as the owner of the license plate was discovered, it was learned by police that there was a warrant on file for Posteal Laskey Jr., for violating the conditions of his probation. Now, an all-points bulletin was issued, "Pick up Posteal Laskey Jr. as a possible suspect for numerous assaults on women and on an open probation violation warrant."

The saga of the Cincinnati Strangler appeared to be coming to a conclusion, but no one could be positive. In any event, the breakthrough brought about as the result of the aborted attempt on the life of Sandra Chapas did not save Lula Kerrick, who — like Rose Winstel — was 81 years old. Kerrick's beaten body was found in the cramped elevator of the apartment building where she lived, The Brittany, located at 104 West Ninth Street, a block and a half from the apartment building where Sandra Chapas and the Halls resided.

At 8:00 a.m. Friday morning, December 9, 1966, homicide detectives responded to a call from District 1 patrol officers that an elderly woman had been found by a neighbor lying on the floor of the ancient elevator, her legs sticking out of the door into the hall. She had been strangled with her own stocking, tied tightly around her neck in two knots. Her purse and its contents were strewn around her body. She had been beaten, but she had not been raped. Was Lula Kerrick victim Number 12? That is a question that may never be answered. Again, as in so many of the other assaults, there were no witnesses and few clues.

Around 9:00 a.m. that morning, detectives went to the residence of Nancy Laskey, mother of Posteal Laskey Jr., at 1820 Freeman. All she would tell them was that her son had his own place at 2201 Reading Road in Avondale. His mother told the detectives that he was probably at work at the Wuest Mattress Company, located at Gest and Evans Street in the city's West End, approximately eight blocks from Nancy Laskey's Freeman Avenue apartment. District 4 police officers were sent to look for Laskey at his apartment at 2201 Reading Road, where he occupied Unit 12. They were told by his landlady that she had seen him leave earlier for work. She told the officers that Laskey was driving a Oldsmobile that had a "white top and a brown bottom."

Shortly after 9:30 a.m., three homicide detectives entered the Wuest Mattress factory's warehouse with a supervisor in tow. Paul Morgan, who looked and dressed as if Hollywood had picked him to play a detective, approached Laskey. The man was wrapping a new mattress with the same type of white binding cord that had been used to choke Barbara Bowman. When Morgan showed him his badge, Laskey calmly and politely said, "I know why you're here. Can we talk?"

In the parking lot of the factory, detectives located a 1962 Oldsmobile two-door, hardtop coupe. The bottom was a light brown and the top was cream colored. It bore Ohio license plate Number 3097AA. The automobile, like Checker cab Number 870, was impounded by the Cincinnati police. Ironically, they were parked in the same garage, next to each other.

Six months before the arrest of Posteal Laskey, the United States Supreme Court had decided the landmark case of *Miranda v. Arizona*, in which the court had struck down Ernesto Miranda's murder conviction because Arizona police officers had failed to advise him prior to interrogating him that he had the right to remain silent and that he had the right to the assistance of an attorney during interrogation.

By December 1966, most police departments across the United States had adopted a statement of rights that were read to each crime suspect who was in custody prior to being questioned concerning the crime or crimes being investigated. These rights became known as "Miranda Rights" and included the following court-mandated warnings to each arrested suspect whom the police intended to question.

> You have the right to remain silent.
>
> If you make a statement, that statement may be used against you in court.
>
> You have the right to have an attorney present during any interrogation.
>
> And if you do not have money to hire an attorney, one will be appointed for you, if you desire, prior to any questioning.

Laskey had been questioned after the murder of Emogene Harrington. He had also been interrogated, as had many ex-cabbies, after the murder of Barbara Bowman. Besides being on probation to Judge Mathews for an October 1965, assault, he had three prior assault convictions. All of the victims had been women. In the 1958 assault conviction, Laskey had been arrested by Lytle Young, the same Lytle Young who was now retired and the property officer for the Hamilton County prosecutor and who had insisted that Laskey was more likely than not the Cincinnati Strangler.

Now, Laskey was in the Crime Bureau, confronted by detectives — Sergeant Russell Jackson, Paul Morgan, Bernard Kersker and Colonel Jacob Schott, the chief of detectives. Laskey was advised of his Miranda rights and interrogated about the death of Barbara Bowman and the other five women, as well as the assaults and robberies of Margie Helton, Virginia Hinners and Della Ernst. He was questioned concerning the attempt to gain entry into Sandra Chapas' apartment the evening before. The interrogation, exhaustive as it was, elicited no statements from the suspect. He was calm. He was, in fact, cool. He denied any knowledge of any of these victims. He knew nothing about the theft of a Yellow cab. In fact, he believed that he was at his mother's place the night that Barbara Bowman was murdered. He knew that his mother would vouch for his whereabouts on August 13 and 14, 1966. Laskey didn't lawyer up — ask for the assistance of an attorney — even though he knew he had the right to do so. He was too cool to admit to anything, and he stayed that way.

Shortly after 2:30 p.m. that Friday, Laskey was taken to the old Cincinnati Workhouse on Colerain Avenue and booked. At the same time, arrest warrants and complaints were being drawn up in the Crime Bureau that would guarantee that Laskey would not hit the bricks again.

That same afternoon, a detail of eight detectives, divided into four groups of two, each group accompanied by a uniformed police officer, circulated throughout the city showing photographs of Laskey to anyone who may have seen him at or near any of the 12 or more crime scenes. As the result of these potential witnesses being contacted and shown photographs of the prime suspect, the homicide squad decided to schedule a formal police lineup for Saturday at 11:00 a.m.

That Saturday morning, Posteal Laskey Jr. was arraigned before Cincinnati Municipal Court Judge Clarence Denning on the probation violation order issued by Judge William S. Mathews. Judge Denning was advised before court by the city prosecutor and homicide detectives that Laskey was a suspect in the strangler murders. The judge was asked to set a high bail, one that Laskey could not make, to ensure that he would be held pending a lineup procedure already scheduled. Judge Denning agreed. When Laskey's probation violation was called, the city's lone public defender, Eddie Fidler, entered a plea of not guilty on Laskey's behalf. Over Mr. Fidler's objection, Denning set bail at $250,000. Later, Fidler would be told why the bail was so high.

At 10:30 a.m., Laskey, now dressed in Workhouse blues, was removed from his cell and driven to the Crime Bureau and placed in a lineup. At this time, he was not represented by counsel because he had not yet been formally charged with a felony.

In a lineup with four other black men, two of whom were Cincinnati police officers dressed in casual clothing, Laskey was viewed by Sandra Chapas; Lawrence and Ethel Hall; Virginia Hinners and Ernest Reams from the New Thought Unity Temple; Della Ernst and Mattie Jones; Clyde and Margaret Vollmer, owners of the Lark Cafe, and Raymond Holstein and Carl Steigleiter, two of the Lark's customers who had seen the young black man enter the bar and yell "cab"; Charlotte Barnhardt and Eileen Aultz, the two women who asked a cab driver for directions on Grand Avenue, the cab driver whom they observed in the back seat of the cab with a white woman; Leroy Smith, who had been Laskey's first fare of the evening of August 13, the passenger who wanted to go to the Katanga Lounge and who had to get change in order to pay the fare; Arthur Scholl, the lot man for Yellow Cab, who had chased a young black man from the Kenner Street storage lot on August 12, the night before cab Number 870 was stolen; and Sol Thompson, the driver for Parkway Cab who picked up the very wet, very winded and very nervous young black man at the corner of Bowman

Street and Mistletoe at 3:15 a.m. Sunday, August 14, and received two wet dollar bills for the fare. In all, 16 potential witnesses viewed the lineup that morning.

Each one identified Posteal Laskey Jr.

By now, the local media had gotten the word that a suspect had finally been arrested in the Cincinnati Strangler cases. The appetite of the press was whetted even more when word leaked out around noon that December Saturday that each of the 16 potential witnesses had positively identified Posteal Laskey Jr.

The only disagreement among these witnesses concerned clothing and facial hair. Those who had seen Laskey only from the front did not mention any whiskers. Those who had seen his profile claimed that he had a short goatee. The photographs taken of Laskey at that time show a wispy goatee clearly visible only from the side. At his trial, Laskey's lawyers would go to great length to establish that the discrepancy about the goatee was evidence of misidentification.

The lineup enabled officers to formally charge Posteal Laskey Jr., with the murder and robbery of Barbara Bowman and the robbery of Virginia Hinners and Della S. Ernst. On Monday, December 12, 1966, Posteal Laskey Jr. was formally arraigned on these charges. Bail totaling $1.5 million was set. There was no longer any chance that he would be released.

Search warrants for both 1820 Freeman Avenue and 2201 Reading Road, Apartment 12, were issued to homicide detectives. The most important items recovered were two jackets (one black leather and one dark slicker) and a red-and-black, lumberjack-style wool shirt.

On December 15, after an exhaustive review of all the evidence gathered, and realizing that of all the homicides, the only one in which there were reliable witnesses was the murder of Barbara Bowman, Prosecutor Melvin G. Rueger presented that case and the robberies of Virginia Hinners and Della S. Ernst to a Hamilton County Grand Jury.

These presentments resulted in the return of Indictment Number 88695, the murder and robbery of Barbara Bowman; Indictment Number 88696, the robbery of Virginia Hinners; and Indictment Number 88697, the robbery of Della S. Ernst. Laskey was arraigned on these indictments on December 16, 1966, and ordered held without bail.

On December 21, he was sentenced to serve six months in the Workhouse by Judge Mathews on the probation violation from October, 1965. On that same day, two former assistant prosecuting attorneys, Burton Signer and Donald Roney, were appointed by the court to act as

Laskey's attorneys on the murder and robbery charges. Pleas of not guilty were entered. The television news broadcast interviews of anyone and everyone who would discuss Posteal Laskey Jr.

Rueger announced that he would discuss the case at the appropriate time, but that this case was not going to be tried in the press like the Sam Sheppard case had been in Cleveland. Dr. Sam's conviction for the murder of his wife, Marilyn, had recently been reversed, and the Cleveland osteopath had been ordered set free by the U.S. Supreme Court because of prejudicial pretrial publicity. Mel Rueger was determined that this would not happen in the cases of *State of Ohio v. Posteal Laskey Jr.*

Posteal Laskey Jr, as he appeared in a police lineup in October 1965.

Verona Apartments, 2356 Park Avenue, Walnut Hills, where Elizabeth Kreco was a victim of rape and attempted murder on October 12, 1965.

Clermont Apartments, 1404-06 East McMillan Street, Walnut Hills, where the caretaker came across Emogene Harrington's body in the basement on December 2, 1965.

Rutledge Apartments, 1210 Rutledge Avenue, Price Hill, where Lois Dant's husband found her beaten, raped and strangled with her nylon hose on April 4, 1966.

This 1962 Oldsmobile was observed near a number of the crime scenes. The license number, registered to Laskey, was not known to police until the morning of the last murder.

Hiking trail in Burnet Woods, Clifton, where Jeanette Messer was walking her wire-haired terrier on June 10, 1966. A strangler left the woman naked and dead; the dog was alive and tied to a tree.

Clifton home, 3480 Cornell Place, where Dr. Carl Hockhausler found his wife, Alice, in the garage, strangled with the cord from her bathrobe.

New Thought Unity Temple in Walnut Hills, where secretary Virginia Hinners was robbed and beaten by Laskey on September 21, 1966. Hinners was a star witness in the Bowman murder trial.

Apartment at 2012 Edgecliffe Point, Walnut Hills, where Della Ernst was accosted on October 4, 1966. She was saved by the caretaker's arrival.

On December 8, 1966, Sandra Chapas raced up the stairs to her third floor room above a restaurant at 14 West Court Street, eluding a man presumed to be Laskey.

The morning of December 9, Lula Kerrick was found dead in the lobby of the Brittany Apartments at 104 West Ninth Street, several blocks from the Chapas incident.

CHAPTER 2

THE TRIAL OF
POSTEAL LASKEY JR.

At 2:00 p.m., Monday, December 19, 1966, I arrived at Room 420 of the Hamilton County Courthouse for an interview with Chief Criminal Assistant Prosecutor Calvin W. Prem. I had been admitted to the practice of law in Ohio on October 19, 1966, and had long held a desire to be appointed as an assistant prosecuting attorney for Hamilton County. The recent resignations of assistants Burton Signer and Donald Roney, who were now slated to be Posteal Laskey's defense attorneys, had created two vacancies in the Criminal Division.

I had never formally met Cal Prem before that day. He was 42 years old, a sun-tanned, handsome man with coal-black hair combed back in the style of the 1940s. He was dressed in a dark blue pinstripe suit, white shirt and red tie. I noticed that his initials, C.W.P., were monogrammed on his left shirt sleeve cuff, just above his gold watch. He was also wearing gold cufflinks and highly polished black shoes. If ever there was a role model for a top-level trial lawyer, Cal Prem was it. Not only was Cal Prem a well-known and feared prosecutor, he also enjoyed a very successful civil trial practice.

I was aware that the purpose of my meeting with Cal Prem was to give him the opportunity to size me up. A week earlier, after learning that Signer and Roney had announced their intention to leave their positions, I had contacted Mel Rueger, by letter, seeking an appointment by him to his staff. I was a brand-new lawyer. I had never tried a court case of any kind. The only exposure I had ever had with a courtroom was the several occasions I had been called upon to testify as a witness. It was obvious that Rueger had orchestrated the interview with Prem so that he could receive Prem's assessment of me. I had the foresight to wear my best suit, polished shoes and color-coordinated tie and shirt.

During the interview, I could overhear a lot of conversations in the hall and adjoining offices about the Posteal Laskey case. On several occasions, Prem had to excuse himself to take a telephone call or to talk to someone in the office about Posteal Laskey. It was obvious that the prosecutor's office was consumed by this case, just the same as the rest of the community. I was duly impressed that Prem had the ability to divide his attention between tasks, a trait that I was to observe in him over the years, meaning that he could have a conversation with someone in his office, take a telephone call and be writing a letter out on a legal pad all at the same time.

My interview with Cal Prem lasted about 45 minutes. It concluded with the words, "We'll be in touch with you."

I prayed all the way back to my office in the Federal Building that Prem had meant what he said. My prayers were answered, for on December 23, I received a telephone call at home after dinner from Cal Prem. He congratulated me and asked if I could start with the prosecutor's office the first week of January. My feet left the carpet with this news. It was one of the greatest Christmas presents I would ever receive.

January 3, 1967, a Monday, was officially my first day in the Hamilton County prosecutor's office. For the next five years, it would literally become my second home. At no other time during my professional career have I enjoyed an experience and received as great an education as I did working for Melvin Rueger and Calvin Prem. Nor did I know that January day just how much I would end up being involved in the Posteal Laskey case, especially being the newest assistant in the office.

Laskey's case was assigned to Common Pleas Court Judge Simon L. Leis Sr. This immediately led to Signer and Roney filing a motion seeking Leis' removal from the case due to the remarks he had made to Laskey when sentencing him on the 1958 assault charge, in which Lytle Young had been the arresting officer. "Men like you should be put out of society for life," the judge had said to Laskey.

Signer and Roney also filed a motion to dismiss the charges against Laskey on the grounds that he had been illegally transported from the Workhouse to the Crime Bureau for a lineup without the presence of a lawyer. They also filed a motion to change venue, claiming that pretrial publicity implying that Laskey was the Cincinnati Strangler would prevent him from receiving a fair jury trial in Hamilton County. For this argument, Laskey's attorneys relied primarily on the 1966 Supreme Court decision reversing the conviction of Dr. Sam Sheppard for the murder of his wife, Marilyn, based on prejudicial pretrial publicity.

Both of these pretrial motions were denied, and Laskey's trial for the August 14, 1966, murder of Barbara Bowman was set for Monday, March 27, 1967.

The trial of the decade commenced on Monday, March 27, 1967.

Except for the media, Judge Simon Leis' third-floor courtroom was not overly crowded. Earlier that morning, before selection of a jury commenced, I was informed by Cal Prem that The Boss, as we all referred to Mel Rueger, had asked him to corral me for duty as a "gofer," meaning that if I didn't have a case of my own to try, I was to sit in the courtroom directly behind Rueger and Prem so that on an instant's notice I could be used to go for a law book or find a witness, or deliver a message.

"Chair cases," as we referred to murder trials where the death penalty was involved, were taken very seriously by the prosecutor's office. Smiles or laughter in the courtroom were forbidden for fear they might give jurors the impression that this was not such a serious matter, and that this perception might affect their deliberations concerning the death penalty — all to the advantage of the defendant.

It was pretty heady stuff for an assistant prosecutor with three months' experience to be invited to sit behind Rueger and Prem in a case with as high a profile as Laskey's. It was an opportunity for which I would gladly have paid an admission fee, if requested.

The first day of the jury selection process was my first opportunity to see Posteal Laskey Jr. up close. As had so often been reported, he was young looking, being 29 years old at that time. He was 5-feet, 6-inches tall and weighed 135 pounds. He had very dark skin and a slight goatee, which could really be seen only when one looked at the profile of his face.

If one were looking directly at the front of his face, the chin whiskers were hidden by the dark shadow of his throat, as photographs taken at the time showed. This, of course, would become an issue created by the defense.

I had been told by Lytle Young that Laskey's hands were way out of proportion to the rest of his body. In short, his hands and fingers were those of a much larger man. Young also told me that Laskey was self-conscious about his hands, and that he normally kept them hidden either in his pockets or behind his back. The first chance that I had to observe his hands was that March 27, when Stanley "Whitey" Heber, chief criminal court bailiff and a retired Cincinnati police detective, brought Laskey into the courtroom.

Whitey Heber was a giant of a man, 6-feet, 2-inches tall, well over 250 pounds, with the chiseled face of a North American Indian. No prisoner ever escaped from Whitey Heber. For this reason, he was always chosen from among the criminal bailiffs to be in charge of escorting murder defendants. He led them to and from courtrooms and the county jail, which in those days was located on the sixth floor of the Courthouse, three floors directly above Judge Leis' courtroom. The instant Heber brought Laskey into the courtroom through the side door, I looked at Laskey's hands, which were cuffed in front of him. Even though his hands were closed, I could tell that they were out of place on this man's small frame. These were the hands of a mighty big man. They were the hands of a strangler, I thought as I watched Laskey take a seat at the defense table between his two lawyers.

After Laskey's hands were freed from the chrome-plated handcuffs, he folded them in front of his body on the counsel table. He must have noticed that I was staring at his hands because several minutes later he slid them off the table and placed them in his lap.

Selection of the jury in the Barbara Bowman murder trial lasted all week. Finally, on Friday, March 31, a jury was impaneled. Four alternate jurors were seated just in case it would become necessary to replace any of the 12 main jurors. As was customary in all first-degree murder trials at the time, the jury was placed on a chartered bus and taken to the scene of the crime. In the Bowman case, it was decided by Rueger and Prem that several sites played an important role in the state's case concerning Barbara Bowman's death. As a result, the jurors were first driven to the Lark Cafe on Vine Street and then to the Yellow Cab parking lot on Kenner Street, the same lot from which cab Number 870 had been stolen on August 13. Next, they were taken to the intersection of Grand Avenue and Ring Place, after passing Barbara Bowman's apartment at 2909 Warsaw Avenue. And, finally, they headed down the hill to the corner of Bowman and Mistletoe, where Sol Thompson had picked Laskey up at 3:15 a.m. on the morning of August 14. The only remark that was heard from a juror was about the odd coincidence that there was a street involved in the case that bore the same name as the murdered woman.

On Monday, April 3, 1967, Mel Rueger made the prosecution's opening statement, outlining for the jury what evidence would be introduced to prove that Posteal Laskey was Barbara Bowman's killer. This date was particularly significant to me, since it was my 30th birthday. Sitting in the courtroom next to Sheriff Dan Tehan — listening to the prosecution's statement, followed by the defense opening statement delivered by Mr. Signer — I learned that Posteal Laskey had been born on June 18, 1937. He was only two-and-a-half months younger than I was. I was at the beginning of a career in the law, and he was probably nearing the end of the process of the law.

During the course of the Bowman trial, I saw Posteal Laskey every day. Shortly after the trial commenced, I became aware that Laskey enjoyed Western novels. The county jail had a small library for prisoners, mainly made up of paperback books. Laskey, as I was told by Assistant Warden Bill Springer, was interested in any Western novel or article that he could lay his hands on. He was particularly fond of books by Louis Lamour and Zane Grey. Several times during the 17 days of the Bowman trial, he came into the courtroom carrying a different Western novel.

The only real conversation that occurred between Laskey and myself came about during one of the numerous short recesses in the trial, when he was permitted to remain in the courtroom at the counsel table under the close scrutiny of Whitey Heber. As usual, Laskey had a Western novel with him, which he would read during the recesses. On this particular day, he was reading a paperback novel titled *The Desperado*. Several times prior to this day, Laskey and I had exchanged casual glances; however, we had never spoken. As he was reading, he realized that I was watching him. He looked up at me and said, "What is your name?" I answered, "Mestemaker." He looked back into his paperback novel for a second or two and then raised his eyes, looking at me with those cold brown spheres. "How do you spell it?" I spelled my last name for him. Once again, he looked back into his book. Then, once again, he looked up at me and, staring into my eyes, he said, "Damn, that's a strange name." We never had the opportunity to talk again. Maybe there was no purpose for further conversation between us.

In presenting the state's case, Mel Rueger was not interested in attempting to prove that Posteal Laskey was the Cincinnati Strangler, even though he personally believed that Laskey had murdered the six other women. His goal was to convince a jury that Laskey had murdered Barbara Bowman, either while robbing her or attempting to rape her — or both.

Of all the cases, the Bowman case was the strongest. There were witnesses who placed Laskey with the victim on the evening of August 13. If Rueger could convince the jury that the murder of Bowman was a heinous crime in which the guilty party should be shown no mercy, Laskey would be sentenced to die in the electric chair. In Rueger's mind — and he was correct — one guilty verdict and one death by electrocution would be sufficient to close the book on Laskey once and forever.

Rueger and Prem's first order of business was to re-create for the jury the scene that existed on Ring Place at 2:30 a.m., Sunday, August 14, 1966. When Ruth Bailey, the first of 25 witnesses, and her friend Raymond Waller happened upon the dying Barbara Bowman, she was lying on her back in the street. Bailey described the girl with her blue dress up around her hips; shoeless, her right foot dangling from her ankle — held there by a sliver of flesh and muscle; her throat cut open so wide they could see her jugular and her wind pipe; a $5 bill and house keys next to her outstretched right hand; blood running from her throat, mixing with rain, and swirling down the storm sewer grate. She moaned and occasionally moved her left leg and her arm as she laid there, eyes wide open as though she had stared into the depths of hell.

After Bailey related the hurried drive to Cincinnati Police District 3, where they alerted Officer Frank Sefton to their grizzly discovery, she was allowed to step down. Hands shaking from the ordeal, she left the courtroom. But she remained in the hall in case she was needed for further testimony.

The next witness was Officer Frank Sefton, who told the jurors that when he arrived at Ring Place behind Bailey and Waller, Barbara Bowman was still alive. "She was moaning — a soft, whimper-like sound. Her right foot was hanging by a thread. There were tire tracks over her right foot. She was bleeding profusely from her throat."

Sefton related the evidence he observed near Bowman, which included the $5 bill, keys, glass beads in the street and more on the back seat and floor of the Yellow Cab. He saw her *Enquirer* folded and lying on the floor of the cab surrounded by more glass beads.

Sefton told the jury that, after Bowman was taken away by the life squad ambulance, he tried to move the taxicab but could not steer it. He then discovered that the left tie rod was broken. He also noticed that there was moderate to heavy damage to the left front fender, caused, he believed, when Barbara Bowman was run down as she ran across Ring and Grand.

Sefton's sergeant had instructed him to remain at the scene and assist the homicide detectives in their search for evidence. Thus, Sefton was able to relate to the jurors that the murder weapon, a steak knife, was found about 10 feet down the street from where Bowman had been found. He also recalled the discovery of her blue high-heeled shoes farther down Grand Avenue, and the finding of her horn-rimmed glasses near a hedge on the west side of the street. Sefton recounted that he was present when her purse was found on Ring Place around 6 a.m., when it started to get light. Then her wallet and identification papers were found thrown into a yard farther east on Ring Place. These finds led police to the conclusion that the killer had run east on Ring Place, discarding Bowman's effect as he ran.

The fourth witness called by Prem was Thomas Tomasick. A local resident who happened on the scene just as Bailey and Waller had driven away to find a police officer. At first, Tomasick had thought he was observing an automobile accident involving the woman in the street and a cab. When he heard a siren drawing closer and concluded correctly that police were coming, he decide to stay and help if needed.

Tomasick described what he saw in a manner that conveyed the true horror of the murder scene. It was obvious to me that the jurors were moved by what they were hearing. Tomasick told the jury that after the ambulance arrived, the police asked him to help them place the victim on a stretcher. But when he looked at her throat and saw her other injuries, he became sick. He could not help because he had to throw up.

The next five witnesses were homicide detectives who had recovered evidence at the scene. They also had taken photographs and the necessary measurements. These witnesses, in the order in which they were called, were Sergeant Virgil Hall, and Detectives James Corcoran, Robert Bluhm and Kenneth Davis. Last in this group was Sergeant Charles Berghausen, who had been sent to St. Mary's Hospital to take charge of the body of Barbara Bowman, who expired at 3:30 a.m. He was required to remain with her body during the autopsy, and to take photographs for use in the trial.

Detective Robert Bluhm testified how he examined Yellow Cab Number 870 at the Police District 1 garage. He could not lift any fingerprints, but he did find a newspaper and glass beads on the floor of the back seat. He also found a single key on a ring in the cab's ignition. It was a duplicate key for a Checker style cab.

For the ninth witness, the scene changed to the evening hours that led to Barbara Bowman's death. Rueger called Betty Beckman, the friend who had picked Bowman up at her apartment and driven her to the Lark Cafe. She recounted how around 1:45 a.m., Bowman said she was tired and called a cab to take her home. Beckman tearfully identified Bowman's dress, shoes, glasses, purse and beads from her necklace. She became unglued as she looked at the black-and-white morgue photos of her friend, wishing she had taken Barbara Bowman home from the cafe that terrible night, rather than letting her call a cab.

The next four witnesses, in order, were Raymond Holstein, Carl Steigleiter, Clyde Vollmer and his wife, Margaret Vollmer. All four identified Laskey as the man who had entered the Lark Cafe at 2:09 a.m. on August 14 and yelled, "Cab." They also saw him walk out with Barbara Bowman behind him, as she bid everyone "goodnight."

Holstein was the only one of these witness to mention Laskey's facial hair. The fact that the other witnesses in the case failed to put a mustache or goatee on Laskey was to be one of his lawyers' arguments that he was a victim of misidentification.

Holstein told the jurors that around 2:00 a.m. a short, slender black man came into the bar, stood by the cigarette machine and yelled, "Cab." At that, Barbara Bowman stood and said, "That's my cab." She then said "Goodnight" and followed the man out the door.

Carl Steigleiter testified that he was sitting next to Bowman at the bar. When he looked up from his beer, the cabby was facing him. "He was very dark; he appeared nervous; he looked like he was going to rob the bar or something."

Both Clyde and Margaret Vollmer identified Laskey as the man who came into the bar and yelled "Cab." Clyde described him as slender, 160 to 170 pounds, about 5-feet, 7-inches or 5-feet, 8-inches tall. Neither of the Vollmers noticed a mustache or goatee.

After the witnesses from the Lark Cafe had placed Laskey in the bar as a cab driver picking up Barbara Bowman, Charlotte Barnhardt and Eileen Aultz were called to relate to the jury their experience with a black man who was in the back seat of a parked Yellow cab on Grand Avenue and who raised his head and stared at them when they stopped next to the cab to ask for directions. Charlotte Barnhardt captured the jury's undivided attention when she testified:

"There was a colored man in the back seat of the cab. He raised his head and looked at us. I said, 'Sir, can you tell us where the Summit Apartments are.' He said nothing. I repeated my question. He stared at me and then he climbed over the seat and started the cab up. As he started to back away from us, I saw a white woman raise up in the back seat just for a short time. Then she laid back down as though she didn't want to be seen."

The impact was electrifying. It was obvious to everyone in the courtroom at this point that Charlotte Barnhardt and Eileen Aultz were among the last of several people to ever see Barbara Bowman while she was still alive — and that they had been Bowman's last hope for rescue. But Barnhardt and Aultz had not realized it at the time.

The following witnesses were individuals connected with one or more cabs. Sol Thompson, the Parkway cab driver who picked a man up in the rain at Bowman and Mistletoe, identified Laskey as his fare. Leroy Smith testified that earlier on August 13, Laskey had been the driver of a

Checker-style cab that had driven him and Debbie Gray to the Katanga Lounge. He noted how the cabby had not turned the meter on until he mentioned it to him. Arthur Scholl testified how it was Laskey whom he intercepted in the Kenner Street cab storage lot on August 12. He testified that he saw a black man that night, who was definitely the defendant, and that he suspected that he was trying to steal one of the Checker-style cabs. He also testified that a Checker-style cab was, in fact, stolen from the Kenner Street lot the very next night. It was Checker-style cab Number 870.

David Shanklin, a dispatcher for the Yellow Cab Company, testified that on the evening of August 13-14, he dispatched cab Number 186 on six calls, the last one being to pick up a woman at the Lark Cafe at 2:06 a.m. Vincent Taylor, a second dispatcher, testified that he monitored six calls for cab Number 186 and that cab 870 received no calls that night. He recalled that at the time, no one knew that cab 870 was on the street. Harlan Blazer, the personnel manager of Taxicabs of Cincinnati, testified that he had hired Posteal Laskey Jr., on July 31, 1962, and that he was assigned to drive cab Number 186, which, in 1962, was a Checker-style cab. Laskey was fired on December 13, 1962, but never turned in his ignition key for the cab he was assigned to operate. Blazer also testified that one ignition key fits all Checker cabs. He had checked the odometer on Checker-style cab Number 870 at the police impound garage at District 1 on August 16 and determined that it had been driven 69 miles on the evening of August 13-14, 1966, but that the meter indicated that only 16 miles were paid miles. He concluded his testimony by stating that it appeared to him that whoever was driving Number 870 that night spent a lot of miles and time "cruising" the city.

Dr. Frank Cleveland, the Hamilton County coroner, testified that he had performed the autopsy on the body of Barbara Bowman at the Hamilton County Morgue on Sunday, August 14. To Dr. Cleveland, the fact that it was Sunday was immaterial since he had been notified at home that the case was one involving a murder. He testified that she had been pronounced dead at St. Mary Hospital at 3:30 a.m., and that his postmortem examination revealed that her jugular vein had been nearly completely severed, resulting in the loss of six pints of blood. He had also found a compound fracture and dislocation of her right ankle. There were multiple bruises and contusions noted on her forehead, face, neck, arms, abdomen and legs. There was an unbroken ligature mark around her neck, which indicated the possibility to him that she had been strangled. Dr.

Cleveland examined and identified the piece of rope that police had recovered on Ring Place. It still had several glass beads imbedded in it, which were identical to the glass beads that had been found on the rear seat and floor of cab Number 870 by Detective Robert Bluhm.

Dr. Cleveland continued his testimony by stating that the death of Barbara Bowman, a 31-year-old Caucasian female, 5-feet, 7-inches tall, 120 pounds, was the result of exsanguination due to five stab wounds of the right side of the neck, which severed the right common carotid artery and the internal jugular vein. In short, Barbara Bowman had bled to death.

When asked how the injuries he noted on Barbara Bowman compared to similarly injured individuals, Dr. Cleveland said, "She was slaughtered."

The last witness called by Rueger and Prem in the state's case caused the most violent reaction from the defense. On April 11, about 10:30 a.m., Rueger asked the bailiff in Judge Leis' courtroom to go to the hall and call Virginia Hinners. The courtroom door opened and in walked the well-groomed, now 54-year-old mother of four, who had faced Posteal Laskey Jr., in the office of the New Thought Unity Center on September 21, five weeks after the murder of Barbara Bowman.

As Mrs. Hinners took the witness stand, she and Laskey made eye contact. I watched Laskey from my vantage point, and it appeared to me that his shoulders sagged as his former robbery victim stared at him. Burton Signer and Donald Roney, on behalf of their client, objected strenuously to any testimony by Virginia Hinners about an incident that, they argued, was unrelated to the crime for which their client was on trial. They knew that her testimony would be highly charged and persuasive.

Mel Rueger and Cal Prem argued convincingly to Judge Leis that Mrs. Hinners' testimony should be allowed under Revised Code Section 2945.59, which permitted testimony of other bad conduct on the part of the defendant if it tended to prove his motive or intent in doing a similar act. Finally, after over a half-hour of oral argument out of the presence of the jury, Judge Leis ruled that Mrs. Hinners could testify.

By this time in the proceeding, being the 13th day of the trial, it was not uncommon for some members of the jury to appear tired and at times somewhat disinterested in further testimony. This is often interpreted in various ways, some believing that jurors have already made their minds up and others believing it is a sign that they have heard enough. Several jurors, in particular one middle-age woman, had begun to look bored. This all changed with the testimony of Virginia Hinners. She recounted the words of her assailant:

"Do you want what the others got? Do you want what the others got? Do you want what the others got? Don't scream. Don't scream. Don't scream. I'll slit your throat. I'll slit your throat."

Every juror in that jury box was leaning forward in their chairs. There was absolutely no sound in the courtroom. The loudest noise was Cal Prem's pen dancing across his legal pad, setting down Virginia Hinners' words.

When Rueger asked Hinners whether the man who had assaulted and robbed her that night in September 1966 was present in the courtroom, she pointed at Laskey and said:

"That's him. I'll never forget that face or those eyes."

Rueger concluded: "Mrs. Hinners, is there any question in your mind that this is the man?"

Hinners: "There is none, whatsoever."

As if he were assisting Rueger in his prosecution efforts, Burton Signer asked Mrs. Hinners whether she had seen her assailant's hands. Her answer was, "I know that he had large hands."

On April 10 — after seven days, 25 witnesses and 87 exhibits — the state of Ohio rested its case.

As was predicted, Laskey's attorneys, Donald Roney and Burton Signer, began calling witnesses whom they hoped would establish an alibi for the accused. They wanted to persuade the jury that on the night Barbara Bowman was murdered he was nowhere near a taxi, the Lark Cafe or the victim. They also intended to show that Laskey was a victim of misidentification because he had facial hair, which most of the prosecution witnesses had failed to observe.

The first witness was Samson Perry, a friend of Laskey. He stated that Laskey always had a short mustache and goatee. He was followed by Paul Binder, who worked with Laskey at the Adam Wuest mattress factory. He testified that Laskey had worn a goatee and mustache for more than a year.

On cross examination by Melvin Rueger, Binder told a hushed courtroom that State's Exhibit 20, a piece of rope embedded with Barbara Bowman's beads, was the kind of rope used at Adam Wuest to wrap paper around new mattresses.

This testimony was a bonus, since Rueger had not known whether Binder would agree that the rope in evidence was identical to that which he and Laskey used every day at the mattress factory. Rueger had gambled, and it had paid off. The defense was shaken by this testimony.

The next witness was Michael Chapel, who had known Laskey for about four years. He told the jurors that he saw Laskey at the Soul Lounge on August 13, saying that when he got there around 10:30 p.m. Laskey was already there.

In rapid succession, Laskey's lawyers called his friend Charles Thompson, his brother, David Laskey, and his mother, Nancy Laskey.

Thompson testified that he saw Laskey at his mother's home at 1820 Freeman Avenue around 1:30 a.m. David Laskey told jurors that he saw his brother at the house at 3:15 a.m., asleep on the living room sofa. Nancy Laskey could only say that her son Posteal was living with her in August 1966 (which was itself untrue) and that he had left the house around 8:30 p.m. on August 13 and that she next saw him around 5:00 a.m. on August 14. "He was in his bed asleep," she said. Mother and brother vouched for Posteal's mustache and goatee.

The defense then called Joseph Riley, who booked bands for night clubs. He testified that he had heard Laskey was playing at the Soul Lounge with a group called The Outlaws, and that he went to the lounge the evening of August 13. He saw Laskey, and he vouched for Posteal's mustache and goatee.

Witness Number 8 was Benjamin Johnson, another friend of the defendant. He related that he arrived at 1820 Freeman Avenue about 1:30 a.m. on August 14, and that Posteal was lying on the living room couch watching television. Of course, he was asked to describe defendant's mustache and goatee.

Defense Witness 9 was not a relative or friend of the defendant. He was George C. Mumford Jr., an FBI identification expert from Washington, D.C. At the request of Cincinnati police, the FBI had sent Mumford here to make a composite sketch of Barbara Bowman's killer. His initial visit was on August 19, four days after the Bowman murder. At the trial, Mumford recounted his interviews with Sol Thompson, Carl Steigleiter, and the Vollmers. He said that based on their descriptions, he was able to draw a pen-and-ink sketch of the suspect, which did not depict either a mustache or a goatee, since none of those interviewed ever mentioned facial hair. He testified that he made a point of asking each witness whether the suspect had any facial hair, and all told him that they had seen no facial hair.

Emmitt Baldwin, a meteorologist for the U.S. Weather Bureau, was called and questioned about the weather on the evening of August 13 and the morning of August 14. His records substantiated that between 2:00 and 2:30 a.m., the Cincinnati area experienced light to moderate rain and that from 2:30 until approximately 3:00 a.m. the rain was heavy. Since this testimony confirmed the state's testimony and there was no dispute concerning the weather, we never understood why the defense offered this evidence.

The final defense witness was Posteal Laskey Jr. He told the jurors that he did not know Barbara Bowman and had never seen her in his life. He testified that he had never been in the Lark Cafe and had not stolen a car on August 13. He denied that he drove Leroy Smith and his girlfriend to the Katanga Lounge in a Yellow Cab or any other vehicle. He claimed that on Saturday, August 13, he had left his mother's house around 8:30 p.m. for the Soul Lounge because he thought that his group, The Outlaws, was playing that evening. Learning that the group was not scheduled, he decided to stay. He recounted that he consumed several beers. He returned to his mother's home around 1:30 a.m. on August 14, watched television and went to bed about 2:30 a.m.

On cross-examination, Laskey denied having any contact with any of the people who claimed he picked up Bowman at the Lark. He denied riding in a cab driven by Sol Thompson. He denied that he had ever been in the New Thought Unity Temple, saying that Virginia Hinners was wrong when she said he attacked her there on September 21, 1966.

Laskey became agitated when Prosecutor Rueger asked him to hold up his hands for the jurors to see. He didn't like Rueger's questions, and his glare said so. And then it was over.

The jury received the Barbara Bowman murder case on the afternoon of April 12. After nine hours of deliberation, during which time they were sequestered and housed overnight at a downtown hotel, they reached a verdict. Their verdict, announced shortly before noon on Friday, April 13, 1967, was "guilty as charged of the murder of Barbara Bowman while committing the crime of robbery."

There was no recommendation for mercy by the jury, which, under the law then in existence in Ohio, meant that the death penalty was automatically invoked. On May 5, Judge Simon L. Leis sentenced Posteal Laskey Jr. to die in Ohio's electric chair for the murder of Barbara Bowman. The execution was set for September 15, 1967. And the lengthy appeal process began.

On June 11, 1967, District 4 police arrested Posteal Laskey's cousin, Peter Frakes, who was picketing against his cousin's conviction. Frakes was accused of blocking a sidewalk in Avondale. This act sparked a race riot — the first to hit Cincinnati during the turbulent 1960s. The presence of the Ohio National Guard was required to quell the rioting over four bloody, flame-filled days. When the riots ended, the entire business section of Avondale was a charred ruin.

In 1972, the U.S. Supreme Court declared the death penalty unconstitutional. All those convicted and sentenced to death prior to that decision were given amnesty. Laskey's sentence was commuted to life, with the possibility of parole. His petition has been rejected three times. He will be eligible for parole consideration again in 2003.

Was Posteal Laskey Jr. in fact the Cincinnati Strangler? There has never been universal agreement. And, short of a confession, there probably never will be. Over the years, some thought has been given to reopening several of the other cases, in particular, the murders of Emogene Harrington and Alice K. Hockhausler. But so many witnesses have passed away and so much evidence has been lost or destroyed that such a trial is unlikely.

One thing is certain: After the arrest of Laskey, the mysterious and gruesome rape-strangulations ended. Whether they ended because the perpetrator had been caught or whether they were unrelated to begin with, will more than likely remain unanswered.

What do you think?

Police mug shots from December 1966 of accused murderer Posteal Laskey Jr. reveal the short goatee that was an identification issue in his murder trial.

The house at 1820 Freeman Avenue, where Posteal Laskey stayed with his mother.

*Hamilton County Prosecutor Melvin C. Rueger and Chief Assistant Prosecutor
Calvin W. Prem presented the state's case at the Laskey trial in April 1967.*
Cincinnati Post *photo, 1965.*

*Assistant Prosecutor Albert J. Mestemaker's assignment to the Laskey trial gave
the 30-year-old attorney an unforgettable crash course in the prosecutorial arts*

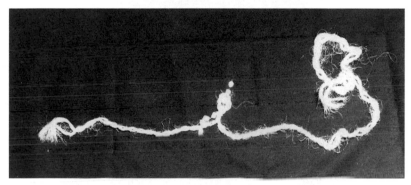

Barbara Bowman survived near-strangulation with a mattress cord and being run down by her assailant in a cab. Her killer finally slit her throat with a paring knife and left her to die in the rainy street of Ring Place, not far from her Price Hill apartment.

No parole for Laskey

Angry letters protested Cincinnati killer's release

From staff and wire reports

Posteal Laskey Jr., serving time in prison for a brutal Cincinnati stabbing, was denied parole Wednesday.

The denial came less than two weeks after a storm of protest reached the Ohio Parole Board, said John W. Shoemaker, chief of Ohio's Adult Parole Authority. Shoemaker said he did not know why the board refused parole.

Laskey, who was convicted in the 1966 stabbing death of Barbara Bowman, 31, a Price Hill secretary, will again be eligible for parole in five years. Laskey escaped the electric chair when Ohio's death penalty was declared unconstitutional.

Earlier this month, outraged Hamilton County Prosecutor Arthur Ney Jr. called for letters protesting Laskey's release. Ney said Wednesday he was pleased with the denial.

Laskey was suspected of committing six other murders that sparked a citywide panic that year, but was tried and convicted only in Miss Bowman's death. All of the other victims were elderly, white women who were strangled to death, putting the city in fear of a "Cincinnati strangler."

Laskey, now 49, was the second of two Cincinnati criminals eligible for parole this year to be turned down. After receiving numerous telephone calls and letters of protest, the parole board last week reconsidered its decision to release Raymond Kassow, 40, convicted for the 1969 murder of Lillian DeWald, one of four women shot to death during a robbery.

"No parole for Laskey," Cincinnati Post, April 16, 1987. Parole was denied then and in subsequent applications. The article also mentions a Delhi Township murder case that involved Mestemaker.

CHAPTER 3

I LOVED THAT OLD MAN

Louis J. Schneider — Judge Louis J. Schneider, where had I heard that name before? Oh, yes, Schneider's Criminal Code. The book that Don Montfort, my mentor in the prosecutor's office, said I had to have. The same book that my boss, Hamilton County Prosecutor Mel Rueger, co-authored. The trial handbook that all Ohio prosecutors in the 1950s and '60s considered akin to the Bible. It was bound in red and weighed about 2 pounds. It was a full 4 inches thick. But every assistant prosecuting attorney carried it to court every day. We believed it was the magic book, that without it we would never win a criminal case. This book was our courtroom Bible because it contained all the criminal statutes of Ohio. It contained all of the elements necessary to prove a crime. It covered procedure from arrest through trial, sentencing, and appeal. In short, Judge Schneider's book, with the text section by Melvin G. Rueger, covered everything from soup to nuts.

Louis J. Schneider had been a Common Pleas Court judge since before World War II. Some lawyers claimed he was a judge when Abraham Lincoln was president. Before that, he had been Hamilton County's prosecuting attorney. He was a gentleman and a jurist of the old school. He wore a green plastic forehead visor to shield his eyes from the glare of overhead lights. He sat on the bench either hunched forward or leaning back in his chair as if asleep. He resembled a wrinkled troll. He was the last Hamilton County judge to have a spittoon beneath his bench to catch his chew of tobacco juice. He refused permission for any lawyer to try a case in his room in a sport coat. No suit, no trial. No lawyer ever approached the bench in Judge Schneider's room, at least a second time, without obtaining permission first. Courtroom demeanor and etiquette were paramount in the Old Man's courtroom. We use to refer to him as "Judge Manners." He was old and bald. There were times during a trial when he would lean his head back in his high-backed leather chair and close his eyes. Next could be heard heavy breathing. Even jurors would nudge each other to look at the sleeping judge. Just about the time everyone in the room was convinced that Judge Schneider had fallen sound asleep, one of the lawyers would say, "Objection" — then the Old Man would open one eye and say either "Overruled" or "Sustained." He never ever missed a beat or a trick.

Judge Schneider's knowledge of the law and the rules of evidence were legend. Most judges have their jury instructions typed up so they can read them without risk of error. This is extremely important to every trial judge. No judge wants to have a jury trial reversed by a court of appeals, especially for giving wrong instructions to the jury. But Judge Louis J. Schneider didn't have to read jury instructions. He had been doing it for so long and his retention of the law was so vast that he was able to recite jury instructions word for word, verse for verse from memory without ever skipping a beat. Time after time, he gave the jury the definition of what constituted evidence beyond reasonable doubt from memory — without ever missing so much as one word. He was truly an amazing man.

I looked forward to trying cases in his room, especially jury trials. That's because trying a case, in particular a criminal case, before Judge Schneider was like being paid to go to school. I knew he had a short fuse, and I knew from experience that it was a big mistake to argue with him. But I had never been known to back away from a fight — partly because by nature I'm not fearful, and primarily because I lack a certain amount of common sense. That, when combined with an active tongue and an aggressive nature, can lead one, especially a young assistant prosecuting attorney, into treacherous waters.

That's just what happened on Thursday, July 3, 1969, while I was try-ing a burglary case before a jury in Judge Schneider's courtroom. The late Anthony Bruenneman was the defendant's attorney. The case, which lacked any eye witnesses, hinged on whether I could introduce evidence that fibers, removed from a piece of plywood that had been broken out of a window frame through which the burglar had entered the building, matched fibers from a sweater that the defendant was wearing when he was arrested two blocks from the burglarized building. Even though the defen-dant had given a statement to the police that tended to implicate him in the burglary, I could not introduce his statement unless I had independent evidence to link him to the crime. This is referred to as corpus dilecti, or the body of the crime. Since no witnesses came forward to say they had seen the defendant crawl through the window, I would not be allowed to introduce his statement to the police unless I could link the clothing fibers found at the scene of the crime to the sweater the defendant was wearing. Without this evidence, the best I could do would be to obtain a conviction for receiving stolen property — to wit, a pair of gym shoes that, because of their minimal value, would amount to a misdemeanor. I wanted a felony burglary conviction, and it all hinged on the sweater fiber evidence. I knew it. Tony Bruenneman knew it. And Judge Schneider knew it. Before the day was over, the jury would know it — and I would be in jail.

Steve Molner was a chemist and criminologist for the Ohio Bureau of Criminal Identification in London, Ohio. After the arrest of the defendant in this burglary case, Detective Bill Brauning had sent the defendant's sweater as well as fibers taken from the plywood window covering at the crime scene to the OBCI for analysis and comparison. The spectrographic comparison, under microscope, of the sweater and the crime scene fibers proved that the sweater and the fibers were one and the same. Molner was my key witness. As a result, Tony Bruenneman knew that his one chance at getting his client acquitted of the burglary charge was to keep the scientific sweater fiber evidence out — in other words, to prevent the jury from hearing this evidence. As a result, Bruenneman lodged an objection to every question that I posed to Molner, including his name and occupation.

Despite the road block that Bruenneman threw in my path, I kept plodding along and finally reached the point in my questioning of Molner where I was ready to ask the $64,000 question, which was: "Mr. Molner, do you have an opinion to a reasonable scientific certainty, and are you able to express an opinion to a reasonable scientific certainty, whether the fibers taken from the crime scene match the fibers contained in the defendant's sweater?"

To this question I knew that Molner's answer would be "Yes." As soon as he would say yes, that he did have an opinion, the rules of evidence would permit me to then ask him what his opinion was. His answer that, which we had discussed before the trial, would be:

"In my opinion as a chemist and a forensic scientist for the state of Ohio, the fibers found at the crime scene and sent to my lab by Detective Brauning are a match with the fibers found by me in the sweater removed the same day from the defendant by the same detective and also forwarded to me for analysis."

This was my whole case. I expected that Bruenneman would object to my question of Molner concerning whether he had such a opinion. What I did not expect was to hear Judge Schneider say, "Sustained." For a second, I felt as though someone had punched me in the stomach, taking my breath away. I looked at Judge Schneider, and he merely shrugged his shoulders and said, "Ask another question." I glanced at Tony Bruenneman who was sitting next to his client grinning at me like a shark. I murmured SOB under my breath, then rephrased the same question by mixing a few key words around. Again, there was an objection. And, again, I heard that horrible phrase, "Objection sustained." I began to feel blood rushing to my face, which then would naturally turn red. I didn't want the jury to get the impression that I was flustered or angry, so I asked, "May we approach the bench?" This is really a signal to a judge — Time out; I need some direction. Only this time, it didn't work. I asked permission to approach the bench, only to hear, "Request denied. Ask another question." Now Bruenneman was grinning like a Cheshire cat. And his client, sensing that I was wounded, was also smiling at me. Now I was really pissed off, and it showed. So I started all over again — and got the same ruling: "Objection sustained." This time, when I asked whether we could approach the bench, Judge Schneider said, "All right, if you insist."

Once at the bench, I explained to Judge Schneider what he already knew: That it was imperative to my case that the jury hear Steve Molner's opinion. At which the judge said to me, "I'm not running a course in evidence." I replied by saying, "Look, your Honor, I am asking this question using what I believe to be proper terminology." Saying "Look, your Honor" was not the best way to start a sentence with Judge Schneider. He raised one heavily haired eyebrow and looked me right in the eye:

"Has anyone ever told you that the shortest distance between two points is a straight line?"

I thought to myself, "What in the hell does that remark mean? This is not a geometry class." It was a good thing the Old Man couldn't read my thoughts. Or could he? He certainly didn't look very pleased with me.

At this point, I said, "Judge Schneider, I have absolutely no idea what a straight line has to do with this point of law. All I am asking this witness is whether he has an opinion to a reasonable scientific certainty if the cloth fibers from the crime scene match the defendant's sweater."

Judge Schneider looked down at his fingers and said, "What is your authority for this question using that phraseology?" Without hesitating, I blurted out, rather sarcastically, "Schneider's Criminal Code." The judge looked at me and said, "Where is that point contained in the book?"

"I'll find it Judge, give me a minute." I paged and paged. Finally, I heard: "Time's up. Ask another question." I was in pain. I looked at the judge, then at Bruenneman, and then at the jury. I thought I could see looks of sympathy in the faces of several jurors. I went to the podium and said, "Judge Schneider, if I ask the same question of Mr. Molner using the same terminology and Mr. Bruenneman objects again, which I know he will, are you going to once again sustain his objection?" Judge Schneider just looked at me as though I had lost my mind. He said, "I will once again tell you that I am not running a class in evidence."

I glanced at my watch; it was 2:15 p.m. The date was Thursday, July 3, 1969. The next day would be Friday, July 4, 1969, a holiday. Besides, my wife and 3-year-old daughter, Tonya, were planning to pick me up at the Courthouse at 4:05 p.m. so we could drive to Lake Forest, Illinois, north of Chicago, to spend the Fourth of July weekend with her parents. If I could get the Old Man to recess for the day, I could get out of his clutches, cool down over the holiday weekend and come back on Monday ready to resume our battle. By then, I would be able to research the evidence law and be prepared to either convince him that my question of Molner was a proper one, or, if he was correct and I was missing some essential word or phrase in the question, I could find the answer and solve the riddle. Eureka! I had the solution.

"Judge Schneider, I have just noticed that it is now after 2:00 p.m., and today is the day before a holiday. Since I am sure that the ladies and gentlemen of the jury and Mr. Bruenneman would like to get an earlier start than 4:00 p.m., I recommend that we adjourn until Monday. And since the defendant is out on bond, this will not require him to sit in jail all weekend."

Judge Schneider looked at me over the green shade of his electric bench lamp and said:

"Now that you don't know how to ask a question, you want to tell me when to adjourn my courtroom for a long weekend. Request denied."

OK, I had one more arrow in my quiver. "Judge, my wife and daughter are coming to pick me up so that we can go to Lake Forest, Illinois, for the holiday weekend. So I need to quit for the day."

"Mr. Mestemaker," he shot back, "We will recess when I say we recess, not before or after. Since my wife passed away, I don't celebrate many holidays anyway. They are all one in the same to me. For the last time, ask another question."

"Judge Schneider," I choked, "I don't feel very well. I think that I am getting sick to my stomach. Can we recess for about 15 minutes?" I knew that this would work, even the Old Man would be moved by a lawyer about to throw up on his beloved courtroom podium. Wrong again. The judge, looking very angry by now, said, "You have wasted almost 20 minutes of everyone's time. I want you to apologize to this jury and move this case along."

"Judge," I said, "I have no reason to apologize to this jury. As far as

I'm concerned, I have not wasted anyone's time. All I am trying to do is my job. With all due respect, if anyone has held up this trial it is you and Mr. Bruenneman."

Did I hear the judge correctly? I thought I heard him say to his bailiff, "Call for the sheriff." No, that can't be right, I must be hallucinating. The judge then looked me in the eye and said, "Sit down, Mr. Mestemaker. Since you refuse to follow my instruction to move this case along, and since you refuse to apologize to this jury as directed, you can sit in the county jail and contemplate your next course of action."

Within a matter of minutes, Dave Culler, who was chief deputy sheriff, came into Judge Schneider's room in response to the bailiff's call. Next to enter the courtroom was the sheriff himself, Dan Tehan, who was also a referee in the old National Football League, a man of national stature — tall, thin and an all-around fine gentleman. After a consultation with Judge Schneider, Sheriff Tehan came over to the table where I was sitting and said, "Mike, I'm sorry: Judge Schneider has ordered me to escort you to the sixth-floor jail to be held for contempt of court."

I stood up and asked, "Judge Schneider, do I at least get to make one telephone call." He smiled slightly when he said, "All right. One call."

I went to the telephone at the bailiff's desk and immediately called the prosecutor's office. Mary Clark answered in her grouchy, old but lovable voice. I said, "Mary, let me talk to the boss. Judge Schneider has ordered me locked up, and I think it may be for the entire Fourth of July weekend." Mary — never one to trifle with, even under the best of circumstances — shot back, "Listen, Mike, I don't have time for your practical jokes, and Mr. Rueger is gone for the day."

"Mary, don't hang up on me. I'm not kidding. Judge Schneider is about to order me to jail, and I need help."

Mary said, "What did you do now, threaten to burn down the Courthouse?"

"No," I said. "Get Cal Prem. I need him down here."

"Cal is also gone," replied Mary.

"Who is there?" I pleaded.

"Len Kirschner is still here."

"Please get him down here now, Mary, and I mean it."

I sat back down and waited for Leonard, the top-ranking prosecutor on duty, to arrive. Since Judge Schneider's courtroom was on the third floor and the prosecutor's office was on the fourth floor, it took Leonard about three minutes to arrive. I hurriedly filled Len in on what was going on. He said that he would take care of it. What a mistake that was. When he informed Judge Schneider of my constitutional right to have bond set and to a formal hearing on a contempt citation, Leonard was threatened with having a cell next to mine. The judge told Len Kirschner that I was in direct contempt for failure to apologize to the jury as ordered, and that I was going to sit in jail until I apologized, even if it took all weekend. Leonard recommended to me in a hushed voice that I apologize. Being 32 years old and bull headed, I said, "Never!" And away I was led to the elevator, to be whisked to the sixth-floor holding cellblock. This may have been my first lesson in never say "Never." Leonard shouted after me that he would stay and talk to Judge Schneider to see what he could do to intervene on my behalf. He kept his word and stuck it out until I was released from jail at 4:15 p.m., later that same day. As the jail elevator door closed behind me, I could hear Leonard say, "Mike, you had better change your mind about apologizing."

Sheriff Tehan and his staff treated me like visiting royalty while I sat in the holding cell. Normally, prisoners have to surrender all valuables, including watch and rings as well as belt and shoelaces. This way you cannot hang yourself from a bar of the jail cell. I was not required to surrender any belongings. I was also allowed to keep my cigarettes (I smoked in those days). Chief Deputy Sheriff Dave Culler had his people get me a Coke and later a cup of coffee and a candy bar. About 4:00 p.m., Leonard Kirschner came up to see me. He told me that Judge Schneider did not want to keep me in jail all weekend. He also related to me that my wife and daughter had arrived at the Courthouse to pick me up to go to Lake Forest. Leonard had talked to my wife who, needless to say, was very upset and angry with me because of my stubbornness. She and my daughter were sitting in Len's office waiting for the outcome of the stand-off between Judge Schneider and me. Leonard said that he had offered to personally post a bond for me, but that Judge Schneider had refused the offer, stating that he wanted me to learn a lesson in humility. I weighed my options and finally decided that I was not going to win Judge Schneider over this way, and I was going to ruin my weekend, as well as that of my wife and our daughter, Tonya. So I sent word to Judge Schneider, through Leonard, that I would apologize for my obstreperous behavior.

Just about 4:15 p.m., Dave Culler and Bill Parsons, the jail warden, brought me down to Judge Schneider's room. My wife and Leonard were in the courtroom. My daughter, Tonya, was playing with the gavel on the bailiff's desk while Judge Schneider made her laugh by winking at her and looking over the top of his glasses. The jury was brought back into the courtroom. Judge Schneider asked me whether I had anything to say. I stood and offered my apology to the court and to the jurors. Judge Schneider thanked me and turned to the jury. He introduced my wife and my daughter to the jurors. He told them that he had decided to grant my request for an adjournment and that they should have a nice July 4 and return on Monday morning, at which time the trial would resume. With those words, the jurors were led out and Judge Schneider said that he would see us on Monday.

On Sunday evening, when I returned from Lake Forest, I called Cal Prem, who was the chief assistant prosecuting attorney in the criminal division. We met in the law library at 8:00 a.m. Monday and found the case law that I needed to convince Judge Schneider that I was asking Steve Molner a proper question after all. When the trial resumed, I was prepared to convince Judge Schneider of the validity of my argument in a professional manner.

Afterward, when Steve Molner was recalled to the witness stand, he was permitted to give his opinion to a reasonable "chemical" and scientific certainty that the crime-scene fibers and the defendant's sweater were one and the same. At 3:00 p.m. that beautiful sunny July day in 1969, that wonderful, intelligent jury returned a verdict of guilty of burglary as charged. I had won the hardest criminal trial up to that time in my brief career, and I had to go to jail to do it.

I have told this story to young lawyers and law school students hundreds of times. Without fail, I have been asked by my listeners each time I relate this tale what action was taken against Judge Schneider for locking me up. No matter how many times I have said that there was no complaint filed against Judge Schneider by me or anyone connected with this incident, they appear astounded. More than once I have heard a listener say, "No judge will ever lock me up and get away with it without a complaint."

My response has always been, and will always be, "I learned more law and more evidence in Judge Schneider's courtroom than anywhere else, including law school. I would never have even considered filing a complaint against him with either the bar association or the Ohio Supreme Court. I loved that old man."

Judge Louis Schneider authored Schneider's Criminal Code, *the standard reference work for the trial bench and bar of Ohio. He was the last judge in Hamilton County to keep a spittoon beside his courtroom bench.*

CHAPTER 4

DON'T LEAVE ANYONE IN THERE ALIVE

On a spring-like, early fall day in 1969, the peace of suburban Delhi Township, 7 miles west of downtown Cincinnati, was shattered when four white, middle-age women were murdered, execution style, during the robbery of a savings and loan. The slaying of four people within less than five minutes was the worst robbery/murder in Greater Cincinnati's history. The fact that all four women were well-known local residents and that one of them, the teller, was the wife of a Cincinnati police officer made the crimes even more heinous.

"Don't leave anyone in there alive." With these six words, spoken by Raymond Kassow on the morning of Wednesday, September 24, 1969, four women were sentenced to death. They did not have the benefit of a jury trial, representation by able trial lawyers, constitutional safeguards or post-trial appeals. In fact, they were not even given the opportunity to pray to their God one last time before they were blasted into eternity.

Lillian Dewald, Helen Huebner, Luella Stitzel and her sister-in-law, Henrietta Stitzel, were gunned down inside the walk-in safe at the Cabinet Supreme Savings and Loan Association at 5162 Delhi Pike, Delhi Township, Hamilton County, Ohio, so that their three killers could divide the $111.05 obtained from the savings institution's cash drawer and leave no witnesses who could identify their maskless faces. Four women — mothers, grand-mothers, loving wives, respected members of the community, hard work-ers, decent, law-abiding, church-going Christians — were murdered. The value placed on each woman's life had been reduced to $27 and pocket change.

Thanks to our court system, their killers are still alive and petitioning for release on parole every three or four years.

If ever there was a valid argument for the retention and use of the death penalty, the murders of Dewald, Huebner and the Stitzel ladies which is still the worst robbery/multiple murder incident in Hamilton County, Ohio's long history — exemplify it.

The only reason John Levi Leigh, Raymond Kassow, and Watterson "Red" Johnson didn't bother to wear masks or disguises the day they robbed the Cabinet Supreme S&L, is that they had already decided no witnesses would be left alive to tell the police what happened and who did it. Dead witnesses tell no tales.

The Cabinet Supreme Savings and Loan was a small thrift, of which Hamilton County at one time had more than 200. It was located in a quiet, residential suburb, a mere 15 minutes drive from Fountain Square in downtown Cincinnati. Cabinet Supreme was a typical savings and loan institution in the 1960s. Its primary activity was to offer its customers a good rate of interest for their savings. The thrift loaned out its customers' savings deposits to people who needed loans to buy homes or automobiles. The association had a special Christmas club savings program so that its customers could save toward their Christmas shopping lists. Remember, these were the days before the proliferation of plastic credit cards. In this era, the association did not even offer checking accounts to its customers.

Cabinet Supreme had two full-time employees, Jerome H. Grueter, secretary and manager, and Lillian Dewald, assistant manager and head teller. They had employed a part-time janitor named Walt, but he had recently been let go because his services and activities were not without some cause for concern. When Walt left his employment with Cabinet Supreme, he felt that he had been treated unfairly. He believed that he had an ax to grind. He also believed that the association kept a lot of currency in that big walk-in safe. He was more than willing to share his belief with others. He did just that. He told Raymond Kassow about this money depository. Raymond, or "Ray," as his friends called him, in turn shared this information with Red Johnson. Red knew just the right trigger man to assist them in striking it rich. His name was and is John Levi Leigh. He was 20 years old in 1969. He was an unemployed, part-time auto mechanic. He was a cool customer. He would kill if told to. He had no conscience, and worst of all, he had no soul.

Walt related to Ray Kassow that the savings association was open for business Tuesday, Wednesday, and Thursday from 9:00 a.m. to 3:00 p.m., on Friday from noon to 8:00 p.m., and on Saturday from 9:00 a.m. to noon. It was closed on Sunday and Monday. Walt also told Ray that regularly on Wednesdays, Jerry Grueter left about 10:00 to 10:30 a.m. to make business calls. This left attractive Lillian Dewald, a woman in her early 40s and wife of Cincinnati police Officer Walter Dewald, alone in the savings association office. The best news that Walt relayed to Ray was that there were no cameras in the office to record the coming and going of customers. There was no alarm system, and the huge stainless steel door to the walk-in vault was left standing open during the hours when the place was open for business.

This setup intrigued Ray Kassow, so much that he decided he needed help. Walt declined any direct involvement in an armed robbery. He was only a weasel. But Walt was willing to share in the proceeds of this expected "big heist" if his information proved to be correct and therefore, valuable. Ray discussed the whole scheme with his friend Red Johnson, who, like Kassow, was a charter member of the "employment challenged" club. These two decided that it would be smart to pay a visit to the Cabinet Supreme Savings and Loan office during business hours to "case the joint." Kassow even decided that one of them should open a savings account to make their visit appear normal. He chose Johnson for this task because Kassow had previously had several run-ins with Delhi Police Chief Howard Makin's department. He didn't want his name on an account card. So Johnson would open up a savings account using $10, of which Ray put up $5. Ray thought he had covered all the bases. However, he was unaware that Chief Makin had a photograph of his face. A mug shot, front and profile, hung on the bulletin board in the Delhi Police Station. A lot of people had seen this picture — several of whom would also see him near the savings association office on Wednesday, September 24, the last day of life for Dewald, Huebner, and the Stitzels.

So it was that on the hot and humid Thursday morning of August 28, 1969, that Ray Kassow and Red Johnson drove from downtown Cincinnati west to Delhi Township. They parked Kassow's car in the Kroger grocery store parking lot next door and walked into the savings and loan office, which was in its own one-story, white building. Jerry Grueter would remember these two men because the date, August 28, was his birthday and the two men who came in struck him as odd. Kassow looked sinister. Grueter was positive he had seen that face before, but he could not recall where. Johnson resembled a large old Labrador retriever with a permanent spacey expression on his broad, pale face. He had the look of a man who never had an original thought his entire life. He was not a leader. He took orders, and Kassow was his first sergeant. He was just the kind of accomplice that Kassow needed for a job like this. He was loyal to Ray. He followed instructions as best he could. He was stupid, but he was an immense and frightening man. He had a strong back.

Johnson followed Ray Kassow's instructions. He approached the counter and asked the lady standing behind the small black plastic desk sign that had "Mrs. Dewald" cut into its face for a card to open a savings account. Lillian Dewald handed him a post-card size green card and told him to print his name, address, and Social Security number and to sign the card at the bottom. She asked him how much he planned to deposit to open his account. He placed two $5 bills on the counter. While Lillian Dewald wrote out a deposit slip, Johnson, with tongue shoved between his teeth in the left corner of his mouth, printed Watterson R. Johnson or Ruth, SS No. 285-24-1603, 1706 Vine St., Cincinnati, Ohio 45210.

Johnson was so slow that he used his exact name and that of his mother. He printed his true Social Security number. However, at the last minute, he decided that he should be devious and clever, so he printed his address as 1706 Vine Street. He actually lived at 1706 Race Street.

While Red Johnson was opening his $10 savings account, Ray Kassow was pretending to read a loan brochure, and then a copy of the savings and loan's annual financial report, while at the same time looking around the office for cameras, especially in the corners near the ceiling. He saw none. He also noticed that the vault door was standing open and that there was a small gate in the cashier counter that led directly to the vault. He casually leaned against the gate. It moved. It didn't have a lock on it. It could be swung open without effort.

As Kassow looked the place over, he was unaware that Jerry Grueter was studying him. Or, if he was aware of it, he didn't seem to care. Something about these two characters unsettled both Jerry Grueter and Lillian Dewald, and they would share their concerns with each other, as well as with Lillian's police officer husband, Walter. Within 10 minutes, Kassow and Johnson were gone. Jerry Grueter got up from his desk behind the counter and walked to the front window and spread the blinds with a finger and thumb so that he could watch the two men leave.

Once the two strange men were gone, Lillian Dewald expressed her fear of them to Jerry Grueter. He told her that he felt the same way. The next day, Grueter mentioned this incident to Chief Howard Makin when he saw him in Frisch's restaurant having breakfast. Chief Makin asked Grueter to describe the men for him. Makin thought that the description Grueter gave him of the dark-haired individual was similar to Raymond Kassow. Since neither man had said or done anything that involved criminal conduct, all Makin could do was make a note of Grueter's description for future use. Makin gave an extra-long glance at Kassow's photograph on the bulletin board at the station house that day.

Lillian Dewald related the incident to her husband the same afternoon that Kassow and Johnson had first come into the savings and loan.

Walt Dewald was concerned enough that he spent six off-days during the next 27 days sitting out of sight in the rear lunch area of the savings and loan office. The two suspicious men never returned while Walt Dewald, 38-caliber revolver on his hip, sat patiently drinking coffee and protecting his wife and Jerry Grueter. Walt could not come in and take up his station on Wednesday, September 24, 1969. He was scheduled to be on duty that day in Cincinnati Police District 3, five minutes from his wife's place of employment.

Raymond Kassow told Watterson Johnson on the night of September 5 that he needed to get two more guns and a third man to help them pull off this job. He had tried to talk Walt into helping, but he refused. He said that he would be spotted the minute he entered the savings and loan. "Red" said he thought that John — that is John Levi Leigh — might be interested in coming in as a full partner. John was out of work and needed money. Besides, John had a mean streak. He didn't take shit off anyone.

So it came to be that on Friday, September 12, 1969, John Levi Leigh had a meeting with Raymond Kassow, Watterson Johnson and the former janitor underneath the Eighth Street Viaduct, which is at the base of Price Hill. At this meeting, Kassow shared all of the details of the savings and loan — including a drawing he had prepared of the office, which he showed to Leigh. He showed Leigh his .25-caliber semiautomatic pistol. He told Leigh that he was working on getting two more guns from a friend. If Leigh was interested in coming in on the deal, could he obtain a fast automobile? Kassow's car was on its last legs and might break down. They needed a fast getaway car. Leigh knew just the car. It was a 1964 Chevrolet Chevelle Malibu convertible. It was blue with a white top. It had a souped-up V-8 engine. It was a "hummer," and it belonged to a friend of Leigh's named Graham Davis. It carried Ohio license plate 5244 AII. And best of all, he had keys to this car because he had recently tuned it up. He could pick this Malibu up anytime. He lived close to Graham. The car was always parked on the street, and Leigh could get it without even asking Graham — if the job was done before noon, which was about the time Graham normally got out of bed.

Leigh was in. Now there were three men to pull the job. If Grueter was out of the office, it would be three men with three guns and a fast car up against one unarmed woman. All they needed to do now was go out to the savings and loan one more time to show John Leigh what the place looked like. But Kassow thought it best to go on the weekend when the thrift was closed and there weren't a lot of people around. Something told Kassow that it would be better that he and Johnson not be seen again near the Cabinet Supreme Savings and Loan building. So it was that on Sunday, September 21, 1969, that the three future killers took a ride out to Delhi. After getting something to eat at the Frisch's restaurant, they walked to the parking lot of 5162 Delhi Pike next door to peer through the two big front windows. They even took the time to walk all the way around the one-story building to check the electric and telephone lines. They were also looking for alarm wires. They saw none. There were none. Leigh was satisfied. He said, "Let's do it."

Wednesday, September 24, 1969, dawned in the Cincinnati area as one of those days when the dry rustle of leaves says summer has ended. The Oak Hills district schools and the numerous parochial schools in the Delhi neighborhood had already been back in session for four weeks. Yellow school buses plied the streets around the Cabinet Supreme Savings and Loan, picking up students and depositing them at any one of a half-dozen schools.

For the first time in a long time, John Leigh had set his alarm clock for 7:00 a.m. He had a job that day, and he didn't want to be late. Leigh picked Watterson Johnson up on Race Street and then returned to his apartment at 543 Klotter Street in Mohawk, just above downtown, where he lived with his wife, Rita. After a few minutes and a peck on the cheek of his wife, he and Leigh drove away in the 1964 Chevrolet Malibu while its owner, Graham Davis, slept off a hangover from a party the night before. Davis never even heard Leigh start the souped-up engine of his Malibu. Next stop was the lot beneath the Eighth Street Viaduct where the men had discussed the robbery previously. Kassow was waiting for them.

It didn't take long for Ray to transfer the .25-caliber semiautomatic pistol and two German-made, R G Roehm .22-caliber revolvers and three cloth bags to the trunk of the Malibu. Leigh said he wanted the .25-caliber semiautomatic because he liked its feel. The other pistols — the .22-caliber Roehms — were what are commonly referred to as Saturday night specials — cheap and easy to acquire. One of them was chrome-plated with imitation pearl grips. The other one was dark blue with black plastic grips. Johnson said he wanted the pretty one. It took Kassow only a minute or two to load all three guns, and the trio was off in the Malibu headed for Delhi. The time now was 8:00 a.m.

Leigh swung the sky blue Malibu into the lot of the big Kroger store at 5080 Delhi Pike and pulled over to the fence near the Frisch's restaurant.

From this vantage, they could watch the front of the savings and loan and walk through an opening in the fence, a mere 40 feet to the front door of the office. At 8:50 a.m., as they sat drinking coffee from Styrofoam cups purchased by Johnson from the Frisch's restaurant, they saw Lillian Dewald arrive and unlock the front door.   About 10 minutes after 9:00 a.m., Jerry Grueter arrived and entered the building. It was Wednesday, and if Walt's information was correct, Grueter would come out sometime around 10:00 a.m. and get in his Ford station wagon to run his errands. About 9:45 a.m., Ronald Carr, an employee of a local construction company, came out of Frisch's, where he had just eaten breakfast. He was carrying a set of blue-prints rolled up and held by a rubber band. His pickup truck happened to be parked behind a blue Malibu convertible. There were three men inside talking and laughing. He could see the man in the right front passenger seat pretty clear. He had seen this man's face before at the Delhi Police Station, on a picture on the bulletin board. He remembered that the guy's name was Kasko or Kossow or something like that. He thought to himself, "What are these three idiots up to?" So he looked at the trunk of the Malibu and wrote the license number down on his blueprints with his 19-cent Bic ballpoint pen. The number on the 1969 Ohio plates was 5244 AH. Just as he started to back his truck out, a guy climbed out of the back seat of the Malibu convertible. He stared directly at Carr. Later that evening, Carr would be shown several pictures by Cincinnati police homicide detectives. He would never forget that face. The photograph that he selected that night had a name on the back. It read "John Levi Leigh."

"God dammit, isn't that asshole manager ever going to leave?" said an impatient Watterson Johnson.

"Calm down, Red. It won't do to get pissed off. I once read that Jesse James waited over six hours in the rain for the right time to heist a bank," laughed Ray Kassow.

"Fuck Jesse James. He didn't sit out in the sun in a goddamn con-vertible with the top up either. Someone get me a lemonade," complained John Leigh.

Leigh was the gopher this time. He had just returned from Frisch's with two cups of coffee and his lemonade when Jerry Grueter walked out and climbed into his 1966 Ford station wagon and pulled out onto Delhi Pike, turning west. Leigh jumped into the driver's seat of the car and start-ed the ignition to pull out behind Grueter. "Don't get too close to him," said Kassow, "We don't want him to spot us."

"Shut up, asshole," yelled Leigh, "I'm driving, not you." It was 10:30 a.m.

Jerry Grueter proceeded south on Anderson Ferry Road, down the long hill toward U.S. 50, River Road, and the Ohio River. As he neared the bottom of the hill, he turned left onto Hillside Avenue. "That's far enough," said Kassow. He ain't coming back soon. Let's get the hell back there and do this job while the bitch is still alone."

At 10:55 a.m., Leigh drove the blue convertible into the savings and loan lot. He drove to the left side of the building and parked next to the Dumpster, where the car was less likely to be seen from the street. As they had driven past a side window, Kassow could see Lillian Dewald on the telephone at her desk. "She's alone," he said.

Leigh got out first and opened the trunk. He picked up the .25-caliber semiautomatic pistol and chambered a round. He stuck the piece in his right front pants pocket. Red picked up the pretty gun, the faux pearl-handled, chrome-plated, .22-caliber Roehm revolver. He put it in his right rear pocket, near his handkerchief. Kassow picked up the dark .22-caliber revolver and stuck it in his belt. He handed a cloth bag to Leigh and another one to Johnson. "Are you guys ready?" Kassow said.

"Yeah, let's get this fucking thing over before I shit my pants," replied Leigh.

Kassow took Leigh by the arm, "I have an idea, Leigh, that woman is probably going to spot me for sure if I stick my head in the door. She may panic and start screaming or try to run out the door. You guys go in first. I'll stay out here and be the lookout. If anyone comes in after you, I'll come in behind them. That way, we'll have them trapped between us. Remember, don't leave anyone in there alive."

When John Leigh and Watterson Johnson walked into the savings and loan office, Lillian Dewald was on the telephone with a customer. Johnson went to a long table that contained deposit and withdrawal forms. He picked up a withdrawal slip form. He started to fill it out. "Watterson Johnson, Account Number 1648, 1706 Vine St." Mrs. Dewald hung up the telephone and walked to the counter. "May I help you, gentlemen?"

Did Lillian Dewald recognize Watterson Johnson? Did she remember him from that frightening Thursday four weeks earlier? No one will ever know. At this point, Johnson walked to the counter — right up to Lillian Dewald. He laid the withdrawal slip on the counter in front of her and said matter of fact, "Yeah, lady, we want to make a withdrawal. This is a stickup."

Leigh pulled his semiautomatic from his pocket and pushed through the small gate in the counter that separated him from Lillian Dewald. He screamed at her, "God dammit, lady. Open the drawer and put all the money in this bag now, bitch, or I'll blow your brains out." Johnson held his chrome and faux pearl-handled revolver on Mrs. Dewald as she, though badly shaken, scooped currency out of the drawer.

The door opened from the outside, and Luella Stitzel, followed by her sister-in-law, Henrietta, entered the savings and loan office. Leigh and Johnson had forgotten to lock the door. Now they had two uninvited women on their hands, "God damn it, Red, I told you to lock the door. We don't need anyone else coming in on us. Where is that asshole Kassow?"

Before these ladies could react, they were both grabbed by Watterson Johnson and pushed through the gate toward the vault. "Get in there and don't open you mouths," hollered Johnson as he waived the chrome barreled, .22-calber revolver toward the safe.

Henrietta had come to the savings and loan that morning to make a deposit to her Christmas savings account. She was 64 years old. Her sister-in-law, Luella, was 61. She wanted to pay a utility bill and make a deposit to her Christmas saving account as well. Both ladies were widowed and lived together at 1438 Denver Avenue. They didn't want trouble. They obeyed Johnson's commands. They went into the vault and held each other as they pressed against the rear wall of the white painted room.

"Where is that goddamn Kassow?" yelled Leigh. "That asshole said that he would come in behind anyone who walked in on us. Hurry up, lady, get these two bags filled. Forget the loose change, just put the rolled money in the bag."

Her hands trembling, 41-year-old Lillian Dewald was doing her best to comply. Leigh demanded to know if there was cash in the vault. She told him there was not. He called her a liar. "Get in that vault, Red, and check those shelves and file cabinets. See if there is any money in there. I don't trust this broad. And tell those two old bags to quit crying or I'm going to blow them away now. There has to be more money in that vault than we've seen so far!"

The front door opened, this time by Helen Huebner, a 46-year old McAlpin's Department Store employee who had been driven to the savings and loan by her husband, Joseph Huebner. They lived at 428 Sunland Drive in Delhi Township. Mrs. Huebner was the mother of three children, ages 23, 18 and 14. They all lived at home. She was there to cash her McAlpin's payroll check. The total amount of the check was $42.50, after taxes. She was carrying a bright red plastic purse. Her husband, Joseph, decided to wait for her outside, so he parked his car in front of the building at an angle where he could see the front door in his rearview mirror.

The time was 11:04 a.m. The robbery had now been in progress for about six minutes.

As soon as Helen Huebner walked inside, she was pushed from behind by Raymond Kassow, who had been standing against the sidewall of the outside corner of the building, where neither the Stitzels, nor Mrs. Huebner nor her husband could see him. "Damn!" said Leigh, "Lock that door before anyone else comes in. Where in the hell have you been, Ray? This whole shit bag is going sour on us. There is nowhere near the amount of money we were promised, and now instead of one goddamn woman on our hands, we have four."

Kassow told Johnson to get Mrs. Huebner in the walk-in safe while he and Leigh looked for more money. They couldn't find any. "We have got to get the hell out of here," Ray Kassow said. "I know it, I know it — shit, shoot all of them. Do it — dammit, John, do it."

Leigh pushed Lillian Dewald ahead of him as he shuffled toward the vault where Johnson was holding Mrs. Huebner and the Stitzels at gunpoint. By now, all three women were crying and begging for their lives. Leigh raised the pistol and shot Luella Stitzel between her eyes. He then fired a bullet into Henrietta's head just above her left ear. Next he turned the gun on Helen Huebner, hitting her in the throat and then the head. Four shots, three women down. Lillian Dewald screamed and bolted toward the doorway of the safe. Leigh fired twice, striking her in the back with each shot. Then the .25-caliber semiautomatic jammed. A spent casing had become caught in the extractor, and it would not feed another cartridge. Lillian Dewald was still alive. She was down on her knees and crying. Leigh grabbed the chrome-plated .22 from Johnson and fired two shots into Mrs. Dewald's lower back, destroying her liver and pancreas. She collapsed forward onto her face, moaning. Her head was lying on the threshold of the vault floor, and her life's blood was creeping across the black-and-white tile floor. It became very quiet. There was smoke and the odor of burned gun powder. The first to speak was Red Johnson. "Jesus, John, you wasted all of them — let's get out of here, now!

"Get the purses, Red." Kassow yelled. "Let's go!"

Joseph Huebner was listening to his car radio. The 11:00 a.m. news had been on about 10 minutes. The announcer was forecasting the weather. Mr. Huebner had begun to wonder why it was taking his wife so long. What could be keeping her, he thought. She's probably in there shooting the breeze with Lillian or Jerry. He glanced at his watch. He looked up into his rearview mirror just in time to see three men running from the front of the building. The third man was carrying several purses. One of them was bright red, just like his wife's. His heart froze. The blue convertible backed out and squealed rubber as it sped out of the parking lot, turning right onto Delhi Pike without even pausing for traffic. Joseph Huebner tried to remember the license number as he ran toward the savings and loan office.

He had a sinking feeling in the pit of his stomach as he entered the S&L. He didn't see anyone when he pushed in past the door. He called, "Helen! Helen!" No answer. He walked behind the counter. He saw Lillian Dewald lying in the doorway of the vault. She was moaning, and blood was coming from her nose and mouth. She did not move. Her stare was fixed. She was dying. He walked around her and saw Luella and Henrietta Stitzel lying side by side in the center of the vault. Then he saw his wife, Helen. She was squatted down on her legs, her back resting against the rear wall of the vault. Blood was running from her head wounds. He yelled, "Helen, are you hurt? Helen, are you hurt?"

Joseph Huebner said later that her head turned to the left, but she would not answer him. Her last conscious sensation on Earth was her husband screaming her name and asking her if she was hurt. Joseph Huebner ran to the phone and called the police dispatcher. "Please hurry, send an ambulance to the Cabinet Supreme Savings and Loan on Delhi Pike. I think that there has been a robbery and four women are hurt bad. One is my wife. Please hurry." The first police cruiser arrived three minutes later. Five minutes after that, Walter Dewald arrived in his Cincinnati police cruiser. His wife, Lillian, was gone. His worst nightmare had become reality.

When Delhi Chief Howard Makin arrived and listened to the description of the three men as related to him by Joseph Huebner, he recognized one description over the others. He had one of his officers bring the photograph of Raymond Kassow over from the police station. When Joseph Huebner was shown the photograph, he said, "That is one of them." Howard Makin instructed Delhi Patrolman John Eschenbach to obtain an arrest warrant for Raymond Kassow. The charges: armed robbery, robbery of a federally and state insured savings and loan, and four counts of first-degree murder. Lillian Dewald had just died, while being put on a stretcher by paramedics.

Leigh, Johnson and Kassow had already arrived at the weed-covered lot under the Eighth Street Viaduct. Kassow took the moneybags. He had Johnson put the contents of the purses into the bags. Then he collected the guns and put them in the second bag. He told Leigh and Johnson to get rid of the purses and to meet him at the Empire movie theater on Vine Street near Liberty Street in a half-hour, where he would give them their share. "Shit, man," said Leigh, "this fucking thing is a loser. You guys got me into this, and there's damn little left to spend."

Leigh and Johnson drove down to the Ohio River and threw the purses in a pile of rubbish. They then drove up to Eggleston Avenue, where the Malibu quit running. They abandoned the convertible and walked 11 blocks to the Empire Theater. Kassow met them in the lobby and handed each of them a handkerchief that was tied in a knot. Each one contained some small bills and change. They were dumbfounded. Johnson was the first to speak this time. He said, "You know, we are going to go to hell for this, and we didn't even clear $30 each. What a crock of shit."

Kassow suggested to Leigh and Johnson that they get out of town as quickly as possible. He told them that he was going to leave Cincinnati as well, and that they couldn't afford to be seen together ever again. Leigh and Johnson would leave town, only to be arrested four days later near Gallup, New Mexico, by a young New Mexico state trooper. Kassow would not get a chance to leave Cincinnati. He was arrested the same evening for the robbery/murders on the warrant ordered by Chief Howard Makin. Thirty-six hours later, after confessing his part in the holdup and killings and naming John Leigh and Watterson Johnson as his accomplices, he led Cincinnati homicide detectives to an old Walnut Hills cemetery where the three pistols and the Stitzel Christmas club books were dug up, still inside the cloth bag furnished by Kassow. The purses were found shortly after Leigh and Johnson's arrests in New Mexico. All three men confessed. Leigh and Johnson first to FBI Special Agent Kenneth Walton. One matter was common to all three confessions: All four women were shot by John Leigh. Kassow had said that Leigh was a killer — Kassow knew of what he spoke.

Hamilton County Prosecutor Mel Rueger and Cal Prem, his chief assistant, decided to try all three men for the death of Lillian Dewald. Even though indictments had been returned accusing the three men of killing each of the four victims, Rueger believed that our office stood its best chance of obtaining three convictions with death sentences if we proceeded to try Leigh, Kassow, and Johnson for the murder of Lillian Dewald since she was an employee of the savings and loan that was the object of the armed robbery. Under Ohio law, the killing of a robbery victim was automatically first-degree murder without the necessity of proving premeditation to commit murder. Due to the fact that each of the three defendants had given separate statements to law enforcement officers, separate trials had to be granted for each man.

Mel Rueger and Cal Prem picked the prosecutorial teams. Rueger chose me to assist him in the prosecution of John Leigh. This was not only a tremendous honor for me, it was the highlight of my career as an assistant prosecuting attorney. Trying a murder case with Melvin G. Rueger was like being asked by Michelangelo to help him paint the ceiling of the Sistine Chapel. It would also prove to be Mel Rueger's last murder trial as a prosecutor, for by January 1971 he would become a Common Pleas Court judge. Other than Cal Prem, I was the only criminal assistant prosecutor in the office in 1969 who Rueger ever assigned to try a case with him, and this was the highest-profile multiple murder trial ever conducted in our county. Cal Prem and Bob Sachs were chosen to prosecute Watterson "Red" Johnson, and Carl Vollman and Fred Cartolano were assigned to prosecute Raymond Kassow.

Common Pleas Court Judge Lyle W. Castle (who had been a partner in the law firm of Smith and Latimer, where I was an associate) was the presiding criminal judge for these cases. Judge Castle kept the Leigh case in his courtroom. He assigned Johnson's case for trial before Judge William S. Mathews, while Kassow's case would be presided over by Judge William Morrissey. Leigh's court-appointed attorneys were chosen by Judge Castle. He assigned Thomas Stueve and my friend Charles E. "Chuck" Hamilton to defend Leigh. The incomparable Cincinnati criminal defense attorney William F. "Foss" Hopkins and Harry Abrams were assigned by the court to represent Watterson Johnson. Gary L. Schneider and Richard Norton were assigned to defend Raymond Kassow. Gary Schneider, by 1969 a defense attorney, had become an assistant county prosecutor at the same time that I had. He and I had earned the nickname the Gold Dust Twins, a label bestowed upon us by Cal Prem due primarily to our shenanigans, both in and out of court. We were fast friends. I had an association with just about every judge, lawyer and police officer connected with these cases, as well as with Dr. Ben Yamagucchi, the chief deputy Hamilton County coroner who performed autopsies on all four of the victims.

In order to coordinate the trials of these three defendants so that there was a minimum of pretrial publicity that might make it difficult to obtain an unbiased jury for each man — as well as to minimize costs and inconvenience to the numerous witnesses who would be called to testify — the judges and Mel Rueger, with Cal Prem's advice and counsel, set the trial dates in a staggered fashion. Their intent was to achieve the best possible climate for both the prosecution and the defense. John Leigh's trial was to start before Judge Castle on Monday, May 11, 1970. Watterson Johnson's trial was to commence in Judge Mathews' courtroom on Tuesday, May 12. And Raymond Kassow's trial followed on Wednesday, May 13, in Judge Morrissey's courtroom.

Today, the media have labeled O.J. Simpson's trial attorneys as "The Dream Team." In fact, Mel Rueger put together the first and the best legal dream team. His prosecutorial team consisted of six prosecutors, two of whom — himself and Cal Prem — had national reputations. The other four assistant prosecutors had a total of 47 years trial experience between them as prosecuting attorneys. I was the rookie of the group with only four years' trial experience, but I had earned a reputation as a fast learner and an even faster talker. Gil Garcetti, the Los Angeles prosecuting attorney, would have been overjoyed to have a staff of trial lawyers equal to the team that Mel Rueger was able to put together for these trials. I don't mean to demean Marcia Clark or Chris Darden, but neither of them could have made first string on Mel Rueger's team.

About two dozen witnesses testified in each of the three Cabinet Supreme trials. Over 42 exhibits were offered and received. A county record of 275 potential jurors were questioned before the final three jury panels were chosen. Each panel was composed of 12 jurors and three alternates. Since most of the exhibits were common to each defendant's trial, they had to be introduced in one case and carried under security to the next case to be identified and marked over again.

While O.J. Simpson's criminal trial lasted more than 10 months and cost the taxpayers of California nearly $10 million, the trials of Leigh, Johnson, and Kassow lasted less than two weeks and cost the taxpayers of Hamilton County less than a half-million dollars. In one day alone, Mel Rueger and I presented the testimony of 14 witnesses and introduced 24 exhibits. We called on witnesses brought in from five states, besides Ohio. There were witnesses from California, Arizona, New Mexico, Tennessee and Kentucky. During the entire trial, we had a total of seven bench conferences with Judge Lyle Castle. In the O.J. Simpson trial, there were days when seven bench conferences were held in one hour. Our closing arguments in the Leigh case lasted less than two hours, far short of the three-and-a-half days for closing arguments in the Simpson criminal trial. Remember, our three trials had 12 lawyers, three trial judges, and 45 jurors to supervise. But there is one thing that the Simpson trial had that we did not. We didn't have television cameras in the courtroom. In fact, in 1969 there were no cameras of any kind allowed in our courtrooms, only sketch artists. Think of how much better off our criminal justice system would be if the no-camera rule were the same today. Federal courts have retained the no-camera rule, for good reason. We wouldn't have judges, lawyers or witnesses checking their makeup or hair before walking into the courtroom. There would be no cameras to play to. There is, after all, no legitimate reason in the law to have criminal trials trying to compete with the Jerry Springer show for Nielsen ratings. This serves no public good.

We did have one logistical problem that had to be handled carefully. To prevent one jury from learning of a verdict in one of the other trials, it had to be understood and agreed that the first verdict would be sealed and, thereafter, the second verdict sealed until the third and final verdict was arrived at. The reason was simple: If one jury found, say, Kassow guilty and either Leigh or Johnson's jury had not arrived at a verdict, those jurors might be influenced unfairly if they learned of the decision in another courtroom before they had reached their own decision. Mel Rueger and Cal Prem worked out an arrangement with the three trial judges that provided for sealing each verdict as it was returned until all three juries had returned a final verdict. They also agreed to sequester each jury — keep them isolated from the other juries or the media — until all three cases were decided. This worked like clockwork, and to their credit, the local media cooperated in this endeavor. Each jury remained isolated from everyone except court personnel until a verdict was reached in each trial.

On Tuesday, May 19, 1970, the jury in the trial of Watterson Johnson returned a verdict of guilty. The jury had to be kept in seclusion, and its verdict sealed. On Wednesday, May 20, 1970, at 10:25 a.m. the jury deciding the fate of John Levi Leigh returned a verdict of guilty as charged. At 3:45 that afternoon, the jury in the trial of Raymond Kassow returned a guilty-as-charged verdict. Now, all three verdicts could be read in court, entered on the record, and made public. We all breathed a sigh of relief. It was over.

On Tuesday, May 26, 1970, at 9:00 a.m. Judge Lyle W. Castle sentenced John Levi Leigh to die in the electric chair at the Ohio Penitentiary in Columbus for the first-degree murder of Lillian Dewald while perpetrating the crime of armed robbery.

John Leigh, Watterson Johnson and Raymond Kassow are alive and well almost 30 years later. In fact, they were recently turned down for the third time for parole. How is it that these three men, all sentenced to die in Ohio's electric chair by a jury of their peers, are still alive? These three killers are alive today solely because in June 1972, slightly two years after their sentencing, the United States Supreme Court in the Case of Furman vs. Georgia, 408 U.S. 238, 92 S.Ct. 2726, ruled that all death penalty cases wherein a jury had imposed a death penalty under then existing laws, were unconstitutional and could not be carried out.

No one bothered to ask Lillian Dewald, Luella Stitzel, Henrietta Stitzel or Helen Huebner whether they felt that the imposition of the death penalty on their murderers might deprive those men of some constitutional guarantee. It was too late to worry about the constitutional rights of these four women.

I'll never forget as long as I live what Gary Schneider told me about his conversation with his client Raymond Kassow on the morning that he was to be sentenced to die by Judge Morrissey. It seems that he and Dick Norton had gone to the jail to fill Kassow in on the day's proceedings. Gary told Kassow that Judge Morrissey was going to sentence him to die, and that he should not become upset in the courtroom because there had not been an execution in Ohio since 1963, and that his chances of being put to death were slim to none.

Kassow looked at Schneider and Norton and said: "Hell, I'm not worried. I know that they are not going to burn us for this. That is why we decided going in that we would not leave anyone alive. That way even if we got caught, we still don't die and we have a better chance of going free if there are no witnesses."

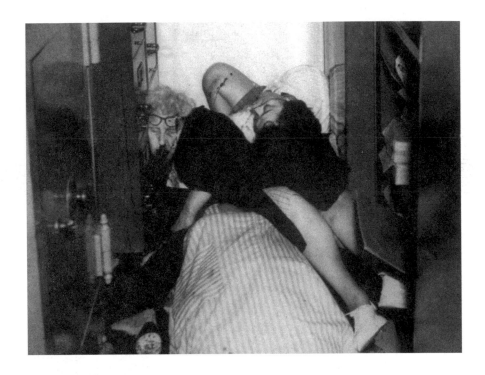

The normal tranquility of Delhi Township was shattered when four women were brutally murdered in the vault of the Cabinet Supreme Savings and Loan in 1969.

Witnesses helped to identify the three city men who confessed to the crime and told where they hid the evidence. One confessed murderer, Raymond Kassow, is shown being interrogated.

The three accused of murder had separate trials. Prosecutor Mel Rueger selected Assistant Prosecutor Mike Mestemaker to join him in trying the alleged trigger man, John Leigh.

Cabinet Supreme Savings and Loan Association at 5162 Delhi Pike, Delhi Township, Hamilton County, Ohio.

The Cincinnati Post

TIMES ✈ STAR

8 Star FINAL
Stocks—Sports
Price 10 Cents
Phones 721-1111

108.   106 Pages   WEDNESDAY, MAY 20, 1970   WEATHER: Fair, warm. Details, Page 54.

LEIGH TO GET CHAIR
FOR SLAYING IN DELHI

John Levi Leigh, 20, of 1509 Pleasant street, today was found guilty of first-degree murder in the slaying of Mrs. Walter P. Dewald, 41, a teller at the Cabinet-Supreme Savings and Loan Assn., Delhi Hills, last Sept. 24, and must die in the electric chair.

The eleven-man, one-woman jury in the Common Pleas Court of Judge Lyle W. Castle did not recommend mercy, making the death penalty mandatory.

Judge Castle set 9 a.m., May 26, for sentencing.

LEIGH DISPLAYED no emotion when jury foreman Frank S. Eisenmann, 24, of 4367 Ridgeview avenue, read the guilty verdict. Judge Castle then polled the jurors individually.

Leigh's young wife, sitting in the courtroom, put her hand up to her face when the verdict was read but made no audible sound.

(Test Accuses Kassow, See Page 54.)

Leigh, wearing a tan jacket, brown trousers and shirt and tie, was handcuffed and led out of the courtroom.

STANLEY HEBER, Criminal Court bailiff, who escorted Leigh back to his cell, said:

"He said he was glad to get it over with and that he would sooner be in death row than in jail here."

At 10:25 a.m. the jury sent word out it had reached a verdict.

JUDGE CASTLE ordered Leigh to be brought to the courtroom and sent a bailiff out to find attorney Thomas Stueve, who with Charles Hamilton, were Leigh's court-appointed attorneys. Albert Mestemaker, assistant Hamilton County prosecutor, represented the state.

The jury then filed into the courtroom — it had resumed deliberations at 9 a.m. today after being sequestered in separate rooms in the Sheraton-Gibson last night —and returned its verdict.

The case went to the jury at 2:15 p.m. yesterday. The jury deliberated for three hours before being sequestered.

LEIGH, and two other men, Watterson (Big Red) Johnson, 22, and Raymond Kassow, 24, were indicted for the murder of four women in the holdup-slaying at the Delhi Hill savings company.

Johnson and Kassow's trials are being held in separate courts.

The other victims were Mrs. Helen Huebner, 47, of 428 Sunland drive, Delhi Hills; Mrs. Louella Stitzel, 61, and her sister-in-law, Mrs. Henrietta Stitzel, 64, both of 1438 Denver avenue.

John Leigh

Watterson Johnson

Raymond Kassow

CHAPTER 5

THAT'S THE MAN

In my more than 30 years as a prosecuting attorney, defense counsel and judge, I have always been aware of the problems inherent in a criminal case in which the defendant's guilt or innocence depends on the eyewitness identification by one person, the victim of a crime.

In cases in which there is a complete lack of independent, corroborating evidence of guilt — such as witnesses not directly involved in the crime, as is the victim; physical evidence, such as fingerprints, hair and blood; recovery of fruits of the crime, such as money, jewelry or other personal property; or an admission or full confession — the case will depend solely on the claim by the victim that the person accused committed the crime. And, of course, the defendant's denial. In other words, as is often stated by those involved in criminal law, the case is a "one-on-one situation."

I recall just such a case assigned to me to prosecute, in which the accused's freedom depended on the validity of the victim's identification of him as the man who robbed and assaulted her. I was convinced that the right man had been arrested and indicted. I remained convinced until it was almost too late for the truth to be uncovered.

By September 1970, William Jenkins, a 32-year-old black man, had been out of work for four months. He was one of the hundred or more employees holding low-skill jobs at a local steel mill to be laid off due to a slowdown in orders for rolled steel. It was no secret that in the southwestern corner of Ohio, the first laborers to be laid off during bad times were Appalachians and African-Americans.

"Bo," as his family and friends called him, was a veteran of two years active duty in the United States Army. After basic infantry training at Fort Knox, Kentucky, he requested and was sent to the Army's Culinary School at Fort A.P. Hill in Virginia. Bo enjoyed cooking and became quite proficient at coming up with tasty dishes made of some of the most bland canned rations that had ever been devised by man. It was said that Bo was good enough that he could transform powdered eggs with sharp cheese and mushrooms into an omelet palatable enough that there were demands by the troops for seconds.

The only service-connected injury that Bo suffered while on active duty occurred the day that a fire started in a grease trap in the mess hall in which he was preparing the evening meal. The flames and scalding grease were fanned by a back draft that caught Bo square in the face as he doused the inferno dancing across the stove and its hood with a fire extinguisher.

The fire caused little property damage. But it did get Bo in the face and on his hands and arms. The injuries were severe enough to be classified as deep second-degree burns; that is, burns that extend necrosis into the derma of the skin, leaving permanent scars. In the case of blacks or dark-skinned individuals, the scarring that results from this type of burn injury is known as leukoderma or vitiligo, and is characterized by patches of stark white skin caused by the destruction of pigment cells.

As the result of his burns, Bo was left with permanent patches of white skin across his nose and left cheek, as well as the back of both hands and his forearms up to his elbows. At first, Bo was so self-conscious about these white spots and blotches on his face and hands that he confided in his close friends that he felt like the proverbial "spotted, dotted puppy." But everyone who knew this amicable, tenderhearted man with a knack for cooking told him that he had no reason to feel ashamed or self-conscious about his appearance. Bo often wore long sleeve shirts. And whenever the weather was right, he wore gloves to hide his hands. But short of wearing a ski mask, he could not hide his face. This problem would eventually cause him a lot more than just self-consciousness.

After discharge from the Army, Bo tried his hand at professional cooking, first at several hotels and finally as a short-order cook at an all-night diner. The problem was the pay. There was just not enough left after payroll taxes to support Bo and his ailing mother. So it was that in October 1969, this 5-foot, 9-inch, 175-pound, muscular black man with white grease-burn scars took a job at the local steel mill on the recommendation of his minister in order to earn the then comfortable sum of $8 per hour, from which he was able to gross $320 per week and take home $263 after taxes, Social Security and union dues. Often Bo was able to get overtime pay by working an extra shift or giving up his Saturdays.

Bo was now earning more money than he had ever seen before. The work was harder than cooking, but he was young and strong. Bo was well liked by his foreman, because he never said "No" when asked to take on an extra chore. He was equally well liked by his fellow employees, for whom he always had a smile and a friendly pat on the back. Bo was a first-class team player.

But that was then, and now is now. September 18 dawned as another day that Bo knew he had to put to use trying to replace the job he had lost four months earlier. It was going to be hot and humid. But at least the sky was free of those dark gray clouds that often spell rain for the steamy Ohio Valley. Besides, it was Friday, and Bo felt that this Friday might bring him a change in his luck. He had a job interview at 11:00 a.m. at the Valley View Grill in Hartwell, a blue-collar neighborhood surrounded by factories and trucking companies. Bo had been given a job lead for a cook's position by a friend of his mother's, Dave Suggs. The friend worked at the trucking company across the street from the restaurant and knew that the owner was looking for a good, reliable short-order cook for the breakfast and lunch crowds.

Bo drove to the job interview in his beat-up Plymouth coupe, which needed brakes, tires and an engine overhaul. He parked the automobile in the lot next to the one-story, concrete-block building. A sign above the front door extended over the sidewalk, identifying this edifice as the site of the best little restaurant in Hartwell, "The Valley View Grill."

Bo climbed out of the old, dark-green Plymouth and headed for the restaurant's front door. He stepped inside, beneath the noisy air-conditioning unit mounted above the main entrance, from which dripped condensation on everyone who dared linger beneath its grillwork. Along the left wall there were 12 booths lined up one behind the other toward the rear of the customer area, capped off by a partition that led to the kitchen. On the right side of this narrow space was a lunch counter and 14 swivel stools bolted to the floor and covered with green vinyl. This counter was punctuated after stool Number 7 by an opening in the counter, which allowed entrance for anyone serving a customer who had chosen a booth over a stool. To the right of the counter was a built-in grill, cabinets and a counter area loaded with dishes, plastic glasses and white coffee mugs. In the middle of all of this sat a very old but still-functioning cash register.

"I'm Bill Jenkins. I'm here about the cook's job," Bo said, his hand extended to shake the hand held out in his direction by a gray-haired man with a toothpick in the corner of his mouth. "Yeah, OK. My name is Ray — Ray Clark. This joint has been in my family for over 40 years. But we ain't ever had a black cook before. My friend and customer Dave Suggs says that you're pretty good. Can you prove it?"

"Sure, OK. What do you want me to cook up for you? You name it, I'll do it," Bo said.

"Pretty sure of yourself, aren't you," Ray grunted. "All right, I want you to cook me up a ham-and-cheese omelet and a couple of those pancakes there," pointing toward a big yellow bowl of batter.

Bo began whipping up some of the eggs he had broken in the mixing bowl, and ladled out enough pancake batter for two 6-inch pancakes. While the cooking test continued, Ray and Bo talked about Bo's age and prior experience. They had one thing in common: both had been in the Army about the same time. Ray had been a mechanic in a motor pool for an artillery battalion. After his discharge, he had come home to work in the family restaurant. He took over management of the place in 1967 after his 66-year-old father suffered a stroke that left him confined, pretty much, to his front porch.

Then the two men sat and chatted as Ray dug into the omelet, offering Bo both of the pancakes, which he washed down with a glass of milk, all on the house as part of the cooking test.

"Pretty good omelet, buddy. The job pay is $4 per hour, and if you want to you can pick up some overtime. I don't carry insurance for my employees, and there ain't no such thing as paid vacation. But I'm easy to work for. You cook good omelets, and I like your attitude. You got the job if you want it."

Ray repeated that he had never had a black man work for him before, noting that some the rednecks who ate in his place might make some racial remarks, but that Bo should ignore them and they would back off if they couldn't get a rise out of him. Bo had been through this kind of warning before. He knew how to keep his cool and assured Ray that he could handle redneck-cracker slurs. He had been doing it for a long time.

"OK, pal. Tell you what. Tomorrow is Saturday. On Saturday, we are open from 6:00 a.m. until 3:00 p.m. Can you start tomorrow? If you work on Saturday, I'll pay you an extra buck an hour. How about it? That's $5 per hour. Hell, that's 45 bucks for a Saturday, OK?"

Bo nodded his head. "Yeah, OK. I'll be here tomorrow at 5:30 a.m. How's that?"

"Good, then you need to take home this income tax and Social Security paperwork to fill out. Bring it back tomorrow when you come in."

Bo stayed at the restaurant and had lunch on the house. As he walked out of the restaurant, he folded up the papers that Ray had given to him to fill out. He waved at the white man who had just hired him as he opened the driver's door of the Plymouth.

"Man," Bo thought, "It really feels good to be able to say I have a job, any job, but a damn job. All right, go for it, man."

Bo was feeling pretty good as he drove in Central Parkway toward

Walnut Hills, which was home for his mother and himself in the two-bedroom apartment they shared on May Street. He turned on the radio to listen to some good jazz music. It was 1:45 p.m. As he turned the dial from station to station on the FM band, he heard the announcement that a World War II B-17 bomber had just landed at Lunken Airport for a weekend of public tours and fly-overs. "Wow, a B-17. I really like those big bombers. I remember making one out of balsam wood. I wonder what ever happened to it? Hell, I don't have anything else to do this afternoon. I might as well drive on over to Lunken Airport to see this old beauty. I wonder what they charge to take a ride on her? Hell, all I've got on me is $6 plus change and no pay check until next weekend. I sure could use some money now. But I'll just go look at this old air warrior anyhow."

Ruth Kreider had worked as a receptionist for 13 years at the Robert A. Taft Sanitary Engineering Center, a federal research laboratory that focuses on pollution. She was a 57-year-old divorcee and the mother of two grown and married daughters. She had five grandchildren and spent alternate Sundays with her daughters and their families.

On this Friday, September 18, she had gone to lunch with two co-workers at a small restaurant on nearby Delta Avenue. She had also cashed her paycheck at a bank in Mount Lookout Square. Now it was 4:10 p.m., and her workweek had finally come to an end. It was a nice, warm, sunny day. Before leaving the building, she recovered the currency from her paycheck from the small bank envelope and counted it again. It was all there: $213.65. She placed the folding money neatly in her billfold. The change went into her coin purse. She straightened her desk and locked the center drawer. She then put the switchboard on automatic answering mode for the weekend.

With purse in one hand and umbrella in the other, this picture of everyone's grandmother — all 5 feet, 4 inches and 128 pounds of her, with silver-gray hair and a friendly smile — left through a rear door and descended to the remote employee lot, where her 1966 Ford Fairlane was parked. The Taft Center is a somewhat isolated property off Columbia Parkway west of the village of Fairfax.

As always, Ruth Kreider had her car keys out and ready to unlock the driver's side to her white, two-door sedan. She knew that a woman alone in a parking lot that far from the street was vulnerable to anyone bent upon harm.

Just as she placed her key into the lock, Ruth's worst nightmare became reality. As suddenly as if in a dream, she saw a reflection in the sun-drenched window of her car: A black man was behind her. As she started to turn her head, a muscular arm was thrown around her neck, and she was dragged backward out of her shoes. She could not scream because the forearm and biceps wrapped around her neck and throat had cut off her ability to breathe. She struggled with her attacker as she was dragged to the edge of the lot and into the shrubs separating the lot from the more open woods behind the Taft center. She was slipping into a breathless world of darkness. Just as she felt that she was going to pass out, her assailant relaxed his grip long enough for her to gulp in a shot of air that came so swiftly her ears cracked as if she had just ascended a mountain road where the air is too thin even for young lungs.

"Gimme the goddamn purse, lady, or I'll break your fuckin' neck," growled the man who had the death grip on her throat.

She pleaded, "Don't hurt me, just take the money and let me live, please!"

As she let go of her purse, it was snapped away from her — the leather strap pulling against her right arm until the pressure eased as the strap passed under her fingers. Just as her assailant pulled the purse to his chest, she saw for a brief second or two a young, muscular black man with white spots or scars across his nose and left cheek. She shrieked and he punched her in the jaw hard enough that she saw brilliant lights roll across her closed eyes and then darkness as she sank into unconsciousness.

The next recollection Ruth Kreider had was being talked to by Herbert Wilson, a security guard at the Taft Sanitation Engineering Center. He had witnessed the last few seconds of the robbery and the assault on Kreider from a third-floor window. He had raced down the metal stairway as fast as his 62-year-old legs could carry him to come to a co-worker's aid. He had seen the black man run into the woods. He could tell investigating police officers only that the man was black with medium-brown skin and short hair and was wearing blue jeans and a gray shirt.

Slowly, Ruth Kreider began to regain her senses. She could recall later that her jaw hurt terribly, so bad that she thought that it was broken. Her left cheek was badly swollen and discolored already. She had a painful ringing in her left ear, which would remain with her even to the date of trial during the last week of November 1970.

Once Wilson had managed to help Mrs. Kreider back into the reception lobby, he telephoned Station X, the old central police switchboard, a system retired once the new 911 emergency call center was established, and requested police assistance and an ambulance to respond to the Taft center.

The first police officer on the scene was a District 7 uniformed officer named Chris Walsh. Ruth Kreider was able to tell the officer that the man who had attacked her and taken her purse was black; that he looked like he was about 30 to 35 years old; that he had short hair, a medium build, was not thin and not fat; was wearing a gray work-type shirt and blue pants, maybe blue jeans. She also realized that she had glimpsed his face only for a second or two, but that he had roundish, pink-white scar marks on his nose and cheeks. "You know, like burn marks."

As Kreider was being placed in the fire department life squad for transportation to University Hospital for X-rays and treatment on her jaw injury, Officer Walsh put out a radio alert for a robbery-assault suspect described as follows:

"Wanted for assault and robbery of employee at Taft sanitation institute: Male, black, approximately 30-35 years of age, 5-feet, 10-inches to 6 feet tall, medium skin, medium build, short hair, no face hair, distinct pinkish-white circular scars on his nose, face and cheeks. Possibly wearing blue, long-sleeve work shirt and denim pants. Amount taken in robbery: $215-$225 dollars U.S. currency plus brown leather shoulder purse containing identification of one Ruth Kreider, female, white, age 57."

District 7 patrol officer Matt Collins was driving southbound on Wilmer Avenue adjacent to Lunken Airport when he spotted the World War II B-17 bomber sitting on the tarmac near a hanger. As he drove closer, he observed a black man walking toward a green Plymouth parked near the gravel apron. He looked long and hard at the man. 5-feet, 10-inches or so, gray shirt, blue pants, medium build. "This guy fits the description of the broadcast I just heard, and I'm only a mile and a quarter from the Taft sanitation institute. I need to talk to this guy."

Collins pulled his police cruiser into the lot, to the rear of the Plymouth, blocking it from backing up so it could turn to leave. The driver had just started the engine. He looked startled as the officer yelled at him: "Turn off your engine, I need to talk to you."

Bo Jenkins stepped from his Plymouth after shutting off his engine.

"What's the problem, Officer?"

"You'd better keep your hands where I can see them," Collins replied. "Do you have a driver's license on you?"

"Yes," answered Bo, as he nervously reached for his wallet.

"Here it is. It's current, too." Bo tried to smile, but his mouth was getting drier by the minute.

Ohio Driver's License issued October 10, 1968, to: William Jenkins;

Date of Birth: October 1938; Age: 32; 1210 May Street, Cincinnati, OH Zone 6; Weight: 175 pounds;. Complexion: medium brown; Height: 5'9"; Race: N; Sex: M.

"Where did you get those scars, buddy?" Collins asked as he studied the driver's license. "What happened to your nose and cheek? You also have similar marks on your hands. How'd you get these?"

Bo was beginning to be frightened that this was more than just one white cop hassling a black man in a white neighborhood.

"Look, Officer, I got these scars when I was scalded in the Army. I just stopped here to look at that B-17 bomber. What have I done wrong?"

"I'll ask the questions. I'm doing the interviewing here," growled Collins. "You own this car? Can I look inside?"

"Sure, Officer. Go ahead. But tell me, what's going on?"

"Stand back from the car and keep your hands where I can see them. OK, nothing on the seat or floor. Open up the trunk!" Bo opened the trunk with his key and raised the lid. Officer Collins moved an old blanket and a toolbox. "Damn. Nothing," he grunted. "Look, pal, where is the lady's purse?"

"Please, Officer, tell me what's going on here. I ain't done anything today but have a job interview and come over here to the airport to see this old bomber."

"So, you're telling me that you haven't been anywhere near the Taft sanitation institute today?"

"No, Sir, I haven't been, not at all."

Collins: "But you do know that it's only a mile or so from here over on Columbia Parkway. And it takes about four minutes to drive to where we are now?"

"Yes, Officer. But, I haven't been there for a long time. Please tell me what this is all about."

"You been with anyone else this afternoon?"

"No, sir."

"How long have you been here at the airport?"

"About 45 minutes," answered Bo.

"Anyone here to vouch for that, pal?"

"I don't know, Officer. There were some other people here when I came, but I didn't know them and they're gone now."

"Well, you fit the description of a guy who beat and robbed a lady in the parking lot of the sanitation institute, and those scars have given you up. Now, why don't you tell me where her purse and the money is, cause you are under arrest. Put your hands behind your back."

Officer Collins handcuffed Bo and pulled his wallet out of his rear pocket. The policeman thumbed the wallet open and observed six single dollar bills inside.

"It'll go easier on you if you just tell me what you did with the purse and the money, buddy."

"Officer, nothing I say is going to change your mind. I don't have any lady's purse or her money."

Next Collins put William "Bo" Jenkins, a very nervous, 32-year-old black man, in the back seat of the cruiser, where he was separated from the officer by a steel screen.

As the cruiser proceeded onto Wilmer Avenue, Bo Jenkins asked the officer what would happen to the Plymouth.

"I'm going to have it picked up and then taken to the district to be searched if that's OK with you."

"Sure, just don't let it set in that lot too long. I left the keys in the ignition."

"You're pretty cool, buddy. I've just arrested you for strong arm robbery and you're worried about your junk car."

When they arrived at District 7 on Erie Avenue in the Cincinnati suburb of Hyde Park, Bo Jenkins was taken into the interview room, where robbery squad Detectives Gus Feldhaus and Frank Sanker were waiting.

A color photograph of Jenkins was taken with a Polaroid camera. A second photograph was shot from the side, then another, then a close-up of his facial scars. And finally one showing the scars on his hands and arms.

While Feldhaus made several telephone calls to locate Ruth Kreider, Sanker advised Jenkins of his "Miranda" rights, and questioned him concerning his activities that day. Officer Collins remained present for the interrogation. The statement given by the robbery suspect was the same given to Officer Collins in the parking lot at the airport. He denied being anywhere near the Taft center that day. He adamantly denied hitting and robbing a white lady.

Feldhaus came back into the interview room and told Sanker and Collins that Ruth Kreider had been released from the hospital, and that she was at the home of her sister, Veronica Hegner, in Pleasant Ridge.

"Here's the game plan," Feldhaus announced.

"Let's take this bird downtown and put him in a lineup with three or four other black guys. I also want to get photographs of him in the lineup to show the victim. I also want to mix his photograph in with some mug shots of other blacks and see who she picks out, OK?"

Jenkins was taken to District 1 and placed in a lineup with three other black men, of whom two were police officers wearing clothing similar to Jenkins'. The third man was a custodian at the high school across the street. Several black-and-white photographs were taken of this lineup and developed immediately.

While this was being done, Detective Frank Sanker was going through the mug photographs looking for photos of blacks as near to Jenkins in appearance as possible. He could not find any photographs showing scars like those on Jenkins' face.

When this task was completed, Bo Jenkins was placed in a holding cell while Detectives Feldhaus and Sanker drove to Pleasant Ridge to inter- view Ruth Kreider and to show her the lineup photos and the mug shot photos.

A half-hour later, Gus Feldhaus called his lieutenant from Veronica Hegner's home.

"Book him, Lieutenant. The victim just picked him out of the lineup and the mug shots. She said that she would never forget those 'Dalmatian' spots on his nose and face. He's the man."

William "Bo" Jenkins was officially charged with the assault and rob- bery of Ruth Kreider at the Taft Sanitary Engineering Center, Columbia Parkway, Cincinnati, Hamilton County, Ohio, on or about Friday, September 18, 1970.

Bo Jenkins was arraigned the next day in Hamilton County Municipal Court. His court-appointed lawyer entered a plea of not guilty. At the request of the prosecuting attorney, the judge set bail at $25,000 on each charge. There was no possibility that Bo's mother could raise 10 percent of $25,000 for a bondsman to have Bo released. This meant he would have to remain in the jail until his trial.

On Monday, September 21, Ray Clark read about Bo's arrest in the morning newspaper.

"I'll be damned, " he said to a customer eating breakfast at the count- er. "I gave this turkey a job Friday to start cooking for me on Saturday. Now I know why he didn't show up. He celebrated his finding a job by going out and robbin' some secretary. Shit, he probably would have stole me blind. Good riddance, asshole."

State of Ohio v. William Jenkins indictment B 70-937 was returned by the Hamilton County Grand Jury on October 6, 1970. On October 19, William "Bo" Jenkins was arraigned on the two-count indictment before

Common Pleas Judge Ralph Kohnen.

"To the charge of robbery, what is your plea?" inquired the deputy clerk.

"Not guilty," answered Jenkins' attorney, Anthony Bruenneman.

"To the charge of assault with intent to rob, what is your plea?"

Same response: "Not guilty to all charges, your honor."

"Will your honor reconsider bond in this case?"

Judge Kohnen, always a stickler in these cases, responded, "I see no reason to alter the bond set by Judge Denning at the arraignment in Municipal Court. Bond will remain at $25,000 on each count. This case shall proceed to trial before this court on November 29, 1970. Agreeable, gentleman?"

"Yes, your Honor," replied the assistant prosecutor assigned to arraignments that week.

"OK, Judge, we will be here," said Anthony Bruenneman for the accused.

The Jenkins case was assigned to me by first assistant prosecutor Cal Prem on October 30, 1970. I read the grand jury transcript and realized instantly that the only direct evidence of William Jenkins' guilt was his identification from photographs by the victim. The money was never recovered. Mrs. Kreider's purse was never found. There was no admission or confession by the accused. In fact, Jenkins steadfastly maintained his innocence.

I telephoned Detective Frank Sanker, with whom I had developed a good rapport. We talked for about half an hour. Sanker told me that there was a lot about this case that bothered him, too. But he told me that he had shown the pictures to Ruth Kreider in the presence of Gus Feldhaus on three separate occasions since September 18th. She had picked out the picture of Jenkins without hesitation each time. "It was the scars on his nose and cheeks," said Sanker. "They make the case strong — much stronger than it would be otherwise. Besides, he could have hidden the purse and money anywhere between the sanitation center and the airport, to be retrieved later."

"In addition," said Sanker, "there is the time factor. The defendant had a job interview with Raymond Clark, the owner of the Valley View Grill, from 11:00 a.m. until just after 1:30 p.m. He even ate lunch there.

"Then he claims that he drove to the Lunken Airport to see a World War II bomber. He got there about 2:05 p.m. He was arrested at the airport by Officer Collins at 4:45 P.M. some 15 to 20 minutes after the assault and robbery of the Kreider woman, which we estimate happened about 4:15 to 4:20 p.m., since she said that she left the building at about 4:10 p.m.

"All of this means that Jenkins was alone from about 1:30 p.m. until 4:40 p.m. He has no witnesses to verify that he never left Lunken Airport between 2:00 p.m. and 4:40 p.m., when Collins first observed him. And remember, the parking lot at the sanitation center and the lot where he was arrested are just over one mile and a quarter apart. He could easily have robbed the victim, stashed the purse and money in some hiding place, and drove to the Lunken field by 4:40 p.m."

"That's cutting it close," I said, "especially since Collins claims that he had observed Jenkins walking toward his car when Collins was driving down Wilmer Avenue. That makes it look to me like Jenkins might have been there for a while, as he has claimed."

"No, I think what happened was he spotted Collins coming down Wilmer Avenue and started headin' for his car to get out of there," replied Sanker.

"Look at it this way, Mr. Prosecutor. He left the restaurant around 1:30 p.m. No one can verify his whereabouts after that time. The assault and robbery occurred at approximately 4:20 p.m. Next, he is arrested about a mile away by Collins at 4:45 p.m. He had 25 minutes to rob that woman and be at Lunken Airport, allegedly to see a B-17 bomber.

"Finally, the positive identification by the victim with those scars and all. For me, that cinches it. I don't really feel that the absence of the money or her purse queers the case. I still believe it is airtight. He did it, and he knows it. Maybe he has convinced himself that he is innocent, or he believes that we can't make the case without the money or the purse!"

When I got off the phone with Sanker, I began to feel more confident that we had a winnable case. I still hoped that between then and November 29, the date Judge Kohnen had set for trial, the money and Mrs. Kreider's purse would be found. Maybe fingerprints could be lifted off these items.

November 30, 1970, was a cold, gray Monday after Thanksgiving week. I arrived at the prosecutor's office at my usual time of 7:30 a.m. and got a cup of black coffee at the vendor's stand next to the courthouse lobby. There was a crowd of about 20 people around the old elevators. Counting heads, I knew I could run the steps to the fourth floor faster than I could get there by cable. Besides, I needed the exercise.

It was about 8:20 a.m. when my favorite gruff old secretary, Mary

Clark, roused me from my review of the evidence in the Jenkins case with the ring of the intercom line on my telephone. Mary told me to get my head out of my bottom because several of my witnesses had just checked in with her. I slid the grand jury transcript back into the manila folder that had printed in bold black face on the upper left tab "Melvin G. Rueger, Prosecuting Attorney, Hamilton County, Ohio," and got up from my desk chair. I swallowed the last of the by now lukewarm coffee from the Styrofoam cup and pitched it into the waste basket as I slipped my suit coat on and headed toward the waiting area where my witnesses sat, nervously wondering how hard this ordeal was going to get before it was finally over.

I opened the solid wood door with the electronic security lock and peeked into the waiting room. The first person I observed was Mary Clark sitting at the reception desk behind the wooden railing. Mary had automatically looked up when I opened the door. Our eyes met. And as I expected, she gave me that same old look — the one that says, "Why in the hell did the boss ever appoint you as an assistant prosecuting attorney?" As she looked away from me, she pointed in the direction of two middle-age women sitting on a small couch facing the door where I stood.

"This is Mr. Mestemaker, ladies. You are now in his care." Mary then looked back at me, "Try to make them feel comfortable here or I'll slip rat poison in your coffee."

As I led Ruth Kreider and her sister Veronica Hegner back through the linoleum-covered corridor, I explained to them that Mary Clark really admired me, but that she didn't want to show any favoritism around other assistant prosecutors. I could tell that the two ladies in my care weren't sure that Mary was teasing me.

Once inside my cubicle of our office, with its four gray chairs, a gray metal desk and one gray file cabinet, I went over the details of the forthcoming trial with Mrs. Kreider and her sister. I removed the photographs of William Jenkins from the prosecutor's office file and laid them on the desk in front of Ruth Kreider. She drew closer and put on her reading glasses: "That's him. I'll never forget that face and especially those scars." I was now fairly satisfied that she would hold up under Anthony Bruenneman's cross-examination.

Shortly after 8:30 a.m., Officers Walsh and Collins, Detectives Feldhaus and Sanker as well as Herbert Wilson, the security guard who came to Ruth Kreider's assistance, showed up. We discussed the order in which I would call the witnesses, what questions I would ask each one of them, and what kind of cross-examination questions they could expect from Mr. Bruenneman.

At 9:00 a.m., I took Ruth Kreider and her sister down to the criminal arraignment courtroom, which, that particular week, happened to be Judge Louis J. Schneider's courtroom. I led the two ladies in and had them take seats in the second row of wooden, church-style benches, which made up the spectators' area in Judge Schneider's courtroom. I pointed out to them the group of prisoners already seated in the jury box under police guard. "These men are being arraigned this morning on indictments that have just been returned." I pointed to a redheaded man in the back row, third from the right. "See that fellow. He is being arraigned for the murder of a woman, whose house he broke into in Bond Hill. If you want to, you can sit here and watch the arraignments while I go outside to talk to Jenkins' lawyer to see if he intends to take this case to a jury trial." As I left the two women, they were intently observing the prisoners seated in the jury box, and whispering to each other about the proceedings that they were witnessing.

I had been outside the double doors to Judge Schneider's courtroom talking to Tony Bruenneman for about three minutes when Veronica Hegner came up to me and said, "I'm so glad that I found you. You have to come into the courtroom right now. Ruth has to tell you something immediately."

"What is it?" I asked, a little bewildered.

"I can't tell you here," said Veronica. "You have to come inside now."

I excused myself from Tony Bruenneman and followed Veronica into the courtroom. Ruth Kreider was hunched forward with her hands cupped over her face. I could tell that she was crying. I had absolutely no idea what had happened to upset Ruth so badly. I sat down next to her and put my hand on her shoulder. "Mrs. Kreider, what is wrong? Has something happened to you?" She looked up at me, tears streaming down both cheeks.

"Mr. Mestemaker, I have made a horrible mistake. That poor young man. He has been in jail for months because of my error. Look at the prisoner in the back row, the fourth man from the left."

I looked up and in the direction that Ruth Kreider was pointing. "Good God!" I thought. "How was it that I didn't notice him before?" Seated in the back row was a young black man with grease-like burn marks on his nose and left cheek. He had a mean scowl. He looked at me, then at Ruth Kreider, and then he turned his gaze away from us. It was obvious that he felt uncomfortable that he was being watched.

I turned back to Ruth Kreider. "Are you now telling me that this guy in the back row is the person who robbed and beat you up?"

She looked at him again and sobbed, "Oh, God forgive, me that's the man."

I immediately took Ruth Kreider and her sister out of the courtroom. Once in the hall, I approached Detectives Feldhaus and Sanker. I had Ruth Kreider report to them what she had just told me. After she informed them that her assailant was in the jury box, I instructed Feldhaus and Sanker to go to the county jail located on the sixth floor of the Courthouse and attempt to interrogate this individual, who Mrs. Kreider had just fingered as her true assailant. I then approached Tony Bruenneman and explained the strange turn of events to him. He and I went into the courtroom, where I pointed the person out to him. Tony turned to me and said, "Christ, they could be brothers. I wonder what the odds are on two men about the same age and build having scars that are nearly identical?"

I asked one of the court officers who the fourth man in the rear row was. He told me that his name was Alonzo Watson and that he was being arraigned for robbing a night clerk in a 24-hour mini market two days ago. I asked to see the arrest record and the police intake form on Alonzo Watson. I took these documents outside and sat down on a bench with Tony Bruenneman to have him present while I compared the vital statistics of William Jenkins and Alonzo Watson. What follows is the comparison:

William Jenkins / Alonzo Watson
Age: 31 / 29
Height: 5'9" / 5'10"
Weight: 175 lbs. / 169 lbs.
Skin tone: Medium Brown / Medium Brown
Scars: Nose, Cheeks, Hands, Forearms / Nose and Cheek
The comparison was uncanny.

As soon as Alonzo Watson was returned to the county jail, he was interrogated by Detectives Feldhaus and Sanker after being advised by them of his Miranda rights. At first, he denied any knowledge of a robbery of a middle-age white woman at the Taft center. Finally, with the approval and assistance of Tony Bruenneman, William Jenkins was brought from his cell to the interview room. As the two men were brought face to face, it was as if there was only one man and a mirror. We then had them stand side by side, at which time they were photographed. It was easy to understand how Ruth Kreider could mistakenly identify William "Bo" Jackson as her assailant.

Perhaps there was a streak of some decency in Alonzo Watson after all. When he was faced with the knowledge that another man had been scheduled to go on trial this very day for a crime that Watson had committed, he admitted that it was he and not Jenkins, who had robbed and beaten Ruth Kreider. He stated that most of the money had been spent on heroin, to which he was seriously addicted. He showed us the needle marks on both of his arms. What about the purse and its contents, which included Ruth Kreider's wallet and identification? He told us that he had thrown it into a culvert pipe in the woods behind the parking lot where the robbery had occurred. The purse and wallet were recovered later that day by Officers Walsh and Collins. This was the missing evidence that I had been looking for the entire time. Now the puzzle was complete.

William "Bo" Jenkins was ordered released immediately by Judge Louis Schneider. Papers were prepared officially charging Alonzo Watson with the robbery and beating of Ruth Kreider. He pleaded guilty to these offenses one week later and was sentenced to 1 to 25 years in the Ohio State Reformatory.

William "Bo" Jenkins became the subject of numerous news stories. He received a lot of job offers and accepted the one he wanted most of all, morning chef at the Sinton, Cincinnati's premier hotel. His name was cleared and he received an official apology from Hamilton County and the city of Cincinnati. He accepted these expressions of regret like a man. Best of all, he accepted a handshake and a hug from Ruth Kreider. They had finally met, after all.

CHAPTER 6

THE DEFENSE RESTS

Esta Pomeroy turned 63 years old on December 25, 1970. Like others who shared her birthday, she had always felt a little cheated at Christmas time. Her husband, Mercer, was also 63. They had been married for a little over 21 years. It was a second marriage for each of them, and it was a happy autumn union between two middle-age, hard-working adults with grown children and an ever-increasing number of grandchildren.

Since 1957, Esta had been the legal owner and operator of Bob's Pony Keg, a typical ma-and-pa mini grocery located in a nearly century old, two-story, brick-and-frame storefront at the corner of Elsmere and Lexington streets in Norwood, Ohio, a blue-collar community bordering the Cincinnati neighborhood of Evanston. The pony keg was purchased in Esta's name due mainly to Mercer's employment with the United States Post Office as a letter carrier. After his retirement in 1971, Mercer supplemented his federal pension by working in the carryout with his wife. In this manner, they were able to be together day and night. Since they resided only one block from the store, they didn't even need an automobile, walking the short distance together each morning and evening on a street where everyone knew them as neighbors and most folks were their steady customers. In the 1950s, '60s and '70s, small operations like Bob's Pony Keg provided a very comfortable income for couples such as Mercer and Esta. Some people considered this particular pony keg to be a gold mine. And in the days before credit cards, most of their business was in cash. The talk on the street was that the store held a lot of cash, especially after the 8-to-5 working crowd had stopped in to purchase groceries, snacks and beverages.

The store was small, the merchandise and cooler area being 14-by-12 feet. A doorway behind the counter next to the cash register led to a small back room containing only 80 square feet. This back room, with a curtain in the doorway to the store proper, contained a table, two chairs, a small refrigerator, a telephone and a bed for Esta to lie down on when her feet started to bother her — which, due to her arthritic problems, was a daily occurrence. Next to the bed was a small table holding a lamp and a radio. The table had one drawer. In it was a loaded .38-caliber Smith & Wesson revolver, kept just in case someone might decide to find out just how much cash the store really did have on hand after it got dark outside.

Esta loved to work her store. She told people that it kept her young to stay busy. She also loved the neighborhood chitchat. Esta was not herself a gossip, but she enjoyed hearing about the goings on in the neighborhood. She often handed out candy to the small ones of the block in exchange for small chores such as Windexing the front door glass or stacking empty bottles in wooden cases.

Mercer often told anyone who would listen that Esta "lives to work in the store." It never occurred to him, even for a second, that his wife would be murdered in her store during a botched robbery.

Monday, February 8, 1971, was a cold and dreary day. About 4:00 p.m., it started to snow. Two young men, Anthony Leon Collins, age 18, and his cousin, Stephen Newell, 19, were sitting in the living room at Collins' house watching television. Both had jobs, but they had decided to knock off this day because of the inclement weather. Collins did not abuse drugs, but his cousin had started a new habit — not only new to him, but one that was new at the time to young individuals in general. Stephen Newell had taken up snorting cocaine. He liked it a lot.

Between the two of them they had about $6 and some change. It was Stephen Newell who first brought up the subject of robbing some place to get some money. Collins' reply was that it sounded like a good idea as long as they could do it and not get caught. He said that going back to confinement was not his idea of fun. Being locked up in the juvenile detention center had left him with a distaste for cages and cells.

But Newell was confident. "Look: it's snowing, and it's already getting dark. There won't be many people out tonight. We could hit that pony keg on Elsmere. You know, the one the old lady and old man run. I've seen the cash drawer open, and, man, they got all kinds of money around. All we need is my grandpa's gun, and it would help if you had one too. We can do it, man."

Collins decided that it was a good plan and that they could probably figure on coming out of the deal with about $500. He had been in the pony keg three or four times before, and he could visualize what the place looked like on the inside. If they waited until it got dark and there weren't many people in the store or out on the street, it would be easy — just like shoplifting cigarettes. He also knew where he could get a gun. It was an old, beat-up .38-caliber revolver that belonged to his father. It had a broken trigger, and the cylinder didn't rotate anymore — but it was a gun. And even if it didn't shoot anymore, it looked real enough to scare the hell out of an old man and an old lady.

Before the duo left Collins' house, he went down to the basement and picked up the ancient Colt revolver from the tool bench. He rotated the cylinder with his thumb and index finger. The trigger didn't work, but the cylinder could be rotated by hand — and the hammer spring worked pretty well. The hammer snapped down real hard when he took his thumb off after pulling it back from the cylinder. He put the pistol in the right-hand pocket of his brown three-quarter-length jacket and went back upstairs, where his cousin was waiting for him in the kitchen.

By the time the two reached the house of Newell's grandfather, approximately 8 blocks from Collins' residence, the snow had let up. There was a good inch or more on the ground, covering the lawns, sidewalks and streets with a heavy wet blanket. It was 30 degrees. Pretty soon it would be dark, and then they would put the plan into operation.

Newell was able to get his grandfather's pistol out of a dresser drawer while Collins kept the old man engaged in a conversation about basketball in the dining room. Newell checked the cylinder to make sure that the gun was loaded. He noticed several loose bullets lying in the drawer behind the pistol. He scooped them up for his cousin. Both pistols were the same caliber. Anthony might want to load the broken gun anyway, just to be cool.

As they walked back to Collins' house, Newell handed Collins three bullets and told him to see if they fit the gun he was carrying. Collins rotated the cylinder, dropping a cartridge into each chamber as it appeared beneath the loading gate in the frame of the weapon. Sure enough, they fit. Collins grinned. "Now we both got heat."

By 7:50 p.m., it was dark and windy. The snow had finally stopped, but there were few people or automobiles on the street as Collins and Newell left the Hudson Avenue residence to walk toward Bob's Pony Keg. They cut through the public park to Elsmere Avenue and went down two blocks to the intersection with Lexington. They could see an automobile standing around the corner with exhaust coming out of its tailpipe. There were two people inside the automobile, a man and a woman. The cousins had observed the woman walk out of the store and get into the passenger side. She was wearing a heavy wool car coat with a fur-trimmed hood. Her name was Diana Payne. The man sitting in the driver's seat was her fiancè. His name was Robert Icenogle. Her father, Ray Payne, was still inside the store, where he was watching Esta Pomeroy ring up the groceries that he and Diana had picked up. Diana had told her father that she would wait for him in the car.

At 8:10 p.m., two other customers walked out of the store. They hardly noticed the two young black men huddled against the front of the store, their heads and necks thrust down in their upturned coat collars. One of the men was wearing a brown three-quarter-length coat and a white knit cap. The other one was wearing a brown, waist-length jacket and a gray chauffeur-style cap. Now the coast was clear. Newell entered the store with Collins right behind him. Newell was startled by the sight of Ray Payne, who turned to walk toward the door. Newell had thought all the customers had left. Both young men quickly turned their heads and stared down at canned goods on a low shelf. Ray Payne glanced in their direction as he walked the six steps to the front door. He didn't concentrate on their faces. He really didn't want to go eyeball to eyeball with the men. Something inside told him he should feel fear.

Once the store was empty of customers, Collins approached the counter to the left side of the cash register. Esta Pomeroy spied him with a mixture of suspicion and fear. He fumbled in his pockets as he asked the woman for a pack of Kools. Mercer Pomeroy was standing in the doorway of the back room. Esta turned her head to the left, opposite the side where Collins was standing, and whispered to her husband:

"Pop, go get the gun. I think there is going to be trouble."

The old man hesitated. He felt a cold chill on his neck. He really didn't want to look at the men standing at the counter. He wasn't sure what he should do. Then Esta shot him a scared glance, which he took to mean he should do what she wanted. Mercer Pomeroy slipped into the back room and fumbled in the drawer for the pistol. Before he had retrieved the gun from its hiding place, he heard a male voice yell in his direction.

"Don't you come out. Don't come back out. If you do, we will kill both of you."

He thought that the next words that he heard were Esta's. He heard, or at least thought he heard, Esta say, "That's a toy gun. I'm not scared by any toy gun."

Next Mercer Pomeroy heard a male voice.

"Hurry up, put it in the sack, put it in the sack. Shit, lady, you're stalling me. Maybe this will hurry you up."

The next sound was a single gunshot. It was followed by a thud as Esta Pomeroy, shot below her left breast, collapsed backward, hitting the wall of the back room before sliding to the linoleum floor. Then the small bell attached to the front door rang as the two men ran out. Then there was silence.

Ray Payne was in the act of handing the groceries into the car to Diana when he heard what sounded like a gunshot. Next he heard the front door of the pony keg slam. He looked up, but he saw no one. Diana Payne looked back when she heard the loud noise and saw two black men as they ran from the store toward the railroad tracks. Robert Icenogle saw the same scene. But neither could describe faces. Both did see the gray chauffeur cap drop to the street just this side of the railroad tracks. It lay in the snow next to the two sets of footprints that hurried off into the dark night, toward the park and Hudson Avenue. It was exactly 8:16 p.m.

The Paynes and Icenogle ran into the store, where Mercer Pomeroy was bent over his wife. He was patting her cheeks and pleading with her not to die on him. Robert Icenogle called the Norwood police department, which, in turn, dispatched the life squad. Within a matter of minutes, Esta Pomeroy was on her way to the trauma center, where she was pronounced dead.

By 10:15 p.m., Anthony Leon Collins and Stephen Le Bron Newell had been tracked in the snow with the help of a police dog to the house of Newell's grandfather. The cousins were found hiding in the attic. They were arrested. The gun used to murder Esta Pomeroy was found in the basement, on top of a cold-air duct near the furnace. The gray chauffeur's cap had been retrieved in the street on Elsmere near the railroad tracks. The police, who tracked the double set of footprints in the snow through the playground in the park, also found a pistol with a broken trigger lying on a walkway. In fact, it was discovered when one of the officers who was participating in the search accidentally kicked the gun as he trudged through the snow.

The indictment returned by the grand jury on March 26, 1971, pronounced that:

"Stephen Le Bron Newell and Anthony Leon Collins on or about the Eighth day of February in the year Nineteen Hundred and Seventy-one at the County of Hamilton and State of Ohio, aforesaid, did unlawfully, purposely and intentionally, while perpetrating or attempting to perpetrate a robbery kill Esta Pomeroy then and there being contrary to the form of the statute in such case made and provided, and against the peace and dignity of the State of Ohio."

On April 9, only one month after I had resigned my position as an assistant prosecuting attorney for Hamilton County, I received a telephone call from my former boss, Melvin Rueger, now Common Pleas Court Judge Melvin Rueger. He said he wanted to appoint me and another former assistant prosecutor, Donald Rolf, to represent an indigent young man who did not have the money to hire his own attorney. This man was 18 years old. He was black, and he was accused of shooting a woman during a holdup of a small grocery. There was a second young man who was also accused of the murder, and two other lawyers had already been chosen to represent him. No one knew for sure which one did the shooting, Rueger told me. But it didn't really make much difference who the actual trigger man was because under Ohio law, both could be found equally liable for the homicide and both could be executed regardless of which one was the shooter. I told Judge Rueger that I would accept the appointment mainly because of who was asking me to accept the case. I recall telling him that I was still a prosecutor at heart, but that if I was to be Anthony Leon Collins' lawyer, I would go full bore and all out to get him acquitted. I recall Judge Rueger saying to me, "That's why I picked you to begin with."

There was really no need to get overly involved in the case anyway. No one in recent history had left the prosecutor's office and straight away gotten someone off on a murder charge, no matter how clever a lawyer he thought himself to be. And I was certainly no more clever than all of those former criminal trial assistants who had gone before me. So, let's face it, we will give the Collins kid the best defense trial possible and hope to hell that we can save him from the electric chair. Forget any thought of an acquittal. This just did not happen in this county, this bastion of conservatism, law and order.

Don Rolf and I first met our client, Anthony Leon Collins, in the jail on the sixth floor of the Courthouse on Monday, April 12. He was a short, thin, light-skinned black kid with curly black hair, sideburns and a mustache. He weighed in at 142 pounds. He was 18 years old, having been born on December 29, 1952. He was 5-feet, 10-inches tall, well proportioned and willowy. He chain-smoked Kool cigarettes and chewed his fingernails. The first thing he told us during our two-hour-long initial interview was that he didn't shoot the lady. This we expected. Then he told us that no one was in the store that got a good look at him. He told us that he and Newell had been put in several lineups by the Norwood police and that he had overheard one detective tell another that none of the witnesses could pick either him or his cousin out as being the men who had attempted to rob and who they said "killed that old lady."

As is always the case, we needed to know whether our client had made a statement. Did he talk to the police? We knew that they had interrogated him. To believe otherwise in a capital murder case would be incomprehensible. So, Don asked him, "Did you make a statement? Did you give a confession to the police?"

Collins stared first at me and then back at Rolf. "Yeah, I told them what happened, but that was only after they told me that they were going to put me in the electric chair, and that Stephen had said that I shot the lady, which I found out he didn't. Then I told them that I wanted to talk to a lawyer, and they just ignored me."

After hearing this, maybe, just maybe, if Collins was telling us the truth, we might have a shot at getting him acquitted of murder, something that had not happened in Hamilton County in a long, long time. If, in fact, there were no witnesses who could put Collins inside the pony keg at the time of the murder, and if we could keep any confession or admission that he made to the police out of evidence, we might have a chance at an acquittal.

We needed to do two things as soon as possible. We had to find out whether any witnesses could identify Collins from the pony keg. And we had to get a copy of the statement given by Collins to the detectives, to see whether we could keep it out of the trial.

Rolf and I discussed how to approach the issue concerning potential eyewitness identification. This trial took place before the rules of discovery had been enacted. We could not obtain a transcript of any witness statements, since there had not been a preliminary hearing. Actually, up to that date, the only place where witnesses had testified in the Pomeroy murder was before the grand jury, which had returned the murder indictment. And since the grand jury proceedings were secret, we were not going to be allowed to review testimony given there.

Then came an idea that, although very unorthodox, we figured might work: a bond hearing. Collins and Newell were being held without bail, which was customary in first-degree murder cases. The authority for refusing bail in a capital murder case is contained in Article I, Section 9, of the Ohio Constitution: "All persons shall be bailable by sufficient surety except for capital offenses where the proof is evident or the presumption (of guilt) great."

Basically, this section means that in all crimes — except a capital crime — bail is available. However, even in a capital case, bail may be set by a court when the proof of guilt is not evident or the presumption is not great.

Two days later, a motion to set bail for Anthony Collins was filed, claiming that he was entitled to obtain a bond on the ground that the proof against him was not evident or the presumption great since no one could identify him. This motion was set for hearing for May 12, and we immediately issued subpoenas for all of the witnesses who had testified before the grand jury.

The hearing was bitterly opposed by the lawyers representing the prosecution. Because such a hearing was really unheard of, the prosecutor's office objected to our being allowed to question any of the state's witnesses under oath concerning their knowledge of Esta Pomeroy's murder. Our argument in favor of this strategy was that we were merely complying with the state Constitution's provision. After listening to these arguments pro and con, Judge Rueger ruled that I could question witnesses to the crime only as it related to their ability to place our client in the pony keg when Esta Pomeroy was shot to death. This was exactly what I wanted to do anyway. The defense had won its first victory in the trial of State of Ohio vs. Anthony Leon Collins.

At the hearing, the first witness whom I called was Mercer Pomeroy. When asked whether the man who had shot his wife was present in the courtroom, he looked around — finally settling his eyes on Collins — and said, "No, sir." He could not identify his wife's killer. He could not identify Anthony Collins.

In order, Ray Payne, Diana Payne and her fiancé, Robert Icenogle, were called to the witness stand and asked whether they recognized anyone in the courtroom from the pony keg. In each instance, these witnesses looked at Anthony Collins, who was seated at the defense table between Don Rolf and myself, and answered by saying, "No."

Our suspicions had been correct. The prosecutor did not have a witness, at least that we were aware of, who could place our client in the store at the time of the murder. We argued that Collins was entitled to a bond because the testimony of the witnesses at this hearing had shown that the proof against our client was not evident or that the presumption (of guilt) was not great.

But Judge Rueger denied our motion to set bail for Collins. This was not a surprise. We had never believed that he would give Collins bail anyway. But we had accomplished our goal: We had determined that the state's witnesses whom we called to testify could not place our client at the scene of the crime, and we had them saying so under oath in open court. They would not be able to change that testimony for the trial. We had pinned them down.

After over a week of effort, we were able to obtain a typed copy of the statement that our client had made to detectives 12 hours after his arrest — without the benefit of having a lawyer present to advise him. The transcript was 10 pages long, representing the entire tape recorded statement made by Collins at the Norwood Police Station in the Homicide Squad Interrogation Room.

There it was on the first two pages — the very same threats related to us by Collins. The request to see a lawyer went unanswered. It revealed the kinds of statements that defense lawyers learn about in law school, the no-no of police interrogation — "threats, coercion, intimidation, lies and denial of counsel." The transcript of the police Q&A with Collins read:

This is Detective Reynolds and Kempf of the Norwood Police Department. We are in the detectives' office. The date is February 9, and the time is now 10:00 a.m. This will be a statement from Anthony Collins in regard to what they did at Bob's Pony Keg concerning the shooting of Esta Pomeroy.

Question: What is your name?

Answer: (Audible sobbing) Anthony Collins.

Q. Do you know what your rights are? They were explained to you last night. Let me explain them to you again. You have the right to remain silent, and anything you say can be used against you in a court of law. You have the right to the presence of an attorney, and if you cannot afford one, one will be appointed to you prior to any questions, if you desire. Do you understand? (There was no response by Collins.)

Q. What is your full name?

A. Anthony Leon Collins (the sound of crying is audible).

Q. What is your address?

A. 3456 Hudson.

Q. How old are you?

A. 18.

Q. Anthony, you realize you are in serious trouble, don't you?

A. Yes sir, but I wasn't in there.

Q. What did you say?

A. I didn't do nothing (sobbing).

Q. Listen to me, all the evidence points to you being there. There's not much question in my mind you were there. The only question in my mind is did you pull the trigger? Are you telling me that your buddy pulled the trigger? Let me tell you something. There was a survey made yesterday in the country on capital punishment, and three out of four want it. There is a damn good chance that you or both of you are going to sit in the electric chair because this crime has got to stop one way or another. (Audible sobbing). They are talking about dusting off the Ohio electric chair. If you think you are sitting there kidding yourself there is a chance you won't sit in it, the only one you are kidding is yourself. There is a damn good chance that you will. And now is the time you have the opportunity to help yourself. Both of you are put at the scene of the crime, but we need to know who pulled the trigger. You want to tell us who pulled the trigger? We will help you if we can, but we got to get down to the facts.

A. (Audible sobbing; voice broken.) He pulled the trigger. I didn't.

(23-second pause)

Q. What, Anthony? How did it happen? Tell what you know about it, so that we can help you — just how it happened?

A. I was getting some cigarettes. Can I talk to a lawyer?

(No response to request for a lawyer.)

Q. You were getting some cigarettes? That your pack that was left on the counter?

A. Yes, sir. Can I see a lawyer?

At this point, the transcript continued on with questions posed to Collins, the answers to which clearly implicated him in the attempted robbery and the shooting of Esta Pomeroy. On several occasions, Collins inquired of his interrogators if he was going to be charged with murder. The answer was as follows:

"That is why we are trying to get the facts straight — so we know what to do, to see if we can help you, OK?"

Beginning on page six of the transcript of Collins' recorded confession to the detectives, he is requested to give a full statement in his own handwriting. His response to this was as follows:

"I don't want to write this stuff down. He (Stephen Newell) is my first cousin."

In an effort to make Collins believe that writing his statement out would help clear him of the murder, the following remarks were made by his interrogators.

"You don't have to write anything about him, other than he done the shooting and pulled the trigger. It could have been an accident. If you don't give us something to go on to prove it was an accident, it does make a difference. It would give the court something to go on too. We have to clear you somehow, and the only way we can do it is for you to tell us what happened."

Collins asked: "Are we both going to be charged with murder? Can I please have a lawyer now?"

Once again, Collins' request for a lawyer was ignored. Instead, his cousin, Stephen Newell, was brought into the interrogation room. Afterward, full confessions were obtained from both Collins and Newell — including an admission that both of them had pistols and that Anthony had the one with the broken trigger, but that they were both real guns, not toys as Esta Pomeroy had believed.

Our review of this statement proved that Collins had told us the truth about the circumstances surrounding his confession. He had been threatened with the electric chair. His repeated requests for a lawyer had been ignored by the interrogating detectives, and he had been the recipient of meaningless promises that his cooperation would lead to his being cleared of the crime of murder.

Our ability to study the transcript of the statements made to detectives by Anthony Collins and Stephen Newell at Norwood police headquarters on February 9, without the benefit of a lawyer's advice, resulted in our filing a motion to suppress the use of this statement by the prosecution in the murder trial of Collins. We were not concerned about its use in the separate trial of Stephen Newell. Newell was represented by two very capable and experienced defense attorneys, and it was up to them to protect his rights to a fair trial.

The hearing on our motion to suppress this statement was before Common Pleas Court Judge Lyle W. Castle on May 20. At this hearing, we placed our client on the witness stand for the singular purpose of establishing the level of coercion and subterfuge employed to obtain a confession from him, and the repeated requests made by him for a lawyer, all of which the officers ignored. Collins' testimony, given in support of the motion to suppress the evidence of his statement to the police, could not be used against him at a trial since it was limited-purpose testimony. He could not be asked by the prosecutor at this hearing whether, in fact, he had been in the store and involved in the attempted robbery of the pony keg and the murder of Mrs. Pomeroy. Despite the fact that we had assured him that he could not be cross-examined by the prosecution about the crime scene, and the hours that we had spent with him preparing him for the hearing, he did poorly on the witness stand. He was scared to death of the whole courtroom scene in general and of Assistant Prosecutor Carl Vollman in particular. Vollman, a tough prosecutor, was like a cobra in a courtroom. One lightning-quick strike on an unsuspecting defendant and the game was over. Although Collins attempted to stick with the script while on the witness stand, Vollman maneuvered him like an expert pilot handles his fighter plane. My notes made while Collins testified in this hearing were ominous:

"Too nervous."

"Appears to be evasive."

"Appears to be untruthful."

"Is not a good witness."

"Will screw himself into the ground at the trial."

After Collins testified, first we called Detective Joseph Crow, the principal interrogator during the questioning of Collins, and then his partner, Robert Kempf. We concluded our part of the hearing by having the detectives play the actual tape of the interrogation for the judge. This was the first time that we had actually listened to the tape of the confession. We believed that this tape was critical to our motion because it clearly revealed the hostility displayed by the detectives toward Collins as well as his tearful reactions, his cracking voice and his sobs as well as his futile attempts to secure the help of a lawyer. I noticed that the judge listened to the tape-recorded confession with great interest. I had the impression that he was troubled by what he heard on this tape. I personally believed that he would rule in our favor and refuse to allow this confession to be used against Collins in his murder trial.

I concluded our part of the hearing on our motion to suppress this evidence by arguing that the statement had not been given voluntarily because the tactics used by the officers, in particular, their threats alternated with offers of help to clear him, overcame Collins' free will to remain silent and that, therefore, his statements had not been freely and voluntarily made, but were rather given out of fear of electrocution and through trickery and deceit. I finished my argument by asserting that the statement should be kept out of evidence because our client's Sixth Amendment right to counsel had been violated by the detectives, who simply chose to ignore his repeated requests to talk to a lawyer. I reminded Judge Castle that the United States Supreme Court had ruled that once a suspect who is in police custody requests a lawyer during interrogation, the officers must stop the interview until a lawyer has been secured and has actually been allowed to advise the suspect.

Judge Castle took our motion under submission, stating that he would give us his ruling in two days. Don Rolf and I believed that he would review the applicable law and rule in our favor. I believe that Carl Vollman also believed that the judge was going to rule that he could not use Collins' confession at the trial. Our confidence made the court's ultimate ruling hard to accept. The judge notified us by official court entry three days later that our motion to suppress the confession given by Anthony Collins to Norwood Police detectives on February 9 was denied, and that the prosecution would be allowed to use the statement at the forthcoming trial. I was particularly disappointed that the judge had failed to cite any legal authority or to explain his reasons for denying our motion.

Now we had to prepare for trial with the knowledge that even though we believed that none of the witnesses, who had been made known to us to that date, could put our client at the scene of the murder, his statement/confession would. We knew that the confession could convict him, and that probably our only chance was to try to discredit the confession. We would not be allowed to attack it on the basis of voluntariness since Judge Castle had ruled that it was voluntarily given by our client as a matter of law. We would be limited to trying to convince the jury that they should not believe in the truth of the confession because of the manner in which it had been obtained.

The trial commenced on June 15 with the selection of a jury, which took two days. The testimony began on June 18, when the prosecutor called the first of sixteen witnesses. As we suspected, the first witness was Mercer Pomeroy. As we had expected, he was the recipient of great sympathy from the jurors as he described the killing of his wife. The next witnesses, in order, were Robert Payne, his daughter, Diana, and her fiancé, Robert Icenogle. As we already knew, none of these individuals was able to identify Collins or to place him at the pony keg. The next two witnesses were friends of Stephen Newell who were at his grandfather's house and who described how excited Newell and Collins were when they arrived, out of breath, scared and wet. There was nothing to be gained by cross-examining these two, especially since they were not permitted to tell the jurors anything that had been told to them by others.

The next seven witnesses were police officers. They had investigated the murder scene, tracked the footprints in the snow through Evanston Park to Trimble Avenue and the front yard of the house where Collins and Newell were arrested, and found the gun that had been used to kill Esta Pomeroy.

Witnesses 14 and 15 were the criminologists. They had dusted for fingerprints, test fired the murder weapon for ballistic comparison, and performed numerous other scientific tests. Then Carl Vollman called his 16th, and what turned out to be his final witness. It was a surprise witness, one whom we had no knowledge of — a witness who had one purpose: to place our client in the pony keg. It was a favorite ploy of Carl Vollman, used by him in more than one murder trial — the mystical, mysterious surprise witness.

Witness 16 walked into the courtroom. She was an attractive redhead in her mid-30s. She raised her right hand and swore to tell the truth. Then she sat down in the witness chair. In answer to Carl Vollman's inquiry, she said that her name was Darlene Paytes. She then proceeded to relate how she had walked into Bob's Pony Keg about 7:45 p.m. on February 8. According to her testimony, when she entered the store there were two male Negroes in the store. Mercer and Esta Pomeroy were standing side by side behind the cash register. She told the jury that there were no other customers in the store and that she walked to the meat cooler, where she picked up lunchmeat. When she got to the counter, she asked for a pack of Winston cigarettes, which were handed to her by Mercer Pomeroy. At this point, she claimed that as Esta Pomeroy made change she observed the shorter of the two black men, who was wearing a leather coat and no hat. She said that he was standing next to the meat cooler. Vollman asked her whether this man was in the courtroom. She stared at Anthony Collins and said that he was the man without the hat. She next stated that as she walked toward the door to leave, the taller black man opened the door for her. She identified this individual as Stephen Newell and said that he was also wearing a brown leather jacket. She left and walked up the street. She did not hear a shot and did not see these men leave the pony keg.

As she completed her direct testimony, Collins leaned over and whispered to me that she was a liar. He said that she was not in the store, and he reminded me that he was wearing a white knit cap at all times that night.

When I commenced my cross-examination of Darlene Paytes, I wanted to know how often she stopped in the pony keg to shop. Her reply was that she was in the place almost every evening after work. I asked her whether there were other occasions when she was in the pony keg that she observed young black men inside the store. She said that she had often seen black customers there, including black men. I asked her whether she would agree with me if I told her that one-third of the stores customers were black. She said that she could agree with that assessment.

Since all of the previous witnesses had placed the attempted robbery and shooting at 8:15 to 8:16 p.m., I asked Paytes how long she had been inside the store. Her answer was no longer than 10 minutes. I reminded her that on direct examination she had testified that she entered the pony keg at 7:45 p.m. I then asked her how she could claim that she had entered the store at 7:45, remained there no more than 10 minutes, and observed two black men inside the store a full 20 minutes before the shooting — when other witnesses had testified that the men did not enter the store until approximately 8:10 p.m. She had no explanation concerning these discrepancies. These questions about times and other details confused her. She was unraveling as a witness. She was not going to be the catch-all witness that the prosecution had expected her to be.

On further questioning, Ms. Paytes was unable to state on which day of the week February 8 had fallen. When asked whether it were possible that she was confused about seeing two black men in the pony keg on the night of February 8, and that she might have seen our client in there on another evening since he had been in the pony keg on several previous evenings, her answer again was, "I'm not sure."

I showed her the white knit cap that our client had told us that he was wearing that night. Since she had already testified that the shorter of the two men, whom she claimed was Collins, had not been wearing a hat, she was unable to identify this knit cap.

I concluded our cross-examination of Paytes by asking why she had not come forward right away to claim that she had been in the store and seen our client and Newell on February 8. Her answer was she didn't realize that the police needed witnesses until a friend told her about Mrs. Pomeroy's death and she called the police to volunteer her help. When I sat down, Collins leaned over and said, "She's lying. That lady wasn't in there that night."

After Darlene Paytes left the witness stand, I fully expected Vollman to call Detective Sergeant Joseph Crowe as his next witness, to have him tell the jurors about our client's confession. Naturally, we would object to that, even if without any hope of success. Then he would ask the judge to allow the jury to hear the actual tape recorded confession. Instead, in a trial full of surprises, I was to receive yet one more surprise. Carl Vollman stood up and announced that pending the receipt of the state's exhibits, he was resting the prosecution's case.

This maneuver meant one and only one thing, and that thing occurred to Don Rolf and to me at the same time. Vollman was holding back the confession of Collins. He was anticipating that Collins would be called by us as a defense witness, and that Collins would naturally deny that he was in Bob's Pony Keg on the evening of February 8. We also figured Vollman was counting on Collins denying being involved in an attempted robbery or the killing of Esta Pomeroy. Then the prosecution would use the Collins confession to impeach him and make a liar out of him in front of the jury. I suspected Vollman believed that the judge had made a mistake when he allowed the confession to be used, and that if he held back and used it only as an impeachment tool of our client on cross-examination, not only would he succeed in having the jurors hear the confession, it would be done in such a way that we could not use the confession successfully on appeal to have any conviction reversed. The trial had turned into a real chess match. Vollman had just made a very clever move.

Fortunately, it was now 4:10 p.m. on June 21, so the judge announced that court would recess until 10:00 a.m. the next morning. This provided Don Rolf and me the opportunity to map out our strategy and to discuss with our client the advantage available if he did not take the witness stand on his own behalf. This created a controversy because Collins was eager to testify, mistakenly believing that he might sway the jurors. Finally, I had to tell him that he was a lousy witness and that Vollman would turn him around eight days from Sunday and would then beat him to death with the taped confession. I won this argument.

On June 22, the final day of the trial, the defense made an opening statement in which we claimed that Anthony Collins had absolutely nothing to do with the attempted robbery and the murder of Esta Pomeroy. We told the jury that the prosecutor had not proven by any stretch of the imagination that our client was involved in this crime. Our first witness was Mary Miller, Anthony Collins' 17-year-old girlfriend, who testified that she had known Collins for about five years and that she had never seen him with a gun or heard that he had been in any trouble. She also testified that Collins called her on February 8 and asked her to come over to his house after dinner, but her mother wouldn't let her because it was snowing and it was a school night. Collins told her that he would come over to her house instead. But she did not see him that night. He called her about 9:15 p.m. to tell her that he was at his grandfather's house on Trimble and that the weather was too bad. She related, in answer to my questions, that he did not sound upset or excited. He did not mention anything about Bob's Pony Keg.

Our next witness was Walter Collins, the defendant's father. His testimony dealt primarily with his knowledge that his son was home most of the day on February 8 and that he did not own a gun. The senior Collins went farther. He volunteered that there were no guns in his house, broken or sound, and that he had never seen either his son, Anthony, or Stephen Newell with a gun.

Our next witness was the Reverend Ardie Brown, minister of the Evanston Baptist Church. He testified that he had known Anthony Collins for 14 years and that he considered him to be a nice young man. In fact, Anthony had even dated the reverend's teen-age daughter. The Reverend Brown considered him to be respectful and of an even disposition. He asserted that Anthony had an excellent reputation in the community for truthfulness and for peacefulness. He did not believe that our client could shoot anyone.

As Reverend Brown left the courtroom, it was obvious to me that the prosecution was anticipating that our next witness was going to be our client. As I stood at counsel table pretending to be contemplating my next move, I glanced at Carl Vollman sitting at the prosecution table facing the jury. He had laid the audiotape from the Collins confession in front of him next to a recorder. He had the typed transcript of the statement given to police detectives by our client in front of him next to his legal pad. Carl Vollman was ready for Anthony Collins. Would Collins ever be prepared for what Carl Vollman would throw at him? The answer to this question was resounding: "No."

I asked the judge for a moment to allow me to consult with my co-counsel and our client. Judge Castle approved my request. For a few minutes, we sat at the defense table huddled together in a hushed conference that appeared to everyone else in the courtroom to be of the most serious nature. However, it was all prearranged. We had decided our course of action with our client the evening before, in the county jail.

Finally, after about two minutes, the judge asked me whether we were ready to proceed. I stood up, facing first the jury, then glancing at the prosecutor. I announced:

"Your Honor, after consulting with our client, Mr. Rolf and I wish to advise the court, counsel and the ladies and gentlemen of the jury that the defense rests."

I heard Carl Vollman gasp. His gasp was heard by the jurors as well. The look on his face was one of disbelief. He had been ready to spring on Anthony Leon Collins like a famished lion. He would have eaten Collins alive on that witness chair. He would have convicted Collins with Collins' own words — words given to a police detective and recorded for all time. Now that option was gone. The prosecution had gambled that Collins would take the stand on his own behalf. He had to. No one ever rested a murder trial without calling the defendant to tell his or her side of the story, at least not in Hamilton County. But it had happened in this case. And the prosecution was stunned. The prosecution was not alone. I glanced at the judge, and his face told me that he wasn't sure that he had actually heard me say, "The defense rests." So he asked me to repeat myself. Again I said, "The defense rests."

The closing argument of first the prosecution and then the defense was followed by the court's instruction of the applicable law. The jury received the exhibits and the verdict forms at 1:06 p.m. on Tuesday, June 22. At 7:52 p.m., the jury foreman notified the court that the members of the jury had reached a verdict. At 8:10 p.m. sharp, we stood on either side of our client as the clerk read the verdict agreed to by all 12 members of the jury.

"We, the jury, duly impaneled in Case Number 97331, State of Ohio versus Anthony Leon Collins, do find the defendant in this case on the charge of attempted robbery and first degree murder ... not guilty."

It could no longer be said in Hamilton County that no one had ever left the prosecutor's office and obtained a verdict of "not guilty" in their first murder trial as defense counsel. Not after *State of Ohio vs. Anthony Leon Collins*.

One week later, in another courtroom before a different judge and jury, a separate prosecution team obtained a murder conviction in the Esta Pomeroy Case against Stephen Le Bron Newell. Mercy was recommended, which saved Newell from the electric chair. Instead, he was sentenced to remain incarcerated for the remainder of his life.

Anthony Collins went home.

CHAPTER 7

LET MY CHILDREN GO

Normally, extradition matters between two states are pretty much open and shut. When someone is wanted for a crime in another state and that person is discovered to be in Ohio, the procedure is that the governor of the state that wants the person requests the governor of Ohio to extradite the fugitive.

The universal laws governing extradition require that Ohio's governor have the person sought, arrested and delivered to the executive authority of the other state if that person has been charged with a felony in the requesting state. These same laws prohibit the governor from inquiring into the guilt of the person whose extradition is sought. In other words, the extradition statutes require only that the paperwork be in order. Even an innocent person has to be returned to the state that has filed criminal charges against him.

This was the exact situation that faced John Slater when he telephoned me from the Hamilton County Jail on May 22, 1974. He sounded desperate. He related to me that he had been arrested at his job with Parker-Hannifin Corporation, where he was employed as a machinist, on three warrants issued by a Leon County, Florida, domestic court judge charging him with three counts of kidnapping. What made this particularly unusual was that John had been indicted in Leon County, Florida, on orders of that county's domestic relations court judge on charges of kidnapping his own sons: Jeffrey, age 11, John Jr., 9, and James, 8. What made these charges ludicrous was the fact that John had been granted legal custody of all of his children in his divorce from his ex-wife, Judith, in 1970 in Palm Beach County, Florida. So we were faced with an unusual legal development in which the Florida judge from Palm Beach County who had granted John Slater's divorce and had awarded custody of his five children to him was now being overruled by another Florida domestic relations court judge sitting in Leon County, Florida, at Tallahassee. The now-remarried mother of the children, Judith, was living with her new husband in Leon County, where she had found a judge who believed that she — and not John — should have custody of Jeffrey, John Jr., and James. Judith had never sought custody of Wendy, 4, because she had never cared for Wendy, having given birth to her in prison. And Jay, their 5-year-old, was now dead.

How could it be that a biological father who had been awarded legal custody of his children by the domestic relations court judge who had heard the divorce case now be the subject of kidnapping charges lodged against him by the order of a domestic relations court judge from another county? This was going to be the linchpin of the request for John Slater's extradition, and it was going to be my job to persuade an Ohio judge to keep John from being hauled back to Florida in chains.

I believed that my first chore was to obtain John's release from the Hamilton County Jail on a reasonable bond in order that he could take care of the four surviving children living with him in Oakley, and to save his job at Parker-Hannifin. I also needed John free from jail to help me prepare a defense to the attempt to return him to Florida to face these preposterous kidnapping indictments, for which he could be sentenced to jail in Florida for up to 75 years.

I was prepared to go to the Courthouse immediately to file a motion to set reasonable bail to gain John Slater's release from jail. But John pleaded with me to first call his new wife, Pauline, to have her pick the children up at 3:30 p.m. at Oakley school and take them to their apartment. He was extremely fearful that some Florida official or a social worker would take his children into custody and return them to their mother in Florida before he could be released from jail and have his day in court. He told me to call Pauline at her office with an insurance company, both so she could get the kids and so she could meet me at their apartment to give me the certified copy of his 1970 divorce decree as well as copies of the children's birth certificates and, in the case of 5-year-old Jay, a copy of the death certificate.

As soon as I got off the telephone with John Slater, I instructed my secretary to type a motion and an entry setting a bond for John. While this was being done, I called John's wife, Pauline, at her job and told her that John had been arrested on his job for kidnapping Jeffrey, John Jr., and James. She began to cry and said that this was so unfair and that all Judith wanted to do was to hurt John. She told me that Judith didn't really want the children, but that they were the perfect weapon to use to get at John. Once Pauline calmed down, I told her that John wanted her to meet me at their apartment to pick up the Florida court papers and to then pick up the boys and Wendy after school and not to let them out of her sight.

Armed with the motion and entry, I first went to 3502 Brotherton Road in Oakley, where John and Pauline resided with the four children. In the space of one year, Pauline had replaced Judith as the mother of the children, both physically and spiritually. I arrived just ahead of Pauline. She met me on the front porch, and we entered the four-family apartment building together. John and Pauline occupied apartment Number 4, which had three bedrooms. Pauline had done a splendid job of turning the apartment into a home during the year that she and John had been married. We entered the apartment through a well-decorated and neatly arranged living room. I followed her down the hall past the boys' bedroom and Wendy's bedroom. She was lucky being the only girl. She had a bedroom all to herself. At the end of the hall, next to the bathroom, we entered the largest bedroom, which was obviously John and Pauline's. Pauline went directly to the closet and opened the door. On a shelf, I could see a gray metal box. I offered to get it down for her, which she accepted. I carried the box into the kitchen and set it down on the table. Pauline opened the box and pulled out a manila file, which had printed on the tab: "Divorce papers."

I opened the file and found the certified copy of the divorce decree, entered November 20, 1970, in Palm Beach County, Florida. Item 4 on Page 2 granted sole and exclusive custody of all five children to the father with reasonable visitation allowed to the mother. Equally important was the fact that this decree did not prohibit John from returning to Ohio with his children to live. His only obligation was to make them available two months each summer to visit with their mother. In other words, John did not have to petition the Florida Domestic Relations Court in order to remove the children from Florida, and there was no requirement that John obtain permission from the court to bring them to Ohio to live. I also found the birth certificates for the children as well as the death certificate for Jay, dated May 10, 1973, from Merritt Island, Florida, in Brevard County.

I placed all of these documents in my briefcase and thanked Pauline for her help. She asked me to hurry to get John released and gave me a message for John: that she would take good care of the children and that he was not to worry, that no one was going to take them away from her.

I arrived at the Hamilton County Courthouse around 2:45 p.m. I went directly to the third floor to the criminal clerk's office, where Chief Clerk Eugene Montesi helped me. Gene and I had been friends since my days in the prosecutor's office. He accepted my motion to set bail for John and time-stamped it into the record. Gene told me that Judge Gilbert Bettman was the presiding criminal judge for May. He said he would telephone the judge for me and ask him to stay in his courtroom until I could make arrangements to have John brought downstairs from the jail and could discuss the case with the prosecutor's office. I was pleased to hear that Gil Bettman was the judge who would hear my motion. He was fair and considerate. He would listen to me and make the right decision. Montesi got off of the phone with Bettman's bailiff and advised me that the judge would grant me a hearing at 3:30 that afternoon.

I ran up the marble staircase to Room 420, the prosecutor's office. I already knew who would represent the prosecutor's office in an extradition proceeding: Leonard Kirschner. Since I had left the office in 1971, Leonard had taken over the prosecutor's office appellate division. In this capacity, he was also in charge of all extraordinary proceedings. I also knew that once Leonard learned what my game plan was, that he would want to handle the matter personally. Leonard was a tough advocate, and he loved mixing it up in a courtroom, especially with his former student.

Leonard was sitting at his desk, surrounded by piles and piles of files, briefs, letters, law books, an apple core and a partly eaten doughnut that was beginning to grow mold. Leonard never was much of an advocate for neat desks. The amazing thing was that despite what looked like the results of a bomb blast, Leonard knew exactly where every scrap of paper could be found, even in a hurry.

Even before I explained my mission, I knew what Leonard's answer would be — he would oppose my motion to have John released on bail. He had already talked to two detectives for the Leon County, Florida, sheriff's office, who were making arrangements to fly to Cincinnati to pick John Slater up for his return to Florida. Leonard wanted John held in jail until he was to be picked up by the Florida officials. He did not want to give John the opportunity to take off with his kids and disappear with them.

I handed Leonard a copy of the motion to set bail. More important, I showed him the birth certificates for the children and the certified copy of the Florida divorce decree dated November 20, 1970, that gave John exclusive custody of all five children. Leonard's reaction was typical. His position was that the issue of whether John Slater could be charged and found guilty of kidnapping his own sons was immaterial to the request for extradition to Florida. Leonard didn't have to, but he went on to remind me that the only issue at an extradition hearing for the court to determine was whether the request for extradition was proper. In other words, if the papers were in order, our judge had to honor the request and order John returned to Florida to stand trial.

Leonard said to me quite clearly that he would object to any attempt on my part to introduce evidence that John was the legal custodial parent of his boys. He was going to oppose me at every turn in the road. I knew that I was in for a good fight. I wanted to win.

I entered Judge Bettman's third-floor courtroom around 3:20 p.m. Leonard was close behind. John Slater had already been brought down from the jail and was seated at counsel table with a deputy sheriff sitting in watch next to him. I asked the deputy to take the handcuffs off of John, that he wasn't going to attempt to escape. The deputy, Dick Hanlin, who knew me from my prosecutor days, nodded and removed John's handcuffs.

While John rubbed his wrists, I told him that I had met his wife and had the divorce and custody papers in my file. I told him that Pauline had by now picked the children up at school and that he could rest assured that they are safe. I introduced him to Leonard Kirschner, who merely nodded in his direction. Leonard never did want to appear friendly toward a defendant in a criminal case. I told John that I wanted him to remain calm even when Leonard argued against his release on a bond. I explained to him that Judge Bettman was very fair and was a compassionate man. We couldn't have found a better judge to hear this matter.

Shortly after 3:30 p.m., the bailiff rapped a gavel on his desk and we all stood as Judge Gilbert M. Bettman strolled from his chamber toward his elaborate, dark-green marble bench. He was a tall, slender, gray-haired man in his early 50s wearing a black robe — the picture of a man that Hollywood would cast in the role of a judge. The judge looked at me and said, "Mr. Mestemaker, I understand that you are asking this court to set a bond to release your client who is wanted for felonies in Florida. Is that correct?"

"Yes, your honor," I replied, as I took my place at the podium reserved for lawyers who were arguing a matter before the court.

"May it please the court: The gentleman seated at counsel table is my client, John Slater. He has been arrested today at his place of employment on open warrants and indictments pending in Leon County, Florida, where he is wrongly accused of kidnapping his three sons. He cannot be guilty of these charges because he has legal custody of all four of his children pursuant to a divorce decree that was entered in Palm Beach County, Florida, in 1970."

At this juncture, Leonard was on his feet interrupting me and objecting to my statements, which he claimed were immaterial since the guilt or innocence of the accused was not a matter for the court in an extradition hearing.

I scowled at Leonard with a deliberate look that said, "Back off until

I'm finished."

"Your honor," I pleaded, "would Mr. Kirschner please be polite enough to allow me to finish my remarks before he makes his statement. I don't intend to interrupt him. I only ask the same in return." It worked. Judge Bettman instructed Leonard to sit down and wait his turn. I resumed my argument by telling Judge Bettman that John Slater had no criminal record either in Florida or in Ohio and that if granted a bond, he would give the court his word that he would not flee with the children as Mr. Kirschner feared. I assured Judge Bettman that I intended to fight the Florida extradition request and that the court had my word that I would see to it that John Slater would not take his children and run.

Leonard got up and attempted to persuade the Judge with the argument that our court's only duty was to honor the Florida governor's request for extradition, and that his office wanted John Slater jailed until the extradition hearing could be scheduled. He concluded his argument by getting on my case for assuring the judge that John would not run off with the children, saying I couldn't deliver on my guarantee.

Judge Bettman patiently listened to each side. He then asked to see the certified copy of the 1970 divorce decree. He studied the document closely, reading each page with great deliberation and care. When he reached the paragraphs in the decree that dealt with custody of the children, he paused. He looked up at me and asked why only Jeffrey, John Junior and James were the subject of kidnapping charges when the decree referred to five children. He wanted me to explain why Jay and Wendy were not also the subject of kidnapping charges. This was my ace in the hole to pull at Judge Bettman's sense of compassion. Leonard did not know the answer to this question, and that caused him for once to remain quiet.

"Your Honor," I said as I again walked to the podium, "Jay is dead, killed by an automobile in Florida. Wendy, the youngest, doesn't even know her mother. She has been with her father ever since the day that she was born to Judith, and Judith has never shown any interest in her or desire to have custody of her. The only children who are now sought by their mother, who apparently has a friend in the person of the Leon County domestic relations judge, are Jeffrey, John Jr. and James."

The judge turned to Leonard and asked how Florida could charge a man with kidnapping his own children after another court in the same state had granted him custody of those children. Leonard's reply, which again, I could have predicted, was that in December 1973 a domestic relations judge sitting in Tallahassee, Florida, had awarded temporary custody of the three boys to their mother and that John Slater had then left Florida with the boys, after which the judge in Tallahassee ordered the Leon County prosecuting attorney to indict John for kidnapping his own sons.

This was the move I had hoped Leonard would make because this opened the door for me to remind the judge that the only Florida judge who had the jurisdiction to make any changes in the original order of custody was the judge in Palm Beach County who had heard and granted John a divorce and exclusive custody of his children in 1970. I added that Judith had attempted to defeat the law by finding a judge in another Florida County arrogant enough to ignore Florida jurisdictional rules and give her temporary custody of the boys, which, in effect, overruled the judge in Palm Beach County — despite his having exclusive jurisdiction over the case.

I could tell by the expression on Judge Bettman's face that he disapproved of the Florida proceedings that caused John to be sitting before him as a wanted fugitive. He sat back and stared at the ceiling for a moment, deep in thought. He then leaned forward and looked at John Slater. He inquired of John as to whether, if he were to release him, he was prepared to give Judge Bettman his solemn word that he would not flee with the children before an extradition hearing could be held. I nudged John to stand up to reply to the judge's question. "Yes, sir. You have my word as a Christian and as a man that I will not run away."

Leonard started to stand to be heard, but Judge Bettman waved him off. "I've heard enough, Mr. Kirschner. Some bond is in order. I will set a bond of $2,000 at 10 percent." We had won Round 1. John would be free as soon as Pauline could get to the Courthouse with $200 to have him released. While John was being taken back to the jail, I telephoned Pauline from the courtroom and told her to get $200 together and come to the clerk's office to get John out of jail.

Leonard and I walked over to the clerk's office to agree on a date for the extradition hearing. Judge William Morrissey was scheduled to be the presiding criminal judge for June. Therefore, he would preside over the extradition hearing. After a telephone conference with Dennis Putoff, the judge's bailiff, it was agreed that the extradition matter would be heard on Tuesday, June 4, 1974, at 10:00 a.m. Leonard asked me what I intended to file to question the validity of the extradition request. I gave that question a few seconds thought, and answered, "Well, Leonard. I think that an application for a writ of *habeas corpus* is the best way for me to go. I do believe that John's detention, whether in jail or under a bond, is illegal in this case because the extradition request is illegal."

Leonard chuckled. "I suspected as much. You and I are in for another good fight, aren't we?"

I smiled at Leonard and said, "What else can be expected when you and I are on opposite sides of any legal matter?"

Shortly after 4:00 p.m., Pauline walked into the criminal clerk's office. "Do you have the $200?" I asked. She nodded her head and reached into her purse. I handed Gene Montesi 10 $20 bills, for which he wrote a receipt with John's name and case number. He then telephoned the jail and instructed the other end to bring John Slater to the clerk's office, that bond had been posted for him by his wife. Within 10 minutes, John was brought down from the sixth floor to the clerk's office, where he and Pauline fell into each other's arms, both of them wiping tears from their cheeks. "Where are the children?" John said in a very concerned tone.

"They are safe," his wife replied. "They are with Mrs. Dolan." Mrs. Dolan was the neighbor in Apartment 2 on the first floor at 3502 Brotherton Road.

"Let's get out of here," I said. We left using the night elevator, which took us down to the Courthouse basement exit, from which we could walk up to Court Street near Sycamore. I walked to Pauline's car with them and told John that we had a shot at stopping the extradition on June 4 in front of Judge Morrissey — if I could get into evidence the history of this case and, in particular, just what kind of a person his ex-wife, Judith, was. I told John and Pauline that we might just force the state of Florida to drop the kidnapping charges if Judge Morrissey became convinced that the extradition request was wrong. I told them to be careful between this day and our next court date and to make sure that they knew at all times where the children were and who they were with. As I left, I told them that I would file an application for a writ of *habeas corpus*, which would require Judge Morrissey to decide the legality of the request for extradition. Three days later, I filed the application for this extraordinary remedy with full knowledge that it was John's only chance to avoid a kidnapping trial in Florida. It was a long shot.

On Tuesday, June 4, 1974, I arrived at Judge William Morrissey's courtroom on the third floor of the Hamilton County Courthouse around 9:40 a.m. John and Pauline were waiting for me. I handed them a copy of the application for the writ of *habeas corpus*, which was accompanied by a memorandum that set forth the history of John's marriage to Judith and how it was that the court had awarded him, the father, custody of five children, one of whom, Wendy, was an infant at the time. I told John to read it over there in the hall to refresh his memory on any necessary points. I told them that I had to convince Judge Morrissey that the judge in Leon County, Florida, had acted illegally and that the ends of justice dictated that John not be sent back to Florida in chains.

As we entered the courtroom, I prayed silently that Judge Morrissey had read my memorandum attached to the application for the writ of *habeas corpus* and the copy of the 1970 divorce decree, as well as the children's birth certificates and Jay's death certificate. I also hoped that he had read Leonard's reply memorandum stating his office's objection to my application — because Leonard had crafted a hard-nosed reply devoid of sympathy for John or his children. If Judge Morrissey, a kind man and himself a father, had read these pleadings, I believed that his sympathy would be with John Slater and his children.

When we entered the courtroom, Leonard Kirschner was already there, discussing the proceeding with three men whom he introduced to me. The first man was Frank Amatea, an assistant attorney general for the state of Florida, who had been sent here especially to assist in the extradition of John Slater. The other two men looked stern and were not very friendly. They were detectives for the Leon County, Florida, sheriff, and were here to see to it that John was going back to Florida. They looked to me like a pair of bounty hunters in business suits.

The minute that Bailiff Dennis Putoff opened court and Judge William Morrissey took the bench, I felt the burden of John's case settle heavily on my shoulders. I had never had the opportunity before this date to fight an extradition proceeding. I knew that attempts to block an extradition request were rare. I also knew that successful challenges to an extradition request by the governor of another state were even more rare, if unheard of. I was sailing in uncharted waters and had wet feet.

Judge Morrissey looked in my direction as he called out the case of *"State of Florida vs. John H. Slater*, demand for extradition to Leon County, Florida, to stand trial on a three-count indictment charging him with the felony of kidnapping, Hamilton County Common Pleas Court Case Number M, for miscellaneous, 74-29. Mr. Kirschner for the governor of Ohio and Mr. Mestemaker for John H. Slater. Are you gentleman ready to proceed?"

"Yes, your honor," I replied as I stood up. "I have filed an application for a writ of *habeas corpus*, and just this morning I filed an additional motion to quash the Florida request for extradition. I have delivered a copy of the latest motion to the court's bailiff and now hand a copy to Mr.

Kirschner. I apologize for filing this additional motion so close to this hearing, but it occurred to me at home last night while I was preparing for this morning's hearing that a writ of *habeas corpus* alone may not legally and procedurally be sufficient to accomplish what we hope, which is a ruling denying the state of Florida's request that Ohio order my client returned to Leon County to stand trial for the crime of kidnapping his own sons. I realize that this may be a surprise to the court and Mr. Kirschner. However, no new law is cited by me, and the issue remains the same. Therefore, I do not believe that this development prejudices Mr. Kirschner and his client, the state. But if it does, I have no objection if he desires a continuance of this scheduled hearing to a later date."

Leonard was hot. He knew that if he asked for a continuance, he risked angering the judge — and what about the three guys who were here from Florida? They would also have to go back to Florida, only to return to Cincinnati later in the month. So, as much as he wanted to request a continuance, Leonard stood up and advised the court that despite defense counsel's last-minute maneuvering, he and Frank Amatea were ready to proceed. Judge Morrissey replied that he was pleased that this matter could go forward as scheduled.

Kirschner asked permission for Frank Amatea to sit at counsel table with him as the representative of the governor of Florida. I told Judge Morrissey that I had no objection to Mr. Kirschner being assisted by Mr. Amatea. With that response, Amatea stepped forward and took a seat at the table next to Kirschner.

"Mr. Mestemaker," inquired Judge Morrissey, "Are you ready to proceed? Do you wish to call a witness? Or do you want to make an opening statement in support of your motions?"

I knew that the only witness I had was John Slater. If I called him, about the only testimony I would be able to introduce without strenuous objection by Leonard was his name, his address, and that he had removed his sons from Leon County, Florida, last December. Then, Leonard would block everything else. Following this, Leonard would be able to cross-examine John. Leonard would eat him alive. By the time Leonard was finished with John, he would be halfway across the bridge to Northern Kentucky on his way to Florida. I really didn't want to have to put John on the witness stand. Since this was a quasi-criminal proceeding, John had the right to invoke his Fifth Amendment privilege against being compelled to testify. So the only way Leonard could interrogate John would be if I called him to testify. This made up my mind for me. "Your Honor, I wish to make an opening statement to tell the court why we believe that this court should refuse to send John Slater back to Florida, and what we expect our evidence will show to prove to you that this extradition request is illegal, invalid and does not serve the interests of justice.

With that statement, Judge Morrissey invited me to proceed. I stood up again and walked to the podium, which I positioned so that I was directly between the court and Leonard Kirschner. This way, Leonard could not see Judge Morrissey without moving, and what to me was more important, Judge Morrissey would not be able to see the expressions and frowns that I knew from prior experience would be forthcoming from Leonard. It really does help when one knows one's adversary as well as I knew Leonard Kirschner.

"Your Honor, gentlemen, may it please the court: We admit that my client is John H. Slater. We further admit the he is the natural father of Jeffrey, John Jr. and James Slater, the three children named in the Leon County, Florida, indictment as the victims of the crime of kidnapping alleged to have been committed by my client on or about December 17, 1973. Beyond that, we deny every allegation made by the state of Florida. We deny these charges because no man can kidnap children that are legally in his custody. In order to show this, I believe that the court will be required to hear and understand the history of John's marriage to his first wife, Judith, who is now remarried and whose name is now Judith Holland."

Leonard started to squirm in his seat. He didn't really want Judge Morrissey to hear about Judith. He stood up and interrupted me by lodging an objection to my opening statement. I countered with this plea, "But, your Honor, I am only stating in answer to the court's inquiry what you need to hear to make a sound ruling in this matter."

Judge Morrissey smiled and stared at Leonard. "Overruled, Mr. Kirschner. This is opening statement. Proceed, Mr. Mestemaker."

Leonard sat down. I could hear his mumbled complaint to Frank Amatea. I resumed my opening statement.

"John Slater's evidence will show and prove that John Slater married Judith, the mother of all five of his children, in 1962. Jeffrey, now 11, was born in 1963. John Jr., now 10, was born in 1964. James, now 8, was born in 1966. Jay, who is dead, was born in 1968. He would be 6 years old now. And Wendy was born in 1969. She is 5. She has lived with her father ever since the day she came home from the hospital."

I continued: "During the 1960s, Judith Slater became very heavily involved in drugs. First, she smoked marijuana. Then, she later became involved in the sale of marijuana. No matter what John did or said, drugs became her whole life. Finally, John could not carry on with this marriage and the exposure of their children to a drug-dependent mother. While Judith was pregnant with Wendy, she was arrested for possession of marijuana. Her father received custody of Wendy upon her birth. Judith has never shown any interest in Wendy. She, in fact, did not request any custodial rights to her five children when she and John were divorced in 1970. As a result, on November 20, 1970, when John was granted his divorce from Judith in Palm Beach County, Florida, the domestic relations court judge awarded sole custody of all five children to their father. As soon as the divorce was final, John moved back to Cincinnati with his children. As you will note, your Honor, in the divorce decree before you, the one I attached to my memorandum; there is no language that prohibited John from removing his children from Florida to another state. Therefore, bringing the children to Ohio to live was legal. At that time, Judith was still in jail on drug charges."

Again Leonard objected. But Judge Morrissey overruled him and invited me to proceed. I glanced at my notes and continued. "Neither John nor the children heard from Judith until 1971, when she called them in Cincinnati from Florida. She told John that she wanted the boys, but not Wendy, to visit her in Florida for July and August. John agreed. She told him that she was alone in West Palm Beach. As it turned out, this was a lie. She was actually living on Merritt Island, Florida, and she was not alone. She was living with James W. Holland, whom she would later marry.

"John placed Jeffrey, John Jr., James and Jay on a plane for West Palm Beach on June 30, 1971. It was the last time that he would see the older three boys until May 15, 1973. It was the last time he would ever see Jay alive. When September drew near, John had begun to be concerned because the boys had only called him once, and that was in late July. He had not received any postcards from them. He attempted to reach Judith at the address she had given him, where she said that she lived in West Palm Beach. Within three days, John learned that she had given him a false address. Several more telephone calls by John about Judith's whereabouts only brought word to him that she no longer lived in Palm Beach County, and that she was no longer living under the name "Slater." John hired a private detective, who charged him $50 per hour plus expenses. After three weeks, John knew no more than he was able to find out for himself. He discontinued the P.I.'s services. He placed ads in several Florida newspapers and even sent photographs of the boys to television stations in Florida with a request that they assist him. Not one television station would display the photographs or cover the story of John Slater's missing sons."

Once again, Leonard was on his feet. When it became obvious to him that Judge Morrissey was not going to stop my opening statement, he only asked that the court note his continuing objection to my opening statement as irrelevant to the extradition matter, and he sat down — resigned in the knowledge that I was on a roll and that the judge was not going to stop me.

"Your Honor," I continued, "John Slater had absolutely no idea where his four sons were or even if they were alive until May 12, 1973, when an old friend of his, who lived in Florida and whom he had not heard from for over four years, telephoned him at his home in Oakley and told him that he did not want to become involved, but that he felt an obligation to John to inform him that 5-year-old Jay had been hit and killed by a motorist on May 10 as he ran across a bridge on Merritt Island, Florida, to show his older brother John a fish that he had just caught. Jay, he learned, had died lying on a bridge as his brother pleaded with him to stay awake until the ambulance came, his skull fractured and his fishing pole with the small sea bass hooked and still flopping next to him. The caller gave John the address where the boys were living with James W. Holland. Where was Judith? John asked the caller. Well, first of all, her name is now Holland, and she is in jail in Brevard County charged with selling 50 pounds of marijuana to an undercover federal agent. The boys were supposed to be in the care of her husband, James W. Holland. But he didn't care about the boys. So they were left to their own devices, and this neglect cost Jay his life.

"Your Honor, John got a flight that night to Merritt Island. When he arrived, he went directly to the address his caller had given him on the telephone. When he rang the doorbell, 11-year-old Jeffrey opened the door, took one look and screamed, 'Daddy! Dad's here — Dad's here!' This brought John and James running to join a tearful reunion between a man and his sons.

"The boys were alone at this apartment. James Holland was gone, probably in a bar somewhere. Their mother, Judith, was still in jail. Their father had the boys pack up their belongings. He left a note for James Holland telling him that he, John Slater, their father, had come to take them home. John and the boys stayed for two more days before they returned to Cincinnati, and that was in order to attend Jay's funeral, held

May 14. Judith was brought to the funeral in handcuffs by a team of female correction officers. It was difficult for John to look at her without pummeling her. He did say that he would always hold her responsible for Jay's death, and that he was taking the boys home. Judith's reply to John was to curse him and promise him that she would get her boys back.

"Judith kept her word. After deciding to cooperate with the prosecutor of Brevard County, which involved naming the source of her supply, she was released from jail. On November 10, 1973, she intercepted Jeffrey, John Jr. and James as they walked on Madison Road in Oakley on their way home from school. Judith had flown to Cincinnati on November 8 and had managed to convince a school office employee at the boys' school to tell her what time classes let out for the day. On November 9, she positioned herself in a taxicab to learn the route the boys used to walk home. On November 10, she employed a cab again. This time, it was not a dry run. This time, Judith had four tickets to Tallahassee, Florida — one adult and three children. As the boys walked on Madison Road, school bags on their shoulders, the cab pulled up alongside of them. Their mother got out and within two minutes had them convinced to go with her to see Disney World.

"By 9:00 p.m., November 10, the boys were in Tallahassee, Florida, where they were met at the airport by James Holland. By 9:15 a.m., November 11, John Slater had reported his sons as missing to both the Cincinnati police and the Cincinnati FBI office.

"Judith and the boys were being traced when her new lawyer, a friend of Domestic Relations Judge James Joanos, convinced the judge in a very one-sided hearing held in Leon County, Florida, on December 4 to grant her temporary custody of the boys. Judge Joanos did not seem to care that the divorce had been granted in Palm Beach County or that a Palm Beach County judge had made a permanent award of custody to John Slater. He did not seem to be concerned that the father of the three boys was not only not present to argue his right to custody, but that he was not even aware of this hearing in which one Florida domestic court judge so easily countermanded a custody order of another Florida domestic relations court judge from another county. In addition, to granting Judith temporary custody pending an investigation, Judge Joanos ordered that the boys not be removed from Leon County by any person without his prior consent.

"This order was not only invalid, your Honor, it was in direct contravention to the rules and laws of Florida. On December 17, 1973, having learned that Jeffrey, John Jr. and James were in Tallahassee, their father flew to Florida and did what Judith had done in November. He picked the boys up and brought them home to Cincinnati. This act led the judge in Leon County to order John Slater indicted for kidnapping his own sons — for which the state of Florida now desires that this man, who only did what any caring father would do, be returned to stand trial for a crime for which he could be sentenced to jail for 75 years, if convicted.

"One final thing, your Honor. Jay was killed by an automobile while Judith had control of these boys. Should John have waited until one of the three survivors was dead before he went to get them and bring them back to Cincinnati?

"Thank you, your Honor. This is what I expect our evidence will show that will enable the court to quash the request for my client's return to Florida to stand trial for kidnapping his own children. I am ready to call my first witness. However, Mr. Kirschner may wish to make an opening statement on behalf of the prosecution."

Now Leonard was in high gear with a full head of steam. He stood up and told Judge Morrissey that if he allowed John Slater to take the witness stand and testify to the matters that I had related in my opening remarks, he would immediately petition our court of appeals for a writ of prohibition to stop the trial court from hearing what Kirschner labeled as irrelevant testimony to the matter of the extradition request.

To this threat, Judge Morrissey replied: "If the testimony were to be as stated by Mr. Mestemaker in his opening statement, I would probably deny the extradition."

Leonard Kirschner again reiterated his position. If the court was going to let John Slater testify to all of the facts that I had made in my opening statement, he, Kirschner, was going to file for a writ of prohibition. Whereupon Judge Morrissey, appearing less than eager to have to respond to a writ of prohibition, called for a recess and instructed Mr. Kirschner, Mr. Amatea and myself to come into chambers for an off -the-record conference.

We entered chambers and the door closed behind us. There was a good deal of posturing and back and forth jabs. But, I stuck to my guns. I told the judge and Kirschner that I believed that our court of appeals would refuse to grant Leonard's request for a writ of prohibition. If that occurred, the extradition request would probably fail. However, in order to avoid this costly maneuvering, I had a proposal to make.

I would recommend to my client that, if the state of Florida agreed in advance and on the record to drop the kidnapping charges, he should return voluntarily to Florida with Jeffrey, John Jr. and James as soon as their school year was over, and that a Leon County, Florida, judge — preferably not Judge Joanos — would review the whole history of the case, including the neglect that caused the death of Jay, and decide whether John was a more fit parent than Judith, or whether custody was to be surrendered to their mother, a known drug addict. I also insisted as part of this arrangement that the boys be placed in a neutral setting in Leon County, Florida, pending a final custody decision, and finally, that the judge in Florida agree to hear from the boys and to take into consideration which parent they wanted to live with.

While Leonard and Frank Amatea went to Leonard's office to call the Florida attorney general for permission to agree to my stipulations, I went back in to the courtroom and laid the plan out to John and Pauline. Initially, John was opposed to returning to Leon County with the boys. But, after I advised him that if we lost here, he would be returned to Florida in chains to stand trial for kidnapping, and on the urging of Pauline, he agreed to follow my game plan.

Within 10 minutes, Leonard and Amatea re-entered the courtroom. Leonard nodded to me that we had a deal. We, in turn, sent word to Judge Morrissey that an agreement had been reached that we wanted placed on the record.

Within minutes, Judge Morrissey returned to the bench, obviously pleased that we had reached an agreement that avoided a writ of prohibition hearing in the court of appeals. We jointly stated the agreement into the record.

- The kidnapping indictments and the request for John Slater's extradition to Florida would be dropped immediately.
- John Slater would return voluntarily with Jeffrey, John Jr. and James on June 21, 1974, to Tallahassee, Florida, for a final custody hearing.
- Wendy Slater would remain in Cincinnati since she was not the subject of any kidnapping charge or custody fights, and the issue of her custody would not be raised by her biological mother.
- John Slater would be free from arrest for any matter involving his divorce or his children while he was in Florida, and the contempt of court charge would also be dropped.
- While in Leon County, Jeffrey, John Jr. and James would be housed in a neutral setting with adults who had no interest in the outcome of the custody fight.

- And, finally, the Florida judge hearing the custody matter would agree to hear from the boys and take their desires into consideration.

Judge Morrissey asked John Slater to come forward. When John was standing next to me at the bench, Judge Morrissey asked him whether he was willing to abide by the terms of the agreement that I had just outlined. John answered that he was satisfied with this agreement.

The judge then inquired of Frank Amatea if he had authority from the state of Florida to keep this agreement. Frank Amatea gave his word that he did, and that all criminal charges pending against John Slater in Florida relative to his sons would be dismissed effective this date.

John spoke up at this point, addressing Judge Morrissey. "I can't let them go back to my former wife."

Judge Morrissey's reply was one that I will always remember: "I can't tell you what the outcome of the hearing in Florida will be, but you and I both will be praying that you and your children will be coming back across the Ohio River on or about July 4."

On June 22, 1974, John and the three boys arrived in Tallahassee, Florida. Through arrangements I had made with Ken Davis, John's attorney in Tallahassee, the boys were placed in Leon County's emergency shelter. Davis also convinced me to agree to permit Judge James Joanos to remain on the case to decide final custody. Davis believed that Judge Joanos realized his mistake from December, and that he would do everything necessary to conduct a full and fair custody hearing.

Judge Joanos heard the final hearing on custody on July 15, 1974. The hearing lasted for nine hours and included testimony from John and Judith, case workers, domestic relations court investigators, children advocates and, finally, the judge heard from the boys themselves. In a final act of irony, Judge Joanos did not rule immediately. Instead, he took the whole matter under advisement, and stated that he would rule within 10 days. This decision terrified John. He could not remain in Florida for 10 more days. He had already used up his entire 1974 vacation. He was forced to return to Cincinnati alone, leaving the boys behind in Florida. This caused him great worry and apprehension. John later told me that this was the longest 10 days that he ever lived.

On Friday, July 26, I received a call from Ken Davis. He read the final order entered that same date by Judge Joanos. "Custody of all three boys to ... their father."

I called John. He didn't need a telephone to talk to me. He could have opened up his living room window on Brotherton Road and I would have easily heard his joy in my office nine miles away in the Kroger Building on Central Parkway in downtown Cincinnati. The boys would be home Saturday at noon.

John had spent almost $10,000 in legal fees, court costs and travel expenses, but he had won. His boys had been let go by the state of Florida.

Mestemaker's client and his sons celebrate a Florida court's award of custody to the father and the return of the children to Cincinnati. Cincinnati Post *photo.*

Leonard Kirchner served in the Hamilton County prosecutor's office for more than three decades. Rob Paris photo, 1976.

CHAPTER 8

I DIDN'T KILL MY SON

1976 was a good year to enter the world. Our country was celebrating its 200th birthday. Any child born that bicentennial year could always answer a quiz as to the number of years of Yankee independence by adding 200 to his own age. But one baby born in 1976 would never have the opportunity to do this math. His name was Robert Edward McGraw Jr. He was born on July 1, 1976. On August 30, 1976, he was murdered. He was 60 days old, 22 inches tall and weighed in at 10 pounds. The fact that he was born during our bicentennial year would never mean anything to him.

When I returned to the office after a long trial and a short lunch of soup and half a tuna-fish sandwich on Tuesday, August 31, I flipped through the opened mail neatly stacked on my desk blotter by my secretary, Karen, and picked up a half-dozen, rose-colored telephone message slips, which were arranged by date and time. Two were from late Monday. The third one was received at 9:05 a.m. that day. It was marked "Urgent." The caller was identified in our receptionist's very neat, feminine handwriting as "Frank O'Neal," a friend and a business agent for Hod Carriers Union Local 90, one of the building trade affiliates and one our firm's clients. When Frank called and said it was 'Urgent,' it was 'Urgent.'

I dialed the number. The telephone on the other end rang three times. I heard the pleasant voice of Lee Baur, Frank's secretary, answer, "Hod Carrier's Local 90. May I help you?"

When I told Lee who was calling, she said, "Oh, good. He has been asking me if you have called since shortly after 9:00 a.m. He is really eager to talk to you."

The next voice was deep and Bostonian — North Side Irish. Frank had grown up in Boston, where his father was an officer in the Cement Mason's Union. Frank was a born union representative who referred to all of his members as his "boys" — even the men who were older than he. Even though we had now known each other for eight years, he still called me "Counselor," and today was no exception.

"Counselor, I need your help. One of my boys has been arrested for murdering his own kid. His name is Bob McGraw. He is only 26 and a good boy. I don't believe that he did it. He needs a good lawyer, and you're the guy to straighten this out for him."

"How old is the child, Frank?"

There was a pause as Frank hollered to Lee: "He wants to know how old the dead child is."

I didn't need to have him repeat what Lee told him. I heard her say "2 months" as plain as if she were on the extension.

I choked. "Frank, I don't know about this. Goddamn! I can't stomach anyone who would hurt his own child much less kill a baby. Can't you get someone else to represent him? I can't stand a child killer. Hell, I'd just as leave pull the switch on one of them myself."

"Look Counselor, this boy is only 26, and he has had a rough time of it. He doesn't smoke, cuss, gamble or cheat on the rotten little broad that he lives with common law, although God knows he probably should considering everything I have heard about her."

"Frank, has he ever been in trouble before?"

The answer was quick. "Yeah, once — as a juvenile, for breaking into somebody's pickup truck and stealing a couple of hundred dollars worth of tools. But clean as a pin since then. Oh, one other thing. His daddy was a Marine. He was a grunt in a rifle platoon in Korea. He was killed in 1951 near the Iron Triangle in North Korea. Second Marine Division, I believe. The boy never knew his dad. He was about 18 months old when his old man caught a piece of Chinese Communist lead."

O'Neal knew from past experience with me that telling me that Bob McGraw had lost his father in the Marines in Korea would soften me up like very little else could.

"All right," I said. "Where is he being held and who will pay our fee?"

"He's in the county jail on a $50,000 bond, and you know that you don't have to be concerned about the money. After all, he is one of my boys."

"I'm going to want about $5,000 for starters, and it may cost more depending on how complex the case is."

"Counselor, you take care of him, and I'll take care of you. You're one of my boys too, and don't forget that."

I hadn't planned to go back to the Courthouse again that afternoon. But here I was at 2:30 p.m., ringing the bell to the lawyers' entrance to the County Jail while being watched by a turnkey on the TV monitor from the camera staring me in the face.

On arrival in the lawyers' room visiting area, I answered the same old question in the same way, "No, I am not carrying a weapon." Then I opened my briefcase for inspection by a corrections officer, who had looked inside of it so often that he knew what I carried in the case as well as I did.

I sat down at a table in the small cubicle reserved for lawyers and prisoners to prepare cases. This cubicle had a sloped ceiling because it was beneath a stairwell. The walls were greenish-gray, as was the floor. There was a beat-up, old wooden table and two dilapidated wooden chairs that creaked when you sat down.

I stood up to greet the purpose of this visit. He entered the room looking like he had just been trapped somewhere. He was about 5-feet, 10-inches tall, very thin, 135 pounds or so. He had blond hair and blue eyes and a very poor excuse for a mustache on his upper lip. In fact, when I first noticed it, I thought that he had snot on his lip. I was about to offer him a Kleenex until I realized that it was hair. When he sat down, I noticed that he had a rosary clutched in his right hand and a pack of filter-tipped Marlboro cigarettes in his left.

"Are you Catholic?" I asked.

"No, but the jail chaplain is Father Bruno. He gave me these prayer beads and said they may help if I used them to talk to God about my problem."

I handed the young man my business card. As so often happened, I was required to pronounce my 10-letter Teutonic last name for him. I always wondered what it would be like to have a last name like Mason, as in Perry. How much simpler life might be.

"Mr. McGraw, I am here at the request of Frank O'Neal, your business agent. On the way up here to see you, I stopped by the clerk's office and obtained a copy of the complaint filed against you by the police. Do you understand that you are about to be indicted for murdering your own child? How old was he?"

McGraw lit a cigarette and looked down at the rosary that he had worked around his fingers. "He is 2 months old."

I looked up from the legal pad that I had started to jot notes on and saw that McGraw had tears welling up over his lower eyelids.

"I want you to know, buddy, that I can't stand the thought of defending someone who would kill their own child. I don't get too upset over what adults do to each other, although that is bad enough. But when someone hurts a child or an elderly person, someone who really can't fight back, I believe that whatever punishment they get short of an execution is too lenient. Now, if, in fact, you killed your baby boy, I want to hear it from you and I want to hear it now."

"Mr. Messmaker, I didn't kill my son."

"Then who did? Do you know who the police believe killed your son?"

"I don't understand what you're asking me, Mr. Messmaker."

"Listen to me: The name is not MESS-maker. It is Mes-TE-maker. Who is in jail for this?"

"I am, I guess."

"Who has been formally charged and is about to be indicted by a grand jury for your son's death?"

"I am, I guess."

"Quit guessing about it. You are the prime suspect. You are the guy who is going to stand trial for murder. And if you are convicted, you can kiss the next 20 years of your life goodbye. If you didn't kill the child, tell me who you believe did."

He turned his head toward the greenish-gray wall and said, "Either Terry or Paula."

"Which one is your wife?"

"Paula is my wife."

"Who is Terry?"

"Our 5-year-old daughter."

"Mr. McGraw, 5-year-old girls don't normally kill their baby brothers. So what about your wife makes you suspect her?"

"Mr. Mes ... temaker. Did I get it right?"

"Yes, go ahead."

"Mr. Mestemaker, Paula was alone with Bobbie all day on the 30th, and she told me that she didn't want him. She even said that she hoped someone would adopt him. She even called him a bastard. But I don't want to get her in trouble. I need her. Terry needs her. So maybe it would be better if I get blamed for it. At least then Terry gets to keep her mom."

"Mr. McGraw, if, in fact, your wife is the person who killed your little boy, do you really believe that you are doing the right thing for your daughter, Terry? Let's suppose that you take the blame for this crime and you go to prison. That leaves Paula scot-free, and she has Terry. What happens if she decides she doesn't want Terry anymore? What happens if she meets some guy and goes wild for him, but he doesn't want her little girl around? Does Terry suddenly die? Think about it. In the meantime, I need you to tell me whom I should interview on your behalf. Let's start with your family."

McGraw gave me a list of names and telephone numbers, starting with his mother, Dolores Johnson, his sister, Sharon Fuller, the welfare case worker, Donna Carson, whom they had contact with in July and part of August when he was not able to find work through the union hall, and, of course, Paula.

"By the way, is Paula your common-law wife."

"Yes," he said with a nod.

"How come you and Paula never married, especially once you had a daughter?"

"I wanted to Mr. Mes ... temaker, but Paula wanted to be able to collect welfare if she was broke and she said it made it easier if she didn't have to tell the welfare people that she had a husband.

"Wonderful!" I said. "Why is it that someone who can't pass a fifth-grade geography quiz knows how to work the welfare system like a pinball machine?

"I am going to go see Judge Gusweiler and see if I can't convince him to lower the bond on you. If I could get a bond of $10,000 at 10 percent, which would be $1,000 in cash, could your mom get you out of jail pending the trial?"

McGraw thought for a few seconds and shook his head. "She may be able to if my Uncle Charlie will help out. He is her brother and has a good job at the Ford plant."

After a little over an hour, my first interview with my new client was over. I felt a little sorry for him, though I still wasn't quite sure that I believed in his innocence. But who knows, I had been mistaken before. Perhaps he didn't kill his son.

What I didn't know was that Paula already had a boyfriend — Chuck Andrews — and that boyfriend didn't care too much about having a girlfriend with small children.

I had decided to represent Robert Edward McGraw, a decision that was not real popular with my wife or the secretaries at the firm. He was considered by all of them, without exception, to be guilty. I decided right then that if this case was to be tried before a jury, I'd better try to pack the jury with men — or Robert Edward McGraw was as good as convicted, if my wife and the firm's secretaries were a barometer.

The first order of business was to try to get Robert's bail lowered to an amount that his mother and her brother, if he would help, could handle. To do this, I had to convince Judge Frank Gusweiler that Robert wouldn't run or hurt anyone if he were allowed out of jail pending the trial.

Frank M. Gusweiler was, by 1976, the dean of common pleas court judges. He was a man of immense presence and even more immense legal ability. He was nearing 70 years and about 6-feet, 2-inches tall, well-built with gray hair, a mustache and a voice that he could sound like thunder whenever he chose to make himself heard above two or three lawyers all talking at the same time.

Gusweiler had been a prosecutor before becoming a judge. As prosecutor, he had presented the people's case in the murder trial of Anna Marie Hahn. She was the first woman to go to Ohio's electric chair. Gusweiler was that good. He was also that well-respected.

While I prepared for a hearing on the motion to reduce the $50,000 bail to as little as I could get the judge to go, I began conducting my own investigation. I went to see Ron Vanetti, who had been assigned to prosecute my client. He, as usual, thought that his case was strong. He told me some details that my client had overlooked during our interview — such as McGraw's admission to Detective Joe Roberts that he had slapped little Bobbie in the face and that the autopsy report indicated facial bruises compatible with a face slap. Vanetti gave me a copy of the autopsy report and a list of his witnesses, which included Donna Carson from the welfare department, two police detectives, the first police officer on the scene and John Lewis, the life squad emergency medical technician who had tried to revive the baby.

Vanetti handed me a Christ Hospital Emergency Room report, which was dated August 23 — seven days before Bobbie's death. "I don't like to spring surprises on defense attorneys whom I like," he said. "You had better look at this ER report. Paula Hill took little Bobbie to the emergency room on the 23rd because he had a cigarette burn on the back of his head, an abrasion on his forehead between his eyes and a swollen left leg. The doctor also noticed dry blood in his nostrils. The mother told the doctor that the baby got these injuries when his sister, who is only 5 years old, pulled him and his blanket off the couch. I have to tell you that the only other person home when this supposedly happened was your client, Mr. McGraw."

I looked the ER report over while Vanetti continued to talk.

"The ER doctor, a Dr. Edward Salinas, and I talked to him two days ago. He didn't believe for a second that the baby received these kinds of injuries by falling off a couch, even if the floor was hard. When he pressed Paula Hill about who else was in the room besides the 5-year-old, she told him that your client was there alone watching TV with the daughter, and the baby was asleep on the couch next to guess who — your client."

Vanetti continued: "When I spoke to Paula Hill about these injuries, she told me that she and your client had been arguing earlier that day over money, and that she had told Dr. Salinas that the little girl pulled Bobbie off the couch to protect your client. She also told me that she and your client had a bad argument the day the baby died. Dr. Salinas reported the incident of the 23rd to the police. Unfortunately, no action was taken, and on the 30th, Bobbie was murdered."

This was just great, I thought. First of all, my client holds back on me. And now I learn that the prosecutor has just about all the evidence he needs to hang young Mr. Robert Edward McGraw. At least Vanetti confirmed one item of information. My client's prior criminal record as an adult was a goose egg, no convictions — and only one as a juvenile, a motor vehicle break-in. At least McGraw had been truthful about his prior record.

My first inclination was to quit this case and try my skills at real estate title searches. My second inclination was to go back to the county jail and wring Robert's skinny neck for misleading me. My third and final urge was to interview McGraw's mother and sister before I confronted him again. One telephone call to Dolores Johnson set up a meeting with her and her daughter, Sharon Fuller, at our office. I also wanted to interview them before attempting to talk to Paula Hill.

In the meantime, I decided to visit several other potential witnesses, the first of whom was Donna Carson, who agreed to see me at her office the following afternoon.

Ms. Carson was a pleasant blond lady of about 45 years of age with a desk full of pictures of her three nearly adult children and a handsome, dark-haired husband whom I immediately recognized as Officer Bob Carson of Police District 3. He was an officer I had known since my days in the prosecutor's office.

After introductions, I told the woman, who asked me to call her by her first name, that I had known her husband for about 10 years. She responded that she knew this and had told him of my contact with her. I couldn't resist asking her what he told her about me. She smiled and said, "He likes you. He says that you are a good lawyer and not to tell you too much." I laughed and got my legal pad out of my case. We both sat down.

"What can you tell me about Paula Hill and Robert McGraw without violating some welfare rule of privacy?"

Donna Carson opened a file. "I first met Paula Hill and little Terry in

January, when she and Robert moved back from West Palm Beach. She was two months pregnant with the little boy who just died. I could tell that she was not happy to be pregnant and wouldn't be upset if she miscarried. Considering that she wasn't married and had one dependent child, she qualified for food stamps, aid to a dependent child and rent subsidy. At the time, she told me that the father was unemployed. After processing her claim, I did not talk to her again until Thursday, August 26, when she called me wanting to know if I had any connections with adoption agencies. She was obviously distraught and said that she had to do something about the baby because she couldn't handle her little girl much less a baby. I tried to get her to bring her husband in with her so that we could chat about this before she made a hasty decision. I told her if she would come in and talk about it I would try to help her if she and her husband agreed that they really wanted to place the child for adoption.

"Paula became very angry when I suggested that she come in with her husband — pardon me, her significant other. I keep forgetting that they are not married. She told me that he would never agree to put 'the little bastard' up for adoption. So it would do no good to come in to see me. She would just have to find some other way.

"I was taken aback by her reference to the baby as a 'little bastard.' I told her that she shouldn't refer to her baby in such terms. She hung up on me. I have not seen or heard from her since. I mentioned this to my husband, and he told me that there was nothing that I could do since Paula had not made a threat against the child to me. But when I learned that the little boy had died, I felt horrible," Donna Carson said.

"Mrs. Carson, let me ask you a question. If you were a betting person, who would you put money on as the one who killed this baby?"

"Oh, golly, I don't know. I have to tell you that I suspect that the father did it. Paula had told me early in the year that he had a bad temper and that he had slapped her around on several occasions when they argued, which she said was usually about money, her friends and his mother and sister. You see, Paula has no family here. The only family that she knows is his."

As I rode down in the elevator from Donna Carson's office, I shook my head. Every woman I had talked to so far believed Robert killed the child. Would I be the next convert?

That afternoon, I had the opportunity to interview Robert's mother, Delores Johnson, and his sister, Sharon Fuller, at my office.

What struck me most about McGraw's mother was her lavender hair and her chain smoking of cigarettes. The sister was extremely thin, almost Twiggy-like, with large brown eyes and a thin but pretty, child-like face.

I began, "Mrs. Johnson, what do you and Sharon know that I can use to help your son?"

"The whole thing makes me sick, Mr. Mestemaker. That baby never had a chance from the day he was born. She started that part-time job at the bar when that little guy was only 3 weeks old. The day she started, I believe on a Monday, she brought Bobbie over for me to watch him. Robert was at work. The baby was soaking wet when she left him with me. He was sucking his little thumb he was so hungry. I asked her about it, and she said she didn't want to nurse him because her nipples were sore. So I told her that she couldn't starve the baby. After she left, I went out and bought him some formula and fed him with a bottle. Then when I changed him, I noticed a bruise on his little chest that covered his entire stomach area. It looked like someone hit him with their fist. I asked her about it, and she said that he fell off the couch. But I never believed her."

At this point, Sharon chimed in with an incident: Paula had told her late in July that she wasn't going to let Robert have sex anymore because she wasn't going to let him get her pregnant again. She had told Sharon that she loved Terry, but she did not want little Bobbie.

Mrs. Johnson urged Sharon to tell me about the day that Paula laid the baby on the front lawn and cursed him. Sharon leaned forward and fingered an ashtray.

"It was about the middle of August, a Sunday."

"The 15th?" I asked.

"I think so" she replied. "Anyway, Paula came over to Mom's. I was there. She was very angry, yelling at us that Robert had gone out to drink some beer with his buddies and left her alone in that hot apartment with two crying kids. She wanted Mom to keep the baby while she took Terry with her to look for Robert. When Mom said no, she laid the baby down on the grass next to the sidewalk and said, 'I hate this little bastard. I am going to put him up for adoption.' I picked the baby up. He was so wet and miserable looking. He looked half-starved."

I leafed through my notes. What had Mrs. Carson told me about adoption? Here it was, August 26 in her interview. On Thursday, August 26, she had received a call from Paula wanting the name of an adoption agency, and on August 15, she was yelling adoption at her mother-in-law and sister-in-law. It was beginning to fall together. Perhaps Robert hadn't lied to me. There were some details that perhaps he wasn't aware of.

"Mrs. Johnson, have you or Sharon told Robert about Paula telling you that she hated 'the little bastard' and that she wanted to put him up for adoption?"

"No, sir, I haven't," Mrs. Johnson said.

"What about , Sharon?"

"No, Mr. Mestemaker, I never told Robert because he was already upset."

"Good! Please, let's keep this between us. It may work out to Robert's advantage that he never knew about the adoption matter. Finally, can either one of you tell me what you know about Paula taking the baby to Christ Hospital Emergency Room on Monday, August 23, one week before Bobbie died?"

"I can," said Mrs. Johnson. "I went to the hospital with her. We took a cab. His left leg was very swollen. He had a burn on his head in the back and a big bruise on his forehead like someone hit him between the eyes. The doctor said he could see dried blood in his nose. Paula told the doctor that Terry had pulled Bobbie off the couch on his blanket. I don't think the doctor believed her. Then he asked her if anyone else was with the baby when this happened, and Paula said Robert was. I knew this was a lie because Robert worked that day. The doctor wrote Robert's name down and told us that he would have to notify the police since the injuries looked a little strange. After we left the hospital, I asked her why she lied about Robert being home. Was she trying to get him in trouble? She told me to shut up and mind my own business."

After my interview with the women, I made a decision not to interview Paula. I was going to try this case pointing the finger of guilt at her. If I did not interview her, she couldn't claim that I had threatened her. I would be a stranger to her in the courtroom, where she would be the surf wader and I would be "Jaws." Besides she didn't have any information that I needed. I already knew what her game plan was. Why let her know mine?

One chore was left today on this case. I wanted to talk to Dr. Paul Jordon about the autopsy he performed on Bobbie. So armed with a copy of the autopsy report lying in front of me, I telephoned Dr. Jordon. He was a pleasant guy who had been a deputy county coroner for about 20 years. He was considered to be a competent forensic pathologist. He taught pathology at the medical college.

"What can you tell me about the McGraw baby, Doc?"

"Do you have the report, Mr. Mestemaker?" the doctor asked.

"Yes, sir. Right in front of me." Our telephone conversation continued:

"Well, the little guy was 60 days old when he expired. He was 22 inches long and weighed 10 pounds. He was normally developed but somewhat under-nourished. His stomach contents were a minimal amount of formula feeding. He had a partly healed, burn-like injury with a scab on the back of his head. There were two faint bruises on the left side of his neck. He had a bruise on his forehead and discoloration of the skin around his nostrils. There was dried blood noted in his nose. In the left leg, induration and swelling was noted, which started in the upper anterior quadriceps region and which extended downward and laterally so that it involved the full circumference of the knee and on down into the lower calf region. His leg had been wrenched rather severely, I'm afraid."

"Please continue, doctor."

"On interior examination, I found recent, three- to four-day-old fractures of the right third and fourth ribs and swelling around the sixth and seventh, all on the right side."

"Doctor, may I interrupt you? Did you know that the baby was taken to Christ Hospital emergency one week before he died, and the X-ray report says nothing about broken ribs?"

"No, Mr. Mestemaker, I was not advised of that. My only conclusion is that the child suffered rib damage between the date of the visit to the hospital and the date of his death. The injury to the ribs was several days old when I observed it during autopsy."

So someone cracked a couple of Bobbie's ribs between August 23 and August 30. Who could it be, and when did it happen? Could it have happened on Thursday, August 26, three days after the visit to Christ Hospital and four days before he died? Could it have happened on the same day that Paula called Ms. Carson wanting help from her to find an adoption agency and when she got angry and hung up on Mrs. Carson?

"Dr. Jordon, could the baby have suffered these rib injuries three or four days before he died?" The answer was music to my ears.

"Yes, Mr. Mestemaker, the injuries that I observed to the ribs could easily have been inflicted three or four days before death. They were definitely not inflicted on the date of death. Based on what I observed, I would say four days before death."

"What exactly killed the little guy, Doc?"

"He died from an acute subdural hematoma on the left side of the occipital region containing approximately 2 teaspoons of blood, which, in turn, caused tracheobronchial aspiration of gastric contents. He also had the fractured ribs, a swollen left femur, a scabbed-over head injury, and numerous bruises and small lacerations. He was a beaten up little guy. Someone gave him a substantial whack on the head."

"Thank you, doctor. You have been very helpful, as always. I guess that I'll see you in court."

Now I believed I had something big to argue in court. These cracked ribs, which were inflicted between August 23 and August 30, might be my ace card.

Two weeks later, I got lucky again. Judge Gusweiler granted my motion to reduce the bail on McGraw. He reduced it to $15,000 at 10 percent. With the help of Robert's Uncle Charlie, he was released from jail in exchange for $1,500 in cash and an order to live with his mother and to stay away from Paula and Terry until further court order.

Robert's trial was scheduled to commence before Judge Gusweiler on January 10, 1977. With the client's approval, a decision was made to take a calculated risk and to waive a trial by jury. This would mean that the judge would make the final decision of guilt or innocence in place of a jury.

When a judge is chosen by a defendant to be the trier of the facts as well as the authority on legal issues, the judge assumes the same role, as do jurors. Just as jurors must be convinced of the defendant's guilt beyond a reasonable doubt in order to convict, the judge sitting in place of a jury is bound by the same requirement.

I had known Judge Gusweiler for 10 years. He was a lawyer's judge. By that, I mean that he was recognized as an expert on law and the rules of evidence. Equally important, he was almost 100 percent free of personal bias. He would call it like he saw it regardless of whether he disliked the type of case, the nature of the crime, the defendant, the witnesses, or, last but not least, the lawyers. Since everyone who I had discussed this case with except my client's mother and sister believed that he was guilty. I had great trepidation about McGraw's chances with a jury, especially if composed of parents. We had to cast our lot with the judge.

The trial started on one of the coldest days of the coldest months in Cincinnati's history. Ron Vanetti was mildly surprised when I announced to Judge Gusweiler that Mr. McGraw had decided to waive his right to a trial by jury. At my request, the judge questioned Robert concerning his decision to waive a trial by jury, asking whether this was a voluntary decision. McGraw told the judge that he understood his rights and what he was doing and that, after consulting with me, he was voluntarily making this decision. I also had taken the precaution of having Robert write this out in his own hand and had it signed by him in the presence of two others.

After opening statements were made, I offered a motion that there be a separation of witnesses so that they could not hear each other's testimony. Judge Gusweiler, as was his practice, granted this motion.

I wanted to be able to call Dr. Jordon as my witness because of the issue of the broken ribs. In order to do this, I needed to keep Vanetti from calling the pathologist during presentation of his case. So I agreed to stipulate the death of Bobbie on August 30, 1976, the cause of his death and what the doctor would say caused his death if he were to testify for the prosecutor. Finally, I agreed to allow the autopsy report to be admitted into evidence as a joint exhibit. This maneuver allowed the judge to review the report while the trial was in progress.

The state's case proceeded along at a fast pace. Vanetti called John Lewis, the EMT for the fire department who had tried to revive Bobbie. He called Patrol Officer Kim Owens, the first officer on the scene where the baby died. He called Detectives Joe Roberts and Elmer Hollister, who had interviewed my client and Paula Hill the night that Bobbie died. He didn't call Dr. Paul Jordon because of our stipulation of his testimony.

Vanetti's next witness was Dr. Edward Salinas, who had treated Bobbie at Christ Hospital on August 23 when Paula brought him to the ER. Dr. Salinas testified concerning the injuries that he observed to Bobbie's head, forehead and left leg. On cross-examination, I asked Salinas whether the baby had been X-rayed on August 23. He responded that X-rays had been taken. I asked him if an X-ray had been taken of Bobbie's chest and abdomen. The doctor answered that there had been two X-rays of the baby's torso. Had the doctor brought these X-rays to court? The answer was yes. At my request, an X-ray viewer was produced in court and the chest X-rays were displayed.

"Dr. Salinas," I said, "do either of these chest X-rays indicate any rib fractures?"

The doctor's answer: "No. They do not show any rib fractures."

At this point, Vanetti looked at me and then hurriedly perused the Christ Hospital ER report prepared by Dr. Salinas on August 23. I realized that Vanetti had not read the entire autopsy report. He was not aware of the rib fractures.

"Dr. Salinas," I said, "if the child had fractured ribs when you treated him, would that be in your report."

"Yes, sir," he answered.

"Is it?" I asked.

"No!" he replied.

Next question: "Did the child have fractured ribs on August 23rd?"

"No, sir. Not when I saw him. He did not have fractured ribs."

"Then, Dr. Salinas, I want you to look at the X-rays again carefully. Do either of them reveal any rib fractures, in particularly to the third and fourth ribs on the right side of the chest?

His answer was as it had to be, "No, sir."

"One final matter, Dr. Salinas. Your ER report states that the child's mother told you that the injuries that you observed were caused when the baby's 5-year-old sister pulled him off of the couch. Is that correct?"

"Yes, it is."

"Did you believe that his injuries happened that way?" I asked.

"No, sir. The injuries that I observed were too severe to have happened by falling off a couch."

"Did you tell Paula Hill and her mother-in-law, Dolores Johnson, who was there with her, that you were going to report this matter to the police?"

"Yes, sir, I did."

"Did all of this cause you to conclude that the father may have caused these injuries to the baby?"

"Yes, sir."

"Did you tell the authorities that the injuries were suspicious and that you suspected the father?"

"Yes, sir."

"Doctor, do you have any real evidence to justify your suspicion that my client caused these injuries to his son?"

"No, sir."

"Did the attitude of Paula Hill and her statements influence you to suspect the father?"

"Yes, sir. I'm afraid they did."

"Do you still feel that way?"

"No, sir, I don't."

"Thank you, doctor. No further questions."

I was pleased that the prosecutor chose not to question Dr. Salinas further. The broken ribs were still my potential ace cards. The prosecution's final witness was Paula Hill. My client had not seen her since the time he had been charged with murder. She had not called him or gone to see him while he was in jail, and he had been ordered to stay away from her as a condition of his release. He had heard the rumors about Paula and Chuck Andrews. It was painful. It was obvious that he missed her and that he still loved her.

When Paula entered the courtroom from a side door, the metamorphous in her appearance was stunning. Her blond hair was styled in a blunt cut. She was wearing makeup, eye shadow and very bright red lipstick. Her wardrobe had improved as well. She was wearing a black leather vest over a white silk blouse, a short black skirt and 4-inch-high heels. She looked quite attractive, and her appearance was not lost on Robert. He looked enamoured of her. But she never glanced in his direction. She stopped in front of the judge, raised her right hand and swore to tell the truth.

From the start of her testimony, it was obvious whom she was going to point the finger of guilt at — and he was sitting next to me, shaking his head in disbelief. She told of being afraid of Robert's temper and how Robert had slapped little Bobbie early in August. She sobbed when shown a picture of her dead son. She recounted the visit to Christ Hospital, testifying that to protect Robert she had told Dr. Salinas that 5-year-old Terry had pulled the baby off the couch.

She told the judge that on August 30, she had gone to Larry's Tap Room only to use the telephone and that the baby and Terry were asleep on the bed when she left. She testified that while she was in the bar, Robert had come home and had been alone with the children until he came over to call the life squad. She said he had threatened her and Chuck Andrews when he found them sitting together in the bar.

Ron Vanetti's final questions of Paula were, "Did you inflict the injuries on Bobbie that he had when he was seen at Christ Hospital on August 23rd?"

"No, sir," she replied.

"Did you inflict the injuries on Bobbie that killed him on August 30?"

"No, sir. I did not. I loved my little boy."

I had purposely not interviewed Paula during pretrial preparation. We were strangers. When I went to the podium, I started my cross-examination by introducing myself to her. I asked her whether we had ever met before or talked about this case.

She looked at the prosecutor and then back to me and said, "No, sir, I have never met you or talked to you."

After a few questions about her childhood in West Palm Beach and how she and Robert had met, I asked her when Terry was born. Her answer was June 15, 1971, and that the child was now 5½.

"Who is Terry living with right now?"

"What does that have to do with this?" she said with a sneer.

"Just answer my question, Mrs. McGraw — or is it Ms. Hill? Which do you prefer?"

"McGraw is OK with me."

"What about Terry," I pressed. "Where is she living now?"

"She is temporarily in a foster home," was her terse answer.

"Why is she in a foster home?" I asked.

"Because I can't keep her right now. I'm not working."

"But you have money for new clothes and a new hairdo, correct?"

"Objection."

"Sustained. Let's move along Mr. Mestemaker," growled Judge Gusweiler.

"Mrs. McGraw, who is Chuck Andrews?"

"A friend. He is only a friend. I know why you are asking me this, and it is none of your business."

"Mrs. McGraw, did you ever tell my client's mother or his sister that, quote, you hated the little bastard and that you were going to put him up for adoption, unquote?"

"No! I did not say he was a little bastard. I may have jokingly said something about placing him for adoption. But if I did, it was only because I was exhausted and angry with Robert for being gone all the time when I needed help with two children."

"Did you ever talk to anyone else about placing Bobbie for adoption?"

"No, I did not."

"Did you refuse to nurse Bobbie?"

"No, only when my nipples were sore, and then I gave him formula."

"Did you ever fail to change him when he needed it or to bathe him regularly.

"Look: Whatever you're trying to do to me Mr. Mestemaker, it isn't going to work. I loved my baby, and I took good care of him. You should ask your client there what he did to Bobbie, not me."

"Thank you. I have no further questions of Mrs. McGraw." I sat down in my chair and waited for the next move.

Ron Vanetti announced that the state was resting its case.

It was 4:10 p.m. Judge Gusweiler stood up and said, "That's all today, gentlemen. The weather looks bad. We may get some snow. I'll see you at 10:00 a.m. tomorrow, God willing. Adjourn court, Mr. Bailiff."

Three raps with a gavel and Day 1 of the trial of Robert Edward

McGraw was over.

On Tuesday, it was the defendant's turn to present evidence. Today was the day to do my best for my client — or he was going away for a long time.

The first witness called was Robert's business agent, Frank O'Neal, who told Judge Gusweiler what a hard worker Robert was and that he didn't believe McGraw had the heart to kill anyone, much less his own son.

The second witness for the defense was McGraw's mom, who wasn't the best witness in the world — but she did OK by her son. She talked about Robert's childhood and how much he loved Paula, Terry and "little Bobbie." She told the judge how wet and miserable the baby was the morning in July when Paula brought him to her apartment to watch him that first day. Paula had returned to a part-time job, and he was hungry because his mother didn't want to nurse him. "It looked to me like she was trying to either drown him in his own pee or starve him to death," she blurted out. Judge Gusweiler sustained the prosecutor's objection and ordered her volunteered observation stricken from consideration.

The next topics covered with Delores Johnson were the bruise that she had noticed on the baby's chest and his mother's explanation that he had got the bruise when he fell off the couch. Mrs. Johnson said she had never believed Paula's explanation. This remark was also stricken, at Vanetti's request — but the judge had still heard it, and I believe it registered.

The next witness to testify for the defendant was his sister, Sharon. She didn't care too much for Paula, and she believed that Paula or perhaps her boyfriend, Andrews, had killed the baby. She was biased, but she was forceful. The main thrust of her testimony concerned the incident in mid-August when Paula had put the baby down on the lawn and said, "I hate this little bastard. I'm going to put him up for adoption." I noticed Judge Gusweiler raise his right eyebrow when he heard this statement. He jotted something on his note pad. When Vanetti cross-examined Sharon, all he accomplished was to piss her off and make her testimony even stronger. At one point, she yelled at Vanetti in answer to a question about Paula being a "good mother."

"She is a tramp!" Sharon responded. "It looked to me like she had made up her mind to starve little Bobbie. She said her nipples were sore. They weren't sore from nursing the baby. Maybe they were sore from Chuck."

"Who is Chuck?" Vanetti asked.

"He is her lover, Chuck Andrews."

"I object!" said Vanetti, surprised at the answer.

"Overruled," said Judge Gusweiler. "You asked the question."

After this exchange, Vanetti didn't want to tangle with Sharon any further.

The fourth witness called on behalf of Robert was the chief assistant county coroner, Paul Jordon. Vanetti looked at me and said, "I didn't think that Dr. Jordon was going to testify. You agreed to stipulate his autopsy report. What's going on?"

"Calm down, Ron. There is something that I may have overlooked, and I just wanted to clear it up. And to do that, I need to call the pathologist."

Once on the witness stand, Dr. Jordon was handed the original of his autopsy report of the death of Robert Edward McGraw Jr.

"Dr. Jordon, did you perform the autopsy on this infant?"

"Yes, sir, I did."

"Your report has already been received by the court into evidence. Is that your report that you are holding now?"

"Yes, sir."

Doctor, the child died from an acute subdural hematoma injury of the head, did he not?"

"That is correct, Mr. Mestemaker."

"Did you by an chance notice any injuries to the back of his head or to his forehead?"

"Yes, sir, I did. He had a partly healed, burn-like injury to the rear of his head. It was scabbed over. He also had bruising of the forehead and a badly swollen left knee."

"Were these recent injuries?"

"No. I would say that they were several weeks old as of August 30. Exactly how far removed, I cannot say for sure."

"But these injuries did not occur close in time to the date of death?"

"No, sir, they did not."

"Dr. Jordon, did your interior exam of the baby reveal any rib injuries."

"Yes, there were ribs that were fractured and swelling around others."

"Which ribs were fractured?"

"Right side, third and fourth ribs, and there was swelling around the sixth and seventh ribs."

"Thank you, doctor. Can you tell the court the approximate age of the rib injuries that you observed?"

"Well, these injuries to the ribs were not the cause of death, and they were not inflicted at the same time as the fatal head injury. I would say that the rib injuries were at least three or four days old, probably four days."

"Then, the rib fractures occurred around August 26?"

"Yes, sir. That would be the approximate date."

"Thank you, Dr. Jordon. The defendant recalls Dr. Salinas to the stand.

"Dr. Salinas, you have testified earlier in the trial that you told the authorities on August 23 that you believed that the baby's father may have caused the injuries that you treated Robert McGraw for on August 23rd. Do you recall that testimony?"

"Yes, sir. I do."

"Do you recall that I then asked you if you still felt that way."

"Yes, sir."

"Doctor, your answer was that you now felt differently, is that a fair statement?"

"Yes, it is."

"Dr. Salinas, what has caused you to change your attitude about my client's involvement in the injuries inflicted upon his son?"

There was a strong objection lodged at this point by the prosecutor. But since this line of questioning had not been challenged the first time, the judge overruled the objection.

Dr. Salinas answered the question regarding his change in attitude: "The child's mother had promised me that she would immediately bring the baby in to see me if there were any additional problems. After I was notified that I was going to be a witness, I was informed that when Dr. Jordon performed the autopsy on August 30th he discovered that the infant had suffered several rib fractures about four days before he died. That would have been three days after I examined him. But I never heard from his mother again. It is not possible for a mother to bathe a baby, change his diaper and hold him and not know that there is something wrong with his rib cage, and it was the child's mother who was with him during this period. I feel badly that I suspected the father. I just wished I had known on August 23rd that Ms. Hill had told her mother-in-law in July, almost a full month or so earlier, that he had received a bruise to his chest by falling off a couch. Because if you look at my notes from the ER room on August 23rd, she told me that the injuries that I treated him for, the scab on the back of his head, the abrasion on his forehead between the eyes and the swollen left leg were caused when his sister, who I believe is 5 years old, pulled the child off of a couch. It is just too much of a coincidence to believe that on two separate occasions such injuries as I noted on August 23rd and Dr. Jordon noted in the autopsy a week later, were the result of the same child being pulled off of a couch by his 5-year-old sister. I have concluded that the child's mother has not been truthful about how the baby received these injuries."

"Thank you, Dr. Salinas. You may step down."

At this time, a decision was made not to put Robert on the witness stand on his own behalf. He had nothing to add and might hurt himself if Vanetti rattled him on cross-examination. Sharon, and then Dr. Jordon followed by Dr. Salinas had set the stage for the destruction of Paula's credibility. I calculated that our final witness would prove once and for all that she was a liar.

"The defense calls Donna Carson."

The courtroom door opened, and Donna Carson entered. She did not realize it but, as she walked toward the witness stand, she was under the constant glare of Paula Hill. Paula, like others who had already testified and would not be recalled, had been permitted by the judge to remain in the courtroom.

After some preliminary questions concerning her employment and her contacts with Paula, Robert, Terry and little Bobbie, I advised the witness that Paula Hill had earlier testified in the trial that she had never talked to anyone about placing Bobbie McGraw for adoption. I then asked Mrs. Carson if she had information to the contrary. The witness looked at me and then frowned in the direction of a still glaring Paula Hill.

"Yes, sir, I do have information to the contrary." She opened her file and continued: "On August 26, I received a telephone call at my office from Paula Hill. She was obviously distraught. I recognized her voice immediately. She told me right out of the chute that she needed to know if I had any connections with adoption agencies, and wanted my help to place the baby for adoption. I tried to talk her out of it, but she became very angry and referred to her infant son as a 'little bastard.' I was shocked by her sudden outburst and concerned with her display of anger. I should have intervened in some way. But I didn't. I never talked to her again. It was only four days later that I received the news that the baby was dead."

"Thank you, Mrs. Carson."

It was over. Except for a brief closing argument, it was over. For good or bad, the case was in Judge Gusweiler's hands — as was my client's fate. Whoever broke those ribs on August 26 was the killer.

The judge retired to his chambers to review the exhibits, especially the Christ Hospital ER report prepared by Dr. Salinas and Dr. Jordon's autopsy report. He returned to the bench after 25 minutes.

"Gentlemen, this case has caused me great concern." The judge started into one of his classic soliloquies. "I have been a judge for 25 years. Yet, I am still astounded by our cruelty toward one another. Parents are supposed to be the nurturers of their children, their protectors, their role models, but certainly not their killers. I believe that in this case, this child was killed by a parent. But I believe that the wrong parent was formally accused and required to undergo the emotional trauma of a trial, which has assuredly only added to the trauma he has suffered through a father's loss of his only son. As I said, I believe that the wrong parent was charged with this child's death. Mr. McGraw, the court finds you not guilty of the death of your son. But I do believe that the guilty party is present here with us today. I certainly hope that the prosecutor and the police will rectify this situation and do it quickly. Mr. McGraw, sir, you are free to get on with your life. I do wish you well."

The silence in the courtroom was broken by my three words: "Thank you, judge."

There were congratulations and hugs all around the McGraw side of the table, but not on the state's side.

Several years went by. I was now myself a judge. Robert now had custody of Terry and had married a very nice girl from Norwood. I heard from them when they announced the birth of their son, who they named Robert Edward McGraw II. There was a new "little Bobby." Maybe Bobby Jr. got to be his guardian angel. I hope so.

No one else was ever brought to trial for Bobby Jr.'s murder. He remains an unavenged angel.

CHAPTER 9

PRETTY WOMAN, BATTERED WOMAN

In mid-1979, June to be exact, few people had ever heard the term "battered woman syndrome." I know that the term meant nothing to me at the time, and it would continue to be unknown by me until it became part of everyday legal jargon in the mid-1990s. This was despite the fact that without knowing it, I had used it as a defense in the murder trial of Debbie Bohanon, who was charged with shooting her former live-in boyfriend, Tyrone Williams, to death on the morning of June 21 of that year.

On June 28, 1979, I received word that Judge William R. Matthews wanted to see me. Being the ever-respectful lawyer, now in the 12th year of law practice, I stopped by to see His Honor at my first opportunity.

Judge Matthews had served as a common pleas judge since 1965. Prior to that, he had been a rural county judge and a practicing lawyer.

The judge was a stickler for promptness. On more than one occasion, he had fined lawyers and locked up defendants who were late for court. He used to delight in coming out of his chambers a minute or two before 9:00 a.m. and sitting on the bench in order to catch lawyers as they entered the courtroom at 9:01 or 9:02. He would look at the big clock on the rear courtroom wall and then at his own watch and announce, "I have been waiting for you. Where have you been?"

One morning in 1968, several assistant prosecuting attorneys sneaked into his courtroom around 8:50 a.m. and turned the minute hand on the wall clock ahead five minutes — to 8:55 a.m. We then seated ourselves at the table directly between the clock and the bench. Judge Matthews came out of his Chambers at exactly 8:58 a.m. — but the courtroom clock said 9:03 a.m. In perfect unison, we chimed, "It's 9:03 a.m. We have been waiting for you, Judge. Where have you been?" He looked at the clock and then his watch and said, "Someone has been up to no good this morning, and he or they had better hope that their identity remains a mystery." It did, fortunately for us, although he really knew who the culprits were.

It was after 2:00 p.m. when I walked into Courtroom 535 and announced my presence to Bailiff Cecil Grey, who had been with Judge

Matthews for 14 years. Cecil had once been the mayor of Addyston, Ohio, and, in that capacity, had presided over mayor's court. Cecil was not a lawyer, but that never stopped him from practicing law unofficially, something he had been doing for over 25 years. Cecil ushered me in to see the judge, who was sitting behind his big desk in shirt sleeves and bright yellow suspenders.

"Sit down, Mike! I want you to take on a homicide case as a favor to me. It's not going to be an easy case because the young lady who is accused of murder wants to plead guilty just to get it over with. She told the police that she shot and killed her boyfriend and that she should be punished. She has already refused two lawyers appointed to represent her merely because they have advised her to go to trial. See what you can do. She needs help, and it will come only from someone who will take charge and be boss. Do me a favor on this one and I won't forget it."

I had learned a long time ago that when a judge asked a favor of me as a lawyer and put it in the terms that had just been related to me, the answer that was expected was, "Yes, sir. I'll do it." I had learned that lesson in the Army. When a superior officer asked a subordinate for a favor in the same fashion, one said, "Yes, sir. Consider it done."

"What is her name, Judge?" I asked.

"Let's see — Debbie Bohanon," he replied. "She's only 23 and a nursing student."

"I'll see what I can do for her, Judge Matthews," I said as I picked up my case to leave.

"OK, Mike. That is all I can ask of you. Just do your best though."

I walked to the elevator, but when the door opened I went down instead of up — which is where the jail was in 1979, up on the sixth floor. I found myself in the Courthouse lobby, at the bookstand, looking for something for a 23-year-old nursing student to read that might break the ice. And then I spotted the perfect ice breaker, a soft-cover novel titled An Army Nurse in Korea. Perfect! First expense of this case: $4.95 for one paperback book.

"Hello, Miss Bohanon. My name is Albert J. Mestemaker. My friends and colleagues call me by my nickname, which is 'Mike.' Here, I have a gift for you — something you can read. The judge told me that you are studying to be a nurse. I saw this book downstairs and thought that you might enjoy it."

I slid the book in front of her. She looked at the cover and started crying. "I'll never be a nurse now. My life is over."

I put my hand over hers and squeezed. "Maybe you shouldn't give up so easy."

"Mr. Mestemaker, I shot Tyrone in the chest with a shotgun. He's dead. How can it not be over for me?"

"I'm not sure at this point, until I hear the facts from you, Debbie. Do you mind if I call you Debbie?"

"No, that's fine. I need friends right now. Will you be my friend?"

I released her hand and responded, "I'll not only be your friend, I'll also be your lawyer if you agree to accept my advice and stop this idea of pleading guilty.

"Judge Matthews has already told me that your first two lawyers are off your case because you don't want to fight. But I will only take the case if you agree right here and now that you will fight back, and I suspect that this is something that is long overdue.

"Now, are you willing to tell me your story from the beginning, and may I tape record it to save time?"

She thought a minute and sighed, "OK, I'll tell you how it all came to be." Debbie's story began to unfold on a Sony recorder.

She was born in Atlanta, Georgia, in 1956, the daughter of a city waste collector and a mother who took in laundry. She had an older brother named Orlando and a younger sister named Verna. She and her brother and sister were very close. She loved her parents deeply and couldn't bear the thought of how they must be reacting to her being in jail for murder. Her parents were going to be in town tomorrow to visit her.

Debbie went on to tell me that when she turned 20, she moved to Cincinnati to live with her aunt until she found a job and could be on her own. She had been a good student in high school, graduating fourth in a class of 235. She wanted to study nursing and become an RN. Not only did she have an aunt in Cincinnati with whom she could live for a while, but also there were three nursing schools affiliated with large hospitals, an ideal setting for embryo nursing students.

Debbie arrived in Cincinnati in July 1976 and immediately took up residence with her Aunt Roberta Taylor near Eden Park in the Walnut Hills section of the city. After several weeks, she landed a job with a large retail outlet for pharmaceutical products. This job was perfect for someone who desired to pursue a career in nursing. Debbie was a quick study. The head pharmacist, Mark Backman, was amazed at how quickly she learned the different categories of medicinal drugs, their effects, side effects, dosages and compatibility with other medications. On more than one occasion,

Debbie questioned a prescription for a certain medication after reviewing the customer's drug profile and verifying that the prescribed drugs should not be mixed together. On each such occasion, the pharmacist found that her concern was justified. She was such a capable pharmacist's assistant that Mark urged her to give up her desire to become a registered nurse and pursue a degree in pharmacy.

Debbie had medium-brown skin and glistening black hair that formed a halo around her face. She had large black eyes set in a small, child-like but sensuous face. She was about 5-feet, 4-inches tall and weighed in at 115 to 120 pounds. She had a very small waist, 18 inches or 19 inches, as well as thin, shapely legs and pleasing curves in all the right places. She was also meticulous about her appearance.

After living with Aunt Roberta for about six months, Debbie had saved enough to rent a small, three-room, furnished apartment on Cutter Street in the West End. She didn't have an automobile, but that was all right with her. No automobile meant no repairs, no gasoline and no license fees or insurance. Besides, she lived 4 miles from work — a 10-minute bus ride. She lived within 7 miles of all of the public institutions of higher learning where she could attend classes in either nursing or pharmacy. All she needed to do was continue to save her money for tuition. She sat down at her kitchen table and listed income and expenses on a note pad. She figured that by the fall of 1977, she would have almost $3,000 saved, enough to get started in school. Things looked good for Debbie.

Tyrone Williams was 31 years old. He was dark skinned, 5-feet, 11-inches tall, 175 pounds, muscular and well-developed. He was a handsome man with bright white teeth and an engaging smile. He was also an ex-con, a hustler, a drug abuser and a man possessed of a short fuse made even shorter by alcohol. He was of the opinion that society owed him a free ride, and it didn't make much difference to him how society furnished it as long as he got it.

Just plain bad luck brought Tyrone Williams into Debbie's life in September 1978. A co-worker had asked Debbie if she could work her shift at the drug store. Normally, because of her nursing classes, Debbie worked evenings. On this particular day, she was working in the afternoon when Williams came in to have a prescription filled.

Tyrone Williams liked what he saw as soon as Debbie greeted him. He turned on the charm and flirted with her while she assisted the pharmacist in filling his prescription. He told her what his name was and wanted to know hers, and why he had not seen her in the store before. She told him that she worked evenings. He told her that he would be back to see her.

This casual atmosphere lasted for about three weeks. Williams would stop in the store and pass the time chatting with Debbie, until her boss finally complained that he was interfering with her work. After that, he would wait for her and walk her to her apartment. On several evenings, they stopped and had coffee. Tyrone was cranking up the relationship.

By September 1978, Debbie was really into her new life. She was close to her 23rd birthday. She had just finished painting her entire apartment by herself, and she had purchased her own bedroom furniture. Her small apartment looked quite homey, filled with the kind of bric-a-brac that young single women love to collect — such as stuffed animals, floppy hats, pennants, glassware and pop art. Debbie was particularly fond of large, colored zoo posters, which adorned her small living room. Her favorite was the one of a big male lion asleep on a tree limb with all four of his legs dangling beneath him in empty space.

After the three or so weeks of casual meetings with Tyrone and an occasional cup of coffee when he was free to walk Debbie home, he invited her to be his date at the wedding of one of his cousins to be held that coming Saturday. Debbie had not had many dates since she had arrived in Cincinnati, a little over two years earlier. She had met several nice young men at her Aunt Roberta's church and had gone out on dates, but there were no sparks and there had not been anything more than just a movie or a church social event.

Debbie had started her second year of nursing school. She was happy, she was radiant. She bordered on beautiful. But she was still a shy Georgia peach and somewhat self-deprecating. She was certainly not stuck on herself. She thought that her breasts were too small and her hips too big. But she could live with these perceived defects, which were really in her imagination and not in any male's perception. She wanted male companionship. She was beginning to like Tyrone a lot.

She really enjoyed herself at the wedding reception, where she met some of Tyrone's friends and family. Only one person concerned her — 26-year-old Latasha Franklin, who took her aside and warned her to stay away from Tyrone for her own good and who then hurried away as Tyrone approached.

"Who is that girl, Tyrone?"

"Never you mind about her, baby," he replied. "She is just a jealous broad I used to date. Stay away from her."

The wedding date was followed by a picnic, followed by a trip to Kings Island Amusement Park. There were goodnight kisses at the door, some touchy-feely, a lot of teasing and giggling. And then, one evening, at 11:00, Tyrone showed up with a duffel bag on his shoulder.

"Debbie, baby, I need a place to stay for a while. I can't tell you why right now, but I really need your help. If you'll let me stay, I can sleep on the couch. Please, Debbie, do this for me."

Debbie was taken aback. She liked Tyrone. In fact, she liked him a lot. But this caught her off-guard. He was asking her to take him in without any explanation. Her parents would never approve of this, but she really cared for him. What to do?

"OK, Tyrone. I can't say no to you. I just hope that you are not in any trouble."

"Later, baby, later. Thank God you said yes! I'll move my stuff in tonight, if that's OK with you."

Tyrone never felt it necessary to tell Debbie that two days earlier he had sold some bad "powder" to a couple of street thugs, who now wanted a pound of his flesh as well as their money. These two didn't know about Debbie, so he was safe in her flat for the time being. Tyrone was placing Debbie in harm's way, but her safety was not his concern.

Tyrone was true to his word about sleeping on the couch and not being a bother. This scene lasted for almost a month, until the evening when Debbie, having taken her shower, came out of her bedroom resplendent in a dainty semi see-through nightgown, which almost made a television-watching Tyrone jump up and cheer.

"Tyrone! You don't have to sleep on the couch tonight. I have needs too, and I need you."

Tyrone had spent his last night on the couch. The sex was good for both of them. Debbie had been a virgin. Now she felt like a fulfilled woman. She was in love.

Several weeks later, Debbie unlocked the door to the apartment after work and saw Tyrone sitting on the sofa with a brown paper package lying on the table in front of him.

"What's in the package, Tyrone?" Debbie said.

Tyrone began to unwrap the paper. First she saw the barrel and then the receiver and stock. "What's this?" she said.

"It's just an old single-barrel shotgun, Debbie. It used to belong to my granddad. You see, he even cut the barrel off so that it's only 15 inches long. But he gave it to me as a keepsake, kind of part of my inheritance.

Can I keep it here?"

"I'm not sure," replied Debbie. "I'm not real keen on guns."

"Debbie, I don't even know if the damn thing will shoot, it's so old. Look, Debbie, I'll show you how to snap it together. See, first the barrel fits into the receiver like this, and then this wood grip fits under the barrel. To load it, all you have to do is turn this little lever to the right and push down on the barrel and it opens. Then you put a shell in the open end, close it and cock the hammer. It's then ready to shoot."

"What's in the other bag, Tyrone?"

"Oh, that. That's just a box of old shotgun shells. I don't know if they are any good, they're so old."

Debbie looked into the bag and opened the box. Removing one of the shells and holding it up, she said:

"Tyrone, if the gun is just a keepsake, why do you need shells for it?"

"Oh, Debbie, baby, you are such a worry wart. Let me put the gun in the closet on the top shelf, and no one will know it's there. Sometime I'll take you to the dump and we can see if it still shoots. If it does, we can shoot rats with it. That's fun."

"Yuck! Shooting rats is not my idea of fun. OK, put it up in the closet. Please take it apart and wrap it up in this blanket. Put the shells up there with it so it is all out of sight."

Just before Thanksgiving, Debbie came home after the drugstore closed for the night. It was almost 10:30 p.m. She was angry to see "Stretch" Davis at her kitchen table with a fifth of whiskey in front of him. What was worse, he was making a thin line out of white powder with a razor blade. He had a straw in his left hand ready to go.

"What in the hell do you two think you are doing in my apartment? Tyrone, you know that I don't approve of this. You are not going to ruin my life with your lousy friends and their habits. I want him out of here, now!"

"Calm down, calm down, baby," replied Tyrone.

"Don't baby talk me, Tyrone. I want him and his drugs and booze out of here."

"OK, OK. You had better take off Stretch. I'll catch you later, man."

As soon as Stretch was out of the door, Tyrone turned on Debbie like a panther. He ripped her blouse open and threw her on the couch. He slapped her across the face, splitting her lip and bruising her cheeks. He then grabbed her by the ankles and pulled her off the sofa and halfway across the living room floor. Debbie kicked at him, losing her shoes. Her skirt was bunched up around her hips. She felt violated. She screamed so loud that Tyrone finally released his grip on her ankles.

As she sat up and tugged at her skirt, she cursed Tyrone. "Get out of here. Take your things and get out of here. No one is going to throw me around and beat me up. I feel like calling the police on you."

Tyrone got control of himself. "Please, baby, please. I'm sorry. I don't know what came over me. I have never hit a woman before. Give me another chance. It will never happen again, I promise."

"Tyrone, I want you out of here. Leave or I call the police. Just go, please."

Tyrone shrugged his shoulders. He packed his clothes while Debbie locked herself in the bathroom and treated her facial injuries. She did not come out of the bathroom until she heard the apartment door close. Then she went into the bedroom and collapsed in tears on her bed, sleeping in her clothes that night.

Debbie's fellow students noticed her swollen lip and bruised cheeks. Her attempt to cover her bruises with makeup was only partly successful. Her boss, Mark Backman, noticed her injuries as soon as she came into work the next afternoon. He suspected Tyrone, but Debbie said, "Please, don't ask me to discuss this with you right now."

Debbie's Aunt Roberta wanted her to call the police the minute she saw Debbie's face. But Debbie told Roberta that she could handle it. She didn't want the police involved in her life. She didn't care for the police in Georgia and didn't know any Cincinnati police officers who she felt she could trust.

Several days later, Tyrone showed up at her apartment. He wanted her to let him come in, but she kept the night latch on the door. He cried, and tears ran down his cheeks. "Please take me back. It will never happen again."

Three weeks later, after numerous telephone calls and visits, Tyrone showed up at the Carmel Baptist Church and slid into a pew next to Debbie. He squeezed her hand and whispered to her. "I'll go to church for you, if you'll have me back."

Tyrone moved back that night. They made love until long after midnight. Debbie had never known such passion in her life. Now she was stuck to this man like glue. She wanted to believe that he was sorry and that he would not abuse her again.

Christmas was the happiest Debbie had ever known. Tyrone was absolutely extravagant. He gave her a beautiful black, knee-length coat with fur collar and cuffs. He gave her a black cocktail dress that was back-less. She looked like a million dollars in it. The most lavish gift of all was a gold-and-diamond tennis bracelet. She was overwhelmed. She had no idea that Tyrone could afford these gifts. He told her he had made some commission money off a real estate deal. She chose to believe him. It was easier this way.

On New Year's Eve 1978, Debbie accompanied Tyrone to a party at the Pink Flamingo Lounge. There were a lot of people there who knew Tyrone. Stretch Davis was there. Debbie ignored him. Latasha Franklin was also at this party. She walked up to Debbie and purred, "You still foolin' with that man, sugar? How many times has he kicked your ass?"

Debbie didn't respond. She walked away from Latasha as quickly as if Latasha had leprosy.

Tyrone had a great New Year's Eve. He drank. He did some amphet-amines and snorted a line of cocaine with Stretch and several other bud-dies. And then, after the party, he beat Debbie up so bad for talking to Latasha that she had to go to the hospital for two days.

When Tyrone had started beating her on the street in front of the Pink Flamingo, other party-goers intervened and drove Debbie to the emergency ward at University Hospital. X-rays revealed that Debbie had two fractured ribs, a broken cheekbone and a dislocated shoulder. She also had numerous contusions and bruises on her face, head, shoulders and arms. Her backless dress had been just about ripped to shreds, and she had to hold it together.

The hospital reported this incident to the police, as was customary in this type of situation. Cincinnati police Officer Jennifer Hill was sent to interview Debbie in the hospital. Debbie told Officer Hill the whole story, but Debbie refused to file a criminal complaint against Tyrone. Officer Hill told her that she was making a mistake and gave Debbie her card, asking her to call if she changed her mind.

On Valentine's Day, Debbie came home from class around 4 p.m. She had to be at work by 5. Her apartment door was ajar. She was afraid to enter alone. She went downstairs and asked her landlady, Mrs. Virginia Carter, to come back upstairs with her. Mrs. Carter brought a cast-iron skil-let with her. On the way upstairs, Mrs. Carter told Debbie that she had heard noises earlier and thought that Debbie had come in early.

When the women walked in the apartment, they were horrified. Someone had spray-painted red hearts on all the walls and furniture. The empty can had been left in the middle of the floor. Debbie entered her bedroom and screamed. "Fuck you bitch" was sprayed on her dresser mirror in the same red paint. Her clothes were all over the room, cut and torn apart. Her dresser drawers were pulled out and thrown on the floor. Her underwear was sprayed red, and other personal items had been cut with a sharp knife.

One of the police officers who responded was Jennifer Hill. She told Debbie that she had been afraid that something like this might happen. Detective Frank Safter canvassed the neighborhood. An elderly neighbor who lived across the street reported that she had seen Tyrone and Stretch across the street earlier in the day but had not seen them enter or leave the building where Debbie lived.

Detective Safter requested the crime bureau to dust the apartment for latent fingerprints, but none were found. At this point, Debbie learned that Tyrone had an extensive criminal record for drugs and violence. On the advice of the officers, Debbie had her apartment door re-keyed. If it had been Tyrone who let himself into her apartment that day, he would have to break the door down the next time.

Tyrone was clever enough to stay away from Debbie's apartment, especially since the police were keeping an eye on the building. He had other plans for her. He could be patient when he wanted to be.

After several weeks, Debbie began to feel more secure. She had not seen Tyrone or any of his friends. She had not received any more calls at home or at work. Spring break arrived, and she had 10 free days. So she bought a ticket on Greyhound and went home to Atlanta to spend Easter with her family. She had asked her Aunt Roberta not to tell her folks about her trouble with Tyrone. Roberta's word was good. Debbie's family still knew nothing bad about Tyrone Williams.

Nursing classes resumed on March 29. On April 3, as Debbie walked home from her job, an automobile came out of the darkness between the streetlights. A passenger jumped out. He was wearing a camouflage jacket and a blue knit cap pulled far down over his forehead. Debbie screamed. She knew it was Tyrone. He pushed her into a walkway between two tenements. He punched her face and held her tight as he forced his lips against hers. Debbie clamped her teeth on his lower lip and held tight. He roared and punched her in the stomach as hard as he could. She saw stars and felt like she would throw up. He pushed his hand into her face and started pounding her head against the side of the building.

"You bitch, I'm going to beat you to a bloody pulp and fuck you for turning on me and trying to get me arrested. I found out that you went to

Georgia. I guess you told your people all about bad-ass Tyrone."

Debbie screamed and struggled. She tried to knee Tyrone in the groin, but he grabbed her raised leg behind the knee and dumped her on her back. Then he pounced on top of her. He tore her jacket open. He ripped her blouse. She was not wearing a bra. When he saw her breasts, he became excited and started to grope at her. He tried to kiss her breasts. Debbie screamed and pushed against him as hard as she could. Close by, a dog barked. A male voice was heard.

"What's going on here?" Tyrone looked up. An elderly black man with a German shepherd on a leash was standing 5 feet away looking down at them.

"I said, what's going on here?" The dog strained at its leash and growled at Tyrone, who pulled himself up and turned, almost knocking the man down as he ran down the street.

"Are you all right, miss? What can I do to help you?"

"Call the police, please, but take me with you. Please don't leave me here alone." Debbie was desperate.

The man helped Debbie to her feet. She clutched her coat shut to hide her nakedness. She had difficulty walking. As the pair started toward the man's apartment, a police cruiser approached. Within 10 minutes, Debbie was in the emergency ward at University Hospital for the second time in five months because of her relationship with Tyrone Williams. Once again, she was giving police officers a statement. What was different this time was that she knew who her assailant was and there was an independent witness, her rescuer, Wendell Jones.

Tyrone was arrested by an officer familiar with this situation, Jennifer Hill, who made it plain to him that he was going to jail for this incident. After being charged with assault and sexual imposition, both first-degree misdemeanors, Tyrone was released on a $2,000 bond with the judge's instruction that he was to stay away from Debbie. By now, Tyrone was completely out of control. He started calling Debbie and threatening "to cut up your fucking whore face." He also said he would cut her heart out "and shove it in your lying mouth." Finally, the telephone company placed recording equipment on Debbie's telephone at the request of Detective Safter. Tyrone made one too many threatening calls to Debbie. He was arrested for telephone harassment — also a first-degree misdemeanor. For violating the judge's order to have no contact with Debbie pending trial, his $2,000 bond was revoked and a new bail set at $100,000. Tyrone would now sit in jail, at least until the date of his trial.

On May 5, 1979, Tyrone was convicted of assault and telephone harassment. The sexual imposition charge was dismissed at Debbie's request because she did not want the further embarrassment that she would have to endure by describing what Tyrone did to her when he ripped her clothing open that night in April.

The judge was far too lenient with Tyrone. He sentenced him to six months in jail but then suspended all but 45 days, after which Tyrone would be on probation for two years with an order for drug and alcohol counseling and to continue to stay away from Debbie.

Both Officer Hill and Detective Safter were disappointed with the sentence. They believed that the judge had failed to recognize the seriousness of this relationship. They believed that Tyrone was capable of killing Debbie. They urged her to move to a different neighborhood. But she said she couldn't afford a move at the time. She agreed to have her telephone number changed to an unlisted number and once again to have all new locks installed at her apartment.

Debbie returned to classes at the nursing school and tried to resume her life. She was still terrified every time she saw any male who even slightly resembled Tyrone.

Around May 30, Memorial Day weekend, she met a young man at her Aunt Roberta's church picnic. His name was Damon Johnson. He was 22 and an engineering student at the University of Cincinnati. He was a co-op student, and at the time Debbie met him, he was on a six week work co-op with the Cincinnati Gas & Electric Company.

Debbie and Damon hit if off right away. She told him what had happened to her and how afraid she was of men. She explained that it would take some time for her to feel at ease with a man again. Damon took her hand and kissed it. He told her that he cared for her a lot and that he was "very patient."

Tyrone Williams was released from jail on June 19, 1979. He had also been very patient.

On June 22, Debbie returned to her apartment after finishing her long day of classes and work at the drugstore. It was 10:30 p.m. It had rained earlier, and there was a nice breeze. When she entered her apartment, she could feel fresh air moving around her. As she passed her bedroom door, she caught a glimpse out of the corner of her eye of a moving curtain in her bedroom window, the one by the fire escape. This startled her because she never left that window open. Suddenly, she feared entering the bedroom. She walked into the kitchen, switching on the ceiling light. She reached for the wall phone, but a hand clamped over her lower face and mouth. She felt the body of her assailant push her into the wall while the telephone receiver was yanked out of her hand.

"Hi, baby! Surprised to see me? You should have left town. I told you I'd be back."

"Tyrone, what are you dong? Are you crazy? How did you get in here? Why aren't you still in jail? What do I have to do to get you out of my life?"

Tyrone spun her around and forced her head back against the wall. He rubbed his index finger over her lips and smeared her mascara with his thumbs.

"You're mine, Debbie the Bitch. The problem is that you haven't learned yet that I'm the man. I'm the boss. All I did in jail was wait for tonight."

Tyrone reached past Debbie's head, ripped the telephone out of the wall, threw the phone on the floor, and then stomped on it.

He grabbed Debbie by the throat and twisted one of her arms up her back and shoved her into the bedroom. He threw her on her bed. He forced her mouth open and stuck a handkerchief in. She started to gag. He pulled a role of duct tape out of his jacket pocket and wrapped the sticky gray tape around her mouth, behind her neck, and back again several times. She could no longer scream. She couldn't even choke. She could feel herself passing out, but she fought to stay awake — to stay alive.

Tyrone had come prepared. He pulled a piece of clothes line out of his pants pocket, rolled Debbie over on her face and tied her arms and hands behind her back. She tried to struggle, but it was no use.

With his knee in her back, he grabbed her slacks with his fingers inside the waistband on each hip and ripped them open — pulling them down, along with her panties, to her ankles and then off of her feet. Her shoes came off with them. He then pulled each of her pink socks off her feet. She tried to kick him in the chest. Tyrone rolled her over and grabbed her legs behind the knees and pushed her knees almost to her face. He then leaned over her and punched her in the jaw, knocking her semi-unconscious.

He rolled her over on her stomach again and spread her feet apart, tying first her left and then her right foot to the corner posts of the foot-board on her bed.

Debbie tried to rise up. Tyrone shoved her head down against a pil-low and with his right forearm against her neck, he grabbed the collar of her white blouse and ripped it down her back, throwing each side off her torso. He then unsnapped her bra and grabbing the straps and the remnants of her blouse, ripped the clothing out from under her body. Debbie was stark naked and helpless.

She was only partially aware of what was happening to her. It was as if she were living a nightmare. She at first thought that she was falling off of the bed but became faintly aware that both she and the bed were moving. Tyrone was sliding the bed against the closed bedroom door. No one was coming in or leaving that room without moving that bed away from the door.

Tyrone turned the bedroom light off, and Debbie thought she saw him taking off his clothes. The next thing she felt was a cold wet towel as it was rubbed on the side of her face and neck and back and on down her legs.

"I want you awake, baby. I ain't going to rape you, but I'm going to butt fuck you good." Tyrone lay down on top of Debbie. In a matter of seconds, he had sodomized her. She passed out.

When Debbie opened her eyes, it seemed like an eternity had passed. She could hear heavy breathing next to her. She turned her head to the right. She stared into Tyrone's face. He was asleep next to her. Their faces were only inches apart. His mouth was open. She could smell the alcohol on his breath. Slowly, she moved an arm. Then it dawned on her that her hands and feet were not tied any longer. She slid slowly to her left, putting her left hand on the floor as she let herself silently down from the bed. It seemed like her body was on fire. Her lips were bruised. Her face was swollen and sore. Her neck hurt. Her bottom was wet and felt like someone had tried to shove a rake handle inside of her. She struggled to her feet. She looked around in the room. It was still dark. Then she remembered that the bed was shoved against the bedroom door. She could not escape this room. She started to cry. She put her hand over her mouth to quiet her sobs. "Please, dear God, don't let him wake up."

There was no phone in the bedroom. She could not possibly move the bed away from the door with Tyrone's weight on it. And even if she could, she could never do it without waking him. "Oh, God, how am I going to get out of this alive? Please help me."

As if a diabolic answer to her silent prayer, she thought of the shotgun on the top shelf of her closet. She had not seen it since the day Tyrone had brought it to her apartment and, at her request, put it on the top shelf of the closet, under a blanket. She wasn't even sure whether it was still there.

Debbie silently crawled to the closet. She reached up and turned the knob. Once the door was open so that it was between her and the bed, she stood up and on her tiptoes reached for the top shelf. She inched her hand under the blanket. She felt the wooden stock, which she slid out and down, next to her body. Then she felt for the barrel. She almost dropped it as she pulled it from beneath the blanket. She felt all around under the blanket for the piece of wood that Tyrone had showed her snapped beneath the barrel. She couldn't find it. She didn't know if the gun would work without it. After long seconds and beads of perspiration, she gave up trying to find the piece of wood. She groped around on the shelf until she felt the cardboard box that contained the shells. She pried the lid open with her right hand and wrapped her fingers around one of the fat, red Number 4, 12-gauge, maximum load shells.

Now she was sitting in her closet, on the floor, in the dark, trying to assemble a shotgun that she had only seen once before in her life. But somehow, she never understood how, she managed to slip the barrel into the notch on the receiver so that when she lifted up on the barrel it actually closed. The sound it made as it closed was loud enough that Tyrone stirred on the bed. Her heart stopped for a second. She quit breathing, but he didn't wake up. Then she slowly and silently pushed that little lever to the right and pushed the barrel down. The chamber swung open. She slid the shell into the chamber and slowly closed it so that this time it made no noise. She remembered that to make it shoot, she had to cock the hammer all the way back. She did this with her right thumb. "Click-click," the hammer sounded as it came back as far as she could pull it.

Slowly but deliberately, Debbie stood up in the closet. She stepped out barefoot on the carpet. Silently, carefully, she walked toward the bed where Tyrone still slept on his face. She then held the shotgun barrel out and touched him on the left shoulder with the muzzle. "Wake up, Tyrone. Get up and get out of my life forever," she sobbed.

He lifted his head and blinked. He stared, disbelieving, at the muzzle of the shotgun. Debbie backed up to the closet door, leveling the barrel at Tyrone.

"Tyrone, I want you to get up and pull the bed from the door. And then I want you and your clothes out of my apartment and my life. You are going back to jail for what you did to me tonight, so help me God."

Tyrone leaped from the bed and faced Debbie in the dark room.

"You fuckin' bitch. I'll kill you for pointing that gun at me. You can't fire it anyway."

Before he could move, Debbie pulled the trigger. The 12-gauge shell exploded. Number 4 shot tore into Tyrone's middle chest, throwing hunks of flesh and blood all over Debbie. Blood spurted from the 3-inch diameter wound, covering Tyrone's chest and abdomen and splattering on the shotgun and Debbie's hands and arms. The sound of the blast deafened Debbie and filled the room with acrid, sulfuric smoke. Tyrone slumped to his knees, staring at Debbie's stomach with sightless eyes. Then he pitched forward onto his face and lay on the carpet, eyes open and blood running from his mouth and nose.

Debbie collapsed on the floor. She sat, holding the gun across her knees, and sobbed. After what seemed like forever, she struggled to her feet and pulled a bathrobe off a hanger in the closet. She laid the shotgun on the bed and slowly, inches at a time, pulled the bed far enough from the door that she could open it and flee her apartment. She went to Virginia Carter's door and banged and hollered. It was 3:15 a.m. Mrs. Carter peaked through her door's peephole. Seeing that it was Debbie, she opened the door immediately.

"What is wrong, child?" she said.

"Call the police, Mrs. Carter. I just shot a man in my apartment. It's Tyrone. I think he might be dead."

Ironically, Jennifer Hill was the first police officer to arrive at 259 Cutter Street, Apartment Number 3. She was a quarter mile away when she heard the dispatcher say, "Shooting at 259 Cutter Street. All units in vicinity please respond." When Officer Hill heard that address on her radio, she knew immediately who was involved. She was mistaken though, because her first thought was, "He has finally killed Debbie Bohanon."

So, Officer Hill was happy to see Debbie sitting in a bathrobe in Mrs. Carter's living room.

"He's upstairs, Officer Hill," said Debbie. "I think I killed him. I'm so sorry, but he hurt me bad tonight."

After the coroner's office had removed Tyrone's body from the apartment, Jennifer Hill took Debbie back so that she could put on some clothes. Dressed in a pair of blue jeans, a University of Cincinnati sweat shirt and tennis shoes, Debbie was once again the subject of an examination at University Hospital. This time, she was subjected to a rape exam both vaginal and anal. The anal exam results were positive for male semen, same blood type as Tyrone, whose autopsy had started about the same time that Debbie's rape exam concluded. After the exam was completed, Debbie was placed under arrest for murder. She had been a guest of the county since that morning, exactly seven days, the longest week of her life.

"Is that all of it Debbie?" I asked her.

"Yes, sir. That's the entire story. All of it, even the details Mr. Mestemaker. I killed Tyrone, and now I am going to have to pay for it. I'm a murderer."

"That is where we disagree, Debbie. It is correct that you shot and killed Tyrone. Killing someone is not necessarily a murder. A murder is an unjustified killing. A killing may be justified, such as self-defense, a soldier in war, or a police officer being forced to kill a criminal. I believe that you were justified in killing Tyrone. He had attacked you. He had beaten you. He had threatened you. Finally, he broke into your apartment, held you captive and sodomized you. I can't accept that your actions deserve punishment for murder."

"But one detective told me that I could have crawled out of the window onto the fire escape while Tyrone was still asleep. He said that he thinks I shot Tyrone to punish him. I don't know. Maybe he is right. Maybe I deliberately shot him because I knew that he would never let me go until one of us was dead. Maybe I killed him to put an end to it once and for all. That would make me a murderer, wouldn't it?"

I turned off the tape recorder and looked Debbie in the eyes. "If you keep thinking like that, you may as well plead guilty to murder. This man terrorized you. He sodomized you. As you say, he would never have left you alone. Now you have a chance to live again, but only if you are willing to help me defend you. Are you willing to do that?"

She looked at her hands. She wiped her eyes. She grabbed my hand, "Please help me. I don't want to go to prison for the rest of my life."

"I'll do the best I can, Debbie. Start praying for both of us."

Carter and Julia Bohanon, Debbie's parents, arrived in Cincinnati from their home in Atlanta on June 30. I met with them and Debbie's Aunt Roberta in my office. Debbie's mother was an emotional wreck. Her father feared that his daughter might not receive a fair hearing because of her race. I did the best I could to convince all of them that race would not be a factor in this case. First of all, because Cincinnati had proven that a black defendant could and usually did receive the same justice as a Caucasian. And secondly, because the deceased was the same race as the defendant in this homicide.

On July 6, Judge Matthews set a new bail on Debbie, $20,000 at 10 percent. It took help from Debbie's parents to raise the $2,000 necessary to have Debbie released, but it was done and I was able to walk Debbie out of the county jail on July 7.

It had always been my experience that the longer a defendant had to sit in a jail cell before his or her trial date, a certain psychological shadow of gloom and defeat would take over the defendant's mental and emotional state. So that by the time of trial, some four to six months down the road, the accused looked and acted guilty of something, and was often therefore found guilty of something.

Debbie's boss at the drugstore cared a lot for her. Her job was waiting. Her landlady held her apartment. So at least she had the support of a family that cared for her, a boss and a landlady who believed in her innocence, and a lawyer who was ready to fight for her.

Something had to be done to snap Debbie out of the deep depression caused by her sense of guilt for Tyrone's death. She was so despondent that I feared that she would either insist on pleading guilty or appear so guilty during a trial that the outcome would be almost preordained. For this reason, I scheduled Debbie to be counseled by a very dedicated and competent clinical psychologist, Dr. Donald Hamilton. As it would turn out, he would become Debbie's cheerleader.

The trial of *State of Ohio vs. Deborah J. Bohanon* commenced before his Honor, Judge William R. Matthews, on Tuesday, November 12, 1979. The charge was murder. The sentence, if found guilty, would be not less that 20 years to life imprisonment.

Every relative and friend of Debbie Bohanon who could be there was in that courtroom. I was surprised to see that even Latasha Franklin, Tyrone's ex-ex girlfriend, showed up. She further surprised me when she patted Debbie on the back as we entered the courtroom.

Monday had been Veterans Day. Everyone around the Courthouse was cheerful. They had just enjoyed a welcomed three-day weekend. But it was November, and it was a cool fall day with a steady rainfall punctuated by thunder throughout the Ohio Valley as jury selection commenced.

It took a day and a half, but by 2:00 p.m. on Wednesday, the prosecutor and I had selected a jury of seven women and five men. Nine of the jurors were white, and three were African-American. None of them had indicated that they knew of Debbie or Tyrone or had read or heard about Tyrone's death. They all had asserted that their minds were open and that they would require the state to prove Debbie's guilt beyond a reasonable doubt. I believed that we had selected a good jury.

The prosecutor's opening statement was textbook. He named all of the witnesses he would call to convince the jurors that Debbie had shot and killed Tyrone Williams without justification — which, of course, would render her guilty of murder. He described their relationship as if Tyrone had been the pursued and Debbie had been the stalker.

It was a classic misstatement of the facts. Even a tabloid reporter couldn't have done better at twisting the facts to suit a particular purpose. Assistant Prosecuting Attorney Allen Nicholson was a master of half-truths.

The defense's opening statement caused mild surprise among the jurors. The jury was told up front that Debbie had, indeed, pulled the trigger of the gun that ended Tyrone's life, but that after they had heard all of the evidence, they would agree that Tyrone had left Debbie no choice except to kill him and that it had been almost the same as a suicide on his part.

In my opening statement I said: "After you have heard all of the evidence in this case, you will be convinced beyond a reasonable doubt that although Debbie did kill Tyrone, she did not murder him. You will be able to conclude that Tyrone, in fact, left Debbie no choice except to kill him. It boiled down to being Debbie's life or Tyrone's. One of them, tragically, had to die so that the other one could live."

The prosecutor called his usual array of witnesses. Tyrone's mother, Mary, identified the photograph of a young black man lying on a morgue table as that of her son. Several police officers involved in the case testified as to their observations at the scene of the shooting. The deputy coroner, Doctor Edward Nosler, detailed the autopsy procedure and explained to the jury that Tyrone had died as the result of a massive gunshot wound to the chest and upper abdomen. He bled to death.

The next two witnesses, although police officers, were obviously supportive of the defendant. First, Officer Jennifer Hill and then Detective Frank Safter related to the jury their contacts with Debbie and Tyrone leading up to the morning of Tyrone's death.

Prosecutor Allen Nicholson completed the state's case with the introduction of the shotgun and sundry other personal evidence relevant to the case. The state's presentation ended the third day of Debbie's trial. It was 4:30 p.m.

Day 4 opened with the defense offering testimony by Debbie's employer, Mark Backman, followed by her Aunt Roberta. The first witness who gave the jury any hint of what was forthcoming was Latasha Franklin; the former girlfriend of Tyrone, who had warned Debbie about him. Over objection of the prosecutor, Judge Matthews permitted her to testify that Tyrone had beaten her up on several occasions and that he had left her alone only after her brother had threatened to kill him if he bothered her again.

Virginia Carter, Debbie's landlady, and Wendell Jones, Debbie's rescuer that terrible night of April 3, when Tyrone brutalized her as she walked home, testified. I began to see expressions on the faces of several jurors that were encouraging. But you never know with a jury until the party is over.

My next witness was Debbie. We had gone over her testimony the afternoon before. She was as prepared as she would ever be. I kept my fingers crossed that she would be able to communicate all of the terrible experiences she had endured at Tyrone's hands, and she lived up to my expectations. She sobbed at certain times during her testimony, when appropriate. It was fairly apparent to everyone in the courtroom that the young lady had lived through a nightmare and that being forced to talk about it was causing her to relive it.

The last witness called by the defense on behalf of Debbie Bohanon was Doctor Donald Hamilton, the clinical psychologist. He certainly did not let Debbie or her counsel down. He told the jury that in his 14 years of practice, dealing with all forms of stress and mental illness, he had never treated anyone whom he believed felt more trapped than Debbie did by Tyrone. He likened Debbie's plight to that of Captain von Trapp of *Sound of Music* fame, who upon being pressed by the Nazis to join the German Navy prior to World War II, fled Austria with his entire family. In Debbie's case, Tyrone prevented her from fleeing by trapping her in her apartment like a crazed animal. And in doing this, Tyrone created the atmosphere that ultimately led to his own death — much the same as committing suicide. Doctor Hamilton testified that Debbie's sudden awareness that the dismantled shotgun was still in her closet next to a box of shotgun shells and her frenzied efforts to assemble and load the gun was further evidence of her terror and sense of helplessness.

In response to a question, Doctor Hamilton stated that Debbie's attempt to awaken Tyrone and make him leave even after she had loaded the shotgun was her last-ditch attempt to resolve the dilemma without further violence. When Tyrone leapt out of the bed and told Debbie he was going to kill her for pointing the gun at him, he had removed Debbie's last hope that she could avoid violence. So she pulled the trigger.

Dr. Hamilton concluded his testimony by assigning a name that he had coined for Debbie's condition. He told the jurors that at the time she shot Tyrone, she was suffering from "von Trapp syndrome." Today, 20 years down the road, I suspect that he would refer to the condition he observed as "battered woman syndrome."

The prosecutor's closing argument was exactly what I expected. He told the jurors that Debbie had pulled the trigger. That it was not self-defense since Tyrone had no weapon and she could have tried to leave the room. "He is dead. She murdered him. She must pay." End of argument.

My summation to the jury was direct. I told them that I believed that Debbie had in reality performed a public service by ridding the community of a predator.

"Ladies and gentlemen, what the deceased did to this young woman, my client, left her no alternative but to resort to violence. It was going to be either him or her. Tyrone chose the game. He set the rules. Someone was going to die. The only move that he miscalculated was who had the last move, and it wasn't him. I can assure you that had it been otherwise, Debbie would be the corpse in this case."

I paused and looked each juror in the eyes. "If you truly believe that Debbie Bohanon purposely and with malice shot and killed Tyrone Williams, then as the prosecutor said to you, it will be your duty to find her guilty of murder. However, if you believe, as I do, that she had no other choice — and you desire to do what is right, so that you can sleep soundly tonight, knowing that you have helped restore a life to this young woman — then your verdict must be, and should in the name of decency be, not guilty."

I sat down, feeling drained and thankful that I didn't have to rack my brain or fear a false move any longer in this case. My part of this chess game was nearing an end.

Out of concern for a possible adverse decision, I urged Judge Matthews to instruct the members of the jury that they could find Debbie guilty of the lessor included offense of voluntary manslaughter; that is, a homicide committed while the perpetrator was in the heat of rage or passion.

The judge believed that I might be making a mistake by requesting this instruction. He was of the opinion that I might be inviting the jury to compromise if they were in disagreement between guilty of murder and not guilty. He opined that this might be a signal to find Debbie guilty of manslaughter, where the possible sentence was much lighter than the mandatory sentence for murder. Nevertheless, being the great judge that he was, he acceded to my request. When the jury retired to deliberate, they had in their possession for consideration four verdict forms: guilty and not guilty of murder, and guilty and not guilty of manslaughter.

Five-and-half hours later, I sat next to Debbie with my right hand on top of her small, clenched, prayerful hands and heard the clerk, Gene Montesi, say out loud for a packed courtroom to hear:

"We, the jury, duly empanelled in this case, do find the defendant, Deborah Bohanon, not guilty of the crime of murder. And we do further find said Deborah Bohanon not guilty of manslaughter."

All hell broke loose in the courtroom. Some spectators applauded. There were even a few muffled cheers and more than a few tears. Judge Matthews quickly regained control of the situation. Debbie was hugging her dad, mom, aunt and me all at the same time. She was obviously exhausted and heartsick to be where she was, even though she had been found not guilty. I knew that it would be a long time, if ever, before Debbie would be free of her sense of responsibility for the death of Tyrone Williams.

I received Christmas cards from Debbie from Charleston, South Carolina, her new city of residence, for about five years. In 1984, I went to her wedding. She married Damon Johnson. The last time I heard from or about Debbie, she had two children, both boys. She was finally free of the "von Trapp syndrome."

Mike Mestemaker in the library of his law firm, Latimer & Swing Co., LPA. He was co-chair of CBA Judicial Selection Committee for the 1979 election. Photo: Cincinnati Bar Association Report, 1979.

PART TWO

THE BENCH – GOOD TIMES

CHAPTER 10

WHERE EVERY DAY IS LIKE A BOX OF CHOCOLATES

Even though I had practiced law before the Hamilton County Municipal Court for over 10 years prior to becoming a judge on March 16, 1981, I was not even close to being prepared for all that can happen in a courtroom on any given day, especially as it relates to the view from the bench.

In some respects, the Hamilton County Municipal Court operates in the same manner as police court in New York City or magistrate court in Chicago. The pace is fast. The types and varieties of cases are limitless. The cast of characters is boundless. A typical criminal and traffic docket, which commences every morning at 9 a.m. sharp, may include criminal trials, traffic trials, probation violation hearings, motions to mitigate sentences, suppress evidence, restore driving privileges, dismiss charges and expunge criminal records — just to mention the more common motions heard each day. Municipal court is a court of constantly changing gears. During any given day, a judge will hear a speeding ticket trial followed by a domestic violence case, followed by a driving under the influence of alcohol case, followed by a theft case, followed by a parking ticket case, and on and on. After the motions are heard, the pretrial conferences are held and the bench trials wrapped up the judge may then have a jury trial to start — hopefully early enough to that there can be a lunch break, but not very often. Quite often by the time any municipal court judge is able to sit down in chambers with a elasticized salad and a wax cup of ice tea, he or she has heard and decided 50 to 60 cases. That can add up to 300-plus each week. This is the reason why I am able to write that between March 16, 1981, and January 3, 1996, I heard and disposed of 26,789 civil, criminal and traffic cases.

In addition to the hundreds of cases each judge hears in his or her own courtroom, there are the two weeks out of every 14 when judges are assigned to special session in either: Room A, the felony criminal arraignment room; Room B, traffic and misdemeanor arraignments; or Room 263, for domestic violence, DUI, and driving under suspension arraignments. When assigned to any one of the special session rooms, there are extra chores to be handled — such as being the duty judge to take care of any and all emergencies, real or perceived; setting bail at night for individuals arrested after 4 p.m. and before 9 a.m.; and, finally, the most joyous duty of all, being hauled out of bed at 2 a.m. to sign a search warrant at the request of police officers, who, for some reason known only to them, would rather serve a search warrant in the nighttime than in daylight hours. I always suspected that there was an annual award for the police officer who had managed to get the most judges out of bed after midnight to sign search warrants.

What follows is the tale, all true, of those people and those situations that made Courtroom 4, Mestemaker, Judge, presiding like a box of chocolates — "you never know what you are going to get."

Fifi

Her Royal Highness, Princess Fifi Running Water Taft Rockefeller, was a woman of indeterminable age who can best be described as resembling a female version of a Norwegian bridge troll. Fifi, in her day, was a Courthouse regular. She would wander from courtroom to courtroom, paying her respects and offering legal advice to all who would listen. Fifi was a study in what was not in vogue in women's fashions. Normally, in warm weather, Fifi would appear in short-shorts or a mini skirt, sometimes worn over spandex workout knee-length tights, very dirty feet, toes stuck into leather thongs of what resembled North Vietnamese jungle sandals, usually a half unbuttoned smock revealing a somewhat misshapen and sagging bosom, a Volkswagen hood ornament hung around her neck by a chain made from a dog leash, binoculars, assorted candidate bumper stickers, topped off by either an orange or lavender wig held down by a construction helmet. Her sunglasses were the latest oversize style from Walgreen's.

Sometimes one lens would be missing, which she would compensate for by covering her eyelid and cheek with similar tinted mascara to fill in for the missing lens. Fifi's wardrobe culminated with her worn briefcase and pockets stuffed with legal forms and bus schedules.

My favorite caricature of Fifi was drawn for me in 1983 by Jeff Harvey, a deputy clerk with a flair for cartoon art. He portrayed our beloved Fifi campaigning for one of her favorite judges. This will always be how I remember Fifi.

The very first time that Her Royal Highness, Fifi, paid an unannounced visit to my courtroom was on May 13, 1981, about two months after I had become a judge. On that date, I was presiding over a jury trial in which the accused was charged with possession of more than 200 grams of marijuana. It also happened to be the day that a Turkish gunman attempted to assassinate Pope John Paul II in Saint Peter's Square in Rome.

Just as I was about to have the clerk swear the members of the jury in, and they were standing with their right hands raised, Fifi burst through the courtroom double doors and hollered as loud as she could:

"Heaven help us, Judge-Honey, some lunatic has shot and killed the pope!"

Several woman on the jury staggered as if they were about to faint. General pandemonium broke out in the courtroom. What made the situation all the more difficult to handle was Fifi's appearance. She was wearing the filthiest tan raincoat I had ever seen. She had galoshes on her feet. She was wearing a Morton Salt girl yellow rain hat and carrying the skeleton of an open umbrella devoid of fabric. Her orange hair was hanging in her eyes. In short, she looked like the Wild Woman of Borneo. It took about 15 minutes to restore order. Thank heaven, as it turned out, Fifi, as usual, had overstated the case. The pope, although seriously wounded, was still alive.

In 1982, Fifi brought me a small cactus plant that I kept on my bench until it finally died sometime around 1988. I believe that it may actually have drowned in one of our numerous courtroom flooding incidents. When Fifi gave me the cactus, she told me that if I spoke softly from the bench and never became frustrated or angry, the cactus would eventually produce a fragrant white blossom. I guess that I failed Fifi's test because the only thing that plant ever produced were small, sharp, finger-piercing needles.

Two days before Christmas in 1986, Fifi came to see me with a gift. She had a fruit basket covered with plastic that was so yellow no one could see through it. The bottom was dripping a gooey liquid that smelled like pickle juice. Before I could react, Fifi shoved the basket into my arms. While I was so handicapped, she grabbed me by my ears and pulled my face down and forward, enabling her to plant a big wet one right on my lips. I broke away and sped to the judge's restroom. I stayed there until Judge Mark Painter brought me mouthwash and Fifi had given up her vigil and left my courtroom. Bailiff Ron Flammer and I compounded this fiasco by opening the cellophane wrapper surrounding my gift — only to release a horde of fruit flies, which had been nesting in the brown bananas and shriveled grapes. We were quickly driven into the hall. The last living fruit fly disappeared from my chamber just after Easter 1987.

In 1989, I was campaigning for my third term as a judge. I had seen Fifi quite often that spring and summer. I was well aware that she was campaigning for me. I was also beginning to think that she was stalking me. For on October 10, 1989, while I was presiding over a jury trial involving a charge of vehicular homicide, Fifi suddenly appeared in the courtroom as if dropped from the ceiling on a wire like Peter Pan. Before Ron, my bailiff, could stop her, she had reached the side of the bench and tossed the dirtiest $5 bill imaginable up and over the rail. It landed in the center of my legal pad. As I tried to advise Fifi that we were in the middle of a jury trial, she exclaimed:

"It ain't much, honey, but it will buy a couple of them handouts with your picture, and there is more where that come from."

As quickly as she had appeared, Fifi beat a path out of the courtroom — shouting at the jury as she left:

"Be sure and vote for 'Honeymaker.' He ain't a kid, but he's still cute."

Just before our court moved from the Alms & Doepke Building into new quarters in the neighboring Courthouse, Fifi borrowed a plant drip pan from my chambers to give water to a dog that some uncaring soul had tied to a parking meter post outside on Central Parkway. It was extremely hot, and the poor animal was nearly dehydrated. Fifi had passed the dog as she was entering the building. Knowing that I had a potted plant in my chambers equipped with an overflow water pan, Fifi came in through the back door, removed the pan from under the plant, filled it with water from the water fountain and took care of the thirsty dog. Had all of this not been observed by Larry Welage, Judge Joe Luebbers' bailiff, I would never have figured out how the overflow pan for my plant came to be on the sidewalk in front of the Alms & Doepke Building.

Fifi has now gone on to that courtroom in the sky, and she is missed. Another era has run its course, and the Courthouse is poorer because of her absence.

Plaster and water

There were times that service as a municipal court judge seemed a lot like aquatic duty at Sea World. Between cascading water and falling plaster, we managed to conduct court, make the national and international news, and maintain some semblance of sanity.

1985 was a banner year. On April 25, I was taken to Christ Hospital from my courtroom by the Cincinnati Fire Division's paramedics, who suspected that I had suffered a heart attack. What had actually occurred was a severe attack of gastroesophageal reflux disease. My esophagus had swelled up in the area of my heart causing lateral pressure against the heart muscle and thus symptoms of a heart attack. Treatment for this problem caused me to absent from courtroom duty until May 10, 1985.

I was very happy to be back to work. Gabe Mulligan, a retired narcotics detective for the Cincinnati Police Division, was assigned to my courtroom at this time as a criminal bailiff. Gabe was one hell of a guy and a longtime friend. When Gabe, who was distinguished by luxurious silver-gray hair, was a narcotics detective, he was fondly known around the University of Cincinnati's main campus as "Gay Muggins."

On the morning of May 20, 1985, before court convened, Gabe was sitting in my chambers, having just returned from a trip to Seattle, Washington. He wanted to hear about my illness, and I wanted to hear about his trip. As I sat at my desk with a cup of coffee, Bailiff Ron Flammer was standing near the desk leaning against a window sill, and Gabe was sitting in a chair next to a file cabinet. Suddenly there was a low rumble directly above our heads. I looked up to see the false ceiling begin to sag toward me, and I jumped up just as the entire ceiling — acoustic panels, plaster, plaster lath and 100 years of dirt and soot — collapsed. Ron managed to get out of the room just as the ceiling let go. I was hit in the head by a piece of plaster but managed to leap into the window well in time to avoid the mother lode. Poor Gabe was trapped. He had just started to get out of the chair when a piece of plaster about the size of a card table hit him across the top of his knees in the same manner that the blade of a guillotine would fall on an unsuspecting neck. As the dirt and dust began to settle to the floor, it was obvious that Gabe was in a bad way. He could not move his left leg at all, and was unable to stand up. Within 10 minutes, Gabe was being carried out of my chambers, ironically, by the same crew of paramedics who had carried me out the door 25 days earlier. As it turned out, Gabe had suffered a severe injury to his left knee, involving torn cartilage. He underwent surgery the next day and was absent from work for over a month, thanks to old plaster, heavy sprinkler pipes and an acoustic ceiling that had hung from the pipes.

It was determined by the fire department investigators and building division inspectors that when the sprinkler system had been installed, the steel pipes were hung from long steel hangers drilled into the original plaster ceiling. To compound the problem, when the acoustic ceiling was installed at a much later date, the supports for the drop ceiling were wired to the sprinkler pipes. As a result, the weight of the acoustic ceiling and the sprinkler pipes became too much for the 100-year-old plaster to handle, and it finally came crashing down. Something had to give, and it did around 8:50 a.m. on the morning of May 20, 1985. Had it let go at night or over a weekend, no one would have been buried in plaster and dust and Gabe would not have been injured. But that would just not do for Courtroom No. 4. If the ceiling was going to cave in there, it would have to happen when the room was occupied by our crew.

The sprinkler system in Courtroom 4 in the Alms & Doepke Building would take revenge on us one more time before we moved to the Courthouse in February 1990. On October 16, 1988, around 11:45 a.m., I was presiding over a bench trial in which a very attractive and well-endowed young woman was accused of engaging in prostitution. The defendant, who was really quite stunning — which is extremely rare in these types of cases — had been arrested when she propositioned a police officer who was masquerading as a potential customer for the young woman's charms. Just as the undercover police officer was testifying as to what services the defendant was willing to perform for the sum of $50, and as if by some prearranged signal, the sprinkler system in our courtroom let go with a torrent of fine spray and enough volume to cool down and dissipate any heat that may have been related to the torrid testimony then being recited into the record. It happened with such precise timing that it was as if the gods had determined that Courtroom No. 4 needed to be cooled down, and in a hurry.

One wet judge, one very soaked court reporter, several attorneys, police officers and the defendant, who at this point appeared ready to enter a wet T-shirt contest, headed for the corridor to dry off. The trial was eventually resumed in a drier courtroom. A maintenance engineer who was inspecting the fire sprinkling system had accidentally broken a seal on a cut-off valve, unleashing the flood that cooled off the courtroom for days and days to come.

More water

The best water story of all involved a Hamilton County Justice Center prisoner named Ricky Malone and a Styrofoam coffee cup jammed into the toilet of the cell in which Malone was being held, which turned out to be directly above Courtroom A, the felony criminal arraignment room on the first floor of the Justice Center, which consists of two five-story buildings designed to house up to 1,200 prisoners, administrative offices, the clerk of court facilities and Courtrooms A and B. As of the date that I encountered Ricky Malone, Courtroom A had been located in this brand-new facility for only 10 months. This complex was so new that the paint still smelled fresh. It also happened to be one year to the day since the life squad had removed me from Courtroom 4 and delivered me to Christ Hospital. It was April 25, 1986.

As the felony lockup docket was being called by an assistant prosecutor for the city of Cincinnati and I was listening to lawyers seeking to represent their respective clients, I began to notice that every three or so seconds a fresh drop of water was appearing on the numerous judicial documents, criminal pleadings and records spread on the bench before me. As the minutes ticked off the clock, the water drops began to fall with more frequency, and they were growing larger. Within several more minutes, what had been a single line of water drops had become a dozen or more lines, beginning to appear as if a curtain of water was developing. While attempting to move my wheeled desk chair and numerous papers from the unwanted shower, I glanced toward the ceiling and observed that the water was flowing from a seam between two ceiling panels directly above the judge's bench. By this time, everyone in the courtroom could see what the judge was watching and could also observe water drops ricocheting off my head and nose. I asked one of the courtroom security officers what was located directly above Room A. He told me that there were jail cells directly above Room A on the second floor, and that the water had to be coming from the cell area. Perhaps it was a broken pipe we thought. Boy, how wrong we were!

As the sheriff's office personnel scampered out of the courtroom to try to find the source of our unwelcome water, the bailiff obtained an umbrella, which he opened and held over my head as we continued to call criminal cases and the indoor rain continued to descend on us. Charles "Chick" Poppe, a veteran news video photographer for WCPO-TV, was in Courtroom A to cover a murder arraignment when the unexpected weather front moved in. Chick couldn't contain himself as he struggled to get his shoulder camera in operation to film Judge Mestemaker holding court beneath an umbrella being held over his head by Bailiff Ron Flammer. Considering that some media types believed Judge Mestemaker to be all wet anyway, the irony of the scene was not wasted on Chick. He was having a ball.

Soon, but not soon enough, the sheriff himself, Lincoln Stokes, came into Room A to advise me that a prisoner named Ricky Malone, who was housed in a jail cell directly above Courtroom A, had stuffed a Styrofoam coffee cup into the neck of the toilet. Once the cup was securely in place, forming a stopper, he had started flushing the toilet over and over until the backed up water covered not only his cell but the neighboring cells and most of an entire cell block with upwards of an inch of standing water. Quite naturally, this overflow from the toilet made its way through vents, cracks and crevices and down until it located the seam in the ceiling of Room A, which had to be directly above the bench, where else? Chief Deputy Sheriff Victor Carelli advised me that as soon as his deputies could get into Malone's cell and subdue him, they would remove the Styrofoam cup from the toilet. This would solve the flooding problem. As soon as the floor upstairs could be vacuumed of overflow water, I told Carelli that if Malone had not already drowned, that I wanted him delivered to Room A for a summary contempt of court hearing.

While we waited for the water to stop coming though the ceiling and for Malone to arrive, I sent for lawyer Eugene Smith, the chief assistant public defender, to represent Malone in the planned contempt hearing. As soon as Smith arrived in the courtroom, I advised him of the task I was assigning to him to handle, noting that as soon as Malone was delivered to the courtroom, I would give Smith whatever time that he required to talk to Malone and decide how he wanted to handle a contempt of court hearing.

We did not have long to wait. As I concluded my discussion with Gene Smith, six sheriff's deputies entered the courtroom in the form of a wedge, escorting a diminutive, angry man who looked around the room as if to say, "What in the hell am I doing here?"

When Malone's gaze finally settled on me, I pointed to the still dripping ceiling directly above me and held up several very soggy sheets of paper for him to see. As if struck by lightening, his heretofore puzzled appearance became a crystal-clear image of understanding. He knew what had taken place, and he also knew why he had been hauled into Room A.

As it turned out, Ricky Malone, who at the time was 33 years old, had accumulated quite a criminal record and quite a reputation while housed in the Hamilton County jail.

On January 24, 1986, he had been arrested for aggravated robbery and felonious assault with a pistol after holding up Lockett's Market at Pulte and Beekman streets in Cincinnati. On April 15, 1986, while waiting trial on the felony charges, he had to be taken to the University of Cincinnati Medical Center after he was found dangling from his cell door with a bed sheet tied around his neck. On Monday, April 21, 1986, after Common Pleas Court Judge Ralph Winkler sentenced him to serve 18 to 25 years, Malone kicked the plate glass out of a courtroom door. Finally, on April 24, he was transferred to a cell on the second floor of the new Justice Center from a cell that he had occupied on the sixth floor of the Courthouse since his arrest in January. As it turned out, Malone was upset about his transfer from the old holding facility to the new one because he had grown to enjoy the company of his cellmate in the old jail. Malone believed that the most effective manner of voicing his displeasure was to flood his cell by stuffing a coffee cup in his toilet. He got his point across and 60 days for contempt of court to boot, which actually meant nothing to him since it would be served with the 18 to 25 years imposed upon him by Judge Winkler.

After both *The Cincinnati Post* and *The Cincinnati Enquirer* ran the clogged-up toilet story, which was, in turn, picked up by United Press International, *The New York Times* carried the story on April 27. I knew that we had gone global when Denise Kelley, an investigator for the Hamilton County Department of Human Services, sent me a clipping from the *Cape Times*, a publication in Capetown, South Africa, which she had read while in that country on April 28. With the article was a note from Denise:

"It's certainly a small, small world after all."

A chain reaction

CINCINNATI, Ohio. — Flushed with anger, a judge convicted a prisoner of contempt by abusing the plumbing in his cell and dousing his honour with toilet water.

Ricky Malone, who was unhappy with his cell in the Hamilton County Justice Centre, faces an additional 60-day stay for pouring his frustrations on to the head of Municipal Judge Albert Mestemaker.

Malone, 33, plugged the toilet in his second-floor cell with a plastic cup on Friday and began flushing.

The overflow from repeated flushing made its way down through the vents and crevices to the floor below, where Judge Mestemaker was holding court.

Soon the judge was forced to dodge water splattering all over the bench. A bailiff held an umbrella over the judge before he finally called a recess.

Malone was brought in shackles to the damp courtroom where the judge charged him with contempt of court after hearing testimony from a guard about the stopped toilet. — UPI

Public restroom

Best: At the Public Library downtown, always clean and with toilet paper.

Worst: At the Justice Center, downtown. A prisoner, to protest his treatment, plugged up the toilets with Styrofoam cups, resulting in a steady flow of effluvium into Mike Mestemaker's courtroom beneath. Some would say justice was done.

Judge Mestemaker conducted court with a protective umbrella raised indoors on April 24, 1986, and the local and international media took note. "A chain reaction," appeared in Capetown, South Africa's Cape Times, *April 28, 1986. "Public restroom,"* Cincinnati Magazine, *November 1986.*

New chambers and more water

In February 1990, the 14 judges of the Hamilton County Municipal Court moved to newly constructed courtrooms located on the first and second floors of the Hamilton County Courthouse. It was like dying and going to heaven. We had new benches, chairs, carpet, tables and witness boxes. We had jury boxes where the second row was a step higher than the first row, as it should be. We had new sound systems — and microphones that actually worked. We had newly papered and painted walls, new lighting and, finally, an attractive gray carpet with the seal of the State of Ohio in the center. We had connected courtroom chambers with new desks and file cabinets. We had genuine vinyl wall paper in these offices, and thick padded carpet.

I had as much fun hanging pictures and diplomas in my new chambers as I had decorating our first wooden clubhouse with World War II pinup posters. Then came the morning of Wednesday, March 14, 1990. Another great flood had arrived.

I knew that something was terribly wrong on the 14th of March when I turned the corner on the second floor of the Courthouse around 8:20 a.m., only to see the bucket brigade in action near the hall door to my brand-new chambers. Overnight some moron, whose identity shall forever remain unknown in the dark recesses of the Hamilton County Courthouse, had left open a window in a fourth-floor, air conditioning compressor room. The temperature that night dipped down to about 15 degrees above zero. A water pipe to an air conditioning unit froze and burst. Down it came — first to the third floor, where it wrecked the chambers of Common Pleas Court Judge Thomas Crush. His office was so wet he even had water standing in his center desk drawer. From Crush's chambers, the water continued its natural downward course to the second floor, specifically, the brand-new chambers for Courtroom 280 — covering the walls, ceiling, the new carpet, furniture and pictures that had just been hung four weeks earlier. Damn, that chamber was gorgeous — if only for one month. Yes, they came in and cleaned everything. They put in a new ceiling. Replaced the wallpaper. They even put in new carpet. But, for some reason, it was never the same again. The place always had a mildew odor about it. Finally, in 1993, when I had a chance to move down the hall to the larger Room 264, I jumped on the bandwagon. Bailiff Ron Flammer and I personally pushed the furniture and books down the hall to the new room. We weren't about to wait for a maintenance crew to help us move to a dryer climate.

Thwarted escapes

Something that few people are aware of are courtroom escapes. But they do happen. Over the years, I have had at least a half-dozen individuals escape or at least attempt to escape — usually as they were being sentenced to jail or being arraigned in Room A on serious felony charges. One day in Room A, a young man whose hair was fashioned in dreadlocks started screaming at me that he was Jesus Christ and that I had no jurisdiction over him. With that, he turned and literally ran over one courtroom security officer as he tried to flee down the aisle toward the main doors to the courtroom. He had certainly chosen the wrong avenue for his escape route because he ran smack into five Cincinnati police officers who had just entered the courtroom. One of the officers was Douglas Mondrell, who is built like The Incredible Hulk. The escapee literally bounced off of Doug's chest and crashed to the floor. I swear that the handcuffs were on his wrists before he landed.

Another attempted escape occurred in my own courtroom, when I was sentencing a male defendant to six months in jail for assaulting a police officer. I could see this one coming because as I passed sentence his eyes started to flit from left to right and then back again. He was obviously getting his bearing in relation to the side courtroom door and where the guards were. As soon as I said how many days his sentence would be, he was off like a flash. He hit the side corridor courtroom door with his hands and shoulder as hard as he could. The problem was that this steel-and-glass door did not open out — it opened in. As he bounced off the door back into the courtroom, he fell into the waiting arms of Criminal Bailiff Cliff Bell. He did not escape from Cliff's bear hug.

On April 19, 1994, I had a young Jamaican man named Boniface Okoli in front of me. He spoke pigeon English, which in Jamaica is a combination of English, Portuguese and Spanish. Most of his sentences started with the word "mon" and end with "you know." Boniface had defrauded his landlord out of a washer and a clothes dryer. I didn't really want to put Boniface in jail, because his former landlord was primarily interested in recovering the $490 value of the two appliances. Initially, after his conviction, I continued Boniface's sentence for 90 days so that he could raise the amount needed for restitution. When he appeared in front of me 90 days later, he didn't have the money despite the fact that he was gainfully employed. I gave him one more 30-day extension but told him that if he didn't have all of the man's money, the next time he had better be prepared to go to the Hamilton County Justice Center.

Perhaps Boniface didn't take me seriously. Or maybe he believed that I would give him another extension. Nevertheless, when he appeared on April 19 and again told me that he had no money, not even a dime of the $490, I said, "Well, Boniface, you are just going to have to sit in jail until you come up with it." Boniface looked me straight in the eyes and said, "Mon, I no go to thee jail, I go to Jamaica." And he was off. Boniface was a 5-foot, 9-inch, slender sheath of muscle and speed. He jumped a chair and headed for the side prisoner door. A black man who was an amputee was sitting in a prisoner chair next to the door. When Boniface side-swiped the chair that this man was seated in, he was sent sprawling on the floor. The collision with the disabled prisoner slowed Boniface down just enough that Cliff Bell was able to grab him from behind. Cliff weighs well over 200 pounds and is a strong man. Nevertheless, Boniface was shoving Cliff backward. At that juncture, my room clerk, Jeff Garner, jumped to his feet and stuck his shoulder in Boniface Okoli's midsection. Jeff, who played football in high school, is a strong young man with a gentle nature. But no one was going to escape in Jeff's presence, especially if he was going to drag Cliff with him. Jeff's powerful shoulder action literally lifted both Boniface Okoli and Cliff Bell off the courtroom floor and forced both of them back against the stand that held the blackboard. As Garner had Okoli and Bell pinned against the blackboard and into the wall, Ron Flammer arrived from the other side of the courtroom and yanked Boniface's legs out from under him. Once on his back on the floor, Okoli was subdued and handcuffed. This felony escape attempt cost Boniface Okoli an additional six months in jail, imposed upon him by Common Pleas Court Judge William A. Morrissey. Cliff had several cuts on his cheek and numerous scratches. Jeff suffered some shoulder discomfort, and Ron, well, the old former professional boxer, Ron Flammer, got his hair messed up. Clerk of Courts Jim Cissel would recognize Cliff and Jeff for bravery and quick thinking. Jeff, in fact, was a pure volunteer since there is not one word in a room clerk's job description that requires or even suggests that part of a courtroom clerk's job duties include apprehending escaping prisoners.

There are times when I still wake up in the middle of the night, listening for the sound of running water, falling plaster, escaping prisoners and Fifi. Withdrawal from the judicial service can take awhile. At least I did not have to deal with "Agent Orange!"

Mike Mestemaker was appointed to the bench in 1981 and immediately began to campaign for election in November 1981. He played catcher in the Don Simpson Scholarship baseball game at Delhi Township Park. Mestemaker had been a pitcher while a student at St. Xavier High School.

Political campaigns are a family affair. Mike's brother, Jerry, came from his home in Florida for a fall campaign event at Flanagan's Landing in 1981.

Princess Fifi Running Water-Taft-Rockefeller was a regular visitor in municipal court and an avid fan of Judge Honeymaker, as she called Mestemaker.

CHAPTER 11

POSITIVE PUNISHMENT

One of the more enjoyable aspects of being a Municipal Court judge for 14 years and 10 months was the relative freedom that such judges had when imposing sentence upon a person convicted of either a misdemeanor crime or traffic offense. A misdemeanor is any crime or traffic offense that carries a maximum possible jail sentence of one year or a fine that does not exceed $1,000 — except in the case of repeat DUI offenders, who may be fined up to $10,000 and lose their driving privileges for life.

Most judges pursue basically the same policy with regard to sentencing, which normally means that a person who is convicted of a crime involving violence against another person can expect to spend some time in jail. In my courtroom, anyone convicted of assaulting a law enforcement officer could generally plan on spending the maximum time of six months in jail unless the police officer who had been assaulted indicated a desire that the convicted person be given less then the maximum sentence.

As is the case with most judges, I have always viewed unmitigated violence as inexcusable conduct — justifying the imposition of a jail sentence as appropriate punishment.

Ironically, the media created an image of me as being soft on men who battered women, which played a large part in my last six months' service as a judge but which was not a true picture of where I stood on the whole issue of domestic violence. Even as I served my last day as a judge — on January 3, 1996 — I had more men who were true abusers of their spouses in jail serving maximum sentences than any other municipal court judge in Hamilton County, Ohio.

The same general policy of jail time was applied to individuals who were habitual DUI offenders or who continued to operate motor vehicles while under suspension of their driver's license (and quite often without so much as a dime's worth of liability insurance). Most judges believe that any individual who is so chemically dependent or who has so little regard for the safety of others that he will continually endanger his fellow man by driving under the influence of drugs or alcohol (or who continues to operate a motor vehicle without any liability insurance, which will compensate another for injuries caused by the offender in an accident) is deserving of as harsh a sentence, fine and suspension of driving privileges as can be imposed by law.

It is always stressful when the judge takes into consideration the hardship that an offender's family will experience as the result of the offender receiving a jail sentence. However, the court must weigh the various factors of each case to determine whether failure to impose a jail sentence will send the wrong message or be a harsher blow to the victim or to society than will be the impact of a jail sentence on the offender and the offender's family.

Once beyond the realm of crimes of violence, there are numerous alternatives available to a trial court judge — such as electronic monitoring of an offender's movements and location, commonly referred to as home incarceration. This is really a misnomer since many offenders who are in this program and who are required to wear an electronic bracelet are permitted to leave their home to go to work or to attend court-ordered counseling sessions, to shop for groceries, to keep necessary appointments, and to go to church services. The main thrust of this form of punishment is the protection of society from further criminal conduct by the offender and the psychological discomfort imposed on the offender. Even though not actually incarcerated in a county jail, the offender is still constantly aware of the limitation of freedom brought about by the restrictions imposed as part of electronic monitoring. In many cases, it is sufficient that an offender be required to serve a sentence at home with the realization that 24 hours each day his or her whereabouts and activities are under scrutiny by a computer, a bracelet and a telephone. Besides, there is the additional benefit of the savings to the community of a significant amount of money when the offender is not eating and sleeping in the tax-supported jailhouse. The average cost of housing a prisoner is $60 to $65 a day, while the average cost of electronic monitoring is $10 a day for — which a gainfully employed offender can be required to reimburse the county. In this latter instance, the offender actually ends up paying for the cost of incarceration, a double punishment for the offender and a double savings for the taxpayer. And it works quite well in those cases where it is employed.

Every offender in the electronic monitoring program is educated to understand that one violation of the rules means serving the original sentence in jail. Few offenders who are in the home incarceration or electronic monitoring program are willing to blow a good deal and end up back in the county jail. This occurs in only 14 percent of the cases where this form of punishment is employed. And it has pretty well been shown that the 14 percent who do violate the rules should have been put in jail in the first place.

Finally, there is a third category of miscreants who commit offenses. These offer the judge who hears the case the opportunity to be creative in the form of punishment. This category is the real thrust of this chapter. So permit me, if you will, to share several of these cases with you — in the area that I have designated as "positive sentencing."

The blue spruce tree

On December 14, 1981, Steven Kurtz, who was then 25 years old, was strolling in Mount Airy Forest with his fiancèe. One of the many matters that they discussed that Sunday afternoon was what kind of Christmas tree would be nice to put up in her apartment. While this subject was still fresh in their minds, they came to a clearing near the lot where Steve had parked his car — and what should appear, as if by magic, but a beautiful, mature, 60-foot Colorado blue spruce tree, growing within 15 feet of the parking lot. Steve's fiancèe made the remark that this tree would be a most beautiful Christmas tree if only it would fit inside someone's apartment.

At this point, it occurred to Steve that while the whole blue spruce might not be suitable as a Christmas tree, at least the top might. So, much the same as the Grinch who stole Christmas, Steve contrived to obtain the top of this tree as evidence of his undying love for his sweetheart.

After dark on December 14, Steve returned to the park with a friend, an ax, a saw and a 50-foot coil of rope. Within 10 minutes, this duo had managed to climb the victim's branches and cut the top 20 feet off of the 40-year-old blue spruce. As the two men dragged it to Steve's car and tied it to the top, they discussed how much of the trunk would have to be cut in order to get the very top part into a tree stand and inside the intended apartment.

With the tree securely tied to the roof, Steve began to drive out of Mount Airy Forest, never giving a thought to the death warrant he had signed for the valuable and beautiful Colorado blue spruce that was now only part of what it had been.

Just as Steve and his companion were about to exit Mount Airy Forest onto Colerain Avenue, they were spotted by a Cincinnati police officer, who thought it odd that someone would be exiting the park after closing time with a large tree top strapped to the roof of an automobile. Needless to say, Steve was stopped by this officer, whose subsequent investigation disclosed the theft of the top of the blue spruce and the death sentence imposed on the bottom part. For as a horticulturist would later testify, the remainder of the tree would die within the next year. As a result, the Cincinnati Park Board instructed the maintenance department to cut down what was left. Result, scratch one valuable and beautiful blue spruce tree.

Next scene: January 7, 1982, City of Cincinnati vs. Steven Kurtz. Charge: Criminal damaging, a second-degree misdemeanor punishable by a jail sentence of up to 90 days and a fine of up to $750, plus court costs, assigned to Room 4, Judge Mestemaker presiding.

By this time Steven Kurtz had consulted with an attorney and been informed that he had little or no chance of being found not guilty if he went to trial. So, he decided to enter a plea of no contest, which in criminal procedure is an admission of the facts set forth in the criminal complaint.

After I heard the facts, including the information that the bottom 40 feet of the blue spruce had to be cut down, I gave the accused an opportunity to be heard. He expressed his sorrow for having been so stupid and for causing the destruction of a valuable tree in a public park. Kurtz's attorney suggested to me that instead of placing his client, who was gainfully employed, in a jail cell — which would probably cause him to become unemployed and unable to pay any restitution — that I provide "innovative sentencing" in this case. I was already way ahead of Kurtz and his lawyer.

While listening to the facts of the case read in open court by the prosecuting attorney, I had been doing some math on a legal pad. Such as, What is the estimated value of a 60-foot tall Colorado blue spruce at, say, $50 per foot — perhaps as much as $3,000. But the maximum fine that I could impose in this type of case was a mere fraction of the value of the tree that was lost. How about the age factor? How long does it take a Colorado blue spruce to grow to be 60 feet tall? At a foot per year, is it 60 years? Or is it 2 feet per year for 30 years? Can a 60-foot tree be purchased from a place that sells trees? What do I do here? What is fair to everyone involved?

"All right, is there anything further from counsel for the city or for the defendant before the court imposes sentence in this case? No, then it is the sentence of the court that Mr. Kurtz be confined in the Workhouse for 90 days and that he pay a fine of $750 plus the cost of the action. Or, if he chooses to cooperate, I will suspend the 90 days in jail and will forgive the entire fine of $750 — on the condition that by June 30, 1982, Mr. Kurtz cause to be delivered to Mount Airy Forest 10 living Colorado blue spruce trees, each being at least 6 feet tall, for planting in Mount Airy Forest at places to be selected by the park's officials."

As was my custom, I gave the defendant the choice. He could sit in jail and be nonproductive, or he could remain free and do something positive. Mr. Kurtz had gained in smarts by this point in his life, and he chose the positive sentence.

This sentence appeared to some reporter to be so unusual that *The Cincinnati Enquirer* wrote about the case on January 8, 1982. The tree sentence was such a novelty that the story ended up on The Associated Press wire and appeared in newspapers around the country. Another article, taken from the wire, appeared in the *Cleveland Plain Dealer* on the same day.

Man Ordered To Plant Trees

A Mount Airy man charged with chopping a 20-foot section from a tree in Mount Airy Forest was convicted Wednesday and ordered to plant 10 more trees in the park.

Steven Kurtz, 25, 5303 Eastknoll Ct., Mount Airy, pleaded no contest to a charge of criminal damaging before Judge Albert J. Mestemaker in Hamilton County Municipal Court.

Kurtz was accused of cutting his own Christmas tree from a Colorado blue spruce at the park on Dec. 14.

Mestemaker ordered Kurtz to plant the new trees—at least 6 feet tall—before June 30. All are to be Colorado blue spruce.

Mestemaker gave Kurtz a $750 fine and a 90-day term in the Cincinnati Correctional Institution, but suspended that sentence and ordered Kurtz to plant the trees and serve a year on probation.

Kurtz's attorney had asked that Mestemaker provide "innovative sentencing" because of the nature of the offense.

"Oh, it'll be innovative all right," Mestemaker replied. "The cost of a 20-foot Colorado blue spruce is more than a new Toyota, you know."

Judge Mestemaker was widely recognized for his innovative sentences. "Man Ordered to Plant Trees," appeared in the Cincinnati Enquirer, *January 8, 1982.*

Don't flick your Bic in Cincinnati

I have never really understood why patrons at rock concerts fire up their cigarette lighters. But according to one police officer, flicking cigarette lighters at rock concerts supposedly encourages the entertaining groups to perform encores.

Cincinnati had already had one rock concert tragedy in 1979, when 11 young concert-goers were crushed to death at a "Who" concert held at the Riverfront Coliseum. Now, in February 1983, I was faced with what to do with five rock concert-goers who had been arrested for flicking their cigarette lighters at two different concerts that had been held in January at the Cincinnati Gardens.

The five defendants who appeared before me on February 2, 1983, could not claim that they were unaware of the prohibition against open flames at the Cincinnati Gardens — since before and during each rock concert an announcement was made over the public address system that anyone violating the ordinance during the concert would be arrested and prosecuted. Perhaps the five defendants who appeared before me had not believed the warning. Perhaps they were so pumped up by the performance they were enjoying that they forgot themselves. Nevertheless, everyone involved believed that their behavior was serious enough to cite them for violation of Cincinnati's anti-smoking or open flame at public events ordinance, a first-degree misdemeanor for which each person convicted could receive six months in jail and a $1,000 fine.

The officers and fire officials explained in court that the five defendants had been warned several times to cease flicking their lighters. In addition Captain Richard Zumwalde of the Cincinnati Fire Division explained that such open flames at concerts are particularly dangerous due to the close proximity of the spectators to each other and the likelihood of a person's clothing or hair being set ablaze by an open flame.

After each of the five defendants had entered no contest pleas and their attorneys had spoken on their behalf, I imposed 30-day jail sentences and $1,000 fines on each of them — and then gave them the option of avoiding jail and $950 of the fine if each would take a conducted tour of the Shriners Burns Institute in Cincinnati and contribute $250 each to that hospital to be used for burn injury research.

Each of the five-concert goers accepted my alternative choice of sentencing and contributed $250 to the hospital. And each of them was given a personal tour of the facility, where they observed the horrible scars caused by burn injuries. I doubt that any one of them will ever flick their Bic again at any rock concert.

On February 3, 1983, *The Cincinnati Post* captured the spirit of the case and the excellent law enforcement work of Barry Andrews and Richard Zumwalde in its article by Barbara Morgenstern:

"The concert ritual of flicking one's cigarette lighter apparently has Judge Albert J. Mestemaker hot under the collar, based on 30-day jail sentences he gave five concert-goes this week," she wrote. "In addition to serving the Workhouse terms, the Hamilton County Municipal Court judge also told the defendants to pay $1,000 fines and $25 in court costs. However, Mestemaker said he would suspend the jail terms if the defendants contributed $250 each to the Shriners Burns Institute.

Officer R.B. Andrews of Cincinnati Private Police cited several   defendants, some at an REO Speedwagon concert Jan. 28 and others at the Phil Collins concert Jan. 30. Both concerts were held at the Cincinnati Gardens.

Andrews said flicking cigarette lighters is a common concert custom that is supposed to encourage encores by performers. The defendants, who pleaded no contest to the first-degree misdemeanor, were cited under a city ordinance that forbids smoking or open flames at public events.

Mestemaker said Capt. Richard Zumwalde, a Cincinnati fire prevention supervisor, gave him the idea for the sentencing.

The judge said when the defendants report back to him Feb. 10, they will have to have a letter from the Shriners hospital, confirming they have donated the $250.

"Maybe they'll even get to see someone who's been burned,"

Mestemaker said. "This has been a tremendous problem for the fire department."

He said tragedies at the Beverly Hills Supper Club and the Who concert make compliance with laws regarding crowds something to be taken very seriously. "Someone is going to be injured very badly if this continues."

Zumwalde said open flames at concerts are dangerous because when people sit in bleacher-type seats, such as those at the Cincinnati Gardens, their clothing and hair could catch fire because of the proximity of the flame to people's heads and bodies.

Zumwalde said Mestemaker's sentencing "sends a message to the county" that breaking this law could cost a spectator 30 days in jail."

High school extortion — no way

Two adult high school seniors accused of running a gang-style protection racket at Forest Park High School. Why do students need to pay for protection inside the confines of one of Hamilton County's largest suburban high schools? As it turns out, the students were forced by fellow students, Michael Brown and James Shelley, to pay for protection from being beat up by Brown and Shelley. There were two other students charged with felony extortion who, because they were juveniles, appeared before a judge in juvenile court.

This criminal case started on March 11, 1983, when Brown and Shelley as well as the other two students were arrested by Forest Park police officers after they had allegedly demanded $5 from a female student, who was then beaten up when she told them that she couldn't pay the amount of money demanded.

The two adult students, Brown and Shelley, were scheduled to appear before me for preliminary hearing on the felony charges on April 6, 1983. Before the preliminary hearing commenced, the prosecuting attorney offered each young man the opportunity to plead to a lessor included misdemeanor offense of coercion — instead of facing the grand jury and a felony trial in common pleas court on a charge of extortion. As in most of these open-and-shut cases, after each defendant and his attorney discussed the plea bargain offered by the prosecution, they chose to accept the deal and to enter pleas of no contest to the lessor offense and avoid the possibility of going to prison — where 18-year-old young men don't fare well.

After the two pled no contest to the charges as reduced by the chief municipal court prosecutor, Terry Gaines, the victims of these two noodniks actually spoke on their behalf, as did other students from Forest Park High School. These students, victims and non-victims alike, actually requested that I not lock the offenders up, but that I order them not to bother their fellow students again. To me that seemed unusually Christian on their part, especially the two young women students who had been roughed up.

Mainly based upon the pleas on their behalf by their own peers, my mind was changed. I had already resolved to send a message to other would-be protection sellers by locking Brown and Shelley up for a while. But their fellow students caused me to rethink my original intention. The result of this process was that each defendant received a suspended sentence on the conditions that they pay a fine, stay away from and not bother or molest any other student. And so that they might learn to have more respect for the purpose for which they were enrolled at Forest Park High School, each was ordered to perform a total of 80 hours community service at the school after class and on the weekends — the amount and type of volunteer work to be determined by school officials. It worked. Not only did this sentence impress the two defendants, but word spread around Forest Park High School to the end that student extortion, at least in that school district, become an extinct crime

BB guns and kittens

On August 2, 1982, 21-year-old Larry Higgs of Cincinnati decided that he would teach his unfriendly neighbor a lesson. So he shot her 6-month-old kitten in the throat with his BB gun. Larry was so brazen that he did the shooting in front of several witnesses. His identity was known, and his crime easy for the prosecutor to prove.

On August 10, 1982, Larry Higgs was convicted of cruelty to animals, a third-degree misdemeanor that carries a maximum possible jail sentence of 60 days and a maximum fine of $500. Fortunately, the kitten did not die — thanks to the expertise of one of our fine local veterinarians.

After all the evidence and exhibits were received and a finding of guilt entered on the record, Larry Higgs and his counsel were given the usual opportunity to address the court in mitigation. This is the time always referred to as begging for the court's mercy. While I listened, I could not help but wonder what Larry would have done had the kitten been able to beg for mercy. Would he have listened and put the BB gun down? I doubted it then, as I doubt it now. What kind of sentence do we fashion in this case? How about ordering Larry to go to the zoo and comb the tangles out of a male lion's mane? Boy, what a sight that would be. Larry would end up looking like he had been shoved through a cheese grater. No, what Larry needed was a good dose of learning to care for sick, injured, orphaned or abused dogs and cats. That is it. We will offer Larry a choice between jail and a fine or probation on a suspended sentence or, a small fine and 40 hours volunteer community service at the Society for the Prevention of Cruelty to Animals shelter, helping care for animals that have been the victims of cruelty and abandonment. Of course, Larry accepted the offer to stay out of jail and to save most of the $500 fine while helping out at the animal shelter.

B-4 METRO THE CINCINNATI ENQUIRER Sunday, August 14, 1983

Man Who Shot Kitten Must Work For Animal Society

Frank Weikel

TURNABOUT is fair play department . . . On Monday the Hamilton County Society for the Prevention of Cruelty to Animals (SPCA) will decide how to best use the services of a young man who has been convicted of being cruel to an animal.

Twenty-one-year-old Larry Higgs admitted to Judge Albert "Mike" Mestemaker last week that he shot his neighbor's kitten with a BB gun. Judge Mestemaker said Higgs said he shot the cat because he didn't like his neighbor.

The six-month-old kitten was taken to a veterinarian and a BB pellet was removed from its throat. It is expected to recover.

Judge Mestemaker thought the best way to teach Higgs a lesson about animals was to give him some practical experience. The judge first got Higgs' attention by slapping him with a 60-day jail term, a $50 fine and six-months probation. The judge then offered to suspend the days in jail if Higgs agreed to do 40 hours of volunteer work for the benefit of animal welfare. HIGGS AGREED!

THAT WAS last week. Well, the SPCA has been contacted and Judge Mestemaker said that Monday the SPCA is supposed to let the court know what kind of "volunteer work" Higgs will be doing.

Frank Wiekel, "Man who shot kitten," Cincinnati Enquirer, August 14, 1983.

Therefore, the sentence of the court was 60 days in jail suspended, $500 fine plus court costs of which $450 was suspended, and 6 months on probation — conditioned upon Larry Higgs staying away from his neighbor and her kitten, paying all the vet bills incurred to remove the BB he had fired into the kitten's throat, and 40 hours volunteer service at the SPCA shelter. I am happy to write that all went well. The kitten shot by Larry grew up to be a healthy feline, and Larry gained a new and everlasting respect for animals by virtue of his volunteer work for our SPCA shelter in Hamilton County. The last I heard, Larry was working with animals on a full-time basis.

Frank Weikel, a metro columnist for *The Cincinnati Enquirer*, heard about the kitten case. Perhaps he liked the theme. Or, perhaps — although I doubt it — the story he did on the case was his way of thanking me. With the assistance of fellow prosecutor Don Montfort, I saved Frank's life in 1969. He was in danger of bleeding to death after walking through a plate glass partition in the Second National Bank Building at Ninth and Main streets, while counting his money instead of paying attention to where he was walking. We grabbed all the handkerchiefs for sale at a nearby vendor stand and applied them to the gaping wound in his leg from where the glass came down like a guillotine. Then he went into shock and wanted to run, but we held him down until the life squad arrived. A truly traumatic event.

In either case, on August 14, 1983, Frank Weikel reported this case in his Sunday column, giving it the top billing — a singular honor, indeed, especially from Frank Weikel.

Don't poach in Hamilton County

Hamilton County, Ohio, has 14 municipal court judges. Between 1981 and 1995, the court had 13 judges who did not hunt game and one who did. Being the only judge on our court who regularly engaged in sport hunting, I had a particular dislike for poachers. So whenever he cited anyone for taking game out of season, fishing out of season, or trapping illegally, Hamilton County's state game protection officer, Mike Serio, hoped that I would be the judge assigned to hear the case. It followed that during my career I had the opportunity to impose several positive sentences in cases involving poaching.

The first of these involved David Jones, Johnny Daugherty and Billy Daugherty. It turned out that on October 23, 1983, David Jones was hunt-

Tough judge has message for poachers

Nature's notebook

Norm Meyer

October 25, during bow season, David M. Jones was hunting deer with a bow while his hunting partner, Johnny R. Daugherty, was hunting deer with a shotgun.

Just outside Miami Whitewater Forest, Johnny Daugherty shot a big buck with his shotgun. Jones shot the same deer with an arrow to make it appear as if it was taken with a bow. They then tagged the deer but did not check it in.

SOMEONE TIPPED off the game protector. When he arrived Billy M. Daugherty was skinning the deer. When the game protector examined the deer he found the bullet hole, and the bullet, and charged all three men with illegal killing, possessing and transporting of a deer.

The men appeared before Judge Albert Mestemaker Nov. 22 and were charged under the Ohio Revised Code 1531.02 — illegal killing, possession and transporting of a deer. This is a third degree misdemeanor which carries a maximum sentence of 60 days in the workhouse (CCI), $500 fine and three years not being permitted to apply for or receive a hunting license.

Johnny Daugherty, 1409 Ludlow Place, Cumminsville, was sentenced to 60 days in jail, 51 days suspended. He must spend three weekends starting Dec. 2 at CCI and was fined $500 plus court costs. His right to receive or apply for a hunting, fishing or trapping license was suspended for three years and he is under one year's probation to Judge Mestemaker. Should he commit any kind of an offense, the full suspended sentence would be imposed.

DAVID M. JONES, 1415 Ludlow Place, Cumminsville, received 60 days in CCI with 57 days suspended, must serve one weekend starting Dec. 2, was fined $500 plus costs and had his right to apply for a fishing, hunting or trapping license revoked for three years, had his archery equipment confiscated and was put on one-year probation.

Billy Daugherty, 1407 Ludlow Place, Cumminsville, had no weapon but was skinning the deer. Judge Mestemaker gave him 60 days with 57 suspended, a $200 fine plus costs and had his hunting, fishing and trapping license for three years and put him on one-year probation.

Judge Mestemaker was quoted as saying "Let this be a signal to all would be poachers of this county. If you are going to poach, it better not be in Ohio."

THIS SHOWS "TIP" is working. It is working only because we have judges like Judge Mestemaker standing behind the game protectors of Ohio and protecting our wildlife.

Lawrence and David Cowell of East Miami River Road were rabbit hunting Nov. 11 at US 50 and Kilby Road in a cornfield when Lawrence Cowell heard movement in the bushes and unable to see what it was, fired his 12-gauge shotgun using No. 6 shot into the bushes. A yearling doe came out and fell dead.

They transported the small doe to their home where David again shot it with his son's toy bow using a tipped arrow head to make it look like the deer was taken with a bow.

MIKE SERIO, our Hamilton County game protector, responded to a tip and found a large group of No. 6 shot in the deer.

The brothers pleaded guilty in front of Judge Mestemaker Nov. 23.

Lawrence Cowell received 60 days in CCI, 51 suspended, was **fined $500 plus costs**, had his right to apply for a hunting, fishing or trapping license suspended for **three years** and was put on one-year probation. He also had his **gun confiscated**.

DAVID COWELL received the same sentence and had his son's bow and arrow confiscated.

These men were lucky it was only a deer in the bushes. It could have been a child.

To avoid tragedy wait until your target comes into full view before firing. Never fire at moving bushes or dark places where it looks like something may be.

Norm Meyer, Tough Judge" Hilltop News, *November 30, 1983.*

ing deer with a bow. It was bow season, and taking a deer with any type of firearm was illegal. Nevertheless, Jones' companions were hunting with a shotgun. On the border of Miami Whitewater Forest, Johnny Daugherty shot a very large buck with his shotgun. Then Jones fired an arrow into the wound caused by the shotgun slug — in an effort to make it appear that the deer had actually been brought down by a legally fired arrow. The two men tagged the buck but did not pass through a deer check-in station. Acting on a tip, game protection Officer Mike arrived at the Daugherty residence, where he discovered Billy Daugherty skinning the illegally taken deer. Upon examining the buck, Serio discovered the slug, which had actually killed the animal. As a result, all three men were arrested and charged with the illegal killing, illegal possession and illegal transportation of the buck.

The three men appeared before me on November 22, 1983. The fact that it was the 20th anniversary of the shooting of President John F. Kennedy in Dallas, Texas, was not lost on me. Johnny Daugherty, who had actually slain the buck with the shotgun, was required to serve three weekends in jail and to pay a $500 fine, much of which would go to the state game and habitat fund, and the loss of all hunting, fishing or trapping privileges in Ohio for three years. His shotgun was confiscated and turned over to the Ohio Division of Wildlife, to be used to teach hunter safety courses.

David Jones, who had shot an arrow into the slain animal in an effort to make it appear that it had been killed in that fashion, received one weekend in jail, a $500 fine and the loss of all hunting, fishing and trapping privileges for three years. Finally, Billy Daugherty, who had been discovered skinning the buck, was ordered to serve one weekend in jail, to pay a $200 fine and the loss of all hunting, fishing and trapping privileges for three years.

Probably the worst case of an attempt to disguise the cause of death of a deer was the killing of a young doe by Lawrence Cowell with a shotgun loaded with No. 6 rabbit shot while he and his brother, David, were rabbit hunting on November 11, 1983. When the young doe jumped out of bushes in front of the two men, Lawrence fired No. 6 shot directly into her face — blinding her — and continued firing at her legs as she ran in sightless circles. Finally, with her legs literally shot out from under her, the doe fell and was clubbed to death. After taking the doe to their home, David Cowell fired an arrow from his son's toy bow into the deer in an attempt to make it appear that this animal had also been taken by bow and arrow.

Again responding to a tip, Officer Mike Seiro discovered the attempted ruse. Both men were charged. They appeared before me on November 23 and pled guilty to illegally killing the young doe. The sentences imposed by me in these cases were similar in nature to those imposed by me on November 22. Although not all of the facts pertinent in the Cowell case were reported in detail, naturalist and renowned taxidermist Norm Meyer captured the spirit in his weekly column in *Hill Top News* on November 30, 1983.

One final story involving positive punishment imposed for illegal hunting activities occurred on February 12, 1986, when Harold Bolton and Charles Mann were convicted of illegal use of a high-powered light to take deer. The practice of blinding deer with a lantern, spotlight or flashlight is called jack lighting. It is illegal because it immobilizes a deer, causing the animal to freeze and stare into the light. People who take deer using this method are not hunters and they certainly are not sportsmen.

The positive penalties employed in their cases were to give each defendant the option of paying a fine or contributing $200 each to Ohio's Turn In a Poacher program (TIP). To their credit, each man chose to make the contribution — which, being made in their respective names, did something positive for them by way of helping restore their reputations as sportsmen. This case was given its just due by *The Cincinnati Post* on February 12, 1986.

---

2 hunters fined for using flashlight

Two Hamilton men convicted today of illegally using a high-powered flashlight to hunt deer were ordered to pay $200 each to "Turn in a Poacher," which rewards whistle-blowers who spot illegal hunters. Hamilton County Common Pleas Judge Albert Mestemaker also assessed Harold Bolton, 23, and Charles E. Mann, 37, both of Hamilton, $51 fines, suspended 10-day sentences and three months' probation for unlawfully transporting loaded weapons, as well as jacklighting, or hunting with the flashlight. Jacklighting, which blinds a game animal, is illegal in Ohio. The men were arrested by Hamilton County Deputy Sheriff R. Schooley about 4:30 a.m. Nov. 27. on Mt. Hope Road in western Hamilton County. Schooley said the men were shining a high-powered flashlight into woods by the road. Mestemaker said the men were caught before they killed any animals.

"2 Hunters fined for using flashlight," Cincinnati Post, *February 12, 1986.*

Vehicular homicide

On November 18, 1986, Eric Wink was convicted by a jury in my courtroom of vehicular homicide in the death of his high school buddy Mark LeTang. The other defendant, Tom Guck, in whose auto, Mark LeTang was a passenger at the time of the accident, was acquitted by the same jury.

This tragic accident occurred on May 10, 1986, after Wink, Guck and LeTang, all buddies at Elder High School in Price Hill, had gotten together for an evening of fun and drinking and to reminisce about their high school days.

Unfortunately, the happy trio had more than enough beer to drink and should definitely not have been operating motor vehicles. Shortly after 1 a.m. on May 10, the Pontiac Firebird Trans Am being driven by Tom Guck, with Mark LeTang as his passenger, was westbound on Bridgetown Road in Green Township while Eric Wink was driving next to them. After they crossed Glenway Avenue, one of the drivers, Wink or Guck, decided to play leap frog.

This game consists of one car speeding ahead and pulling into the other car's lane and then slamming on its brakes. This causes the passed vehicle to immediately change lanes to avoid rear-ending the vehicle now in front. The act is repeated as the vehicle taking evasive action speeds ahead, pulling in front of Vehicle Number 1, slamming on its own brakes, and causing that vehicle to repeat the evasive action earlier taken by Vehicle Number 2.

As the two vehicles sped west on Bridgetown Road, this leap frog game continued until something went terribly wrong and Guck tried to go around Wink on the right side. Wink swerved to block Guck's attempt, which caused Guck to lose control, hit the curb and flip. As the Trans Am was in mid-air, Mark LeTang was partially thrown from the car and crushed to death as the Trans Am landed on its roof. Mark's death was immediate — and horrible for his friends to see. Neither Eric Wink nor Tom Guck will ever forget the sight of their buddy dead beneath Tom's Trans Am.

I was surprised that the jury had decided to convict Wink and acquit Guck, and I told them so. I told Wink that he alone had not caused Mark LeTang's death, and I wanted Tom Guck to hear how I felt.

It would have been proper to sentence Eric Wink to a lengthy jail sentence for the death of his friend due to alcohol, speed and negligence.

However, I believed that the entire community would benefit more and Eric Wink would remain more conscious of his responsibility if he were required to visit area high schools and lecture high school students about his personal tragedy of drinking alcohol and then operating a motor vehicle in a manner that cost his friend his life.

When I made this order, I believed that if his lectures saved one life it would be worth the effort. For the next year, Eric Wink was required to actively seek speaking engagements at area high schools under the supervision of a municipal court probation officer. I hope that many lives were affected and perhaps enhanced by Eric's speeches. How many lives were saved, no one can ever know. But it was a positive approach. On November 19, 1986, David Wells covered this case and reported on the sentence in the following *Cincinnati Enquirer* article:

Man ordered to give talks about DUI

BY DAVID WELLS
The Cincinnati Enquirer

A 19-year-old Green Township man convicted of killing his high school chum in an auto accident must spend the next year telling other high school students about the dangers of drinking and driving, Municipal Judge Albert Mestemaker ruled Tuesday.

Eric Wink was convicted by a jury of vehicular homicide and driving under the influence at the time of the May 10 accident that killed Mark LeTang, 19, Cleves-Warsaw Pike.

LeTang had been riding in a car driven by Tom Guck, 19, also of Green Township. All three men were 1984 graduates of Elder High School, and had been partying together before the 1:10 a.m. accident on Bridgetown Road.

According to testimony in the two-day trial, both cars were westbound, when Guck tried to pass Wink on the right side. Wink's car swerved, causing Guck's car to run off the road and overturn.

LeTang was crushed under the rolling car. Guck, who police said was speeding and trying to make an illegal pass, also was charged with vehicular homicide, but was found not guilty in the case.

Mestemaker said he did not believe that Wink was solely responsible for LeTang's death, despite the jury's decision to acquit Guck. "You alone did not cause the death of Mark LeTang," the judge said.

He went on to say that he hoped Wink's lecturing other young people "will do more to rectify the death of Mark LeTang than any other fine or jail sentence I might impose . . . If you save one life by your story it is well worth the effort expended."

The judge said a lecture on the devastating costs of drinking and driving from a teen-ager like Wink might be better received by other young people than the same message from parents or teachers.

He ordered Wink to actively seek out and accept speaking engagements at high schools in the Greater Cincinnati area.

In addition to the lectures, Mestemaker

David Wells, "Man ordered to give talks about DUI," Cincinnati Enquirer, *November 19, 1986.*

There is a proper place in criminal and traffic cases for positive punishment approaches. Society cannot afford to lock up every criminal. There are not enough jail cells or enough money to accomplish that. Balance is the secret to this phase of the judicial system. Where jail is called for, use it. Where a positive approach to rehabilitate and to educate is the better approach, choose it.

Judge Mestemaker and wife, Judy, campaigning for re-election in 1989.

"Give light and the people will find their own way"

The Cincinnati Post

Editor	Editorial Page Editor
Paul F. Knue	Byron P. White
Managing Editor	Associate Editor
C. Wayne Perry	James L. Adams

125 East Court Street, Cincinnati, OH 45202 (513)352-2000   Thursday, October 26, 1989

Editorial

For municipal court

Most people arrested in Hamilton County for minor offenses — traffic violations, petty theft, domestic violence — end up in the county's municipal court. Those who sit in judgment in this "people's court," therefore, should possess the legal ability and judicial temperament to assure ordinary citizens — innocent or guilty — that justice has been done.

A municipal court judge must not only be competent but also innovative and willing to use alternative forms of sentencing at a time when prisoners are being released prematurely because of jail overcrowding.

Sixteen candidates are running for eight municipal court seats. The races include three head-to head contests and a field race of 10 candidates jockeying for five seats. In the two-candidate races, we recommend voters choose the following on Nov. 7:

■ **Albert J. Mestemaker.** Mestemaker probably makes the news more than any other municipal court judge — whether he is getting hit on the head by a piece of falling ceiling in the courtroom or for walking off the bench in anger.

Eccentric though he may be, Mestemaker is regarded as one of the best minds on the bench. He listens carefully to both sides and arrives at the kind of decisions that have earned him the title of "umpire." He also has an astute understanding of the law unmatched by many of his colleagues.

■ **Mark P. Painter.** Painter, who has been on the bench since 1982, has won a reputation as one of the brightest and best judges in the municipal court. A jurist who enjoys writing legal opinions, he has had 26 decisions published in national law books and is the co-author of "Ohio Driving Under the Influence Law." He has earned six more productive years in the municipal court.

"For municipal court," Cincinnati Post, *October 26, 1989. Judge Mestemaker won easily with 101,285 votes.*

CHAPTER 12

THE ANIMALS' COURT

When I was sworn in as judge of the Hamilton County Municipal Court, I had already had 10 years experience practicing both criminal and civil law in this particular court. My experience as a trial lawyer handling all types of cases in the municipal court had left me with the belief that municipal court is the court of the people. This reference to the "People's Court" is by no means to be confused with a court established in a communist nation such as Red China, where just about every institution begins with the word "people." No, the reference to our court being the people's court means that the municipal court is the only court that most individuals ever have personal contact with during their adult lifetime. If a person receives a traffic citation requiring a court appearance, the case is heard in municipal court. The same holds true for misdemeanor crimes and civil cases up to $10,000. So, for most individuals, it is truly a people's court.

Besides being a court for the people and by the people, I discovered soon after I ascended this lofty bench that municipal court also handles cases involving animals and household pets. Animal cases are never routine or run of the mill. Some are sad, like the puppy shot six times by a police officer. Some are uproariously funny, like the caiman living in a bathtub. All of them were interesting, as were the humans who came to court with or because of them. Perhaps I was drawn to these cases because I must confess to being somewhat of an animal lover. I have been ever since I tried, without success, at the age of 10 to save a robin that had a broken wing. The truth of the matter is that I really wanted to be a veterinarian.

Not all chickens are poultry

In 1981, the village of Fairfax, Ohio, had on its books Ordinance Number 15-1962, titled "Regulating the Keeping of Animals In The Village of Fairfax, Ohio." Section II of this village ordinance read as follows:

"It shall be unlawful to harbor any animals within the village of Fairfax, Ohio, with the exception of dogs, cats, and other small animals and birds strictly considered as household pets and only upon a non-commercial basis."

On August 5, 1981, Officer C.R. O'Brien of the Fairfax Police Department issued a criminal citation to Kathy A. Gratsch of Fairfax that charged her with the misdemeanor offense of "Keep(ing) animals in the Village other than animals strictly considered household pets, to-wit: chickens."

The citation ordered Ms. Gratsch to appear before His Honor, the mayor, in the Fairfax Mayor's Court to answer this criminal charge in a trial set for August 21, 1981. Her chickens had been observed in the yard of her house by neighbors as well as a Fairfax police officer. So it appeared that this was an open-and-shut case. Ms. Gratsch would appear in Mayor's Court. The witnesses against her would testify that she was keeping chickens on her property in violation of Village Ordinance 15-1962, Section II. The mayor would rule that chickens are not household pets. And as a result of that, Ms. Gratsch would be found guilty as charged. She would then be fined and ordered to destroy or to move the chickens out of the village of Fairfax. The mayor of Fairfax had never met or had to deal with Kathy A. Gratsch or her chickens, Miss Prissy and Ms. Sanders. He and I were to learn that a determined woman and two hens can be formidable advocates for people's and animal rights.

Fairfax resident Kathy Gratsch was allowed to keep her pet chickens, Miss Prissy and Ms. Sanders, when the judge ruled the village ordinance was unconstitutionally vague in regard to chickens.

As everyone predicted, Kathy and her pets had their trial in mayor's court. And despite the presentation of photographs into evidence of Miss Prissy and Ms. Sanders dressed in various costumes for such holidays as Halloween, Thanksgiving, Easter and Christmas, the mayor did rule that the two pets were not, in fact, pets, but rather were poultry, and as such could not continue to reside in the village of Fairfax. Short of a successful appeal by Ms. Gratsch to the Hamilton County Municipal Court, Miss Prissy and Ms. Sanders were headed for the country or the stew pot. Ms. Gratsch filed a timely appeal of the mayor's decision with the clerk of Hamilton County, and I probably do not have to tell you which judge received her appeal for a new trial.

Kathy Gratsch's case was set by our court assignment commissioner for a trial in my room, to commence on September 10. Unfortunately, Ms. Gratsch never received word of her trial date, and she failed to appear as ordered on that date. As a result of Kathy's failure to appear, I issued a warrant for her arrest and set a bond of $500, which would require her to pay $50 to be released on bond. Fortunately, Kathy learned that afternoon that she was supposed to have been in my courtroom at 9:00 that morning. She hurried down to the Courthouse and came into my office just as I was getting ready to leave for the day. After listening to her explanation, I walked with her to the clerk's office (since it was after 4:00 p.m.) and signed an order recalling the arrest warrant and the $500 bond in order that Kathy would not have to put up $50 to go home that day.

In some manner known only to the journalistic world, the media got wind of Ms. Gratsch's brush with the law. And the next day, the following article appeared in *The Cincinnati Enquirer*.

Chickens almost send woman to the pen

FAIFAX — Kathy Gratsch came close to spending the night in jail Wednesday. She failed to appear in court for a hearing. Her crime: she keeps two pet chickens.

In Fairfax it is illegal to have very much other than dogs or cats as pets. Chickens are definitely out. But the Fairfax woman finds it an unlikely offense to be jailed for.

GRATSCH, 28, of 6003 Murray Ave., almost ended up in jail when Hamilton County Municipal Court Judge Albert J. Mestemaker issued a warrant for her arrest. Mestemaker ordered Gratsch to post a $500 bond for failing to appear at a hearing in his courtroom.

The hearing was called by Fairfax Prosecutor Patrick D. Lane to change the date of Gratsch's trial from Sept. 10 to Sept. 14. Lane said he sent Gratsch a notice that he intended to change the trial date. He added that he telephoned Gratsch's home and told her brother of the date and time of the hearing.

After rushing downtown to talk to Judge Mestemaker before the courts closed, Gratsch said (the judge) was "very apologetic" and canceled his action against her.

"I ALWAYS did have pet chickens — ever since I was a little girl," Gratsch said. The chickens she is keeping now in her fenced-in back yard were given to her by her brother as chicks last Easter. Gratsch said neighbors have not complained about the chickens.

"This is my house," she said. "I don't tell people what to keep as pets."

Lane said the city prohibits any animal except "dogs, cats and other small animals and birds strictly considered household pets and only on a non-commercial basis."

Gratsch said she believes she is being singled out for harassment. She was cited for keeping chickens in 1979 in a case that was later dismissed. Rabbits have been sold openly in her neighborhood, she said. "I had ducks last year and nobody said anything about them."

Neighbor Michael Orchin of 3998 Watterson said he believes the city is wasting resources on the case. "How many hundreds of dollars have gone into these chickens?" he asked. "Her family is chicken crazy, I guess — they've always got chickens. She has pictures in her photo album and all," he said.

The case did not go to trial on September 14 either, because on that date an additional witness required by the village prosecutor was unavailable. At least on the second date there was no need to issue another failure to appear arrest warrant for Kathy Gratsch. She was in court at 9:00 a.m., ready to defend herself and her pets.

The next date set for her trial by our assignment commissioner was September 24. By this date, the media had taken great interest in this case. As a result, the courtroom was about as crowded as I had ever seen it. The prosecuting attorney for Fairfax commenced his case by stating that he would prove that Ms. Gratsch lived inside the village of Fairfax, and that she was continuously in violation of Ordinance Number 15-1962 for keeping chickens in and around her home, and that chickens are not by any stretch of the imagination small animals or birds that can be considered household pets.

Kathy Gratsch, who had throughout this case acted as her own attorney, came to the courtroom prepared for trial with a stack of printed material. She brought dictionaries, photo albums containing pictures of her "pets" dressed in various seasonal costumes, encyclopedias and the American Audubon Society's annual list of birds that are considered pets in different cultures. Kathy Gratsch did not deny that she harbored chickens at her house, although she was not particularly enamored of the word "harbor" as used in the ordinance in place of "possession" — because "harbor" to her made it sound like she was hiding fugitives from justice. Her position was that Miss Prissy and Ms. Sanders were her pets, her friends and members of her extended family — as well as her personal property, a liberty the village of Fairfax should not be allowed to deprive her of without compensation.

During the course of her testimony, Ms. Gratsch read various definitions from several dictionaries to support her position that her particular chickens were, in fact, pets. For example, one definition stated that a chicken is a common domestic fowl. Another definition stated that chickens are any one of a number of various birds or their young. Ms. Gratsch read various accepted authorities that included chickens in the definition of bird. Her next move was to introduce into evidence the photo albums that she had with her showing Miss Prissy and Ms. Sanders in various poses to prove the cleanliness and livability within the confines of her house. The chickens were in costume or at play. One photograph contained a sign, which cautioned passersby that they were approaching a chicken crossing at her front walk. Chickens! They are small. They are fairly clean. They are certainly not a danger even if they do escape from their residence. They do qualify as private property, and in this case their owner showed ample proof that she considered them as pets if not also as companions. It can be said with certainty that anyone who makes Halloween costumes for their chickens certainly does not consider them to be fowl.

As this case developed and headed for a conclusion, it became apparent that it rested on three legs — not to be confused with drumsticks. First of all, I would be required to determine whether chickens were birds as exempted from the ordinance. The next issue was whether chickens could be considered household pets — and thus also exempt from the ordinance, if their owner intended that they be raised and cared for as "pets." The third and final issue, which had not been alluded to either by the village prosecutor or the defendant, was the question of the constitutionality of the ordinance as it applied to the facts of this case.

There could be no disagreement that the village of Fairfax had the power to ban the possession (or harboring) of animals that would represent a threat to the peace, safety and welfare of the commonwealth. Therefore, the village could ban possession of, say, a Bengal tiger or a crocodile. But we were dealing with chickens. Could chickens kept in a house and a fenced-in yard be considered a threat to the peace, safety and welfare of the village of Fairfax, Ohio? The obvious answer was no. However, the ordinance limited the types of animals permitted in the village to be those "strictly considered as household pets."

First of all, who was to make the strict consideration as to what animal was a household pet? And what guidelines were in place to be employed in making such a decision, especially in the case of chickens — which, after all, had been proven by Ms. Gratsch to be birds? The answer to both questions, again, was in the negative. The ordinance did not provide any criteria dealing with birds intended by their owner to be kept as household pets, and there were no guidelines in place relative to any animal covered by feathers.

The trial lasted almost two hours. It was punctuated with giggles and applause, mostly in favor of Ms. Gratsch. The court rendered its decision by finding that the ordinance in question as it applied to the facts of Ms. Gratsch's case was unconstitutionally vague and that she must be found not guilty of illegally harboring a prohibited animal in Fairfax, Ohio. So, Ms. Gratsch won her case and saved Miss Prissy and Ms. Sanders, who lived out the remainder of their lives in Fairfax, Ohio.

The case was reported in the media, and I took a lot of good-natured ribbing over it from my colleagues on the bench as well as lawyer friends. They repeatedly referred to my decision in this case as a real "Clucker."

The caiman caper

On April 26, 1990, Patricia Lowenstein, of Norwood, Ohio, sprayed Nancy Jacob's pet caiman with her garden hose. As a result, Ms.

Lowenstein was cited and charged with criminal mischief, a third-degree misdemeanor that carries, upon conviction, a possible sentence of 60 days in jail and a $500 fine.

This turned out to be another animal trial in which the judge received more advanced education in the area of "household pets." First of all, I wondered, what is a caiman? A caiman, sometimes also spelled "cay-man" after the Caribbean Islands of the same name, is defined in Webster's Collegiate Dictionary as a South American "crocodilian" similar to an alligator but which superficially resembles the African crocodile. This particular caiman was named Rex, and he was the "household pet" of Nancy Jacob and her husband, who resided with Rex in a two-bedroom apartment in Norwood. They had acquired Rex when he was a small hatchling, called thus because he started life inside an egg. By April 26, 1990, when criminal mischief was allegedly committed by Patricia Lowenstein, a next-door neighbor, Rex was 4-feet, 8-inches long and weighed in at 110 pounds. Norwood, Ohio, is not considered a prime habitant for a 5-year-old, adult male caiman — which, by the way, is referred to as a "bull."

Like all other cases that come before the municipal court, the caiman caper came to be in my courtroom because after she was cited to court for criminal mischief, Ms. Lowenstein entered a plea of not guilty — thereby deciding she wanted to have a trial in this case. Our ever-vigilant assignment commissioner rolled this case in the selection computer and up popped my number. The case was mine!

Ms. Lowenstein, who had decided to appear and represent herself, was instructed that her case would go to trial in my courtroom on June 11, 1990, at 9 a.m. sharp. The prosecuting attorney then issued subpoenas for all the witnesses needed to prove a case of criminal mischief. Mr. and Mrs. Jacob were requested to bring a photograph only and "please" leave Rex at home.

The Lowenstein case was called by Assistant Hamilton County Prosecutor Thomas D. Heekin Jr. about 11:30 a.m. At that point, I had already heard approximately 20 to 25 more-mundane matters. So I was ready for a change of pace. Little did I know exactly how much of a change of pace I was actually in for when this case was called for trial. However, we were not going to have a trial. After discussing the facts of the case in the hall outside my courtroom with the Jacob family and Ms. Lowenstein, Mr. Heekin offered her an opportunity to plead guilty to a lesser included offense of disorderly conduct, which, in this case, was a minor misdemeanor. Apparently, after hearing the facts, Mr. Heekin believed that the lesser charge was more appropriate in this case. After discussion, Mr. and Mrs. Jacob advised the prosecutor that such reduction was agreeable to them. The defendant, Ms. Lowenstein, accepted the offer of the prosecutor and agreed to plead guilty to a minor misdemeanor charge of disorderly conduct, for which she could not be ordered to serve a jail sentence. The maximum penalty for a minor misdemeanor is a fine of $100 plus court costs. This is quite a bit less than the possible penalty of 60 days in jail and a $500 fine if she were to be found guilty of criminal mischief, as she stood charged in the complaint.

After I was advised that Ms. Lowenstein had decided to accept the plea bargain, I advised her of her rights and the maximum possible fine and court costs and concluded by asking her whether she understood her rights and whether she was entering a plea of guilty to the lesser offense voluntarily. As in the case of most defendants who appear in court without a lawyer, Ms. Lowenstein's response to my inquiry was, "Judge, that's fine, I just want to get everything over with."

To which I replied, "All right, plea of guilty is accepted to a minor misdemeanor of disorderly conduct. Let the record reflect that the defendant waives the issuance of a new complaint and enters a plea of guilty to disorderly conduct. Please give me the facts of this case, Mr. Heekin."

I was told that Rex spent most of his time in the Jacobs' bathtub in their first-floor apartment's bathroom, which had a small window with the sill above the tub. Whenever he wanted to, Rex could stand on his hind legs in the tub and rest his front legs and feet on the window sill. This enabled him to watch the coming and goings of people and other activity at the house next door, which was occupied by the Lowenstein family. As I listened to this testimony, I had a vision of walking into a bathroom only to observe a nearly 5-foot-long caiman from the rear stretched up along a bathroom tile wall, rear feet firmly planted in water and front feet perched on a window sill and long snout up against an open window screen watching the neighbor next door.

As it turned out, April 26, 1990, was a warm, balmy spring day in Norwood. Nancy Jacob had opened the window so that the bathroom could air out. She had also added several glass items to the window sill, such as bath salts, bubble bath and shower gel. She was aware that Patricia was outside her parent's home next door watering her mother's roses with a hose equipped with a pistol-style nozzle. After Nancy left the bathroom, Rex waddled in and slid over the side of the tub into his comfortable 18 inches of water. Perhaps Rex heard the garden hose outside of his window.

Perhaps he caught the scent of Patricia Lowenstein. In either event, Rex decided to stand up in his tub and take a look outside to see what was going on. When Rex observed Patricia, who was watering roses next to the side of the house closest to Rex's window, a distance of no more than 15 feet, he let out a low, rumbling growl. When Rex growled, he startled Patricia, who looked toward the source of the growl — only to observe to her sheer terror the snout of what appeared to her to be some kind of prehistoric lizard staring at her. She had absolutely no clue that her parents' neighbors were housing Godzilla on Courtland Avenue in Norwood, Ohio.

Patricia's reaction was natural and instantaneous, or so she claimed. She swung the hose nozzle around in the direction of the growling sound and found her mark — spraying Rex straight in his long kisser with a steady stream of water. Rex let out one more growl and retreated down the wall into his tub to avoid further contact with Patricia or her garden hose equipped with a hard-spraying pistol nozzle. No one was injured, and none of the items placed on the window sill was broken. However, Mr. and Mrs. Jacob heard the noise and rushed into a very wet bathroom, passing the retreating caiman on the way. They were upset over this incident because they believed that Patricia's act of spraying Rex through the open bathroom window was deliberate. Yet they did not call the Norwood police right away. Instead, they thought the matter over for several days before

Rex, the caiman that lived in a two-room apartment in Norwood, became the subject of a dispute that ended in Judge Mestemaker's court.

reporting the incident to the police. Three days after the incident, Patricia answered her parents' door, only to be greeted by a police officer who advised her that he had a warrant for her arrest. Those were the facts of this case, plain and simple, said Mr. Heekin.

I inquired of the Jacobs whether anything was damaged in their bathroom as the result of this incident, and they advised me that there was not any damage or injuries to anyone including Rex, the caiman who had only been frightened when sprayed directly up his snout. The chief complaint was a wet bathroom.

I asked what Rex normally ate and was advised that he dined on a fare of raw chicken and an occasional fish. I then couldn't resist asking where Rex slept, to which Mr. Jacob replied "anywhere he wants to." I should have seen that answer coming. At this point, I was provided with a photograph of Rex. After viewing Rex's photo, the following exchange occurred, according to the hearing record:

> The Court: What do you feed him; I guess anything he wants to eat?
> Mr. Jacob: Yeah.
> The Court: I haven't seen that many teeth since I attended a dental academy display. Ms. Lowenstein, do you have anything to say before I make a finding in this case?
> The Defendant: No, sir, except that I didn't do it intentionally.
> The Court: Anything further from the prosecution?
> Mr. Heekin: No, Judge.
> The Court: Do the Jacobs want to say anything?
> Mrs. Jacob: No sir.
> The Court: The finding is that Ms. Lowenstein is guilty of disorderly conduct, which is the charge that you have entered a plea of guilt to. Do you understand that Ms. Lowenstein?
> The Defendant: Yes, Judge Mestemaker.
> The Court: Is there anything, ma'am, that you want to say before I impose sentence — which we stated earlier was a fine of $100 plus court costs, which now are $32, for a total possible amount of $132?
> The Defendant: Just that I am sorry for any inconvenience that I caused.
> The Court: OK, Ms. Lowenstein, I am not going to impose the $100 fine. But I will order that you pay the court costs of $32.

The Defendant: Thank you very much, Judge Mestemaker, that is nice of you.

The Court: Pay the costs then, ma'am. This is a very interesting case. I will call it "The Alligator Caper." Don't spray the alligator anymore.

With these words of sage advice, representing many years of judicial learning, the caiman case ended as far as it concerned my courtroom and the criminal case of *Norwood, Ohio, vs. Patricia Lowenstein*. However, there were still a few shock waves for Mr. and Mrs. Jacob, especially in light of the fact that neither the city of Norwood nor their landlord had known about Rex until the complaint was filed against Patricia Lowenstein. Chickens in Fairfield are one thing, caimans in Norwood are quite another. It appeared rather quickly that Rex would have to find another place to live, with or without his owners. Apparently, this was accomplished, as it was later reported to me that Rex was living well and happy at a reptile farm open to the public and that his former owners visited him frequently. It is certainly a lot more tranquil on Courtland Avenue in Norwood these days. Adios, Rex.

The pig that did not get to market

Penelope is a Vietnamese pot-bellied pig. She does not belong to the Viet Cong or the ARVN (Army of the Republic of Vietnam). She belongs to Tommie Murphy, from whom she is inseparable as their photograph shows.

Penelope and Tommie live in Montgomery, Ohio, with their parents. Well, at least with Tommie's parents. Penelope has a litter box that she uses all of the time when nature calls. She eats low-fat foods such as cabbage, carrots, lettuce, cucumbers and an occasional apple or banana. She is impeccably clean, loves to be bathed and scented, and — unlike Rex the caiman — loves to be sprayed with a garden hose. As far as housing accommodations are concerned, Penelope has a fenced-in rear yard to play in, which includes a sand box. She sleeps on an oval throw rug at the foot of Tommie's bed on the second floor of a nice brick-and-frame residence in the lovely suburban city of Montgomery, which is located in northeastern Hamilton County. All in all, Penelope lives in pig heaven.

This scene of swine serenity remained just that until 1994, when it came time for Tommie to start attending nursery school. It was very trau-matic for Penelope to stand each morning by the gate in the rear yard and watch her buddy get on the school bus. She had no idea where he was being taken or how long it would be before he returned home. That being the case, Penelope would take her station by the gate near the driveway and wait until shortly after noon, when the same small yellow bus would drop Tommie off. That was the happy time for Penelope because it meant lunch, a nap and then playing in the yard, unless, of course, it was raining — in which case she and Tommie played in the finished basement or watched TV together.

Even though Tommie's daily climb up the steps of that yellow bus began to become routine, it still bothered Penelope that he was leaving without her and that she did not know when he would return because Vietnamese pot-bellied pigs have an undeveloped sense of time. Finally, one day, someone forgot to latch the backyard gate — and when Tommie climbed the steps of the school bus and the door closed behind him, Penelope took advantage of the opportunity and decided this was her chance to find out where the yellow bus took her friend each morning. Unfortunately, a school bus moves much faster than a pig, and within sev-eral blocks it was out of Penelope's sight. Undaunted, our perseverant pig kept up her fastest pace, hoping that she could deduce where the bus had taken her friend. As Penelope wandered along the berm of Pfeiffer Road, she was sighted by a Montgomery police officer who was on routine patrol. Penelope's guardian angel was definitely on duty, since the officer who spotted her also recognized her as belonging to a local family. He was able to entice Penelope to enter his cruiser with a Tootsie Roll. She was returned home in the rear seat of the cruiser, separated from her chauffeur by the steel screen between the front and rear seats — just the way dangerous criminals are transported.

Several weeks later, Penelope's adult male owner, the father of Tommie, was required to appear in court for failure to confine one pet Vietnamese pot -bellied pig named Penelope. After hearing the facts of this case, I decided that no one should be fined because, after all, Penelope let herself out of her yard without any direct help from a human being. However, the law is the law — even though some unknown individual had failed to make certain that the gate was latched, which allowed Penelope to leave the back yard and not remain confined on her owner's property, I had to find her owner guilty. In mitigation, I concluded that Penelope's apparent reason for her journey was an understandable one. In addition, her display of superior intelligence in remaining on the berm and not roaming in the middle of Pfeiffer Road called for mercy by the court and the imposition of $42 court costs but no fine and certainly no jail time. Penelope's gate is now equipped with a self-locking latch, which I am told is pig proof.

Penelope, a pot-bellied pig, lived in Montgomery with her friend, Tommie.

Frenchie

In 1994, Frenchie was a very young-looking, 10-year-old, female, mixed-breed, longhaired shepherd. She was owned by Frank Fiorini of Delhi Township, who, in all other respects except for the care of a dog, may be a decent individual. But with regard to Frenchie, Mr. Fiorini was not a friend of animals.

In 1994, Mr. Fiorini had property in Delhi that had a rather large and wooded rear yard. For some unknown reason, he chained Frenchie to a large tree in a weed- and insect-infested area of the yard where the only sources of shelter from the elements, including a very hot summer sun, were the leaves and limbs of the large tree to which her chain was attached. As if these conditions were not bad enough, Fiorini went out of town and Frenchie, as is often said, was a victim of the "out of sight, out of mind" syndrome. Within a matter of days, Frenchie was out of water and food and had been attacked and badly injured by a much larger dog, which had wondered onto the Fiorini property. Due to Frenchie's diminutive size and her inability to escape from her chain, she was a severely handicapped target for the larger dog, which was able to inflict severe bite wounds on Frenchie's back and hind quarters. It only took 24 hours or so for the flies to lay their eggs in Frenchie's open wounds and even less time for the maggots to spawn and start destroying flesh. Finally, Frenchie's pitiful cries of hunger, thirst, and pain caught the attention of a neighbor, who, after several calls in an attempt to locate Frank Fiorini, took matters into his own hands and rescued Frenchie. Upon realizing just how ill the dog was, the Good Samaritan took Frenchie to Dr. Richard Seaman, a veterinarian on Anderson Ferry Road, who spent days treating Frenchie for the injuries, acute infection and malnutrition. Fortunately, after five days or more of constant attention, Frenchie turned the corner and began to eat solid food. Dr. Seaman had, quite frankly, saved her life.

In the meantime, Fiorini had returned from his trip, whereupon he was cited to court for cruelty to an animal. When Mr. Fiorini appeared before me with an attorney, he decided he wanted a trial on this charge. Of course, it was his right to have since he had entered a plea of not guilty and truly believed that he was not guilty of this offense for the reason that he did not intend to be cruel or to neglect Frenchie.

At Fiorini's trial, the neighbor who rescued Frenchie testified. He had also been thorough in his actions by taking several photographs of Frenchie as she appeared before he removed her from the Fiorini property and took her to Dr. Seaman's office for emergency medical care. This witness testified that he had seen Fiorini tie Frenchie up in the rear of the property and how long she had been there without any attention from Fiorini or anyone else.

Dr. Seaman testified concerning Frenchie's injuries and her deplorable condition when she was brought to his office. The Society for the Prevention of Cruelty to Animals witness testified that he had cited Mr. Fiorini for cruelty to animals and that records of the SPCA license section revealed that Fiorini was Frenchie's registered owner. He also testified concerning the scene of the overgrown lot where Frenchie had been kept, including his observation of empty water and food containers. This witness had also taken photographs, which were received in evidence at the trial.

After the prosecution had rested its case, the defendant testified on his own behalf. He admitted that he was Frenchie's owner. But he denied that he was in any way responsible for what happened to her. He attempted to absolve himself of any responsibility by testifying that someone else was supposed to be caring for Frenchie's needs while he was out of town.

After hearing this testimony and studying all the exhibits, I entered a finding of guilt of cruelty to an animal against Fiorini. I decided after listening to his attorney's plea for leniency to treat Fiorini better than he treated Frenchie. Instead of a putting him in jail (where he no doubt deserved to be placed, even if it were only for a long weekend), I suspended the 90-day jail sentence and most of the possible $750 fine on the condition that Fiorini reimburse Dr. Seaman for the fair and reasonable value of the veterinarian services he rendered on behalf of Frenchie. Another condition that I placed on the defendant was that he surrender custody of Frenchie to the SPCA, where she was already being cared for. And, finally, I set the condition that he not purchase or acquire another dog without my prior written approval. Fiorini agreed to all of these conditions of his probation.

After this trial, Harold Dates, the SPCA's general manager, and I agreed that my granting of custody of Frenchie to the SPCA was conditioned upon all possible avenues being exhausted in an effort to find a good home for Frenchie. As the result of this agreement, Frenchie got a wonderful new home where she would never have to worry about food and water or fear abuse again.

The Hamilton County SPCA, through the efforts of Harold Dates, had an agreement with WKRC-TV to feature a program every Saturday morning as part of the station's Saturday news format called "Adopt a Pet." This segment was hosted by Mike Buresh, a reporter for this station, and weekly features Harold Dates and animals from the shelter that need new homes. On Saturday, November 5, 1994, Harold appeared on "Adopt a Pet" with Frenchie, who was an instant star. After Harold told Mike Buresh and the viewing audience Frenchie's story, the calls poured in to the SPCA by the hundreds with offers of adoption. Frenchie had a new home by 3:00 that afternoon.

I was fortunate enough to be given a video of the "Adopt A Pet" show featuring Frenchie and a photograph of Frenchie and her new owner as they appeared outside the animal shelter that same Saturday afternoon. She and her new mistress looked so happy together. It became a relationship well-deserved for Frenchie, the charismatic lady from Delhi.

Freddie the parrot

Freddie involved the case of the homeless parrot. Freddie was a bright red-and-green adult male parrot who had been taught to talk. In fact, Freddie not only had a pretty well-developed vocabulary, he could also mimic other animals. In short, Freddie was quite a bird.

Freddie's mistress had been placed on probation by me earlier in the year, but due to her having violated the conditions of her probation, I sentenced her to serve 15 days in the county jail. At her sentencing, the defendant became very distraught — not so much because I had sentenced her to serve 15 days, but because she had no one to care for Freddie while she was a guest of the county and she feared that something might happen to him. In order to be a reasonable judge, I told her that I would personally see to it that Freddie would be cared for in her absence. As soon as court was over for the day, I telephoned Norbert Mahlman, who, at the time, was the president and general manager of the Hamilton County SPCA. Norbert graciously agreed to help out. That same afternoon, Freddie was picked up at the defendant's apartment with the assistance of her landlady, who let the animal shelter officers into the apartment, and off Freddie went to the SPCA shelter just as if he was going to summer camp.

At first, Freddie was kept on his stand in the front office where the employees could show him attention, to keep him from being lonely. This turned out to be an unsatisfactory arrangement, due primarily to Freddie's desire to talk to everyone all day. It was bad enough that Freddie chattered all day, but the things he vocalized were worse. First of all, he greeted every woman with a shrill wolf whistle. Every time one of the ladies who worked in the office left the area, she was greeted with this tribute when she returned. Then Freddie would spend long periods complaining that he had no food or water, which, of course, was not correct since his water and food supply were located in containers attached to his perch. Finally, he would go off on a binge of shouting "Shit" or "Fire" in alternate rhythm. This made some conclude that Freddie may have served a stint in the artillery.

In an effort to preserve some decorum in the office, Freddie was moved to a small open area between two sets of dog runs. There he could not see the dogs, and they could not see Freddie. However, they could all hear each other. It didn't take long before Freddie learned to imitate the bark of each dog in these two runs. So, as you might imagine, the dogs barked and Freddie barked. It was great fun for Freddie. The more the dogs barked, the more Freddie responded with gusto — until the humans who worked at the shelter could stand it no longer. Poor Freddie had worn out his welcome. After eight days, he ended up in a room all by himself, where he chose to entertain himself by yelling "Help" every 10 minutes or so. Finally, after 15 days, which must have seemed like an eternity at the animal shelter, Freddie went home to Price Hill.

Unfortunately, not all of the animal cases handled by me in my courtroom between 1981 and 1996 were entertaining or humorous. I imposed a six-month jail sentence upon a racetrack employee who angrily stabbed a valuable thoroughbred horse in the chest and legs with a pitch fork because the 3-year-old animal had leaned against the man while he was cleaning the thoroughbred's box stall at River Downs Race Track. The injuries suffered by the horse ended his racing career. I have never understood the kind of blind anger that would cause someone to go after a beautiful animal with a pitch fork. I believed then, as I do now, that a jail sentence was in order in that case.

Two other animal cases left an indelible mark on my memory for the brutality and tragic consequences. The first was the case of the North College Hill dog, and the second was the Bybee Kennel case. Both are worth dealing with as a finish to my interesting judicial career with our friends, the animals of Hamilton County.

The six-times shot puppy

Throughout my judicial career, I have considered myself to be a strong advocate for our law enforcement agencies. I have many police officers among my close friends. For these reasons it has never been easy for me to find fault with the actions of a police officer, especially when it is a judgment call, that is to say, any matter where the officer had to rely on his own judgment in an emergency situation. Since a judge does not witness an event that ends up in the courtroom and can never look into another's mind, it is the worst kind of Monday morning quarterbacking to be required by the judicial oath to second-guess the actions of a police officer. This is in no way made easier when one knows the officer personally.

Maggie was a 6-month-old female German shepherd owned by Sherry Kratzer, a 22-year-old secretary. Maggie was shot six times by North College Hill Officer Daniel Davis when he responded to a call from a neighbor that a frightened dog was running around loose in her fenced-in rear yard.

This was a civil case in which Ms. Kratzer was asking that the city of

North College Hill or Officer Davis or both be ordered to pay her $5,300 for the negligent and wrongful shooting death of her dog, Maggie.

The facts of this case alone were as unusual as the actions of the police officer. The story unfolded during an extremely heavy thunder shower on a June day in 1980, replete with resounding thunder claps and brilliant lightening strikes. As it turned out, Maggie was very frightened of thunderstorms. Maggie had, that morning, been placed in the garage where Ms. Kratzer lived because it was raining. There was food and water in the garage, and her owner thought Maggie would be safer in the garage than tied up in the back yard.

Sometime around noon, when the thunderstorm had reached its peak, Maggie went through the open window and through the back yards on Mulberry Street until she ended up in the fenced yard at a neighbor's home. The neighbor saw Maggie frantically roaming the inside fence line of the back yard trying to find a way out. When the lady went outside and tried to approach Maggie, Maggie growled at this unknown woman. As the woman testified at the trial, the puppy appeared to be extremely frightened and distraught. She called the North College Hill Police Department and reported a stray dog in her back yard.

Within 10 minutes, Officer Daniel Davis arrived at the location after being dispatched by radio. The information given to him on his police radio was "stray dog in rear yard on Mulberry Street, reported to be frightened by storm."

The neighbor lady came out of her home just as Officer Davis drove his cruiser into her driveway. She took him to the back yard, where he could observe Maggie running around still trying to find a way out of the fenced area. Since she was going to one corner, the neighbor believed she was trying to get out to go home.

After observing Maggie for several minutes, Officer Davis returned to his cruiser and got a rope from his trunk, with which he proceeded to fashion a lariat. As he started back up the driveway, the neighbor observed the officer unsnap the strap of his holster, which, she testified at trial, scared her. She inquired of Officer Davis, "You are not going to shoot the dog, are you? Why don't you call the SPCA?" The neighbor testified that Officer Davis told her that it would not do any good to call the SPCA because the agency would not respond unless the dog was tied up. Norbert Mahlman testified that such a statement was incorrect, and that had Officer Davis called the SPCA on his police radio or through his department's dispatcher, an SPCA unit would have responded within 45 minutes.

As Officer Davis walked up the driveway with his holster unsnapped, the neighbor stated that she feared that he intended to shoot the shepherd. Officer Davis entered the gate near the driveway and approached Maggie, who was trying to avoid him. He began trying to lasso the frightened animal, which made her more terrified. Finally, she stopped running and crouched down. As Officer Davis approached her, she let out a low steady growl. Officer Davis testified at the trial that at this point in time, Maggie lunged at him. However, the neighbor lady disputed this testimony, stating, under oath, that the dog began to whimper and actually started backing away from the advancing police officer, who is over 6 feet tall and weighs well in excess of 200 pounds and also, on the day in question, was in full blue uniform and armed with a .357 Magnum revolver, a baton, chemical mace, handcuffs and 2 feet of looped rope.

Regardless of whether Maggie was moving toward Officer Davis or away from him, the stillness of Mulberry Street was suddenly shattered by gunfire. By the time it ended, which was a mere matter of seconds, six shots had been fired and six shots had found their mark. Six-month old Maggie was dead, her body riddled by six .357 Magnum, solid-point, 280-grain bullets. The neighbor was so upset that she retreated into her home and would not come out until after the SPCA arrived and removed Maggie's body. All she could repeat over and over was, "Why didn't Officer Davis call the SPCA first?"

During the trial, Officer Davis was asked, in addition to why he did not radio for help from the SPCA, why he had not used his chemical mace or his baton if he feared that Maggie was about to attack him. To these questions his reply was that he didn't know.

As if to add insult to injury, when Sherry Kratzer went to the North College Hill Police Department three days later to recover Maggie's collar and to ask Officer Davis what caused him to shoot her dog, he responded to her inquiry by writing her a citation for permitting Maggie to run loose on the day he killed her. Ms. Kratzer was acquitted of this charge at a trial held before another judge.

After hearing the evidence in the civil case, I ruled that Officer Davis had acted in haste and had been negligent in his decision to shoot the dog as opposed to seeking other solutions such as calling the SPCA to tranquilize the aroused dog or waiting for backup or calling for the fire department to respond with a net. I believed that the animal's death was unnecessary. I further ruled that it had not been shown satisfactorily that the shepherd was chasing or worrying Officer Davis, which are necessary elements of the

Ohio law that permits someone to kill a dog.

The inability of the officer's attorney to produce evidence that Maggie was chasing or threatening Officer Davis at the time of the shooting meant that the killing was unnecessary and, in effect, an act of negligence.

Sherry Kratzer had sought a judgment in the sum of $5,300 — claiming that Maggie was worth that amount because she intended to use her for breeding purposes. However, since Maggie was only 6 months old when she was killed and had never produced puppies, a claim of future value for breeding purposes was speculative and could not be proven by her owner. My award of $284 was based upon testimony concerning the cost of replacing Maggie with a similar shepherd, plus the veterinarian bills that Ms. Kratzer had incurred for Maggie. I also suggested that the city pay the damages so that they would not come out of Officer Davis' pocket. After the Kratzer trial was over, I contacted Dolores "Dee" Dunn, the law director for North College Hill, to determine whether the city would pay the award to Ms. Kratzer so that Dan Davis would not have to pay it out of his own pocket. Dee, being a true advocate, did not agree with the decision I had made with regard to the evidence but did agree with me that Officer Davis had not acted maliciously when he shot the dog and that if he had, in fact, been negligent or had acted rashly, it was out of fear and not to seek to punish a 6-month-old pup. Further, we agreed that since the officer had been dispatched to secure the dog and since his actions, right or wrong, were done in the performance of his duty as a North College Hill police officer, any judgment awarded in favor of the plaintiff should be borne by the city and not the officer, individually.

The city of North College Hill paid the judgment out of the city treasury. Sherry Kratzer used the money to purchase a replacement for Maggie. But in her heart, Maggie lives on, as her photograph and her collar kept on a bedroom chest of drawers proves.

CHAPTER 13

SLEEPING ON HOMECOMING NIGHT CAN BE DEADLY

I can still recall from high school days how much effort was devoted to fall homecoming, the game and the big dance held each year after what we hoped would be a gridiron victory. Now, in 1987, as a judge, I would always remember Norwood High School's homecoming and 17-year-old John Fenton.

October 17 was a warm, very sunny fall day. My wife, Judy, and I had made plans to have dinner at a downtown restaurant with Jack and Rachel Rosen. Jack was a colleague of mine on the bench. We had become close friends, and regularly the four of us would get together for a late dinner and conversation.

Just after midnight, we said our goodbyes to the Rosens and started our half-hour drive west to our home in the village of North Bend. It was a clear evening with a full moon and a sky filled with stars.

Shortly after we passed the old Amtrak station on River Road, I noticed that the automobile in front of us was being driven extremely slow for the conditions. As I drew closer, I noticed that the vehicle was starting to weave — first left, then right and then left again. Judy noticed it at the same time and voiced concern that I not get too close, since the driver might be intoxicated.

After a few hundred more feet, I was close enough to the vehicle to determine that it was a two door Nissan. I could see through its rear window. There was no head visible above the backrest of the driver's seat. I thought out loud, "My God, there's no driver."

In the amount of time that it takes to count to three, the dark Nissan made one more swerve to the right, and then, as if the driver were making a left-hand turn into a driveway, the car sped across the eastbound lane and struck a steel telephone pole dead center. The crash caved in the entire front of the vehicle, as if the auto had arms to wrap around the roadside pole.

There wasn't much time to think. I pulled our car over to the curb in front of the crashed Nissan, which by now had smoke and sparks shooting out from under the buckled hood. There were what appeared to be small flames dancing around the exhaust manifold. I could smell battery acid. But, amazingly, the engine was still running and the headlights were still on.

The driver was unconscious. The force of the impact had thrown him forward against his steering wheel, breaking his jaw and a collarbone, and then his body was catapulted back so hard that he had broken the seat back, which was lying on top of the rear seat, behind his head. He looked as though he were in a recliner.

I could smell burning insulation, and the sparks continued to bounce on the street beneath the front of the caved-in grille. I tried to rouse the driver, who appeared to be young, but I could not. I did manage to get the driver's door open after putting my right foot against the side panel behind the door and pulling on the handle with both hands. Finally, after several loud creaking sounds, the driver's door popped open. At the same time, I yelled to my wife to get away from the Nissan, which I feared was about to burst into flames. At this point, Judy took off running toward the Super America station located about a block farther west in order to have a clerk call 911 for police, fire, and a life squad. I reached in and turned off the ignition switch. The engine sputtered several times and died.

As Judy ran down River Road, I tried to pull the young man up and out of his Nissan. But I couldn't move him because his seat belt and shoulder harness would not release. Apparently, in the collision with the telephone pole, the buckle to his seat belt had jammed. It was later determined that the seat belt buckle was actually bent double.

As I was struggling to pry the seat belt away from the driver's waist, I became aware that there were several younger men standing behind me offering assistance. I asked if there was a knife available among this trio. This question was answered for me with the swish and click of a 6-inch switchblade knife. I took the open knife so graciously provided and reached back into the car, first cutting the lap belt and then the shoulder harness as it crossed the victim's chest near his throat. Now that the seat belt and shoulder harness were severed, I was able to drag the unconscious victim out of his Nissan with the help of two of the young Good Samaritans. The third one retrieved his knife.

We carried the young, bloody motorist down the sidewalk far enough to get him away from the still smoldering Nissan. He was bleeding fairly heavily about his head and face, and his left shoulder was obviously injured. Besides a lot of blood, I noticed that he had baked beans in his hair and on his jacket. The odor of bacon and beans was fairly prevalent.

However, despite any earlier suspicions, there was a complete lack of the odor of any alcoholic beverage on this poor soul.

While my young helpers stayed with the injured motorist, I ran back to his Nissan and found a book bag and a blanket, which was also covered with baked beans. There were also several casserole dishes lying on the rear seat and floor. The back seat looked like there had been a food fight inside the Nissan.

I removed the book bag and the blanket. I accidentally dragged the remains of a bright red-and-blue striped tie out of the car. The tie had no knot, and it was in two pieces. It was at this point that I realized that while cutting the seat belt harness away from his chest I had also cut the lad's necktie off just below the knot. After all, it was dark that night.

I returned with the book bag, which I placed under the victim's head; then I covered him with the blanket. Since he was still bleeding heavily from a gash under his right jaw, I made a compress with my handkerchief and held it as tightly as possible against his jaw in an effort to stem the flow of blood. It did not take very long before I had almost as much blood on me as our injured friend had on himself.

Gradually, he opened his eyes and started moaning. About the same time, my wife returned, saying that the police and an ambulance as well as a fire truck were on the way. For some reason that will never be known, when my wife mentioned "police," my three helpers and the switchblade knife disappeared in their automobile, never to be heard from again by us.

Within another minute or so, I was able to learn from our injured friend that his name was John and that he had been on his way home when the accident occurred. He was in a state of shock and kept asking me how bad his injuries were. I lied and told him that it was no more than a scratch, but he didn't buy that story because of all the blood that he could see on my white shirt. He knew that the blood he saw was his and not mine. He complained that his shoulder hurt him very much and that he was having trouble breathing. I was afraid to move him again, fearing that he might have broken ribs that could puncture a lung.

Suddenly, a Cincinnati police cruiser whizzed past us, and then another. As the third cruiser approached, lights and sirens activated, Judy ran into the street and flagged it down. Luckily, this police cruiser was being operated by Sergeant James Whalen, a friend and the son of then Cincinnati Police Chief Lawrence Whalen. Apparently, the first two cruisers had sped by in response to a report that the Super America station was being robbed. Judy was sure that she had told the clerk on duty to call and report an automobile accident with injuries in the 2700 block of River Road. How the dispatcher came to send police to a robbery at that Super America was just comic relief on a bizarre evening.

With the help of Jim Whalen and his radio, the cruisers that had gone onto the Super America returned. Soon, a fire engine and an ambulance arrived. The firefighters quickly extinguished the charred Nissan while the emergency medical technicians attended to John Fenton with a variety of tourniquets, slings, bandages and braces. He was placed on a stretcher, wheeled to the ambulance and whisked away to the University of Cincinnati Medical Center for necessary repairs.

Jim Whalen had taken John's wallet for safekeeping. An examination of its contents turned up a driver's license, a small amount of cash and a card that told us that in case of an emergency please notify the Reverend Thomas A. Fenton, 5318 Delhi Drive in Delhi Township.

As it turned out, John's father was the new pastor of the Delhi Hills Baptist Church. Yet John's driver's license listed him as a resident of Norwood, Ohio. I was questioned concerning whether I suspected that John had been consuming alcohol before the accident. I explained to the officer that I had not smelled or observed anything that would lead me to believe that alcohol was the cause of John's accident. As it turned out, this was correct. A blood test administered that morning at the hospital revealed that there was absolutely no alcohol nor evidence of drugs in John's system. John had quite simply fallen asleep behind the wheel of his Nissan, lost control, and hit a pole.

At the insistence of Jim Whalen, I washed my hands and arms with a special medicated soap located in the fire engine. He was concerned about possible blood contamination, as I guess we all are these days. There was no problem.

On Sunday afternoon, Judy and I drove to the UC Medical Center to visit John. It was then that we met his father, mother, and his older sister. They were happy to meet us, and it became a little embarrassing as I was hugged and squeezed. John was a mess. He had suffered a broken jaw, broken collarbone, broken hand, a 4-inch gash in his jaw, a black eye, bruised ribs and a slew of cuts, scratches and facial bruises. But he was alive, and that was what really counted.

As it turned out, John, who was a senior at Norwood High School with a perfect 4.0 scholastic average and the student chosen to be valedictorian of his graduating class, had worked at his part-time job all day Saturday. He had prepared dinner for his girlfriend, which he delivered to her home to be consumed there. Part of the meal John had prepared consisted of baked beans. At least now that mystery was solved. After dinner, John and his date placed the leftovers on the floor of John's Nissan before leaving for Norwood's Homecoming Dance. After John took his date home, he started his drive to his parent's house in Delhi to spend the night there and to return his mother's casserole dishes. By the time John started out River Road, he had been up for 18 hours, had worked a full day, cooked a meal, attended a dance where he drank nothing but soft drinks, and finally had fallen asleep behind the wheel of his Nissan on his way to his parents' house. Not only was there no alcohol or drugs involved in John's accident, the investigating officers decided that John should receive no form of traffic citation. Whether my presence had any bearing on the decision that a traffic citation was not called for is up to conjecture. I can only say that it was a single-car accident and the only person injured was John Fenton. As far as property damage, scratch one Nissan.

On October 27, 1987, Steve Hoffman, a reporter for *The Cincinnati Enquirer*, wrote a very well-thought-out article about John's accident and the value of seat belts.

The publicity given to John's accident by Steve Hoffman's article caused almost immediate repercussions from officials at Norwood High School. John and his parents were notified that John would not be allowed to attend classes at the high school for his final semester; that he would not be allowed to graduate from Norwood High in June 1988, and finally that he would not be his class valedictorian since he would not be graduating from Norwood High School.

Had John's automobile accident caused this reaction from his high school administration? Had he violated a school rule by falling asleep at the wheel of his Nissan and almost killing himself? No, the actions of the Norwood school district had absolutely nothing to do with his automobile accident, but it had everything to do with the fourth paragraph of Steve Hoffman's article, in which he wrote: "Young Fenton was en route home to Delhi Township from Norwood High School's homecoming dance when he fell asleep at the wheel on River Road early that Sunday and hit a utility pole."

John was not kicked out of the high school he had attended for three-and-one-half years because of an auto accident. He was expelled because a newspaper article had innocently stated that his home was in Delhi Township, which is not in the Norwood School District but rather in the Oaks Hills School District. Thus, the administration of the Norwood

School District had decided, based on one newspaper article, that a senior with a perfect 4.0 scholastic average, a National Merit Scholarship finalist and the recent recipient of a full four-year scholastic scholarship in physics and mathematics from Harvard University in Boston was not going to be allowed to graduate with his class as its valedictorian because his home was publicized as being outside Norwood.

Until August 1987, John, his sister and their parents had resided in Norwood, where John's father was the minister at a Norwood Baptist Church. Shortly before John commenced his senior year, his father was offered the pastorship of the Delhi Hills Baptist Church, located on Foley Road in Delhi Township. A house went with this assignment. The offer was too good for John's father to refuse. But John did not want to leave Norwood High School after three years to transfer to Oak Hills High School, where he had no friends and would have a different curriculum to digest during his final year of high school.

When John's parents decided to accept the position in Delhi, they met with officials in Norwood and explained the residence problem. It was suggested that John find a place in Norwood to live to comply with the school district's residency requirement. So then it was decided that a furnished room would be rented for John in Norwood by his parents. In this way, John lived in Norwood during the school week, using his furnished room to study and going to Delhi on the weekends to be with his parents. During any given week, John slept at least four nights in Norwood and usually three in Delhi.

However, now that John's story had been published, a small but vocal group of parents demanded that John be expelled from Norwood High School, claiming that his rental of a furnished room inside the Norwood School District was a mere ruse. Bowing to pressure, the superintendent notified John's parents that John had been determined by the district to be a nonresident since his parents and natural guardians now resided in the Oak Hills School District in Delhi Township, and that John would have to transfer to that district as soon as possible.

In one fell swoop, all of John's educational achievements and acknowledgments — so hard won and earned — were on the verge of being stripped away from him. He was faced with the possibility of having to transfer to a strange school, where he knew no one, and also the possibility that the differences in the two school systems' curriculum could delay his graduation from high school beyond June 1988, which, of course, would cost him the four-year scholastic scholarship at Harvard — which at the time had a total value of approximately $160,000. Now, $160,000 is a lot of money to any family, much less the family of a Baptist minister.

Acting on sound advice, the Fentons brought legal action against the Norwood school system in common pleas court to prohibit and enjoin the district from expelling their son, who by now had only six months of high school to complete graduation. Their case was assigned to Judge Richard A. Niehaus, who, after hearing testimony and evidence, ruled that John was, in fact, a legitimate resident of Norwood by virtue of his having a furnished room in Norwood and spending most of the school week there. Judge Niehaus ruled that the fact that John's parents, who were also his natural guardians, lived in another school district was not determinative of John's residential status, provided that his residence in Norwood was with the knowledge and consent of his parents — which, of course, it was. In addition, Judge Niehaus determined that John's parents and John had discussed the matter of his residency with school officials prior to their move to Delhi. He ruled that there was sufficient evidence for the court to find that the Norwood school officials involved were aware that John would be living in a furnished apartment in Norwood after his parents moved to Delhi.

Judge Niehaus's sensible and equitable decision allowed John to finish his senior year at Norwood High School. I received an invitation to John's graduation in June 1988 at Cincinnati's Riverfront Coliseum. John delivered an inspiring valedictorian address. He expressed his gratitude to Judy and me.

John not only went on to Harvard University, he graduated from that institution in 1992 with high honors. Today, John is married and pursues a successful career. He is a credit to his parents, his family, and his community.

Certainly, in this case, the fine tooth comb of justice saved a life, a graduation, and a scholarship. The system can do wonders when given the opportunity.

By the way, I gave John a graduation gift in 1988. It was a very handsome bright red-and-blue striped tie. I owed him one.

A seat belt, municipal judge helped save car wreck victim

—

BY STEVE HOFFMAN
The Cincinnati Enquirer

Seventeen-year-old John H. Fenton is another living testimonial to the merits of seat belts.

His father, the Rev. Thomas A. Fenton, and Hamilton County Municipal Court Judge Albert J. Mestemaker last week credited the seat belt in his 1983 Nissan with saving young Fenton's life Oct. 18.

The Norwood High School honors senior suffered a broken jaw, collarbone and hand and a partially collapsed lung.

Young Fenton was en route home to Delhi Township from Norwood High School's homecoming dance when he fell asleep at the wheel on River Road early that Sunday and hit a utility pole.

Mestemaker, who was driving behind Fenton, managed to cut the seat belt wrapped around him, remove him from the car and summon a Cincinnati life squad, which rushed him to the hospital.
"The only reason he is alive today is that seat belt," said his father, pastor of the Delhi Hills Baptist Church.

"He's lucky he had the seat belt on, he didn't hit an oncoming car or a nearby house," Mestemaker said.

"I had been dancing for four hours and I did not feel tired," said John Fenton later, speaking through his wired jaw. "I thought I could make it home. I guess I didn't."

The wreck occurred on westbound River Road in the Riverside-Sedamsville area.

Mestemaker said he and his wife were on their way to their North Bend home at the time, about 1 a.m..

"We were right behind him, we had just heard the radio report about the two Milford High School football players who were killed and then suddenly, this car made a sharp left turn, crossed the street and wrapped itself around the pole," he said.

Mestemaker estimated Fenton's car was traveling 25 to 30 mph when it hit the pole. He said traffic was "fairly light."

"There was smoke and sparks coming from the hood and I was afraid it would burst into flames. The door was caught and I had to put my foot against the car to jerk the door open."

Fenton was in a reclining position because the seatback had broken, Mestemaker said. "I couldn't release the belt or slide him out. He was out (unconscious) at first, but then he came to and began moaning."

Mestemaker managed to cut the seat belt when one of three young men, who stopped to offer help, supplied a knife.

"I even cut off the end of John's tie," said Mestemaker with a laugh.

He managed to drag Fenton away from the car to a nearby sidewalk and used the youth's book bag under his head as a pillow.

"He didn't panic; he's a great kid," the judge said. "We were both soaked with blood."

The Mestemakers visited Fenton at the hospital the next day.

Fenton hopes to return to school some time this week .

"He's very fortunate," said his father.

The youth started his final year at Norwood High with a perfect 4.0 scholastic average. He was a named a National Merit Scholarship semi-finalist in September.

PART THREE

THE TIME OF ADVERSITY

CHAPTER 14

HANG THIS JUDGE

After 14 years and 25,476 cases heard and decided, there were days on the bench when even the great King Solomon would have been tempted to order the two claimants of motherhood to be split in half instead of splitting the baby.

Not only was 1995 a re-election campaign year for me, it was the fourth in 14 years. Like the others, it would be a contested race — no free ride available for this judge. It would also be the first time I had to run in a judicial district instead of countywide. The new judicial districts, which had been created in 1992 by federal court order, were intended to achieve racial diversity among the judges. This affirmative-action scheme was anathema to a majority of the judges. Of our court's 14 judges, three were members of the racial group intended to be assisted by the scheme — and those three judges had all been elected countywide.

March 1995 was a tedious month. It marked my 14th anniversary as a municipal court judge. I also learned that my opponent in the November election was to be a Western Hills lawyer who had strong connections among Elder High School alumni. Elder is a large Catholic boys' school with a long tradition of kinsmanship among its alumni, all of which foretold a hard campaign ahead for me.

At the same time, our criminal and traffic caseloads had increased almost 50 percent. And as a result of the brand-new, mandatory arrest law in domestic violence cases, which became effective on March 9, the number of these types of cases increased from a previous high of 3,991 in 1994 to 6,329 cases in 1995, a total increase of 59 percent. There is no other crime in Ohio that mandates an arrest — not even in a case where murder is involved. As luck would have it, I was scheduled to be the arraignment judge the week that the mandatory arrest law became effective, adding to the docket over 150 cases in one day alone.

And, to boot, I was dealing with persistent chest pains. They began by radiating from the chest down into the left arm, ultimately causing numbness in the left hand. The pains had started in December, and by March, they were becoming more frequent and more painful and lasting a little longer. But if we don't think about the problem, it will go away. So, we will work around it and double our daily aspirin dosage.

Despite all of the negativism, I was still considered as a law-and-order, firm-but-fair, no-nonsense jurist by prosecutors, defense lawyers and police officers — and even as an "umpire" by the *Cincinnati Post* afternoon newspaper, in which it had been written:

> Eccentric though he may be, Mestemaker is regarded as one of the best minds on the bench. He listens carefully to both sides and arrives at the kind of decision that has earned him the title of "umpire." He also has an astute understanding of the law unmatched by many of his colleagues.

And even though my record of judicial service included well over 100 jury trials with only 17 reversals by the court of appeals — representing one reversal for every 1,499 cases decided — the reputation that had been built over 28 years as a lawyer and judge was now, in 1995, to come under attack by the media. So aggressive and repeated were these media attacks that the storm raged out of control as if fueled by gasoline.

Ignited initially by a young female reporter for *The Cincinnati Enquirer*, the metropolitan morning newspaper, the media blitz zeroed in on the handling of domestic violence cases, even resurrecting the Orr case from 1992, as well as marriage orders and an alleged racial slur. The controversy would continue unabated from mid-July until November, when the voters, by then duly influenced, made their decision.

One columnist, Cliff Radel of the *Enquirer*, delivered his personal indictment on July 21st, when he wrote:

> Hang this judge. Albert Mestemaker is guilty of holding domestic violence cases in utter contempt. Before another woman takes a fist in the face, voters should sentence him this

fall to an early retirement for ordering spouse beaters to marry
their victims. Dismissing a battered wife's charges as "absurd"
and sending her home into the fists of her abusive husband,
Mestemaker's actions became a death sentence. Charles Orr beat
Delores Orr to death October 21, 1994.

Radel concluded with a reference to Nicole Simpson, murdered ex-
wife of O.J. Simpson, and a thinly veiled comparison between the actions
of "this judge" and the brutal murder for which Simpson was then on trial.
There is little doubt that the O.J. Simpson trial had catapulted the subject
of domestic violence and family abuse into the national limelight. God
help a male judge who was running for re-election in 1995 and who would
be branded as soft on domestic violence. According to Radel, I was as guilty
of Delores Orr's murder as was her ex-husband, Charles.

By 1995, advocacy groups had secured the passage of new laws
regarding domestic violence, such as:

- Victimless prosecution, wherein the case is able to proceed to trial
  even if the victim fails to appear to testify. This feature was previously available only in cases of homicide, where the victim is
  deceased and unavailable as a witness.
- Mandatory arrests of the accused in all family violence cases,
  regardless of the absence of evidence of violence or injuries, thereby depriving police officers of their normal exercise of discretion.
- Mandatory arrests of parents on the unsworn statement or accusa-
  tion of abuse by a child.
- The requirement that each complaint of domestic violence be
  investigated by at least two police officers and that they treat the
  case as if it were a homicide.
- The issuance by the arraigning court of temporary protective
  orders, which usually means that the alleged offender must find
  somewhere else to live until the case is over.
- The automatic confiscation of any firearms, even though not
  involved in the alleged offense.
- The prohibition that any person who has been convicted of
  domestic violence may not possess a firearm or ammunition. This
  last piece of federal legislation pushed through by the Bill Clinton
  administration affects anyone who must carry a firearm in his or
  her profession, such as police officers and military personnel.

So it was that on March 9, 1995, Ohio House Bill 335 — known as the

Victimless Prosecution Bill — became law in Ohio. Not only did Ohio's new domestic violence arrest and prosecution law contain the aforementioned characteristics, it also expanded the definition of household members to include former spouses, children of former spouses, and same-sex partners, including former same-sex partners. Partly as an outgrowth of the failure of Milwaukee, Wisconsin, police officers to remove a 14-year-old boy from serial killer Jeffrey Dahmer's apartment, Ohio's new mandatory arrest law placed a heavy personal burden on any police officer who declined to make a physical arrest in a domestic violence encounter — to the end that in many cases after the new law became effective, officers began to arrest both combatants in instances when it could not be determined who the aggressor was and who the victim might be. The result of this phenomenon was the courts being forced to arraign two individuals in two separate cases wherein the alleged abuser was the victim in one case and the victim was the alleged abuser in the other case. In 84 percent of these cases, both parties indicated their desire not to prosecute the other. Further compounding the complexity of this legal morass was prosecutorial refusal to file charges against individuals who falsely accused another of the crime of domestic violence!

The new mandatory investigation and arrest law created one hell of a logjam in the number of domestic violence cases that had to be processed. During February 1995, the last month before the new law became effective, 294 domestic violence cases were processed in Cincinnati and Hamilton County. Under the new law, the number increased in March 1995 to 687 cases, an increase of 393 cases or 134 percent — and this judge was on the front firing line.

Shortly, after the enactment of the new investigation and arrest law, the county prosecutor adopted a "No dismissal policy" under which the victim was not permitted to have the charge dropped even if there had been no injuries and no history of violence in the relationship. Since the prosecutor for the city of Cincinnati had not adopted the same policy, cases that originated inside the city could be dismissed if the victim requested a dismissal. Meanwhile, those that originated outside the city — in areas under the county prosecutor's jurisdiction — would not be dismissed.

Suddenly, where the arrest occurred became an issue of prosecution versus non-prosecution.

What follows are several examples of the types of domestic violence cases disposed of by me after the new law was enacted. The names of the parties have been changed to spare the individuals involved additional embarrassment.

Early in March 1995, one domestic violence case involved a 52-year-old woman who was the sole caregiver for her 27-year-old, mentally retarded son who resided with her. The son had struck his mother in the face during a disagreement about taking his medication. She had called the police only because the young man had become so distraught after he struck her that he threatened to commit suicide. Once the investigating officers learned that her son had struck his mother, she was advised that they were required to arrest her son for domestic violence. Despite the woman's pleas that they not arrest her son, she was told that there was no choice in the matter.

When the case was called for trial four weeks after the incident, the mother requested that the case be dropped. She stated that she had not been injured and that her son had not meant to strike her. He had no prior record for violence and was visibly upset about hitting his mother. The mother did not want her son to have a conviction for domestic violence, which she feared might mean that he could not continue to live with her, and he had nowhere else to live. She also feared that a conviction for domestic violence might cause her son to lose his monthly Social Security disability check, which was vitally necessary for his support. The police officers who made the arrest were not opposed to a dismissal of the case. Only the assistant prosecutor remained adamant that the case not be dropped without a conviction, regardless of how the victim or the police officers felt. After listening to the prosecutor's objections for about 10 minutes, I granted the mother's request and dismissed the case "at the request of the prosecuting witness."

On April 6, 1995, JoAnn Smiley was arrested for domestic violence after hitting her fiancée in the leg with a Frisbee.

On April 8, 1995, Richard Kline, a 74-year-old Marine veteran of World War II, was arrested for shoving his 22-year-old granddaughter in his kitchen after she called her 72-year-old grandmother a "bitch."

On April 11, 1995, 86-year-old Bailey Smith, who required the use of a wheelchair, was arrested for striking his 19-year-old nephew with his cane after he learned that the young man had forged his signature to and cashed the older man's Social Security check to buy crack cocaine.

On May 2, 1995, Ernest Hayes was arrested for domestic violence after a scuffle on the front porch of the family residence with his 17-year-old daughter, who had been grounded for seeing a boy against her parents' wishes. She went to a neighbor's home and called 911, alleging that her father had assaulted her. At trial, she recanted her story, admitting that she had called the police because she knew if she accused her father of domestic violence he would be arrested and removed from the family home, and that she wanted to get even with him for refusing to allow her to continue to see a young man who was abusing drugs. Except for the last case, the prosecutor's office objected to each dismissal by the court.

The stage was now set for the final act that would provide the local print media with sufficient fodder for sensational and controversial reporting that, in some respects, outdid the more familiar efforts of the "tabloid press." Or, as one reporter said: "Who does he think he is that he can try to force his 1950s morals on he rest of us?"

CHAPTER 15

MARRIAGE ORDERS AND RACIAL SLURS

Scott Hancock and Yvonne Sevier

"Judge Mestemaker ordered a convicted abuser to marry the woman he abused as punishment for domestic violence."
— Kristen Delguzzi, reporter, *The Cincinnati Enquirer*

"The femi-Nazis will get this whacko judge."
— Rush Limbaugh, on his radio talk show

"Believe it or not folks, some unbalanced judge in Cincinnati believes marriage is the best punishment for men who beat up their girlfriends."
— Paul Harvey of "NOW you know the rest of the story" fame

"Hang this judge."
— Cliff Radel, *Cincinnati Enquirer* metro columnist

"An Addyston man has nine months to marry the woman he punched in the mouth or risk imprisonment."
— Kristen Delguzzi, reporter, *The Cincinnati Enquirer*

"He is completely out of line. Why should anybody think that if they were married, he wouldn't hit her again? The offense of the judge is almost as bad as the offense of the abuser."
— Zauzi Smith, president of the Cincinnati Chapter of the National Organization for Women, as reported in *The Cincinnati Enquirer*

"Cincinnati, Ohio, U.S.A., local judge orders brutally beaten woman to marry her assailant."
— *Morning News* of London, England

As of July 13, 1995, Scott Hancock and Yvonne Sevier had been living with each other for four years. Their daughter, Lindsey, was almost 3 years old. They were living in a home owned by Scott's father, James Hancock, located at 144 First Street in Addyston, Ohio. As related to me by Addyston police officers, Yvonne had an older child who was living with her parents. Yvonne was also several months pregnant with a second child of Scott's.

Yvonne was unemployed. Hamilton County welfare records revealed that she was receiving benefits from the Hamilton County Department of Human Services, and Scott was listed as residing with Yvonne while unemployed. As a result, Yvonne was receiving ADCU (Aid to a Dependent Child Father Unemployed) for Lindsey in the sum of $341 a month. Yvonne was also receiving $318 a month in food stamps as well as $300 or more a month in rent subsidy. Since she was residing with Scott in a home owned by his father, it was believed that the senior Mr. Hancock was receiving the rent subsidy money. Yvonne was also receiving welfare medical insurance benefits for herself and her daughter at a monthly cost to Hamilton County of $300. Therefore, at the time Yvonne Sevier appeared in court as the victim of a domestic violence charge in which Scott was the defendant, she was receiving approximately $1,259 a month in public assistance for herself and Lindsey. Scott, by his own admission, was living with Yvonne and enjoying the food and subsidized rent paid for by the taxpayers. There was one big problem: At this time Scott, was gainfully employed.

There is a notation in Yvonne's file at the Department of Human Services indicating that in June 1995 the client received benefits through error due to the failure on the part of a caseworker to verify the child's paternity and the father's employment status. At the time, Yvonne was receiving food stamps for three people.

By July, the Department of Human Services had become suspicious. An investigation was about to be launched concerning the eligibility of Yvonne to continue to receive benefits. Scott, at this time, had other problems. He had been arrested in Addyston on April 23, 1995, on charges of driving under the influence of alcohol, driving under suspension, failing to maintain reasonable control of his automobile, and leaving the scene of an accident. And now, at age 25, Scott had a new and more serious criminal charge to face. For during the early hours of Saturday, June 24, 1995, Addyston police officers were called by a neighbor to stop a fight between Scott and Yvonne on the sidewalk near their shared residence. This was not the first contact that Patrol Officer Mike Schmit of the Addyston Police

Department had with Scott and Yvonne. However, it was his first contact that he had with them since the new domestic violence arrest procedure had become law in March.   When he arrived at 204 First Street and observed Yvonne with a cut on her lower lip, he asked what had occurred. Perhaps in honesty, or perhaps out of disdain, Scott told the officer that they had been arguing and that a scuffle had followed during which he pushed her in the face, cutting her lip. At this point, Officer Schmit told Scott that the new domestic violence arrest law required him to arrest him for domestic violence.

Once the fact that Scott was being handcuffed and being placed in a cruiser for transportation downtown settled in Yvonne's mind, she leaped into action. She told Officer Schmit that she did not want Scott arrested. Then she told the officer that nothing had happened. When he asked her what happened to her lip, she said that it was no one's business. She stated that she would not sign a complaint against Scott. This argument failed, since Officer Schmit told her that he would sign the affidavit and complaint as the arresting officer, thereby putting the matter out of Yvonne's control.

It was not until the officers threatened to arrest her as well that Yvonne backed off and stopped interfering with the arrest of Scott Hancock.

Shortly after 9 a.m. on Monday, June 26, Scott Hancock was brought out of lockup before the arraigning judge. Yvonne was present. First she attempted to drop the charge of domestic violence, which she was told would not be permitted for several reasons — one being that the police officer and not she had signed the affidavit and the complaint, thereby rendering her a victim-witness but not the prosecuting witness. The prosecuting witness was by law the person who signed both the affidavit and the complaint under oath; to wit, Officer Mike Schmit of Addyston. Having failed to gain a dismissal of the case, Yvonne's next tact was to plead with the judge to reduce the bail that had been set on Sunday by another judge. She told the judge that nothing had happened and that she was not afraid of Scott. Besides, Scott had to get out of jail or he would lose his job. Of course, she did not tell the judge that she was receiving ADCU on the basis that Scott was unemployed. The judge agreed to reduce the bail to $2,500 at 10 percent, and he granted Hancock's request of a two-week continuance so that he could hire a lawyer.

Yvonne had several hundred dollars with her, which enabled her to hand the clerk $250 plus a $20 state fee. It cost her $270 to spring Scott from jail and to take him home with her, even though a protective order had already been issued by the judge — which required Scott to stay away from the house and away from Yvonne. Neither of them had any intention of obeying this order, or, for that matter, any other court order.

But Scott had a real dilemma. He had hired attorney Dean Pruitt to represent him in Addyston on the DUI charge. He had paid Pruitt a retainer to secure his services. Now, he had to decide whether to call Pruitt and tell him that he was also facing a charge of domestic violence, which would cost him more money — or whether to try to go it alone, meaning represent himself. Yvonne helped Scott make his decision by telling him that he didn't need a lawyer on the domestic violence case because she fully intended to go back to court with him on July 13 and get the charge dropped. Because of Yvonne's promise not to prosecute, Scott did not call Dean Pruitt and tell him that he needed him to defend against a domestic violence charge. Yvonne would handle the problem for him. Yvonne Sevier and Scott Hancock appeared together in Room A on Thursday, July 13, 1995, before me. They had no idea that they were on the threshold of international notoriety. Neither did I.

On July 13 when the Hancock case was called and Scott and Yvonne entered Room A together, holding hands, Yvonne was primed to do her part to get this domestic violence case dismissed. She immediately approached Assistant County Prosecutor Penny Cunningham and told her that nothing had happened — that it was all a big mistake. She became quite irritated when Ms. Cunningham advised her that the case would not be dismissed. The debate between Ms. Sevier and Ms. Cunningham occurred while I sat observing the interaction. Finally, after Yvonne had said for at least the fifth time that Scott had not struck her and that the charge was a lie, Hancock spoke up and said: "Why are you saying this. I admit I hit you, but you started it."

At this point, I finally interceded. I asked Scott whether he had an attorney. He said that he did not. I asked him whether he wanted another continuance to obtain an attorney. He replied that he wanted to get the case over with. He did not want to have to come back to court again on this case. I then inquired whether he wanted to sign a waiver of attorney and enter a plea that day, advising him that he could be put in jail for six months and fined $1,000. He responded by saying that he wanted to get it over with. "I'll sign the waiver of attorney and enter a plea of guilty."

I suggested instead that he sign the waiver and enter a plea of "no contest" — because a "no contest" plea admitted only the facts and was therefore not as onerous as a plea of guilt. He followed this advice, signed the waiver, and entered a plea of no contest. As soon as I heard the words "no contest," I asked him whether he was doing this voluntarily, and reminded him again that he could be sentenced to six months in jail and fined $1,000. He then verified that the signature on the waiver was his and that he had signed it voluntarily.

The preliminaries having been accomplished, I asked Ms. Cunningham to read the facts, which were: "Your Honor, may it please the court. The defendant, Scott Hancock, on or about June 24, 1995, in the village of Addyston, Hamilton County, state of Ohio, did knowingly cause physical harm to one Yvonne Sevier, a person living with him as his spouse, by striking her in her lower lip."

That was it. Those were the facts. When Ms. Cunningham was finished, I asked Scott whether he had anything to say. He said, "No." I said, "Guilty of domestic violence." I then turned to Yvonne Sevier and asked her how serious her injury was. I could not observe any mark on her face. She told me that her lower lip had been split, but that it had healed. Again, she said that nothing had happened. I told her that we were beyond that. Now all I wanted to hear was what they both had to say to me before I passed my sentence on Scott.

As was my custom, I began asking them questions. Their answers informed me that they had been living together for several years, and that they had a 3-year-old daughter named Lindsey. I asked them whether they were married; they said that they were not. I asked them why they were not married; the response was that they were planning to get married. They were saving money to get married, and they wanted to get married. I asked them about the drinking. Both admitted they drank too much beer, and that the only time they fought was when they both had too much to drink. I advised Scott that a marriage license cost only $35 and that I guessed that he spent more than that amount each week on beer. He agreed with me that he did. I then asked them if it wouldn't be better for their 3-year-old daughter if she had a married mommy and daddy. They said that of course it would be better. I then said, "Why not do it? Why not sanctify your relationship with a wedding."

I then said to them, "I will tell you what. I am going to give you a choice. Stop drinking and fighting and break up. Or, for the sake of your daughter, get married. The choice is yours. I probably can't order you to get married, but I know that I can order you to stay away from each other. Of course, who knows if even that is enforceable today? But I want you to make a decision: I want you to tell me now what will it be."

Scott and Yvonne looked at each other and then at me. "We will get married," Yvonne said. "I don't want to break up."

Scott stated that he would choose to get married as well. He wanted his daughter to "have a good home."

I had been looking at Scott's record, which I had before me. I noticed that he had no criminal record, and — most important — nothing indicating violence. He had been convicted six times since 1989 of minor traffic offenses. I then noticed that he had traffic cases pending in Addyston. I asked him what they were. He told me about the driving under suspension and leaving the scene of an accident on private property after losing control of his automobile. I asked him if that was all; his answer was, "Yes." In fact, Scott was lying to me about his traffic cases. He concealed the fact that one of the charges pending in Addyston was a DUI. And for some unknown reason, the record before me did not show a pending DUI charge. I was to learn about the DUI from Dean Pruitt.

After questioning Scott about his pending traffic cases, I asked him and Yvonne whether they had anything further to say to me before sentence was to be imposed. They said that they did not. The following exchange then took place.

> The Court: The sentence of the court is as follows. Serve 120 days in the Justice Center. I will knock off 60 days because you were honest enough to plead "no contest."
> The defendant: But, your Honor ...
> The Court: Wait a minute, Mr. Hancock, I'm not finished. I will suspend the 120 days and place you on nine months probation with the following conditions. One, family counseling; two, alcohol counseling for both of you because you both drink too much beer. Three, you and Yvonne are to sanctify your relationship with a wedding or break up, what will it be?
> The defendant: Marriage!
> Ms. Sevier: A wedding!
> The Court: OK, a wedding, and no fighting. Remember Mr. Hancock, if you touch her again you will spend 120 days in jail. Do you understand me?
> The defendant: Yes, sir.
> The Court: All right, now, in addition, I will fine you $1,000, but if you have no more arrests or convictions, I will forgive $900 of the fine and you will have to pay only $100 plus court

costs. Do you understand me? Is it worth $900 for you to stay
out of trouble and also stay out of jail?

The defendant: Yes, sir.

The Court: Any further questions?

Ms. Sevier: No, your Honor.

The defendant: No, sir.

The Court: Then fine. Report to this probation officer sitting
here. She will tell you where to report. Call the next case.

So, it was that this case ignited the media firestorm. Apparently, a
reporter had been sitting in the courtroom during the disposition of the
Hancock case and called the local news desk, alerting the courthouse
reporter to a possible story.

The *Enquirer's* courthouse reporter, Kristen Delguzzi, reached me at
home that evening and asked me at to explain the sentence to her.
Although I was reluctant to give her an interview, I explained that I had not
ordered Yvonne to marry Scott Hancock as some form of punishment, but
rather had given them a choice, which was to stop fighting with each other
or break up once and for all. I told the reporter that when they said that
they did not want to be ordered to break up I then told them to sanctify
their relationship with a wedding. Despite this explanation, the story was
carried the next morning stating that the judge had ordered an abused
woman to marry her abuser as a form of punishment.

The article first published on the front page of *The Cincinnati Enquirer*
on July 14, the day after the couple appeared in court, stated:

> An Addyston man has nine months to marry the woman
> he punched in the mouth or risk imprisonment under a sen-
> tence imposed Thursday by Hamilton County Municipal Judge
> Albert Mestemaker.
>
> The couple, whose argument on a sidewalk near their
> Addyston home turned violent June 24, has a young child
> together.
>
> The judge ordered Scott Hancock to seek counseling, enter
> an alcohol treatment program and marry his girlfriend, Yvonne
> Sevier.
>
> In court Thursday, Sevier professed her love for Hancock.
>
> "Maybe someone needs to nudge them along to get mar-
> ried," Mestemaker said. "I happen to believe in traditional

American values: boy meets girl, boy asks girl out, boy and girl go steady, boy and girl get married, and then boy and girl start raising a family," Mestemaker said.

The article was picked up by The Associated Press wire service and reported first nationally and then internationally, becoming more distorted with each repetition, in the same manner as a shipboard rumor in the Navy. It wasn't long before the story was being reported as:

"Brutally beaten woman ordered by a judge to marry her attacker."

On July 26, a group whose members called themselves the Lesbian Avengers held a mock wedding ceremony on the steps of the Courthouse. The groom was carrying a baseball bat and the bride had her arm in a sling and a cervical collar on her neck. As part of this ceremony, the participants handed out handbills referring to me as "Judge Mess-maker" and urging onlookers to express their ill feelings toward me at my home, supplying my address for the occasion.

Hancock and Sevier were offered $10,000 plus expenses to go to New York and agree to be married on a nationally televised show. I was contacted by producers of the *Today Show, Good Morning America* and *48 Hours* — just to name a few — who wanted me to debate my sentence with legal scholars and leaders of women's advocacy groups on national television. I quickly declined all offers to appear on TV or radio talk shows. In my mind, the affair was already a circus. My appearance or public remarks would only make matters worse.

In the meantime, Scott Hancock and Yvonne Sevier had a change of heart. They advised the court through attorney Dean Pruitt that they preferred not to get married. At the time, I did not know that Yvonne was receiving over $1,200 per month in welfare assistance, or that she was expecting a third child. As a result, I did not understand the true reason for their decision to remain together but to remain unmarried.

As the result of a conference with Dean Pruitt and the prosecuting attorney, I made the decision to rescind the controversial marriage order. I also offered Scott Hancock the opportunity to re-enter a plea of not guilty to the domestic violence charge and to have his case re-assigned to a different judge. Hancock declined the reassignment offer, stating directly to me: "I don't want another judge. I am satisfied with you."

Still being unaware that Hancock had a pending DUI charge in Addyston, which would soon be transferred downtown to our court, I did not realize that he had an ulterior motive for not wanting another judge.

His intention was to have the domestic violence case resolved before our court system became aware of the pending DUI charge, which he believed would draw jail time, especially if it were discovered that he had lied to me about the nature of his pending traffic cases.

Scott Hancock's legal problems have continued to this day.   On January 6, 1999, while still living together and still unmarried, he and Yvonne had another altercation, which led to both of them being arrested and charged with domestic violence. Since Hancock had a prior domestic violence conviction, the new charge was a felony — for which he could be sentenced to prison for a year.

The prosecutor dismissed the charge that had been filed against Sevier in order to secure her testimony against Hancock.   However, this maneuver backfired because Sevier disappeared on March 29, the date of Hancock's scheduled trial. Without her as a witness, the prosecutor could not proceed to trial. So the new felony case of domestic violence against Hancock was dismissed. As soon as this occurred, Sevier re-appeared and resumed living with Scott Hancock as if nothing had ever happened between them, the same as they had in 1995. Once again, they used the system to their advantage and won. As usual, it was the taxpaying public and the justice system that lost out.

Even though the common pleas court judge who was assigned to preside over Hancock's felony domestic violence trial could have granted the prosecutor a continuance and ordered Sevier held in jail as a material witness until the next trial date, it was obvious to court observers that neither the judge nor the prosecuting attorney desired to continue to be burdened with Scott Hancock and Yvonne Sevier. And truthfully, I for one can accept and understand that position.

Richard Gambrell and Patricia Wilson

One couple said, 'I do' after judge told them to
— Headline in *The Cincinnati Enquirer*, July 22, 1995

The media hype about the Gambrell case was the most puzzling to me. All I ordered was that Richard Gambrell do something that he and his fiancée — Patricia Wilson, the mother of his two sons, Justin, age 2 years, and Ryan, age 3 — had said that they were planning to do anyway, which was to get married on June 30, 1995.

Richard Gambrell was 22 years old when he appeared before me. He continuously operated a motor vehicle on the streets of both Hamilton County and Clermont County while under various driving suspensions, including at least one court-ordered suspension.

The first time that Richard Gambrell was before me was on December 6, 1994, as the result of his arrest on October 18, 1994, by Deputy Sheriff Chris Ketteman on charges of driving under a financial responsibility suspension, driving under a point suspension, driving under administrative suspension, driving with an expired driver's license and possession of an open flask. Mr. Gambrell's cases were assigned to me to be tried on December 6, 1994. On that date he was convicted and given a suspended six-month jail sentence, a fine and a one-year, court-ordered driving suspension — due in large part to the fact that he was driving without so much as a dime's worth of insurance and drinking a can of beer while doing it. The last piece of advice that I gave Richard Gambrell on December 6, 1994, was: "Don't get caught driving again while under my court-ordered driving suspension. If you do, you will go to jail."

Exactly three weeks to the day after that warning, he was arrested by the same deputy sheriff, Chris Ketteman, while driving eastbound on Beechmont Avenue toward Clermont County. Of course, as usual, Gambrell, who cared very little about the rights of other citizens, was once again driving an automobile without any liability insurance — and this time under a court suspension.

Just to indicate how bad Richard Gambrell's luck was, not only was he arrested on December 27, 1994, by the same deputy sheriff who had arrested him a mere 21 days earlier, he also ended up with the same judge for both cases. To compound his problems, the judge remembered him.

As soon as Gambrell found out that his latest traffic arrest cases had been assigned to me, he told his appointed public defender lawyer, Winnie King, that he was not going to plead to anything. He insisted that his case had to go to trial because, as he said to her, "I can't afford to get convicted of driving under this judge's court-ordered suspension. He has already told me that if I got caught again I was going to jail."

Richard Gambrell's defense to the latest traffic charges was simple and direct. He claimed that his fiancèe, Patricia Wilson, was driving the automobile, not him, and that he was seated in the right front passenger seat the whole time. Basically, his testimony was to the effect that Deputy Sheriff Ketteman was lying when he testified, under oath, that he had observed Richard Gambrell driving the automobile. Ketteman said that as he made a U-turn on Beechmont Avenue to pull Gambrell over, he could see Gambrell sliding over the top of Patricia Wilson, who moved into the driver's seat. So, when the deputy pulled the vehicle over, Patricia was behind the wheel and Richard was seated in the right front passenger seat.

At the conclusion of Gambrell's latest trial before me, on March 28, 1995, I found him guilty as charged and sentenced him to six months in jail with the following admonishment:

"Any judge that lets this man out of jail can be guaranteed that within three weeks he will be caught driving a car again because court-ordered suspensions mean nothing to him."

The cell door had hardly closed behind Richard Gambrell before I started receiving telephone calls from Patricia Wilson and the defendant's mother. When I wouldn't speak to them on the telephone about the case, they both started writing letters to me. One letter from Patricia stated that their two boys cried themselves to sleep every night for their daddy. Another letter contained a copy of a letter purporting to be from a pediatrician, which asserted that the children were suffering from emotional stress due to their father's imprisonment. Another letter from Patricia claimed that she and Richard had already set a wedding date for June 30, 1995, their older son's birthday, and that if I didn't let him out of jail by then their wedding plans would be ruined. Gambrell's mother's letters, of which there were two, dealt with her son's newly found sorrow for his violation of the law and her belief that he had finally learned his lesson now that he was behind bars. She also enclosed a letter from his employer that voiced praise for the defendant's high work ethics and credibility. Finally, I started receiving letters from Gambrell himself from the Hamilton County Justice Center. He pleaded with me to let him go home to Patricia and the two boys. He promised that he would stop driving and drinking. He said that all he wanted to do was marry his fiancée on their son's birthday on June 30 and lead a decent life for his wife and his children.

On April 12, 1994, Winnie King was in my courtroom representing a different defendant. When the case was concluded, I called Ms. King to the side bar and gave her all of the letters that I had received on behalf of Mr. Gambrell. Ms. King read the letters in the courtroom. After she had given the letters back to my bailiff, Ron Flammer, I suggested that she file a motion to mitigate Gambrell's sentence and to have it set for hearing for the last week in April.

Winnie King followed my suggestion and promptly filed a motion to mitigate sentence on behalf of Richard Gambrell, setting forth in motion the reasons for mitigating the sentence to be the same matters as those set forth in the various letters — such as the children's need to have their father home; the mother's need to have him as her help mate; the maintenance of his employment, which depended on his being released from jail; and, finally, the need to carry out the planned wedding scheduled for June 30, 1995.

The motion to mitigate the sentence filed by Ms. King was set for hearing on April 25, 1995. Present for this hearing were Ms. Gina Saba, the original trial prosecutor on behalf of the state of Ohio, Ms. King on behalf of the defendant, the defendant Richard Gambrell, his fiancèe, Patricia Wilson, and the defendant's mother. The defendant's mother had also brought with her a new letter of support from her son's employer.

Ms. King spoke on behalf of Mr. Gambrell, urging the court to grant her motion to mitigate his sentence. Ms. Saba, the assistant prosecuting attorney, was given an opportunity to voice any objection on behalf of the prosecution to the motion. When asked whether she wished to be heard, Ms. Saba said, "No, your Honor." In other words, the prosecution chose not to oppose the defendant's motion. I wish now that she would have opposed the motion.

The following represents the hearing that concluded with the so-called marriage order.

(*Morning session — April 25, 1995*)
The Court: This is Mr. Gambrell, who absolutely refuses to stop driving under suspension. Correct?
Ms. King: Only now he has learned his lesson, your Honor. He has been locked up, has a family to take care of. Has a job working for Michael Vining Custom Homes. His mother is here. I have a letter from the children's doctor, who states how his two kids are affected by his absence. It is a hardship on the family not having their dad around.
Mr. Gambrell wrote you a letter apologizing for his behavior and telling you the positive impact incarceration has had on him.
The Court: What did you want to say, Mr. Gambrell?
Mr. Gambrell: I would like to say I think I have learned my lesson this time. Me and my fiancèe are planning on getting married in June. My little boy's birthday is next month.
The Court: How old will he be?

Mr. Gambrell: Two.

The Court: How many children do you have?

Mr. Gambrell: Two. I have one 3 years old and one will be 2. I have been taking GED classes since I have been here. I live behind Clermont College. I plan on getting my GED, if you let me out of here. I have been going through AA meetings since I have been here.

The Court: Do you need help with the drinking?

Mr. Gambrell: No, sir, I don't think I do.

The Court: Why are you going to AA meetings in jail?

Mr. Gambrell: Well, I think it has helped me a little bit going through them. It has encouraged me to quit drinking, I do believe. I have not had a drink, to start with.

The Court: How long have you been locked up now?

Mr. Gambrell: A little bit over 38 days.

The Court: Did you go in March 28? Isn't that when we had your trial?

Mr. Gambrell: Yes. I was locked up before that. I have been locked up since the 18th.

The Court: That was because you didn't come to court when you were supposed to?

Mr. Gambrell: Right.

The Court: Have you been locked up since the 18th of March?

Ms. King: That's right. His mother would like to say something.

The Court: Yes, ma'am.

Defendant's mother: Richard has a full-time job with construction. On days he doesn't work because of bad weather, I do own my own business, and Richard will be working with me.

The Court: I am trying to determine how that affects this.

Defendant's mother: I will go and pick up Richard.

The Court: So there won't be a temptation for him to drive?

Defendant's mother: I will pick him up. I live 15 minutes away.

Mr. Gambrell: My boss is willing to pick me up every morning, too.

The Court: Ms. King.

Ms. King: Nothing further, your Honor. Thank you.

The Court: You had one involvement with drugs earlier this year. What was that? Marijuana?

Mr. Gambrell: Yes, sir.

The Court: So you are going to get married?

Mr. Gambrell: Yes, sir, June 30.

The Court: You have already set the date?

Mr. Gambrell: Yeah, we have some of the stuff paid for, and everything.

The Court: You are in jail and you set your wedding date. You must have had some premonition.

Mr. Gambrell: We set our wedding date a few months ago.

The Court: You set it before you went to jail?

Mr. Gambrell: Yes, sir.

The Court: What was the date?

Mr. Gambrell: June 30.

The Court: Good. I will make that a condition of probation so your two sons will be legitimate. You understand what I am saying?

Mr. Gambrell: Yes, sir.

The Court: You have two little boys?

Mr. Gambrell: Yes, sir.

The Court: State wish to be heard?

Ms. Saba: No, your Honor.

The Court: Are these all county cases?

Ms. Saba: County.

The Court: The motion is granted. He is credited with 38 days, and we will suspend the balance of the days at this time on each case. And I am going to place Mr. Gambrell on one year's probation. There is an order for alcohol counseling and drug counseling, if needed. And he is to go ahead and get married by June 30. Maybe that will change his lifestyle. I hope it does. We'll have a $200 fine on the A charge, and $100 on the B charge, and $100 on the C charge, and they are all payable through probation. He is to report to probation as soon as he is released today Any questions?

Ms. King: Nothing further. Thank you.

The Court: He can have his letters back.

The journal entry in this case places two conditions of probation upon Richard Gambrell. The first one is that he receive drug counseling, and the second condition is that he get married June 30, 1995 as planned.

On July 18, a deputy court clerk called me to tell me that the same

Cincinnati Enquirer reporter who had written the Hancock-Sevier article was checking through my case files in the clerk's office trying to find any other case in which I had made marriage a condition of either the court's sentence or probation.

As the result of her search, she discovered the Gambrell case and decided to give Richard Gambrell and Patricia Wilson a public forum to vent their wrath — with suggestions from her. She interviewed them at their home on July 20, and her article about them appeared in the *Enquirer* on July 22.

It should be noted that the reporter did not contact me before she wrote her article. Therefore, her article failed to include my position and motivation for the marriage order. Even more mysterious is her apparent failure to read the transcript of the April 25 hearing. Had she ordered and read that transcript, which she could have obtained in one working day for a minimal fee to the court reporter, she would have learned that the subject of marriage was first broached by Gambrell and Wilson — initially in their letters to me — and by Gambrell in court on April 25 when he said:

"Me and my fiancèe are planning on getting married in June. My little boy's birthday is next month — June 30."

The Court: "So you are going to get married?"

Mr. Gambrell: "Yes, sir, June 30."

Why the reporter chose not to interview me as the judge or why she apparently did not review the hearing transcript before she interviewed the Gambrells and wrote her article shall remain unknown. Nevertheless, what follows is what she wrote for the July 22 issue of the *Enquirer*:

One couple said, 'I do' after judge told them to

A Clermont County couple said 'I do' in May because they were ordered to get married by Hamilton County Municipal Judge Albert Mestemaker.

Mestemaker, who vaulted into the spotlight last week after he ordered an Addyston man to marry the woman he abused, told Richard Gambrell on March 28 that he had to marry his girlfriend of eight years by June 30 or risk being sent to jail for violating his probation.

So Gambrell and his girlfriend, Patricia, found a justice of the peace. On May 23, the parents of two toddlers were married.

The Gambrells are among three couples — all with children — who Mestemaker sentenced to marriage. The

Gambrells, who live in Batavia, are the only ones to honor the judge's unenforceable order.

Unlike the other two cases, Gambrell was not before Mestemaker on a charge of domestic violence.

The 22-year-old was convicted of driving with a suspended license and was sentenced to jail. When Gambrell asked the judge to modify the sentence so he could help support his family, Mestemaker asked if he was married.

"I told him I had future plans to get married," Gambrell said.

Mestemaker then made a wedding a condition of probation. So the couple forsook the ceremony they had in the works and rushed to get married.

"I didn't get the wedding I wanted because I was afraid Rick would go back to jail," Patricia, 23, said.

"I think he owes us a big apology," Gambrell said.

In her article, the reporter sets the date of the marriage order as March 28, when, in fact, the hearing held to review Gambrell's jail sentence, which was the result of his lawyer's efforts to get him out of jail, occurred on April 25.

Her article also levels a claim that Patricia didn't get the wedding she wanted because they had to hurry up and get married because she was afraid Rick would go back to jail. How could the reporter have squared these statements of Patricia with the court transcript, which has Gambrell claiming before the judge that they had already set their wedding date for June 30, and that they had even paid for "some of the stuff"?

This is the same Patricia who also claimed to Deputy Ketteman that she, and not Richard, was driving the vehicle on December 27 — and accused the officer of picking on Richard.

It is highly doubtful that the questions concerning this reporter's lack of accuracy in this instance will ever be answered. She has moved on to a job in New Orleans. Was this merely a case of sloppy reporting? Or is it possible that she actually obtained a copy of the court transcript and then purposely altered the facts to make the story more sensational? She apparently believed the story to be one of importance, since she took a photographer with her to the interview. Or, as some have suggested, a few of whom are even her journalistic colleagues, is it possible that her interest was to do injury to a judge? Regardless of the reporter's intent, evil or not, the Gambrell story has never been able to pass a smell test.

Sara A. Whalen and Kenneth Collins

This case represents the third of three instances in which marriage was a consideration in a sentence imposed by me in any type of case. All three of these cases occurred between March and July 1995.

This particular case was disposed of on April 13, when Sara Whalen appeared in court accused of committing the crime of domestic violence against her boyfriend of eight years, Kenneth Collins. It was obvious from the beginning that Collins was a reluctant witness who did not want his partner convicted.

The facts of this case were that Sara Whalen and her boyfriend, Kenneth Collins, with whom she had been living for over seven years and with whom she had a 2-and-one-half-year-old son, had been in an argument over money. Sara became angry, and a pushing match started. It ultimately led to Kenneth being scratched on his face, arm and back by Sara's long fingernails. Since the police officer had actually signed the complaint, the prosecutor would not dismiss the case even though Collins, the victim, had not wanted a complaint filed against Sara and did not want to be forced to testify against the mother of his son.

The trial transcript of this case reveals the following:

(Morning session — April 13, 1995)
Ms. Saba: Your Honor, on the criminal docket, Sara Whalen. It turned out Mr. Owens is on vacation.
Mr. Smith: I am here in lieu of Mr. Owens. Both parties are here. This is a case where the officer filed a complaint. My understanding is that the alleged victim did not wish to have a complaint filed. With the state of affairs with domestic violence, we are going forward. They want to resolve this with a no contest plea. Everyone will agree this was mutual combat.
The Court: First-degree misdemeanor?
Ms. Saba: Correct.
The Court: Did you tell her she could receive a possible six-month jail sentence and a fine of $1,000?
Mr. Smith: Yes.
The Court: Plead no contest? Correct?
Ms. Whalen: Yes, sir.
The Court: Plea is accepted. Statement of facts.
Ms. Saba: Facts are, on or about March 18, 1995, Hamilton

County, state of Ohio, the defendant, Sara Whalen, did cause physical harm to Kenneth Collins, a person living as a spouse. They had been living together for seven years. There were injuries to Mr. Collins' face, arm and back, and scratches, and pictures of those that the officer saw.

The Court: Anything on the facts?

Mr. Smith: The officer noted this was mutual. They were tussling back and forth.

Mr. Collins: It was mutual.

Mr. Smith: Fortunately, he wasn't injured. It was not her attacking him. It was him standing there, and it got out of hand. That's all I have.

The Court: Guilty. Mitigation.

Mr. Smith: My client has no criminal record. She is 25 years old, works at Cincinnati Medical Laboratory as a phlebotomist. The parties had a 2-and-a-half-year-old son and are planning to get married soon.

Mr. Collins: This summer.

The Court: You are not married yet?

Mr. Collins: No.

The Court: Why not?

Mr. Collins: We are planning to do it.

The Court: We will take care of that. You will get married. That will be a condition of her probation.

I don't know what happened to the institution of marriage. Let me tell you what. When I got married, peopled got married first and then had children. There seems to be some confusion about that order now. Most people I have in front of me now have children all over the place and have no intention of getting married.

Mr. Collins: We have every intention.

The Court: Do you file a joint tax return?

Mr. Collins: No.

The Court: Marriage has a lot of nice things about it. Do you think maybe some counseling would be a good idea?

Mr. Collins: Her mom offered to pay for it.

The Court: We have all kinds of good counseling.

Ms. Whalen: I am trying to maintain my job. I started my job three weeks ago.

The Court: We will work your job in. Anything further from the state?

Ms. Saba: No, your Honor.

The Court: Anything further from the defendant?

Mr. Smith: No.

The Court: Ninety days, suspend 90 days, nine months probation. There are two requirements of probation, and one is marriage counseling for both of you. You are to go together to joint counseling and you are to go upstairs to probate court and get a marriage license and get married. The fine is $41 plus costs. Ms. Whalen can pay that through probation.

Long after this case was heard and after the dust had settled, newspaper dust that is, an attorney who was representing Kenneth Collins in an unrelated matter advised me that they were now married and getting along quite well. "They are now happily married. They believe that what you told them was correct considering what their life style was like in 1995. They wanted me to tell you that they believe that you treated them fairly, and that the reporting was inaccurate."

In retrospect, and after long consideration, a virtue of hindsight, it should be stated that, in general, an order of marriage is not a good idea — and its legality is questionable. But there were only three instances when this situation occurred, and all three cases had in common the fact that the couples were living together as though they were already married. They each had children together who had been born outside of marriage. And in each case, they told me that they wanted to get married and were planning a wedding. And in one case, Gambrell and Wilson, a wedding date had been set.

As we start a new century, concerned about family values and the future of our society, two-parent families are still considered by most to be the best situation for the proper raising of children. Media types such as Judge Judy, Doctor Laura, and Rush Limbaugh regularly stress the importance of marriage to a stable family life. In this climate, can it truthfully be said that a judge who advocates marriage for couples who have children together is a whacko?

Edna Ellery — racial slur

It is an honor for a lawyer to be chosen from among his fellow lawyers to be a judge and to be looked upon by society and held in the high esteem accorded to judges. Therefore, regardless of personal problems — health, stress or fatigue — a judge must at all times display patience and dignity, and employ common courtesy toward all members of the public who appear before him. Courtroom courtesy is clearly a duty owed to the public.

A judge should never seek to be extreme, peculiar, spectacular or sensational in his judgment or in his conduct on the bench. There are four basic axioms that apply to all judges:

(1) Hear courteously.

(2) Answer wisely.

(3) Consider soberly.

(4) Decide impartially.

Proper courtroom demeanor applies to everyone who appears before a judge, and especially to the judge himself. Even though judges are human and may be influenced by personal beliefs and reactions to events that occur in or out of the courtroom, any intentional remark or reaction can unduly influence the appearance of justice and propriety — especially when comments from the bench are made needlessly. Therefore, any remarks that appear to be ethnically or racially biased are the most insidious and harmful remarks that any judge can make. Such remarks will surely give the appearance that justice, at least in that courtroom, is color dependent.

One judge of the Hamilton County Municipal Court who retired in 1993 commonly referred to African-American men or women who appeared as defendants before him as "boy" or "girl." In one case, he told a white male defendant who was constantly violating the law: "Quit acting like a nigger."

This judge was extremely lucky that, for some unknown reason, the local media failed to expose his behavior — especially in light of the fact that other judges, lawyers, and in some instances the public were aware of his conduct. Perhaps the media weren't interested in such remarks made by a jurist who spent his formative years in Tennessee.

Another local judge who has served in a judicial capacity for over 25 years once told an African-American woman who was being sentenced to prison on several counts of welfare fraud that he wished that he had the authority to order her to be sterilized because, "You people breed like rats."

Fortunately for him, he did not make this remark in a year in which he was seeking re-election. While the media reaction to his comment was swift and scathing, it lasted only so long as it took him to apologize for his remark and to defend it by saying that it was said out of pure frustration caused by the number of people who cheat the taxpaying public out of welfare funds. He survived this controversy and today is one of the senior judges of the common pleas court for Hamilton County and a widely respected jurist.

Judges must remember that whenever they make a derogatory remark to a member of any racial or ethnic minority, confidence in the judicial system is damaged. A judge must remember at all times that individuals are not before the court as members of any race or ethnic group but are there as individuals. A case in point involved a judge in Wisconsin who was suspended from his judicial duties for a 1994 incident in which he advised a Hispanic defendant at sentencing that upon his release from prison he should "get out of town and go back to Puerto Rico ... because you can't make it in a civilized society."

While his beliefs about the problems of our society may have been acceptable in another setting, the expression by a judge of these thoughts from the bench is never acceptable.

These examples set the stage for the Edna Ellery incident. I did not intend my remarks to be interpreted as a racial slur, but that was how they were perceived, and for this I was seriously taken to task by the media and reprimanded by the Ohio Supreme Court.

Edna Ellery lives with a man named Marvin Young. They are not husband and wife. On August 14, 1994, Edna Ellery called 911 to report that Marvin Young had struck her and pushed her. When the police officers arrived at the residence, they found an intoxicated Marvin Young and an intoxicated Edna Ellery. The Cincinnati police officers who arrested Marvin Young for domestic violence reported that both parties were drinking beer, that both were intoxicated and that an argument had occurred during which Edna Ellery was struck in the face by Marvin Young.

Since this incident had occurred in Cincinnati, the city prosecutor rather than the county prosecutor was responsible for the Young case. At his arraignment on August 15, 1994, Young was represented by the public defender. A plea of not guilty was entered, and Young was released on a $1,000 at 10 percent bond. It is not unusual in domestic violence cases for the victim to put up the bond money to obtain the release of her assailant.

So it was in this case that Edna Ellery put up $135 (10 percent plus the processing fee) to secure the release of Young. In addition to posting his bond, Edna Ellery took Young home with her — even though the judge had issued a standard temporary protective order that forbade Marvin Young from going near Edna Ellery or her residence.

The Young case was set for a non-jury trial before me on September 6, 1994. On the trial date, a plea bargain was entered into between Mr. Young's attorney and the city prosecutor, in which a trial would be avoided by Marvin Young pleading guilty to a charge of domestic violence under the section that states that the defendant threatened the victim instead of the section that states that the defendant actually struck or injured the victim. The difference in possible penalties is quite significant. If convicted as charged, Marvin Young could have been sentenced to six months in jail and fined $1,000. Under the plea bargain reduction, the maximum jail sentence is 30 days and the maximum fine is reduced to $250. Needless to say, Marvin Young was willing to accept this offer by the prosecutor, who had secured Edna Ellery's permission to reduce the charge from a first-degree to a fourth-degree misdemeanor.

After the facts were stated in court, the charge of domestic violence was reduced. I was advised that Edna Ellery had initially told the prosecutor that she didn't want to proceed with the case and that it was her desire to drop the charge all together. Her reluctance to prosecute the man with whom she was living, and as it turned out she was supporting, prompted the prosecutor to offer the defendant the opportunity to dispose of the case with the plea to the lesser offense of threatening domestic violence.

It was apparent that alcohol had played a significant role in this case and that both the victim and the defendant abused alcohol in the form of beer, consumed quite liberally on weekends, when they were home together. This was borne out by the fact that Young was arrested on Sunday, August 14, at their home, and both were intoxicated at the time.

Partly at the request of Edna Ellery, who stated that she did not want Young to be locked up, and with the knowledge that she had posted his bond and had taken him home with her despite the temporary protective order, a sentence was fashioned with the view toward helping this couple overcome a persistent alcohol problem. As a result, I sentenced Marvin Young to serve 30 days in the Hamilton County Justice Center and suspended this sentence — choosing to place the defendant on probation for nine months, conditioned upon him immediately going to Alcoholics Anonymous, obtaining a sponsor, and attending regular meetings. I instructed Edna Ellery to also stop drinking and participate with Marvin Young in alcohol counseling. She told me that she would honor this condition. A fine of $150 was imposed, which the defendant was permitted to pay off in installments through the probation department.

Ten months later, on the morning of July 5, 1995, Marvin Young's probation officer came to see me before 9 a.m. to advise me that Marvin Young was to be in front of me that day for violating the terms of his probation. He advised me that Young was now in jail, being held on a charge of felony domestic violence in which Edna Ellery was once again the victim. I was also advised that neither Young nor Ellery had adhered to the terms of probation set by me on September 6, 1994. Specifically, Young had failed to report regularly to his probation officer. He had failed to enroll in Alcoholics Anonymous, had failed to obtain a sponsor, and had failed to attend any meetings or to verify any attendance. He had also paid only $16 of his fine in nine months. And, most seriously, he was now facing indictment before the grand jury on a felony charge of domestic violence. In addition, Ellery had failed to join AA and attend meetings.

I was also told that both Marvin Young and Edna Ellery continued to drink heavily each weekend, and that she still constituted their sole support. The probation officer added that he believed if Marvin Young were let out of jail again he was going to "do serious harm to Ms. Ellery." Not surprisingly, this probation officer proceeded to tell me that Ms. Ellery was attempting to get Young out of jail again, and that she was once again attempting to drop the latest charge of domestic violence, which, of course, was not going to happen since the new charge was a felony.

Finally, Young's probation officer told me that he really felt sorry for Edna Ellery because she was a poor, hard-working "Mexican" lady who had no family in Cincinnati, and that he believed she would be much better off if someone would tell her to break off her relationship with Marvin Young and return home to her family with her children. From this statement, I concluded that Edna Ellery was a Mexican national living in the United States in a very dangerous relationship. This set the stage for an uncalled for and very serious blunder on my part. The forum had now been erected upon which I would embarrass the victim of a crime by reference to her ethnic background and do tremendous damage to myself as a judge.

What follows is the entire transcript of what was said by me to Marvin Young and Edna Ellery in open court on July 5, 1995. As before, the public defender was representing Marvin Young, and he was very familiar with the case.

(Morning session — July 5, 1995)

Mr. Sauter(prosecutor): Marvin Young on the criminal docket.

Mr. Johnson (public defender): Probation violation. Plea is no contest.

The Court: Failure to report for initial interview. They say he never came in. Defendant has another pending probation violation before Judge Gaines, July 13 of '95. Defendant is currently locked up in Queensgate. Defendant also has a new case pending

Mr. Johnson: I am not sure about the —

The Court: Felony domestic violence. Has he been indicted already?

The defendant: No. That's not me.

Mr. Johnson: He may not have been aware of it, if it just came out. He may be going through arraignment on that this coming Friday.

The Court: Do you know whether or not this felony arrest involves this same person?

Mr. Johnson: That, I do not know.

The Court: This was a fourth-degree domestic violence, and he had 30 days suspended.

Ms. Ellery: When this happened, he had been drinking, and we got into an argument.

The Court: He was supposed to go to AA meetings and quit drinking. Do you still drink, too?

Ms. Ellery: Sometimes.

The Court: Are you the same lady on the present case pending where he is locked up now? He has a felony. And how many times have you had him arrested?

Ms. Ellery: About three times.

The Court: Do you think you folks are done? You cost the taxpayers $10,000. When will it stop? Where are you from?

Ms. Ellery: El Paso, Texas.

The Court: Ever think about going home?

Ms. Ellery: I got kids here.

The Court: Why is America being punished? Did we do something to you folks? We have to pay for all your crimes. Did we do something wrong? Could we get foreign aid from your native land for you being here? Now he has a felony. Who is his felony attorney? I know, the taxpayers are paying for him. Did we do something to your country? Did they send you here to get even with us for something? Montezuma's revenge? How long has he been locked up? I will give him the balance of the 30 days. No sense having him on the street.

Mr. Johnson: He has been locked up 19 days.

The Court: Credit 19 days. Is he being held on some kind of a high bond, Mr. Johnson?

Mr. Johnson: $1,000 bond, 10 percent.

The Court: You say that the grand jury has not reported out on that?

Mr. Johnson: If they have, he has not been made aware.

The Court: Has he been locked up 19 days?

Mr. Johnson: Yes.

The Court: Serve 11 days, terminate probation. And the case is closed. Serve the fine with the days.

(Proceedings concluded.)

An apology was tendered by me to Ms. Ellery by telephone shortly after the incident. The Young case and the revelation of my remarks to Edna Ellery became public domain only after I issued the order of marriage on July 13 to Scott Hancock and Yvonne Sevier.

After the Hancock-Sevier case was heard, a telephone call was made from a member of the staff of the prosecuting attorney for Hamilton County to the newsroom at WXIX-TV, advising the television station's news staff to investigate and follow up on an important tip that on July 5, Judge Mestemaker had insulted a Hispanic lady by telling her to go back to Mexico.

WXIX-TV's news director immediately dispatched a reporter to the Courthouse with instructions to obtain a transcript of the July 5 hearing and, in particular, my remarks to Edna Ellery. She was not interested in a transcript of any other hearing that had been held in the case, telling the court reporter:

"I need the transcript of the judge making a racial slur to a Hispanic lady, including a remark about Montezuma's revenge."

That evening, July 18, a WXIX news anchor reported this story and referred to me as a "jerk." He asked a colleague, "How can we get rid of this guy?" At which point he was told that I was up for re-election in November. Looking at the lens of the camera, the anchor said:

"Did you hear that, folks? He's up for re-election. This is your chance to get rid of this jerk."

All in all, I have to admit that when it came to what I said to Edna Ellery on July 5, I truly was a jerk. There was no excuse for what I said to her, and I regret it to this very day.

The Lesbian Avengers*
request the honor of your presence
at the ceremony of deadly matrimony
of
Ms. Beaten Belinda
and
Ms. Abusive Alice
mandated by the Honorable
Judge Mess-maker
on Wednesday the 26th of July
to be held at the Courthouse
on Main Street.
If you too are fuming over Mestemaker's "family values," stand up and speak now...
or forever hold your peace.
Ill wishes and regrets may be sent to
Judge Mestemaker himself
at 2521-19 Cliff Rd., North Bend, OH.
* a direct action group focused on issues vital to lesbian survival and visibility.

Flier issued by the "Lesbian Avengers," which was circulated in the vicinity of the Hamilton County Courthouse.

Patricia Wilson repeatedly petitioned the court to grant early release to Richard Gambrell, alleging that the couple had planned and paid for a June wedding to take place prior to their son's birthday. Ryan was 3; Justin 2.

—15.

6

JOURNAL ENTRY

ASE: C/95/TRD/001247/A

TLNO: 1934025   TICKET: 00/00607327   ARREST DATE: 12/27/94

● VIOL: 4507-02B /ORCN   JUDGE

     UNDER FRA OR SAFETY SUSP

EFENDANT: GAMBRELL, RICHARD   SEX: M   DOB: 2/05/73

LEA: _N/G_ . FINDING: _Gne_ .

IS THE SENTENCE OF THIS COURT THAT THE DEFENDANT BE COMMITTED TO THE CUSTODY OF THE SHERIFF OF HAMILTON COUNTY

AYS: _180_ SUSP: _142_ CREDIT: _38_ STAY: _____ COMMITTED: _____

INE: _200_ REMIT: _____ SUSP: _____ STAY: _____ COMMITTED: _____

COST: _CRC_ REMIT: _____ SUSP: _____ STAY: _____

PROBATION: _Out of a_ YRS/MOS/DAYS: _____ PAY PROB: _____

     DRIVING SUSP: _3_ YRS/MOS/DAYS   EFFECTIVE DATE: _____

DRIVING CONDITIONS:

NO privileges - This was an aggravated case all DLS are

Consecutive

FRA COMPLIANCE - _____ FRA/NON COMPLIANCE - _____ PREVIOUS DUI CONVICTIONS: _____

CONDITIONS: ① _A/C & Drug Counseling is mandatory_

② _A is to get married 6-30-95. As planned_ ①

● 4/25/95

ATE: 3/28/95   SIGNATURE OF JUDGE: _Mike maher_

Judge's journal entry granting the petition for release of Gambrell, July 28, 1995.

CHAPTER 16

THE DISMISSED DOMESTIC VIOLENCE CONTROVERSIES

Ronald and Donna Kraus

Judge Mestemaker presided over the case of a man who abused his wife of 17 years. He said the man was legally, technically guilty of domestic violence, according to court transcripts. But then, the judge said he had no intention of putting the man in jail and found him not guilty.
— Kristen Delguzzi, *The Cincinnati Enquirer*, July 22, 1995.

As of 1995, Ronald and Donna Kraus had been married for 17 years. They had two sons, ages 11 and 8 years. Neither parent had ever been in a criminal courtroom before in their life. Ronald Kraus had absolutely no criminal record. His only mistake was having a physical argument with his wife, Donna, after March 9, 1995, when the mandatory domestic violence arrest provision became law. This case was so weak that Steve Adams, the assistant county prosecutor who tried the matter, made an opening statement that included the following remark: "This is a domestic violence case. But for a policy, we would probably be dismissing the case, a policy of non-dismissal." Whenever a prosecutor makes an opening statement such as in this case — instead of a traditional opening statement in which the prosecutor outlines what evidence he intends to introduce in order to prove that the defendant is guilty — a signal is sent to the judge that even he, the prosecuting attorney, does not believe that he can prove that the defendant is, in fact, guilty. Just such a signal was sent to me in the Kraus case. I thought that I understood what the assistant prosecutor was saying to me. Adams was telling me that he had a lousy case, but that because the Hamilton County prosecutor's office had taken a position in March 1995 that domestic violence cases would not be dismissed — except in very rare instances, such as the state's inability to locate witnesses — he was obligated to present his evidence, which even he did not believe credible, and then let the judge make a finding of not guilty. Sometime between July 17 and 20, Kristen Delguzzi, the Cincinnati Enquirer reporter who had originally reported the Hancock-Sevier case, obtained a copy of the Kraus transcript. She did not order it from the court reporter, which leads one to the conclusion that she must have obtained it from one of her several sources in the county prosecutor's office. In this case, I was told that she received it from Adams, who had ordered it from the court reporter. During the week of July 17, Delguzzi was writing almost daily stories critical of my handling of domestic violence cases. She received the Kraus transcript in time to include it in her article that was carried in *The Cincinnati Enquirer* on Saturday, July 22, 1995. She wrote:

> More recently, on June 2, Mestemaker presided over the case of a man who abused his wife of 17 years. He said the man was "legally, technically guilty of domestic violence," according to the court transcripts. But then, the judge said he had no intention of putting the man in jail and found him not guilty. Mestemaker said he was concerned because, "We, as a society, have allowed everything that goes on within the family to be controlled and supervised by the government."

The Kraus trial was certainly unusual in at least one respect. It was the first time and the only time that I, as a judge, ever asked the victim of a crime what the victim wanted the court to do with regard to a finding of guilt or innocence. Mrs. Kraus requested that I find her husband not guilty of domestic violence. I obliged her request. The exposure of Ronald and Donna Kraus to the Hamilton County criminal justice system commenced March 10, 1995. On that day, they became embroiled in an argument during which Donna accused Ronald of lying to her, and he tried to resolve the argument by leaving their home. The testimony of Donna Kraus revealed that the physical aspect of the verbal argument developed after she threw a telephone at her husband, a man who would later be labeled by the reporter as an "abuser." Her relevant testimony was as follows:

(Donna Kraus, questioned By Mr. Adams:)
Question: Were you with Mr. Kraus, Ronald Kraus, on March 10, 1995?
Answer: Yes.
Q: And were you at your home on Zion Road?
A: Yes, sir.

Q: This happened in the state of Ohio, Hamilton County?

A: Yes, sir.

Q: Did you happen to get into some type of argument with your husband?

A: Yes, sir.

Q: About what time was it?

A: In the evening time, maybe 7:30, 8 o'clock.

Q: Had either of you been drinking prior to this?

A: No.

Q: What was the argument about?

A: We were arguing about something that started at work. I accused him of lying to me. And when he came home, he started packing up his clothes to leave.

Q: What proceeded to happen from there?

A: After he left — I didn't want him to leave, but he left anyway — he went to where he was staying. And then I followed him there. We got in an argument at their house. When I got there, he was on the phone. I grabbed the phone out of his hand, and I threw it at him. He was trying to ask me to leave, and we were kind of scuffling, pushing each other. I finally left. When I left, he had his clothes in his truck. I took the clothes out of his truck, and threw them in the yard and left to go home.

Q: Did he follow you home?

A: A few minutes later, he came home. I was in my room. Actually, I was in the kitchen when I heard him come in. We started arguing, and we went to our room, the bedroom. That's when we started pushing and yelling and screaming and fighting.

Q: Who started pushing, yelling, screaming and fighting?

A: We both started.

Q: Who made the first push?

A: I don't remember who made the first push. We were yelling and screaming at each other.

Q: And what did your husband grab you by?

A: He grabbed me by my bra. I had a shirt on and a pair of shorts, and he ripped my bra off.

Q: Did he rip anything else off?

A: He ripped my shorts off and threw me down.

Q: How did he throw you down? Did he pick you up first?

A: Picked me up and threw me down.

Q: Did you fall down on the ground?

A: Right on the carpet in my room. Yes, sir.

Q: So you were lying on the ground before you got up?

A: Yes.

Q: Was you husband still standing?

A: He was standing there getting ready to walk down the hall to leave.

Q: Were you in any pain at that point in time?

A: No. I was just scared.

Q: Did you feel he would cause you further harm at that point in time, immediately after he threw you on the ground?

A: No, sir. I did not. I thought he was going to leave. I wasn't sure if he was going to leave. That's when I called 911. When I heard his truck start up, I said, "Forget the 911 call." And she said, "Ma'am, we cannot do that." They dispatched the police to my house. When they showed up at my house, they asked me if there was domestic violence. I said, "Yes, sir, there was." They stated, "What happened?" I explained what happened. And then they said, "We are going to have him arrested." I said, "I don't want him arrested. He is gone." They said, "By the new law, we have to go and arrest him."

Q: You admitted you thought domestic violence went on. When you told them that, what was your idea of domestic violence at that point in time?

A: We were arguing. He picked me up and threw me down (indicating).

Q: You are indicating?

A: But we were both arguing.

Q: That didn't hurt at all?

A: That we were arguing?

Q: That you were picked up, thrown on the ground.

A: Yes, I told them that.

Q: Did it hurt you at all that you were picked up and thrown on the ground?

A: Yeah. It hurt when I got thrown down, but I wasn't in any pain. After it happened, it was over.

Q: But it was an immediate sense of pain?

A: Yes.

Mr. Adams: Nothing further.

The Court: Mr. Pruitt.

Mr. Pruitt: A couple questions.

(Cross-examination by Mr. Pruitt:)

Q: Did you suffer any bruises or were you harmed in any way after this event took place?

A: No, sir.

Q: In the emotion of the moment, what was taking place at your home between Ron and you this particular night? Have you had occasion to reflect on it since then?

A: Yeah.

Q: Did you feel like when these events took place, Ron was try-ing to hurt you?

The witness: Was he trying to hurt me? I think he was trying to get my attention.

Q: The answer is no?

A: No.

Mr. Pruitt: I don't have any questions.

Mr. Adams: State will rest.

At this juncture, I became convinced that the assistant prosecutor realized that he could not make a case of domestic violence because even though the arresting officer was present to testify, he did not call him as a witness — electing instead to rest after the testimony of Mrs. Kraus. This is very much a standard procedure when the prosecutor believes that call-ing additional witnesses will not salvage a bad case. I used to follow this procedure when I was a prosecutor. It is a way of not wasting everyone's time when more witnesses will not mean more evidence of guilt. The other thought that crossed my mind that caused me to believe that Adams was not "pushing" the case was the fact that Donna Kraus had clearly testified that at no time was she injured, and that she did not feel that her husband would cause her harm. One of the necessary elements of domestic violence as a first-degree misdemeanor is proof that physical harm was caused to the victim. In this case, it was obvious that Donna Kraus had not been physi-cally injured or harmed. I concluded that Adams had recognized his fail-ure to elicit testimony of physical harm from Donna Kraus, and that he was prepared for a court finding of not guilty. The only other witness who testified at this trial was the defendant, Donald Kraus, whose testimony was generally the same as his wife's. Relevant portions of his testimony were as follows:

(By Ronald Kraus:)
A: "I left the house, took my belongings and went to where I had been staying with my sister. She came in the house, took the phone out of my hand, hit me with the phone. I kept trying to get her to leave. She wouldn't leave. I tried to push her out of the room. She broke the glass out of my gun cabinet. She left, took the portable phone, threw it in the yard, got in my truck and took my personal belongings — a briefcase, check book, billfold, clothing — and threw them on the ground and left. I didn't pay much attention to all this. I didn't know what had happened. Later on, my sister and brother-in-law came down and told me my clothes were all over. So I go to my truck to check for things. All my belongings are gone — my clothing, briefcase, checkbook, so forth. So I go back to my own home to try to retrieve them. At that time, tempers were flaring. I walked in the house, go in the bedroom to find these things, didn't find them, started to go back outside and look inside her car, which was locked, went back in the house. At that time we got into a shoving match, I don't know who started what. She bit me on the hand. When she bit me on the hand, that was basically when I went off. At that time, I went to get out of the house. Previously, when I tried to leave the house earlier, she got in the truck two or three times and wouldn't let me leave. I had another set of keys, was the only reason I could leave. As I was going out of the house, we were still scuffling. The only thing that entered my mind was, if she doesn't have clothes on, she won't come outside and try to get in the truck when I leave. That was why I tore her bra off and her shorts.

(By Mr. Pruitt:)
Q: Donna also testified that you picked her up and threw her on the ground.
A: I probably did. In the heat of the moment, I couldn't tell you exactly what happened.
Q: Was she struggling with you at that time?
A: Yeah, we both were.

Q: She bit you on the finger previously?

A: Bit me on my hand.

Q: Whatever she was doing, you were holding onto her, she was struggling, attempting to hit you?

A: Correct.

Q: Ultimately, I take it that you left home, and that was the end of the incident?

A: Yes.

Q: But for you spending a substantial amount of time in jail before you were released?

A: Yes.

Q: Did you attempt to cause your wife physical harm?

A: I didn't have the intention to.

Mr. Pruitt: No further questions.

The Court: All right, sir. Step down. Anything further, gentlemen?

Mr. Pruitt: No further witnesses. We rest.

The Court: Rebuttal.

Mr. Adams: No, your Honor.

The Court: Argument.

At this point I fully expected the assistant prosecutor to submit the case to me for decision without oral argument. Based on all the evidence before the court, he had failed to prove that the victim had been injured. He had also failed to prove that the defendant had intended or attempted to injure or cause physical harm to his wife. And finally, since he had failed to call the arresting officer as a witness, the case boiled down to the classic one-on-one situation where the evidence is of equal weight — which is a far cry from evidence beyond a reasonable doubt, which is necessary before there can be a finding of guilt in a criminal case. Before I could enter a finding of guilt in this case in which I was the trier of the fact, there being no jury, I had to satisfy myself that I was convinced beyond a reasonable doubt that the state had proven each and every element of the offense of domestic violence. Based on the nature of the evidence in this case, my answer to this question was, No, I was not convinced beyond a reasonable doubt that Ronald Kraus had been proven guilty of the crime of domestic violence. Instead of submitting the case, the assistant prosecutor launched into a closing argument that included a lecture to me on his concept of what the law of domestic violence is in Ohio. I have to admit that I grew weary of the argument being presented and made a very injudicious and discourteous remark to the prosecuting attorney. My response to the legal lecture was swift: "When I want you to teach me law, Mr. Adams, when I want you to lecture me on the law — I will ask you." Of course, this made him very angry, and perhaps caused him to feel the need to seek revenge.

Having now heard all of the evidence, I pondered whether there could be even a technical finding of guilt in this case before I finally asked Mrs. Kraus whether she really wanted me to find her husband guilty of domestic violence, which question she answered in the negative.   The transcript of this exchange follows:

> The Court: He may be legally, technically guilty of domestic vio-
> lence. I understand the problem. This lady doesn't want her
> husband of 17 or 18 years in jail. Therefore, I don't have any
> intention of putting him in jail. I am concerned about what's
> happened in the past and what their present situation is. I am
> concerned about the future. I am concerned about domestic
> violence cases. I am concerned about where we are headed as a
> society.   Do you folks have children?
> Ms. Kraus: Yes.
> The Court: How many?
> Ms. Kraus: Two.
> The Court: What are their ages?
> Ms. Kraus: Eleven and 8.
> The Court: Because, folks, we, as a nation, have ceased to be
> responsible people, which we have since 1945. The state legis-
> latures in every state, including the one you folks live in, have
> written laws that deal with how you behave toward each other.
> Our legislature has passed laws that control how you behave
> toward your children. You can now be arrested and brought to
> court for child endangering, if some outsider feels that you have
> disciplined your children too aggressively. The legislatures have
> now passed laws that govern the way you treat your household
> pets, if you have pets, because you can be brought to court for
> cruelty to animals. So what have we done?
>   In the 50 years since 1945, we, as a society, have allowed
> everything that goes on within the family to be controlled and
> supervised by the government. Now, I am going to ask you
> something I have never asked anybody before. Do you want me

to find your husband guilty of domestic violence?

Ms. Kraus: No, sir.

The Court: Not guilty. I would hope you folks are mature enough that nothing like this will ever happen again. Are you?

Ms. Kraus: Yes.

The Court: Are you?

Mr. Kraus: You won't see me again.

The Court: I asked you if you are mature enough to never allow anything like this to happen again?

Mr. Kraus: Yes.

Mr. Pruitt: Thank you, your Honor.

(Proceedings concluded.)

While I did say on the record that Donald Kraus may be legally, technically guilty of domestic violence, this statement was not even necessary on my part. Nevertheless, in her article published on July 22, the reporter wrote that I had said that the "man was legally, technically guilty of domestic violence, according to court transcripts." There is a significant difference between the word "may" and the word "was." This misquote changed the entire meaning of what was said by the court. Since the reporter stated in her article that her source was court transcripts, it is known that she had possession of the court transcript before she wrote the article. She wrote this article in such a way that it would appear that the judge had stated that a man who had been abusing his wife for 17 years "was" guilty of domestic violence, but then said that he had no intention of putting this "abuser" in jail, and accomplished this by finding this "abuser" not guilty. Since we know for certain that the reporter had access to the Kraus transcript before she wrote her July 22nd article, why did she fail to report that the judge had actually asked Mrs. Kraus whether she wanted her husband to be found guilty of domestic violence, to which her answer was "No, sir"?

Could it have been that including this exchange in her article might have changed the tone of her report, and may have made it less controversial?

Equally puzzling or amusing, depending on one's point of view, is how the reporter handled the manner of informing her readers that Ronald and Donna Kraus had been married for 17 years. The statement that "Judge Mestemaker presided over a case of a man who abused his wife of 17 years" gave many readers the impression that I had found a man not guilty of domestic violence who had been abusing his wife for 17 years. This was, to say the least, a clever way of relaying this information to her readers if, in fact — as some have stated — she desired to put her own slant on this story.

Later, Dean Pruitt told me that my decision and my lecture to Mr. and Mrs. Kraus probably saved their marriage. He told me that they were content and resolved to make their marriage work. Ron and Donna Kraus and their two sons are still a family unit. And after all, this is the most important outcome of the Kraus case.

Delores Orr and Charles Orr

On May 11, 1994, Delores Orr, 50, was granted a divorce from her husband of 29 years, Charles Henry Orr, 51, by Domestic Relations Court Judge Patrick Dinkelacker in Case Number A9304101. Pursuant to an agreed property entry, Mrs. Orr, the mother of five children by Mr. Orr, was granted the right to retain possession of the marital home located in the Cincinnati suburb of Forest Park. Less than six weeks later, Mrs. Orr permitted her ex-husband to move back into the home, despite warnings from her friends and co-workers that she not allow him to do so. Mr. Orr, who was extremely jealous and possessive, was between jobs and prevailed upon his former wife to allow him to live in a small apartment that had been constructed in the basement for one of their adult children. He promised her that if she allowed him to live in the basement apartment, he would not come upstairs and would not interfere in any way in her activities. This was a promise that he would not be able to keep for very long. Less than five months later, on Friday evening, October 21, 1994, Mrs. Orr, a very attractive woman, was in her bedroom preparing to go out for the evening when Charles Orr — having overheard her plans and suspecting that she was going out on a date — climbed the stairs to the first floor of the house and trapped his ex-wife in her bedroom. He beat her so savagely that her skull was fractured and her front teeth were literally knocked down her throat. As she lay on the bedroom floor semi-conscious, he looked down at her bloody face and shouted, "Don't die on me, bitch! I want you to see what I've done to you."

Delores Orr died of her injuries the next day. Her ex-husband was immediately arrested and charged with murder, for which he would be sentenced to prison for 20 years to life on July 18, 1995. Delores and Charles Orr were not strangers to me. On May 30, 1992, Charles Orr was arrested for domestic violence at the couple's home. This was after he had made a fist, which he stuck under her nose, and told her during an argument that if she didn't shut up he would kill her. Since this was a case where there was no actual assault, Orr was charged under the "threat" section of the domestic violence statute, which is a fourth-degree misdemeanor. The maximum sentence for this is 30 days in jail and a fine of $250. This was the one and only domestic violence charge ever filed against Charles Orr. The domestic violence case was dismissed in my courtroom at Mrs. Orr's request on September 16, 1992. They continued to live together until about May 18, 1993, when she sued him for divorce. As if by fate, the Orr case became news again on July 18, 1995, when he was sentenced to prison for his ex-wife's murder and the media recalled that I had been the judge before whom the 1992 domestic violence case had been dismissed. This coincidence was almost too good to be true — for the news media. It was no secret that I had been the judge assigned to handle the domestic violence complaint filed by Mrs. Orr in May 1992, since I had been interviewed extensively in October 1994 when Mrs. Orr was murdered. However, the fact that Charles Orr was being sentenced for her murder the very week after the Hancock-Sevier case became a major news story prompted a renewed media interest in the 1992 domestic violence case.

So it came to be that the same *Cincinnati Enquirer* reporter who wrote the articles about the Hancock-Sevier case as well as the Gambrell and the Kraus cases ordered a copy of the final hearing held before me in the Orr case. At this hearing on September 16, 1992, Mrs. Orr, who was already residing with her husband again, requested that the charge against him be dismissed. This is known as an RPW dismissal — at the Request of Prosecuting Witness. The reporter did not bother, for a reason known only to her, to obtain court transcripts for the two hearings held July 8 and September 9. This was significant. After reading only the final hearing transcript, the reporter arrived at conclusions no more valid than those that might be reached by one who reads only one chapter of a book. Suddenly, I was the cause of Delores Orr's death just the same as if I had held her while the man she had divorced, the man she was not supposed to have living in her home, killed her with his fists. Both a reporter and a metro columnist for *The Cincinnati Enquirer*, who had recently become my most vocal critics, wrote about my involvement in the Orr homicide with a renewed vigor. Several of their remarks are repeated here:

> Mestemaker made the comments during a 1992 hearing in which he threw out a complaint filed by a woman against her

husband. "This man is living with this lady under the same roof," he said in the 1992 case. "And I'm to believe that he represents a threat to this lady when ... she's voluntarily living with him?

"Oh, come on, folks, come on. Let's get with the program. This is absurd. ... This case is dismissed."

— Kristen Delguzzi, *The Cincinnati Enquirer*, July 21, 1995

Hang this Judge. Albert Mestemaker is guilty of holding domestic violence cases in utter contempt. Before another woman takes a fist in the face, voters should sentence him this fall to an early retirement.

— Cliff Radel, metro columnist, *The Cincinnati Enquirer*, July 21, 1995

According to Radel's tortured logic, I had sent Dolores Orr home on September 1992 into the fists of her abusive husband, to be killed by him a full two years later. In Radel's untrained mind, this made me an accomplice to her murder despite the fact she had allowed her then ex-husband to move back under the same roof with her. Radel failed to inform his readers of this last fact. The two-year span and the presence of Charles Orr in the marital house after divorce did not fit into his column. My involvement with the Orr domestic violence case commenced on July 8, 1992, when the case was first in front of me for trial. John L. O'Shea was the assistant prosecuting attorney representing the state, and Saul Fettner, a public defender staff lawyer, was representing Charles Orr. At this hearing, at which Mrs. Orr was present, an agreement was reached between the attorneys and the Orrs that if Mr. Orr attended and completed the four-week AMEND counseling program, the domestic violence charge would be dismissed at Mrs. Orr's request. It was also at this hearing that Delores Orr requested that the temporary protective order be dissolved so that Charles could return home to be with her and their children. What follows is the court transcript of the July 8, 1992, hearing:

(Morning session — July 8, 1992 proceedings)
Mr. O'Shea: Good Morning, Judge.
The Court: Good Morning, Mr. O'Shea.
Mr. O'Shea: First on the county docket is Charles Orr. Is there a Charles Orr present or Delores Orr? Ma'am, are you Delores

Orr? Could you step over here, please? Do you still wish to prosecute?

Mrs. Orr: No, sir.

Mr. O'Shea: Judge, there is a domestic violence. The prosecuting witness is with me. She tells me that she does not wish to prosecute.

The Court: Well, I'm sorry to hear that, but you can tell her that we don't do it that way.

Mr. O'Shea: Right.

The Court: I assume they are husband and wife.

Mr. Fettner: Your Honor, it's a 27-year marriage.

The Court: Well, why don't we have Mr. Orr go to the AMEND program, and then, you know, we can dismiss it. I have no objection to dismissing the case after the AMEND program. OK? That's for the good of both parties.

Mr. Fettner: That will be fine, your Honor.

The Court: That's a good choice. Let's set it over for like the first week of September, or something like that, for status report. Have you got your book with you?

Mr. Fettner: Your Honor, let me suggest September 9th, a Wednesday.

The Court: Did you say the 9th?

Mr. Fettner: Ninth.

The Court: How about September the 9th, '92, at 9 a.m. for status report on the AMEND referral?

Mr. Fettner: OK. Thank you, your Honor.

The Court: Now, I see where Judge Rosen, it appears I'm not sure who the arraigning judge was on June the 1st, because I can't tell from the signature.

Mr. Fettner: Judge Painter. Well, I've got a notation of Judge Painter.

The Court: OK. He granted a temporary protective order. Does this lady still want that?

Mrs. Orr: No, sir.

The Court: You don't? OK. You don't want that anymore?

Mrs. Orr: No, sir.

The Court: We can dissolve that at her request. Dissolve the TPO at Mrs. Orr's request. OK, so we won't have any problems, then, with regard to working around the temporary protective order. And here is the AMEND referral form, Mr. Fettner.

Mr. O'Shea: Thank you, Judge.

The Court: OK, folks.

(Proceedings adjourned until 9/9/92 at 9 a.m.)

By September 9, 1992, Mr. O'Shea, the assistant prosecutor who had entered into the agreement with the defendant and his attorney, that if Mr. Orr completed the basic four-week AMEND counseling program, the case would be dismissed — if Mrs. Orr still desired a dismissal — had been rotated to another courtroom. Carol Wiggers was now assigned to handle the case, having replaced O'Shea. She was apparently unaware of O'Shea's agreement with Fettner and his client about a dismissal if Mr. Orr completed the four-week AMEND program.

The prosecutorial rotation plan followed by the Hamilton County prosecutor's office has always resulted in problems of continuity, because one assistant prosecutor is not assigned to stay with a particular case from beginning to end. Often, as many as three or more assistant prosecutors will handle one case before its conclusion — each often unaware of any agreements or offers that were made to a defendant by the other assistant. This is exactly what happened in the Orr case. Not only does the record clearly reveal that Carol Wiggers was unaware of the agreement entered into by John O'Shea, it is obvious that she did not know that the AMEND program staff had recently adopted a new 10-week program. In fact, neither Mr. Fettner nor the court was aware of the new extended program. What follows are the transcripts of the last two hearings on this case.

(Morning session — September 9, 1992, proceedings)

Ms. Wiggers: On the county criminal docket, Charles Orr.

Mr. Fettner: Good morning, your Honor. This matter is here to show completion of the AMEND program. He has a certificate. This is the 15th of August.

Ms. Wiggers: For the record, I want to state, also, that it says "Recommendation for further treatment, 10-week AMEND program." It is the state's recommendation ...

The Court: The what, 10 weeks?

They've got another program down there?

Ms. Wiggers: Ten weeks.

The defendant: I didn't know.

The Court: I've never heard of the 10-week AMEND. It baffles

me that they go through a program, they give a certificate —
why would they give the man a certificate?

Ms. Wiggers: I don't know, your Honor.

Mr. Fettner: Your Honor, this is a 27-year marriage.

The Court: Is she here today?

The defendant: No.

Ms. Wiggers: Delores Orr?

The defendant: She's on vacation.

The Court: I'd rather hear from her than from these folks from
AMEND.

Ms. Wiggers: I have had some contact with her. I think she's
still fearful, your Honor. And at this point, the state would
request a continuance in order to obtain the presence of the
prosecuting witness before this matter is completely dismissed.

Mr. Fettner: Your Honor, can you tell us who signed that report,
if there is a signature?
Is it legible?

The Court: You're welcome to give it a try. The answer is no,
Mr. Fettner. I cannot tell you who signed it. It could have been
anyone.

The defendant: I don't even know who this person is. He wasn't
even the counselor over at the program.

Mr. Fettner: I have no objection to the court reviewing if the
man has any kind of history of anything like this, as far as his
rap sheet.

The Court: Quite frankly, I would like to hear from Mrs. Orr.
Could we set this down one day next week, and could you get
Mrs. Orr to come in?

Ms. Wiggers: That would be fine, your Honor.

The defendant: She won't be back until Sunday.

Mr. Fettner: Mr. Orr has indicated she's in Stanford,
Connecticut, on vacation, won't be back until Sunday.

The Court: When?

Mr. Fettner: She'll be back this coming Sunday.

The Court: I'm scheduled to be in my room on the 16th of
September, and it will be up to you, Ms. Wiggers, whether or
not you wish to bring in this person from that program. You
know, I don't understand this. They marked everything
"acceptable," and they grant a certificate of completion, and

then they want him to attend a new 10-week program, which I
have never heard of and the prosecutor, Ms. Wiggers, has never
heard of. Well, we will see about this on the 16th.
(Proceedings adjourned until 9/16/92 at 9 a.m.)

Thus, at Ms. Wiggers' request, the Orr case was again continued to
another date so that she could secure the attendance of Mrs. Orr, as well as
the counselor from the AMEND program who would be able to explain
why the agency was recommending an additional 10-weeks counseling session even though it had issued a certificate to Mr. Orr stating that he had
successfully completed the four-week program.

Ms. Wiggers did have Delores Orr present on September 16, 1992.
However, again she failed to have the counselor present. She did at this
hearing refer to a report from AMEND that purportedly claimed that there
was a possibility of future violence. However, Ms. Wiggers had not taken
the necessary steps to obtain the report in order that the court could read
it. At no time during this final hearing did Ms. Wiggers offer the court tangible evidence to support her claim that Charles Orr, now living at home
with his wife, would harm her in the future. What follows are the relevant
portions of the court transcript from September 16, 1992. This is the one
and only transcript of the Orr case that the reporters secured and used as
their source for the several articles on this tragic case.

(Morning session — September 16, 1992)
Ms. Wiggers: On the county criminal docket, Charles Orr.
Mr. Fettner: Your Honor, this is to show completion of AMEND.
I have his certificate.
Ms. Wiggers: Your Honor, this is the case where the AMEND
certificate was presented.   At the same time, Corbin Hobbie,
who's the AMEND counselor, presented that with an indication
that the likelihood of continued abuse, on a scale of low to
extremely high, was extremely high.   And he also further recommended that he spend 10 weeks further in the program. I
then subpoenaed Mrs. Orr, so that she would be available.
The Court: Oh, yeah.   That's right.   Mrs. Orr was to be here
today. Here's what we wrote on the judge's sheet on the 9th:
"Continued by the court, at request of prosecuting attorney, to
9/16/92 so that we can hear from Mrs. Orr. OK, swear in Mrs.
Orr, please.

The bailiff: Raise your right hand. (The witness was sworn.)
The Court: Ma'am, have a seat in the witness chair, please. Ms. Wiggers has some questions she wants to ask you.

Delores A. Orr, being first duly sworn, was examined and testified as follows:

(Direct examination by Ms. Wiggers:)
Q: Ma'am, will you please state your name for the record, spell your last name.
A: Yes. My name is Delores A. Orr, O-R-R.
Q: And are you married to Charles H. Orr?
A: Yes, I am.
Q: Did you have occasion to sign a domestic violence complaint against him?
A: Yes, I did.
Q: And do you recall speaking to me this morning with respect to your concerns as to how things might proceed in the future?
A: Yes, I did.
Q: And based on your contact — are your presently living with Mr. Orr at this time?
A: Yes.
Q. Based on your contact with him, do you have any concerns, you want to express to the court regarding your concern for your safety or the possibility of future abuse from Mr. Orr?
A: Yes, I'm a little uncertain whether or not something else will happen if he gets angry enough.
Q: Do you recall me mentioning to you that the AMEND program had recommended an additional 10-week program?
A: You mentioned it to me?
Q: That the AMEND program had recommended additional treatment?
A: Yes, you mentioned that to me.
Q: And based on your experience with Mr. Orr and how things proceeded, do you feel that would be something you would feel would be in your best interest?
A: Yes.
Mr. Fettner: Objection, your Honor.
The Court: In her best interest?

She can answer what she thinks may be in her best interest. Overruled.

A: Yes, I do.

Q: How long have you been living with Mr. Orr now, since this case was filed?

A: Since July the 8th.

The Court: I'm sorry. I don't understand. You're not living with him now, are you?

The witness: Yes, sir.

Mr. Fettner: Your Honor, the TPO was dissolved as of July the 8th.

The Court: OK.

By Ms. Wiggers:

Q: Have there been any further episodes of violence towards you from him?

A: No, there haven't.

Q: Has there been any behavior towards you where you felt that you might be somewhat threatened or felt concerned for your safety?

A: No.

Q: Do you feel there is a possibility that there may be further abuses to you in the future?

Mr. Fettner: Objection.

The Court: Overruled. I mean, admittedly, here's a lady who's living under the same roof with this man — so, knowing that is the basis, she can answer. Are you voluntarily living with him? I mean, he's not holding you in the house, is he?

The witness: No, sir.

The Court: You choose to live with him?

The witness: I choose.

The Court: And now you are being asked, even though you choose voluntarily to live with him, do you have reason to feel that he might hurt you?

The witness: I'm uncertain.

The Court: Please?

The witness: I'm uncertain.

By Ms. Wiggers:

Q: Do you have some concern for your safety, ma'am?

The Court: From him?

What Ms. Wiggers is asking you is, do you have some concern for your safety from Mr. Orr?

A: OK. I think that if I was to upset him to the point — I'm not sure. Would think that he would — you know, I'm not sure. But I don't — I don't plan on doing that. Ms. Wiggers: OK. And, ma'am, is this your husband, Mr. Orr, sitting here in the courtroom?

A: Yes.

Ms. Wiggers: Thank you. I have no further questions.

Mr. Fettner: Just a couple questions.

(Cross-examination by Mr. Fettner:)

Q: You've been married 27 years?

A: Yes, sir.

Q: And you've been back together now almost two-and-a-half months?

A: Yes.

Mr. Fettner: I have nothing further.

The Court: Ma'am, did you ask a judge to dissolve the protective order?

The witness: Yes, sir.

The Court: Who was the judge that you asked, me?

The witness: It was you.

The Court: And so I dissolved it at your request, and you moved back home with him?

The witness: Well, he moved back in with me.

The Court: He moved back in. And nothing else has happened?

The witness: No, sir.

The Court: And he went to the AMEND program?

The witness: Yes, he did.

The Court: And he completed the AMEND program as agreed?

The witness: Yes, sir.

The Court: OK. Thank you, ma'am. You can step down. *(Witness excused.)*

The Court: OK.

Ms. Wiggers: Your, Honor, if I could be heard, briefly.

The Court: Sure.

Ms. Wiggers: I called the AMEND program. I attempted to get

in touch with Mr. Corbin Hobbie. He's no longer with the program. I did speak with Gilda Tennent to find out what the status is, what does it mean to the AMEND program when they issue the certificate. She verified to me the AMEND certificate is nothing more than a certificate of attendance. It is not any kind of representation as to what they feel is accomplishment or successful completion.

The Court: Then why do we use them?

Ms. Wiggers: I began to wonder that myself, your Honor. Based on the recommendation of this counselor, the state would request that the court order Mr. Orr to go through the further 10-week AMEND program, since it will be beneficial.

The Court: But his lady — wait a minute. Wait a minute. Look, this lady asked me to dissolve the protective order and has this man come back home. And I asked her, is he holding you there. No. And then she is asked, well, does she think that maybe some time in the future he might hurt her. And her answer was, well, I guess if the circumstances were right, he might. Well, I mean, how can we conclude from that this man represents a threat to her?

Ms. Wiggers: I think we can do it, your Honor, because after going through a four-week program dealing specifically with his counselor, who has training in this area, this counselor was concerned there was a likelihood of further abuse.

The Court: Then have the counselor come in here. Who is this Mr. Hobbie?

Ms. Wiggers: Corbin Hobbie.

The Court: Have him come in. Mr. Flammer, get AMEND on the phone. Get Mr. Corbin Hobbie in here.

Ms. Wiggers: Corbin Hobbie is no longer with the AMEND program. That's why I spoke with Gilda Tennent.

The Court: Corbin Hobbie is no longer with the AMEND program? I don't understand where this started. I don't understand who started it. But now these people have taken to the position that they are going to run the court system, and they are going to have all these programs, and we're going to have 10 more weeks of this, and 10 more weeks of that. And this man is living with this lady under the same roof. And I'm to believe that he represents a threat to the lady, who he's — she's voluntarily living with him?

Oh, come on folks. Come on. Let's get with the program. This is absurd. Ms. Wiggers, this is absurd. I'll tell you why it's absurd. This program is absurd. The case is dismissed at Mrs. Orr's request. The prosecution has a right to appeal this ruling. Ms. Wiggers: Please note the state's objection.

Several issues surfaced in this hearing that merit consideration. Mr. Orr was living at home with Mrs. Orr and their children. This was at Mrs. Orr's request. Mr. Orr had competed the AMEND program and had received his completion certificate. Mrs. Orr, appeared in court and under oath stated she wanted the case dropped. Therefore, the judge did not "throw it out," as Ms. Delguzzi later reported. It is also apparent from a review of this transcript that Ms. Wiggers did not have her AMEND counselor in court ready to testify. Nor did she offer whatever report she claimed to possess into evidence. As a result, the court was deprived of any supporting testimony or written documents that might have substantiated Ms. Wiggers' allegation of possible future violence. And, finally, it should be pointed out that the court advised Ms. Wiggers of her right to appeal the dismissal if she chose to do so. Ms. Wiggers never appealed the dismissal and took no further action with regard to this case. Much too late to benefit Delores Orr, the AMEND program commenced forwarding written reports from their counselors directly to the municipal court judges in December 1994. After Delores Orr's tragic and senseless death at the hands of her ex-husband on October 22, 1994, George Lecky and Amanda Garrett of *The Cincinnati Post* wrote on October 24, 1994:

Friends said they couldn't believe Orr would hurt his ex-wife because he was anxious to reconcile with her, even giving up his pipe when she declared their home a no-smoking zone. Until a couple of years ago, Orr worked for General Electric. From there he went to work at an encyclopedia company, where he was a successful salesman.

On October 25, 1994, Adam Weintraub, a reporter for the *Enquirer*, wrote of Delores Orr's death as follows:

Delores Orr filed a domestic violence complaint against her husband in May 1992. "My husband, Charles Orr, and I got into a very heated argument today," she stated in the complaint. "He came at me three or four times, drawing his fist back to strike me, and told me ... that if I didn't shut up, he would kill me."

The court granted a protection order but later dissolved it at Delores Orr's request. Municipal Court Judge Mestemaker, dismissed the case September 16, 1992, at her request.

On October 26, 1994, Amanda Garrett wrote an in-depth article in the *Post* about the Orr case, in which she stated:

What happened to Delores Orr is a tragedy, said Hamilton County Municipal Judge Albert Mestemaker, but "as a judge I can't forbid two adults from ever having further contact with each other. Judges can't protect everyone. The police can't protect everyone. It's impossible," he said. Had he been convicted, Orr would have faced 30 days in jail and a $250 fine. But he dodged a trial and jail time by agreeing to complete the four-week AMEND program in domestic violence. "It is either AMEND or letting them walk in a lot of cases ... and at least this way they have a shot at getting some sort of counseling," said Hamilton County Prosecutor Joseph Deters.

Amanda Garrett further wrote in this same article:

The day her husband enrolled in the AMEND program, Mrs. Orr asked the court to remove the temporary protection order. She never called the police again, but did file for a divorce later this year. In June (1994), however, she agreed to reconcile with her husband. Mestemaker said that the Orr case is not all that unusual.

"She actually secured a divorce and then took up living with him again," he said.

"When you have homicidal maniacs, you are not going to be able to cure them in some program that tells you not to hit girls," Deters said. "There are very bad people who will continue to beat and kill their spouses no matter what they have heard .... And the system will never be able to protect them in all cases."

Had the Orr case proceeded to trial instead of being dismissed at Mrs. Orr's request, Mr. Orr would more than likely been found not guilty — since the threat of domestic violence voiced by him on May 30 was what is referred to under Ohio law as a "conditional threat."

In her affidavit filed on May 30, 1992, Mrs. Orr wrote:

"My husband, Charles Orr, and I got into a very heated argument today and he came at me 3 or 4 times drawing his fist back to strike me and he told me while he drew his fist back that if I didn't shut up he would kill me." In several cases involving a threat, the Ohio Supreme Court as well as the Court of Appeals for Hamilton County have reversed convictions for domestic violence while holding that the existence of a conditional threat standing alone is insufficient to sustain a conviction.

In one case reviewed by the Court of Appeals for Hamilton County, the victim was told by her drunken husband that, "If I had a gun, I would shoot you." The appellate court set aside the conviction in this case, as it has in others where the allegation of domestic violence involved a conditional threat, and where there has been no showing by prosecutors that the accused attempted to carry out the threat or that any physical harm actually occurred. These cases have also held that where there is a threat standing alone, a conviction cannot be upheld unless the prosecutor has shown that the victim believed that the threat was imminent and that it would be carried out, and that the ability to prove this is an essential element of the offense. It is reasonable in this instance to infer that Delores Orr did not believe that she was in imminent danger of harm, since she asked the court to rescind the temporary protective order. In addition, it was at her request that the case itself was dismissed. On the other hand, had the Orr case proceeded to trial and resulted in his conviction of a fourth-degree misdemeanor domestic violence as the result of the threat, the maximum sentence that the court could have imposed would have been 30 days in the Hamilton County Justice Center. Mr. Orr would have been entitled to credit for the night he spent in jail on May 30. Therefore, he would have served his maximum sentence by October 15, 1992 — a full two years before he beat Delores Orr to death. Had he been ordered to attend an additional 10-week AMEND counseling program, he would still have had two full years before he killed her.

No judge or prosecutor or police officer or counselor could have prevented this senseless tragedy. Nor should any member of those groups be deemed responsible for Delores Orr's death. On July 31, 1995, I had a meeting with Ann MacDonald, the executive director of Women Helping Women, in which we discussed the Orr case. During this meeting, Ms. MacDonald said to me:

> "Judge Mestemaker, please don't hold yourself responsible for Delores' death. Her friends and co-workers, as well as members of my staff, including myself, told Delores that she should not allow Charles to move back into the home after their divorce. We all told her that now that they were divorced she should stay away from him. We told her that he was so jealous of her that he was a constant threat to her, and we really feared for her safety. But just like a fatal attraction, Delores ignored everyone's advice. And she paid for it with her life. You are not responsible for this tragedy. No one but Charles and perhaps Delores are. It truly was a case of fatal attraction."

Several days later I had occasion to discuss the same subject with Peggy Caldwell, a senior crisis counselor for Women Helping Women. Ms. Caldwell had become friendly with Delores Orr during the 1992 domestic violence case and maintained a close contact with her to the date of her death in October 1994. When Peggy Caldwell learned in June 1994 that Delores Orr had allowed her ex-husband to move back into the residence only one month after their divorce, she expressed her concerns. But Delores Orr told her that she was not afraid for herself. She told Peggy that she believed that Charles had changed since their divorce and that he would not hurt her. According to Peggy, Delores Orr allowed her former husband to move back into the home in mid-June 1994, one month after their divorce became final. This arrangement appeared to be working until the evening of October 21, 1994, when Charles Orr was apparently told by one of the children that his former wife was getting ready to go out on a date with a man. Enraged, Charles Orr came upstairs from the basement and trapped his ex-wife in her bedroom, where he beat her until she was beyond recognition and salvation. Peggy concluded our conversation by saying: "Judge Mestemaker, Charles Orr was an evil man. He killed Delores, not you. We begged and pleaded with her. But she had her mind made up. No one could have prevented what happened to Delores except maybe God, and none of us are God."

Cliff Radel would write one final story about Delores Orr. In his metro column published by *The Cincinnati Enquirer* on October 23, 1996,

Radel wrote about the excellent work of Ann MacDonald of Women Helping Women. In this column, which dealt with a new committee called the Domestic Violence Death Review Panel, Cliff Radel referred to the late Delores Orr with these words:

> Deaths from domestic violence are down in Hamilton County. In 1989, there were 24. This year, there have been five. People tell Ann MacDonald: "Be happy, we're under 10." She hears that and sees another face. On a Sunday in 1994, as she sat in church, a friend slid into the pew behind her. The friend, a social worker, leaned forward and said these chilling words: "One of the women I worked with was killed."
>
> The woman was Delores Orr. A victim of years of domestic abuse, she was beaten to death by her husband. This happened despite repeated police visits, court appearances and counseling sessions. This is the kind of case Ann MacDonald is working to prevent. "She was a real woman who had a family who cared about her," Ms. MacDonald said. "She was not a statistic. She must not be remembered as a number. She must be remembered as a person." That's why Ms. MacDonald sees Delores Orr's face every time the panel meets. "I have high hopes," she said, "that in two years, the panel will be up and running. And it will have gathered enough facts to be making meaningful recommendations to reduce the number of deaths from domestic violence." Ms. MacDonald will be pleased. But she won't be happy until the deaths are reduced to her favorite number: zero.

Even in this final column, Radel could not or would not reveal the entire Delores Orr story — tragic as it is. He could have at least warned all women that once they divorce a man who behaves like Charles Edward Orr, never — never — let him come home to live with her. It won't work. Delores Orr paid for that error with her life. But then, no one has a crystal ball to tell them what the future holds — not even judges. If I could turn the clock back to that morning in September 1992 when the only domestic violence complaint Delores Orr ever filed against Charles Orr was dismissed at her request, I might have forced the parties to go to trial. And, if Charles Orr was found guilty of the fourth-degree domestic violence as charged, I might have sentenced him to serve 30 days in jail — or I might have placed him on probation for a year. Either decision would more than likely have saved me from a public lynching by the local print media. Tragically, though, neither move would have spared the life of Delores Orr. After her husband spent 10 more weeks in counseling or 30 days in jail, she would no doubt have still taken him back. Only Delores Orr had the capacity to save Delores Orr. Sadly, she chose to follow a different path.

Delores Orr was beaten to death by her jealous ex-husband, Charles, in October 1994, two years after the couple appeared before Judge Mestemaker.

Holiday card sent to Judge Mestemaker in December, 1994 by Ann MacDonald expressing appreciation for his efforts on behalf of Women Helping Women.

CHAPTER 17

THE POLITICS OF LAWYERS RATING JUDGES

On Wednesday, October 12, 1995, the Cincinnati Bar Association publicly announced its judicial candidate ratings for the Hamilton County Municipal Court elections in November. Of the 14 candidates for nine judicial seats, only two candidates were rated as "Not Recommended for this Office at this Time" — despite the fact that six years earlier, in 1989, they had both been rated "Recommended and Preferred" by the Cincinnati Bar Association.

The two candidates who received the "Not Recommended" rating — which is essentially the same as being black balled — were two longtime incumbent judges with over 66 years combined legal experience and 32 years combined judicial experience. One judge ran unopposed and was re-elected. The second judge was opposed in his bid for re-election, and he was defeated despite the fact that he had over 14 years experience as a municipal court judge. His name is Albert Joseph Mestemaker.

1995 was only the second time in the controversial and often tumultuous history of the bar association's ratings for the Hamilton County Municipal Court that this candidate review was conducted for seven judicial districts — as opposed to a number of countywide races for the municipal court, which, after all, does have countywide jurisdiction.

The first time that the bar association conducted judicial candidate ratings for municipal court by judicial districts occurred in 1993, when seven judges were elected, one for each of the seven judicial districts created in 1993 pursuant to a federal court order. The remaining seven judges were then scheduled to be chosen in 1995 — in order to have two judges for each judicial district, being the allotted 14 judges authorized for the Hamilton County Municipal Court.

Under the new system, there is no requirement that a judge actually reside in the district from which he or she is elected. Every judge elected has jurisdiction over all municipal court cases regardless of whether they occurred in the judicial district that elected that particular judge or in a district in which that judge was not required to seek voter approval.

In other words, since 1993, a resident of Hamilton County who has a matter pending in the Hamilton County Municipal Court has only two chances out of 14 of having his or her case heard by a judge for whom that citizen had an opportunity to vote. Further complicating this was the 1988 agreement between the two major political parties that certain judges — based on racial considerations — would not be opposed at election time. The result is that for a particular district race, the voters may have as their only choice either to vote for the person whose name appears on the ballot or to cast no vote.

By the time of the 1995 ratings, I had heard and decided a total of 26,441 civil, criminal, and traffic cases. During that same period, I had received my fair share of publicity and media coverage, some good and some not so good. However, it was my outspoken opposition to the mandatory arrest law in domestic violence cases, which became effective on March 9, 1995, and my order of July 13, 1995, that Yvonne Sevier and Scott Hancock either quit fighting, abusing alcohol, get off welfare and sanctify their relationship with a marriage in order to give their child a decent, stable home life, or separate from each other that led to the media frenzy and mass criticism that my opponent made good use of to win the judicial seat in District 7 by 738 votes.

My involvement and knowledge of the mechanics of the judicial rating process employed by the Cincinnati Bar Association goes back to 1973, when I was appointed to membership on the committee, then known as the Judicial Selection Committee.

The ballot used by the bar association to rate all judicial candidates remained unchanged from 1973 through 1978. Each ballot requested that the voting lawyer answer 10 questions with a "yes" or "no."

The 10 standard questions were as follows:

1. Would he/she be courteous toward litigants, witnesses and counsel?

2. Is he/she susceptible to his/her own bias or to other pressure which would affect his/her judicial discretion?

3. Would he/she be attentive to arguments of counsel and (trial court) testimony of witnesses?

4. Does he/she possess the temperament to deal with litigants, witnesses, and counsel in a considerate and judicious manner?

5. Does he/she have legal ability for the particular office?

6. Does he/she have sufficient actual experience in the practice of law or as a judge?

7. Would he/she be punctual in opening court and in keeping appointments?

8. Do you trust him/her?

9. Would he/she carefully study authorities submitted and render prompt decisions with appropriate findings?

10. Is he/she of good reputation in the community and of good character and integrity?

After a voting lawyer had completed answers to the 10 standard questions, he or she was then asked to assign an overall rating to each candidate being rated.

The overall rating categories that were employed between 1973 and 1978 were:

1. Outstanding
2. Well Qualified
3. Qualified
4. Not Qualified
5. Not Rated

Over the intervening years, there had been increasing criticism of the rating categories by judges and non-judges alike. Many judges and lawyers questioned the rating of "Outstanding" because the term as applied to a judge or, in particular, to a lawyer running for the first time for a judicial post was subject to so many interpretations. What does "Outstanding" mean?

There was an almost bitter resentment of the "Not Qualified" rating as being particularly demeaning to the candidate being so rated. If the candidate was an incumbent judge, such a rating led to the obvious question of how did he or she become a judge in the first place? Equally damaging was a "Not Qualified" rating being assigned to a lawyer seeking to become a judge. Such a rating, when made public, caused considerable embarrassment to the lawyer. In certain cases, it had been known to materially affect a lawyer's relationship with his or her clients who questioned the capabilities and effectiveness of a lawyer who was considered by his or her colleagues to be "Not Qualified" to be a judge. If a lawyer is not qualified to be a judge, is he or she qualified to represent people who require the services of a capable lawyer?

As a result of the dissatisfaction by a majority of the members of the bar association, a decision was made by the executive board to appoint a blue-ribbon subcommittee to study the advisability of revamping the system of rating judicial candidates. In January 1978, I was appointed co-chairman of this committee and instructed to hold hearings, interview judges and lawyers, and to report our findings and recommendations to the executive committee of the bar association. It was the bar association's goal to make the rating process more impartial, more credible with the public, and as free of political or personal rancor and pressure as possible. An additional task, and one which was not finally implemented until 1996, was a study and a recommendation by the subcommittee that only lawyers who had actual firsthand dealings with and knowledge of a particular incumbent judge or a lawyer seeking a judicial post be permitted to rate that judge or lawyer. It serves no rational purpose to have lawyers whose entire practice is devoted to real estate title examinations to rate trial judges in whose courtrooms they have never appeared. Less than 15 percent of all lawyers practice criminal law. Nevertheless, every lawyer who votes to rate a judge was expected to know how that judge handled criminal cases.

After a six-month study, the subcommittee made the following recommendations to the committee as a whole and, in turn, to the executive committee.

- That the bar poll ballot then in use and referred to earlier be retained for the time being;
- That a system of limiting voting to lawyers who could show that they possessed actual, firsthand knowledge of a judicial candidate's qualifications and personal qualities be devised to do away with the hearsay problem with many of the ratings assigned and that the overall rating categories to be assigned to individual judicial candidates be revised to be:

1. "Highly Recommended" (formerly Outstanding.)
2. "Recommended" (formerly Highly Qualified.)
3. "Not Recommended at this Time" (formerly Not Qualified.)
4. "Not Rated."

As part of the new rating categories, an additional device called the "Preferred Rating" was devised to be employed in any case in which two candidates for the same judicial post received an identical rating, but one was preferred over the other for election by the bar association. In this event for example, two candidates for the same judgeship might receive identical ratings such as "Recommended" but one was more experienced or knowledgeable in certain areas. That candidate would then be assigned the overall rating of "Recommended and Preferred."

The substitution of "Not Recommended at this Time" answered the objections of those members who had expressed their concern over the use of the term "Not Qualified."

My last rating meeting as a member of the Judicial Selection

Committee occurred in October 1980, by which time non-lawyers who had been appointed to the committee had been given the right to vote on incumbent judges and judicial candidates despite opposition by a significant number of lawyers on the committee.

I began my own judicial career on March 16, 1981, when then-Governor James A. Rhodes appointed me to replace a judge who had resigned his position on the Hamilton County Municipal Court. I ran for election in 1981, for re-election in 1983, and again in 1989. In 1989, I was serving the first year of a two-year term as the presiding and administrative judge of the Hamilton County Municipal Court. My relationship with the Cincinnati Bar Association had always been cordial, even though I had not been a member since 1981.

In 1989, I received a rating of "Recommended and Preferred" in a countywide field race that included 10 candidates seeking election for five judicial positions. At that time, I had served as a judge for eight years.

The judicial rating process for 1995 commenced for me on July 27, 1995, when I received the standard biographical information request from the judicial rating committee. This form was accompanied by a letter from James A. Vogele, chairman of the committee, which complimented me for my decision to seek re-election to a third full term as a municipal court judge. Item 13 of the biographical information form requested the names of 10 local lawyers who had opposed me in litigation prior to my becoming a judge. The purpose of this request was so that the members of the subcommittee rating me could contact these lawyers for their assessment of me as a trial lawyer. It was not until after I had received a "Not Recommended at this Time" rating that I personally contacted nine of the 10 lawyers listed by me for Item 13. These nine lawyers, to a person, told me that no one from the subcommittee or the bar association had contacted them to request their assessment of me.

Item 15 of the same form requested the names of at least 10 lawyers who had contested matters in my courtroom within the past year. The purpose of this request was to enable the members of the subcommittee to contact and discuss with these lawyers my handling of cases as a judge. In response to this request, I furnished the subcommittee the names of 18 lawyers who not only had appeared in my courtroom once within the past year, but who had actually appeared before me at least once each month — or 12 times — in the past year. Since the purpose of requesting the names of lawyers who appear before any judge is to obtain firsthand information from lawyers who have had an opportunity to measure a judge's demeanor, temperament, patience and diligence, as well as knowledge of the law and rules, I purposely gave the committee the names of lawyers who had appeared before me at least once per month. At least eight of the lawyers named in this category actually appeared before me on a weekly basis, several as often as two or three times per week. Again, as with the lawyers listed in Item 13, after the bar association announced its 1995 judicial ratings on October 9, 1995, I personally contacted each lawyer listed by me in answer to the request contained in Item 15. To my dismay, I learned that only four of these 18 lawyers had actually been interviewed concerning me.

After my unfavorable rating, I discussed this matter with Ernest F. McAdams Jr., the chairman of my subcommittee. He advised me in a letter dated October 23 that 32 lawyers were interviewed. I have no reason to doubt the truth of this statement. However, the point is that most of the lawyers whom I listed to be interviewed were never contacted concerning my qualifications to continue to be a judge. If the bar association chooses not to interview the lawyers listed by the candidate, why continue the practice of requesting the judges and candidates to furnish the names of particular lawyers to be interviewed?

As had been done each year since the bar association commenced its judicial rating activity, the bar poll ballots for 1995 were mailed out by August 25, with a request that they be completed and returned to the accounting firm that tabulates the poll results by September 22, 1995. In 1995, ballots were mailed to 3,500 members of the Cincinnati Bar Association and non-member local lawyers. This was a far cry from the 1,400 that were mailed out in 1966, when I began practicing law. Of the 3,500 ballots sent out, only 413 were completed and returned for tabulation. The total number of local lawyers who actually voted to rate the judges and judicial candidates running for election in 1995 represented a mere 12 percent of the total number who received ballots. Most lawyers throw the ballots in their waste paper baskets. Of the 413 ballots returned, 307 lawyers rated me. The percentage of the total number of lawyers who received a ballot who rated me was a mere 9 percent.

According to court records, a total of 522 lawyers had appeared before me in the six years since I had last run for re-election, in 1989. These records indicated that the total number of lawyers who appeared before me at least once every six months during the same six-year period approximated 208. Despite the fact that at least 522 lawyers had firsthand knowledge of me in my judicial role through personal contacts, only 307 lawyers rated me in 1995. How many of the 307 lawyers who did rate me on the bar poll ballot had actually appeared before me as a judge can never be determined due to the nature of the bar poll ballot itself, which did not require the name or signature of the voting lawyers, thus guaranteeing anonymity to those voting. This had also been an area of criticism of the bar's rating process because a lawyer who had a personal dislike for a judge or judicial candidate can caste a very negative vote and remain anonymous.

On September 5, I was notified in a letter from James A. Vogele, chairman of the Judicial Rating Committee, that the subcommittee assigned to rate my judicial qualities consisted of four lawyers:

- Ernest F. McAdams Jr., chairman
- Mark C. Bissinger
- Matthew T. MacLeid
- Margaret A. Hilvert

Each candidate has five days to present an objection to any assigned member of the subcommittee if a conflict exists. I was not aware at the time of any conflict with any of the individuals assigned to rate me and notified Mr. Voegle accordingly. The chairman of the subcommittee assigned to rate me, Ernest F. McAdams Jr., was a senior assistant prosecuting attorney for the city of Cincinnati. I had known him since 1979. We have been on a first-name basis for years. When I became a judge in 1981, he was a staff attorney for the public defender's office. As a result, he tried hundreds of cases before me as a defense attorney. In the mid-1980s, Mr. McAdams switched sides and became an assistant Cincinnati prosecutor. After that, he prosecuted hundreds of cases in my courtroom. The result is that he knew me very well as a judge as well as personally and could almost predict my reaction to a particular case or situation.

The second member of the subcommittee was Mark C. Bissinger. He was admitted to practice in Ohio in 1983. I did not know Mr. Bissinger professionally or socially. To the best of my recollection, he had never appeared before me in any capacity. Nor did I know whether he possessed any experience practicing in municipal court. However, since I possessed no knowledge of him, either positive or negative, there was no reason to object to his assignment as a member of my subcommittee. As it later turned out, Mr. Bissinger proved to be a supporter at the final rating meeting. He had formed his opinion based upon our one meeting.

Matthew T. MacLeid, the third member of my subcommittee, had been an attorney since 1963. I had known him since 1966. His main area of law was civil litigation with an emphasis on collection law. He appeared before me at least once a month during the 14-plus years that I served as a judge. In addition, I knew Matt personally as a lawyer before I became a judge. We were not social friends, but I have a great deal of respect for Mr. MacLeid as a lawyer and as a gentleman.

The fourth and final lawyer assigned to my subcommittee was Margaret A. Hilvert. Ms. Hilvert was admitted to practice in the courts of Ohio in 1989. I have never met Ms. Hilvert professionally or socially, not even as of the time of this writing. I also knew that she had never tried a case of any type before me, and to the best of my recollection, she had never appeared before me for any purpose. In short, Ms. Hilvert was unknown to me, and I was unknown to her. I concluded with regard to Ms. Hilvert that since the public revelation of my suggestion to several couples that if they were going to continue to live together that they be married, having a woman on my subcommittee would actually be a plus. I believed that once Ms. Hilvert and I met, and I was afforded the opportunity to explain these cases to her, that she would have a better understanding of me and the reasons behind my rulings. As a result, I lodged no objection to Ms. Hilvert serving as a member of my rating subcommittee, even though I did not know her. My decision not to object to Ms. Hilvert turned out to be a mistake on my part. I never had the opportunity to meet and talk to Ms. Hilvert. Why? Because Ms. Hilvert never bothered to attend either of the two face-to-face meetings that I had with my subcommittee. Even though her excuse, relayed to me by Ernie McAdams, was that she was out of the city on a pre-planned vacation, she never made any effort on her own to meet with me at some time convenient to her or to telephone me to discuss my qualifications.

Since my second and last personal meeting with my subcommittee had taken place on Monday, October 2, and in light of Ms. Hilvert's unfortunate absence from that meeting, I telephoned her office on Wednesday, October 4. I was advised then that Ms. Hilvert was not available to speak to me. Despite the message, she never returned my call. To this day, I have still not personally met Ms. Hilvert. I later learned that Ms. Hilvert was a member of the same law firm as Peter L. Cassady, who in 1995 served as co-chairman of the Hamilton County Democratic Party's Judicial Selection Committee. In this capacity, Mr. Cassady was instrumental in the selection of my opponent for the 1995 election. Also in this capacity, he was responsible for performing services to assist his party's candidates to win the judicial seats for which they were running. The extent of Mr. Cassady's involvement in the campaign of lawyer James Patrick Kenney to defeat me for re-election to a third full term as a judge was revealed in an article that appeared in *The Cincinnati Post* on August 7, 1995, in which Sharon Moloney wrote in her "Political notebook" column: "The Democrats are going to go all-out and work very hard for Jim Kenney," says Peter Cassady, co-chairman of the Dem's Judicial Selection Committee.

Despite this obvious conflict of interest and serious ethical problem, Ms. Hilvert chose to remain on my subcommittee as a non-participating member. I have since been advised that when the general rating meeting was held on October 9, she joined in speaking against my endorsement for re-election. This was her way of becoming a participant.

Ms. Hilvert had an ethical obligation to advise the chairman of the Judicial Rating Committee that she had a conflict that prevented her from serving as a fair and impartial member of my subcommittee. This would have enabled Mr. Vogele to appoint an individual to replace her who would have actively participated in the rating process, and who would have been fair and objective in assessing me. Only Ms. Hilvert can answer questions concerning her motive for concealing her predetermined attitude toward me, as well as the obvious conflict of interest that should have disqualified her from being a member of my rating subcommittee.

On Friday, October 6, three days before the bar association's general rating meeting, a close friend of mine who is a member of the Judicial Rating Committee stopped by my office to tell me that "the word is out. You will not be recommended by the bar association for re-election." He told me that he didn't want to upset me, but that he felt that I should be aware that "the deck has been stacked against you." He was to be proven correct.

The general rating meeting for 1995 was held at the bar association's offices on Monday, October 9. It should be said at this time that the candidates being rated are never permitted to appear at this meeting. It should also be noted that these meetings are secret — closed to the press and the public. Nevertheless, as in almost every situation, secrecy has its flaws — and statements made tend to leak out to interested individuals.

The above-mentioned friend contacted me after the bar association had announced its rating for the 1995 judicial races. As he had predicted, I was rated "Not Recommended for Re-election at this Time." I was told that two members of the bar association's board of trustees had put in an appearance at the meeting. My informant considered this to be highly unusual.

The two trustees were both women. One was a common pleas court judge; the other was an adjunct professor of law at the University of Cincinnati College of Law, who, according to this witness, appears to have attended to ensure a "Not Recommended" rating for me.

The witness stated that when this lady arrived, the meeting had been in progress for over a half-hour. As she sat down at the conference table, she asked, "Has Judge Mestemaker been discussed yet?" When told he had not, her reply was: "Good. Then I am in time."

Judge Mestemaker was still to be rated by the committee. Ernest McAdams gave the subcommittee's report, which concluded with the unanimous recommendation of the three "participating" members that the judge receive a rating of "Recommended." As soon as McAdams finished his report and recommendation, one Cincinnati Bar Association trustee spoke up as if by prearranged signal. She asked this question:

"Would someone please explain to me, just what exactly is this man's definition of domestic violence?"

The thrust of the criticism was against retaining a judge who had so little respect for women that he would order a woman to marry her abuser. The tone of the statements were so slanted that, as one lawyer later said, "*The Cincinnati Enquirer* reporter could have been given the assignment of rating Judge Mestemaker. The script was hers."

One lawyer on the committee, Barbara K. Barden, who had practiced law before me almost daily for over 12 years, stood and took on this assault as if she were the judge's champion. As it was related to me, Barden informed those detractors who did not personally know Judge Mestemaker, and had never appeared in the judge's courtroom in any capacity, that their comments were both misinformed and out of line.

Despite the fact that the members of my subcommittee who had attended meetings with me voted unanimously that I receive a "Recommended" rating, their vote and recommendation were ignored. Ernest McAdams, as chairman of my subcommittee, did not include Margaret Hilvert because she had never participated in the rating process, except for her comments at the general rating meeting. Further, despite the fact that of the 307 lawyers who had returned ballots — of which 59 rated me "Highly Recommended" and 103 rated me "Recommended," for a total of 162 favorable votes against 137 "Not Recommended" and eight not rated — the committee voted, after listening to the long and withering attack, that Mestemaker was to receive a "Not Recommended" rating.

This vote was significant for several reasons. First of all, it is extremely rare for the Judicial Rating Committee to ignore the poll of the bar association's members and the legal community and give an incumbent a rating other than the one reflected by the bar poll. In my case, the bar poll rated me as "Recommended" for re-election. Secondly, it is unheard of for the committee as a whole to refuse to accept the recommendation of a particular judge's subcommittee. In my case, my subcommittee, led by Ernest McAdams, rated me as "Recommended" and urged the committee as a whole to assign that rating to me.

Finally the board of trustees for the Cincinnati Bar Association decided to let stand the rating assigned to me by the Judicial Rating Committee as a whole. This was another slap in the face to the subcommittee assigned to assess my judicial skills and qualifications. One result of this final vote was the resignation from the Judicial Rating Committee by two of the four members of my subcommittee. One matter is certain. The local press, in particular the articles written about me in *The Cincinnati Enquirer*, formed the basis for the "Not Recommended at this Time" rating. Between the efforts of several reporters and a few members of the Cincinnati Bar Association, my judicial career was soon to be over. On October 16, I received a list of the names of all of the 50 members of the judicial candidate rating committee for 1995. A review of the members by me revealed that of the 50 members, 11 were lawyers who regularly appeared before me in my capacity as a judge. The remaining 39 were individuals who did not know me personally or who had never appeared before me. The analogy that I have employed on several occasions, when being asked how I felt about the "Not Recommended" rating received by me under these peculiar circumstances, has been that I felt the same as a student would who receives a passing score in a math test — but who nevertheless receives a failing grade because the teacher doesn't care for him and asks other teachers who don't know the student what grade they believe the student should receive.

While I received a "Not Recommended at this Time" rating, my opponent — who certainly was not as well known as me — received the advantage of being "Recommended" for election. My opponent's ability to advertise that he was rated "Recommended" by lawyers while I was rated "Not Recommended" proved to be a great assistance to him in his Election Day victory over me by 738 votes out of 27,986 votes cast in our race in Judicial District 7. After the bar association's ratings were made public, I received a letter from Ernest McAdams dated October 23 in which he wrote:

The subcommittee assigned to interview you unanimously recommended that you receive a "Recommended" rating. The entire Judicial Candidate Rating Committee then voted for you to receive a "Not Recommended" rating. Finally, as a result of that process, I resigned from the Judicial Candidate Rating Committee, putting my reasons for doing so in writing, chief among them being that lawyers who did not practice before you carried way too much influence.

Apparently the "Not Recommended at this Time" rating that I received caused such an uproar that on October 24 the president of the Cincinnati Bar Association, Terrence M. Donnellon; the bar association's executive director, John C. Norwine; and the president-elect of the bar association, Michael H. Neumark, met with me in my chambers at the Courthouse at their request. These representatives of the Cincinnati Bar Association, to a person, expressed their disappointment with the rating that I had received. Mr. Donnellon stated that he believed that the bad press that I had received since the Hancock-Sevier story broke on July 14 had unduly influenced a significant number of lawyers, and even more particularly lay persons, on the Judicial Rating Committee to vote against my receiving a favorable rating. He told me that the lawyers who had contact with me as a judge, a lawyer, and as a human being knew that I was a capable judge. I told this group that I now believed that it would be highly unlikely that I would be re-elected. I gave as my reason for this belief the constant barrage of bad press, the "Not Recommended" rating by the bar association and my belief that my opponent would use these negative factors to his advantage. Mr. Neumark told me that he believed that I was being overly pessimistic and cited the several examples in which incumbent judges who had received unfavorable ratings from the bar association had still been re-elected. This meeting concluded with my suggestion that changes be made in the rating process to allow only those individuals who actually knew and who had contact with a particular judge to rate that judge concerning his or her qualifications, and that everyone who voted to rate judges and judicial candidates on the bar poll ballot be required to sign their name to the ballot.

On October 30, I received a very kind letter from John C. Norwine, executive director of the Cincinnati Bar Association. The conclusion of that letter was as follows:

"It may seem a little bit hollow at this time, but I personally wish you the best in the election and I expect to see you on the bench for many years in the future. "

On October 31, 1995, the Cincinnati Bar Association published its 1995 judicial endorsements. The endorsements were mailed out to local businesses, corporations, political and social groups, as well as to lawyers. In order to gain as wide a distribution as possible, the endorsement flier was inserted in both local daily newspapers to ensure that readers would receive the bar association's advice as to which judicial candidates the public should support on Election Day. This flier claimed, among other matters, that the association's poll was the result of participation by more than 3,500 Cincinnati Bar Association members. As discussed earlier, the truth was that of the 3,500 lawyers claimed to have been polled about the 1995 judicial candidates, only 413 had voted — and only 307 of that number had rated me. To claim that the poll was based on 3,500 votes was clearly misleading and, in my opinion, beneath the Cincinnati Bar Association.

By the end of October, I had basically concluded that my judicial career would be over after the election on November 7. Despite this feeling, my wife and I continued to campaign right up to the last minute. I was very pleased that I won the absentee ballots by a margin of 57.5 percent, or 1,086 votes, to my opponent's 804 votes. However, this proved to be a short-lived victory because over the weekend before Election Day, Mr. Kenney's committee caused over 13,000 fliers attacking my handling of domestic violence cases to be mailed to all registered women voters in Judicial District 7. Even my wife and stepdaughter received one of these mailers. No effort was made by Kenney's campaign committee to mail these negative flyers to registered male voters in our district. They were aimed solely at women — with the intention to influence women voters. It worked. Most of the registered women voters who reside in Judicial District 7 received this mailer on Monday, November 6, 1995, the day before Election Day. We had no time left to respond to this advertisement.

This last-minute flier distributed by Mr. Kenney's campaign committee was designed for him by Scott Seidewitz, a young executive at Procter & Gamble and an active Democratic Party pollster. This flier capitalized on the criticism of me by *The Cincinnati Enquirer* and my handling of several domestic violence cases. The flier mailed out by my opponent proved to be the deciding factor in our election campaign. On Election Day, he received the votes of over 5,000 previously uncommitted female voters to win the vote 13,558 to 12,538 — a margin of 1,020 votes. Since I had won the absentee ballots cast by 282, the total vote difference between my opponent and myself was 738 votes — equivalent to 2.3 votes per precinct, or 51.3 percent to 48.7 percent. The most ironic part of this whole episode is that both my unfavorable rating by the bar association and my opponent's mailer were based on my alleged soft attitude toward men who abused their partners. The irony lies in the fact that during this entire period and up to my last day as a judge, January 3, 1996, I had more abusive men serving jail sentences for domestic violence than any other judge in Hamilton County.

The 1995 rating results probably caused more discord among local lawyers than any rating results in recent memory. By then, most of them were familiar with the reasons behind my "Not Recommended" rating. In the spring of 1996, Michael H. Neumark, incoming president of the Cincinnati Bar Association and the association's board of trustees, determined to address the problem and to decide whether the bar association should even continue to rate judges and judicial candidates — and, if so, how to take bias and partisan politics out of the rating process. The result of this latest attempt to cause the ratings to be fair was a judicial rating ballot for 1996 that, among other changes, required each voting member or lawyer to sign a certification in connection with the ballot that the individual voting was rating only those judges and judicial candidates whose work he or she has personally observed in the past four years. This would certainly have made a difference to me in 1995, in particular with regard to people who had never observed my work as a judge or as a lawyer.

The ballot adopted for 1996 also reduced the previous 10-category questionnaire to four categories, which I believe to be at least more relevant and to the point. They were:

1. Integrity, character, objectivity.
2. Legal experience, knowledge, ability.
3. Respect for and courtesy to litigants, counsel and witnesses.
4. Diligence

Also, gone are the former ratings of:

1. Highly Recommended
2. Recommended
3. Not Recommended at this Time
4. Not Rated

These four ratings have been replaced with a point system of from 1 to 10, with 10 as a perfect score.

The new system of rating incumbent judges and judicial candidates for the 1996 court of appeals and common pleas court races was approved by the Cincinnati Bar Association's board of trustees on July 29, 1996. The ballots were mailed out on August 21, 1996, to be completed and returned to the association by September 13, 1996. On October 1, 1996, the results of the new rating process were released and published the next day in both local newspapers.

With regard to the new rating system adopted for 1996, Cincinnati Bar Association President Michael Neumark was quoted as saying:

> There is a relatively narrow spread between the top and the bottom of all candidates and sitting judges. They are all above a certain level. One conclusion might be that they are all of relatively the same level.

> But I'm saying that's only one interpretation. Someone else may say it's very significant if there's a 1-point difference between two candidates. We haven't decided that.

If the Cincinnati Bar Association hasn't yet decided the significance of its rating system after all of these years of failed attempts to make the method of rating judges and judicial candidates objective, then the time has come for the Cincinnati Bar Association and the trial lawyers to get out of the business of rating judicial candidates and thereby trying to influence the voters who to elect to be their judges. The courts belong to the people — and not to those who profit from the justice system or who have a special agenda to promote.

Too many judges shape their decisions based on fear of the media, advocacy groups, and lawyers — in that order. Judges who make decisions based on who they will please or who they will offend are not doing justice.

An equally serious flaw in the rating process conducted among lawyers is the failure of the new rating system to address the practice of block voting. Block voting is a device employed by large law firms and other large groups of lawyers to guarantee that judges who are friendly toward their firm's type of practice and their clients receive the highest scores on the bar poll rating. Under this system of voting, one of the group's members is assigned the task of coordinating how the group rates the judges. "Friendly" judges and judicial candidates thereby receive good marks, while others deemed "less friendly" to the law firm's particular type of practice or clientele receive lower marks.

Generally unknown by the public or the media is the fact that with approximately 120 staff attorneys, the Hamilton County prosecutor's office is the second-largest law firm in Cincinnati. These 120 lawyers are members of the bar association and therefore eligible to vote in the judicial rating process. Block voting by this group can virtually determine whether a judge or judicial candidate receives a favorable rating or one that is unfavorable.

As Joseph Deters, who was the prosecuting attorney for Hamilton County in 1995, said in a June 13, 1999, interview with *The Cincinnati Enquirer* on this very subject:

"You're (the prosecutor's staff) the farm team for the judiciary in many respects. That office is looked upon by everybody as the political powerhouse of the Courthouse. You have highly educated, highly motivated, ambitious young lawyers who want to be involved in politics."

Deters went on in the article to explain how the prosecutor's office can and does affect judicial races.

"Mr. Allen (the current Hamilton County prosecuting attorney and Deters' handpicked successor) can say, 'This year we're going to work on judge so and so's campaign,' and that project becomes very doable when you have 115 lawyers on your side. Who else can do that in the city? Nobody."

These recent remarks by Joe Deters, now state treasurer of Ohio and himself a highly educated, highly motivated, ambitious young lawyer who is involved in politics, says it all. It explains why few, if any, sitting judges are willing to buck the county prosecutor's office.

During the late spring and summer of 1995, I had several high-profile disagreements with several assistant prosecutors assigned to the county prosecutor's Municipal Court Division concerning their policy of pursuing totally groundless cases, including domestic violence cases, even when they knew that no crime had been committed. I believed then, and still do, that this policy hurt a lot of innocent people. The proper role of the publicly funded prosecutor's office is to pursue justice, not to seek convictions at any price.

By the time the 1995 judicial rating process commenced, my "heretical" views were well known. I was probably the least-popular judge among assistant county prosecutors.

Hypothetically speaking, of course, if 120 assistant prosecutors did give me an unfavorable rating for re-election in 1995, that number represented 39 percent of the total of 307 lawyers who rated me. Since the total unfavorable ratings that I received numbered 137, the 120 represented by the prosecutor's staff — if, in fact, this occurred, represented 88 percent of the total of my unfavorable ratings. The impact of this group of block votes would certainly be devastating to any judge's chances for an overall "Recommended" rating.

One thing is certain: Not one member of the county prosecutor's municipal court staff offered to work on my campaign in 1995. Their help would certainly have been welcome, and it might have changed the outcome of the election.

Since my experience in 1995, I have been asked whether I believe that the system of lawyers rating the judges can ever be rendered objective. After 30 years experience, I now have to say that I do not believe that the system will ever be more than a popularity contest. There are many sincere and dedicated lawyers who try to be fair and objective when it comes to rating judges. The problem is that they are outnumbered by those who vote with their emotions and their self-interest in mind. In the final analysis, only the voters should rate judges. They are the group to whom the courts are responsible and for whom justice is intended.

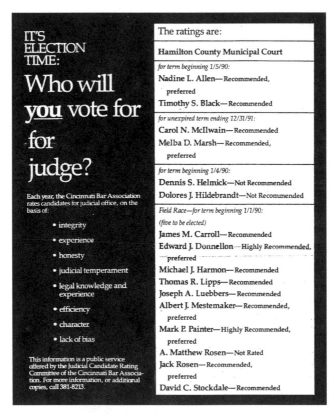

Albert J. Mestemaker had consistently received positive recommendations from the Cincinnati Bar Association, as evidenced by this rating sheet from the 1989 election.

PART FOUR

END OF AN ERA

CHAPTER 18

THUMBS UP OR THUMBS DOWN

Once a gladiator bested his opponent on the floor of the Coliseum in Rome, the audience would decide the fate of the vanquished. If he had displayed courage and tenacity and had fought well, he was likely to be the recipient of the "thumbs up" signal — which meant that his life would be spared. On the other hand, if those in the stands felt that he had fought poorly and without valor, he would receive "thumbs down" — and the victorious gladiator was required to deliver a deathblow.

In reality, life is much like a gladiator fight. We win some, and we lose some. When we do lose, we hope to be afforded the opportunity to snap back. But in politics, it has long been an axiom that there are no second chances. In politics, when one loses, the game is over. So, when voters signal "thumbs down," the political life of the vanquished is generally not spared.

When a *Cincinnati Enquirer* reporter wrote that I had ordered a domestic violence victim to marry her abuser, I was dumbfounded not only by the distorted reporting but also by the immediate storm of controversy that erupted around me — which then led to more accusations and, in turn, more controversy. Suddenly, every pronouncement that I had ever made from the bench that criticized individual lifestyle choices was fodder for another media report and feedback from every advocacy organization in existence.

I was born in 1937. Every draft-age male member of my family had gone off to serve our country in World War II. (Grandfather's attempt to re-up was rejected, so he volunteered as an air raid warden.) I had attended Catholic schools for 16 years. I was taught that it was wrong for two adults to live together and have children without the kind of commitment inherent in the sacrament of matrimony. I had been taught that sexual intercourse between members of the same sex was a sin. I had been raised to believe that it was a sin to lie or cheat or be disrespectful toward others. So when individuals appeared before me who had cheated the welfare system, stolen from their employer or their neighbor, or punched a parent, a teacher or a police officer, my sense of outrage became aroused.

I was not able to change the way that I was raised. Nor could I separate my job as a judge from my personal code of morality and what was right or what was wrong. I had been raised in a home in which there was a very thin line that separated right from wrong, or good from evil. There was absolutely nothing ambivalent about the discipline imposed on my sister, my brother or myself when we broke the rules.

At the time that it was reported, although not quite accurately, that I had ordered Yvonne Seiver to marry her abuser, Scott Hancock, the president of the Cincinnati Chapter of the National Organization for Women referred to me in an *Enquirer* article as a "Neanderthal" and said that I just didn't "get it." I was surprised by her remarks, but then I realized that when she made them, she was unaware that both Yvonne and Scott had told me in open court that they loved each other — and that they wanted to get married and give their daughter, Lindsey, a stable home. She was unaware that they had told me that they were saving money to get married and that they had pleaded with me not to make them stay away from each other.

But, by the end of the month of July 1995, when the criticism was at its peak, I was beginning to question myself whether my ideals of what was good behavior and bad behavior were any longer relevant. Perhaps, I thought, my critics — and there were many — were correct. Perhaps I was an anachronism in this so-called modern era. I recalled that one local talk show host asked her listeners: "Who does this judge think he is, trying to impose his 1950s morals on the rest of us?"

Or perhaps Cliff Radel of the *Enquirer* was correct when he wrote in his metro column: It's time to "hang this judge." Voters should "sentence him to an early retirement this fall." I never did understand how I could enjoy early retirement if I was hanged first, as Radel suggested. Or maybe he felt that I should be punished twice.

Sometime around 3:30 a.m. on Wednesday, August 2, 1995, I sat up in bed — soaking wet and gasping for air. I had just dreamed that a M48A1 Patton Main Battle Tank, the model I had been commander of in 1959, '60 and '61, had rolled across my body, crushing my chest. I had gotten out of bed, thrown up in my bathroom, taken an aspirin, smoked a cigarette with a glass of orange juice and returned to bed. There I lay, with pain radiating into my left shoulder and arm. This occurred in the midst of the storm of protest over my handling of the Hancock-Sevier, Ellery and Gambrell cases. I was physically unable to go to the Courthouse on August 2. I did return to my judicial duties on August 3, not knowing that I had suffered my first heart attack.

On August 3, I had lunch with my close friend Doctor Set Shahbabian, one of the most respected neurosurgeons in the Midwest. He was very concerned about the media assault on me and he wanted to let me know that he and his wife, Sheila, were in my corner. He also wanted me to make an appointment to have a physical exam and an EKG, because he told me that he did not like my skin tone, which he described as being on the gray side. I purposely refrained from telling him about my dream. I didn't want Judy to learn about it from him or anyone else.

Fortunately, by the third week in August, the media had found another story to follow, the O.J. Simpson murder trial, which kept all of the media outlets mesmerized with its daily shocking or bizarre revelations and the goal of Simpson's attorneys to portray the frame-up that they alleged was being orchestrated against their client by the Los Angeles police and in particular, Detectives Mark Furman, Tom Lang and my friend and acquaintance, Phil Vannatter. Due to this coverage, for a least a few weeks, I was not news. This enabled me to return to presiding over an orderly and sane courtroom. But it would not remain quiet for long.

On October 10, the Cincinnati Bar Association announced its ratings and recommendations for the 1995 judicial races. My opponent was rated as "Recommended." I was rated "Not Recommended at this Time." As a close friend who was a member of the judicial rating committee said to me, "They could have just as well allowed the *Enquirer* reporter to assign you your rating. It would have been the same, and it would have saved a hell of a lot of argument."

The bar association's ratings were released exactly one week to the day after O.J. Simpson had been found not guilty of the murder of his ex-wife, Nicole Brown and her friend Ron Goldman, in what some have described as the most brutal case of domestic violence in the 20th century.

Everyone was discussing domestic violence. In one week, this topic had become the single-most important issue in the 1995 judicial elections — not only in Cincinnati, but everywhere in the nation. This was no time to be accused of being soft on domestic abusers. Suddenly, I was a news item once again. Now I had become the poster child for despised judges. My opponent was to use this turn of events to his ultimate election advantage.

When the absentee ballots were tabulated, I had received 1,086 votes to my opponent's 804. I had won this part of the election by a percentage margin of 58 to 42. This lead was to be short lived. For on Monday, November 6, the day before the general election, 13,000 women voters in my judicial district received a single-sheet mailer, which contained several excerpts from the *Enquirer* articles written about me by Kristin Delguzzi on the subject of domestic violence. The flier then called for a change, asserting that my opponent believed that domestic violence should be treated as a serious offense — implying that I did not treat it as such.

On November 7, some 26,096 registered voters cast their ballots in the 7th Judicial District. Of these voters, 14,091 were women. This represented 54 percent of the Election Day vote. Some 13,558 voters chose my opponent. And 12,538 indicated their desire that I be retained. The margin of victory for my opponent was 51 percent to my 49 percent that day. He won the election by 738 out of 27,986 votes cast. Was it merely a coincidence that my opponent's mailer was sent to 13,000 women on November 6 and he received 13,558 votes the next day?

On November 7, 1995, I was fired from a job for the first time in my life. I had held several part-time jobs when I was a student. I had served in the Army. I had worked as a federal treasury agent before and while attending evening law school. After graduation and admission to practice law in Ohio in October 1966, I was appointed an assistant Hamilton County prosecuting attorney in the Criminal Division, a position I held for over five years. Between 1971 and 1981, I was a partner in the labor law firm of Smith and Latimer (later Latimer and Swing) as chief civil and criminal trial lawyer. During that same period, I was hired by my alma mater, Chase College of Law, where I taught criminal law and criminal procedure. Also in 1974, I was hired by Anderson Publishing Company as the co-author of that publisher's *Ohio Criminal Practice and Procedure* manual, which is now in its fifth edition and a 26-year working relationship that I value highly.

In more than 15 years as a practicing attorney and 14 years as a judge,

I had never had a complaint filed against me either with the Ohio Supreme Court or the Cincinnati Bar Association by a client, a lawyer, a judge or a private citizen. Now, I was the accused in a disciplinary complaint that had been filed against me with the Office of Disciplinary Counsel for the Ohio Supreme Court by an attorney from Columbus, Ohio, named Joseph L. Maas, whom I had never heard of or met. He had filed a complaint and requested an investigation of my remarks in the Edna Ellery matter as well as the so called "marriage orders." He had filed his complaint on July 25, 1995, with the Ohio Supreme Court's Office of Disciplinary Council in his capacity as director of the Ohio Commission on Spanish Speaking Affairs, a position to which he had been appointed by Ohio's governor.

With regard to the allegation that I did not treat domestic violence as a serious offense, the record says otherwise. As of December 31, 1995, the last month for which I received a report from Sheriff Simon L. Leis Jr. concerning the number of prisoners in the Hamilton County Justice Center who had been sentenced to jail by me, there were 52 individuals in jail — of whom 11 were men who had been convicted of domestic violence. This represented more individuals jailed by me for domestic violence than any other municipal court judge then on the bench.

My tough stance on domestic violence and my support of victims of this particular crime was continuously recognized by Ann MacDonald, executive director of Women Helping Women, who, on several occasions, wrote to me, thanking me for my support of her agency's goals.

Nevertheless, the voters of Judicial District 7, influenced by a half-dozen print and electronic media reporters and further persuaded by my opponent's last minute flier, were of a mind to terminate my judicial service after nearly 15 years.

There was no reason to suspect that the voters had turned me out over the way that I ruled in other criminal cases or in serious traffic cases such as vehicular homicide or DUI's. Nor were the voters concerned about my disposition of the numerous civil cases filed in our court. Judges seldom receive publicity about their handling of civil matters unless the case is extremely high profile, such as was Judge Norbert Nadel's handling of the Pete Rose baseball banishment case in 1989. Normally, the public pays little, if any, attention to civil cases or trials. By December 1995, I had reduced my civil caseload to 41 pending cases. No. I was quite simply let go because the voters of Judicial District 7 had been led to believe that I was some kind of a loose cannon who could not be trusted to handle domestic violence matters. This was to become my legacy.

As of January 3, 1996, my last day in office, I had been a judge for 14 years, nine months and 18 days — and had heard and decided 26,789 cases. I had been reversed on appeal in 17 of those cases — less than one hundredth of a percentage point. I was proud of this accomplishment.

I was not the only judge to be taken on by the media for controversial decisions. The editorial page editor for *The Cincinnati Post*, a daily afternoon newspaper, had become an accomplished judge basher by 1995. In 1991, he jumped on my case on the editorial page for clearing my courtroom of spectators after a woman with an unruly child had called my bailiff, Ron Flammer, a mother-fucker when, for the fourth time in a half-hour, he had requested that she take the child out of the room.

In 1994 the same writers tore into Judge Mike Allen when he set $100,000 in bonds on Dr. Stanley Broadnax, M.D., the ex-Cincinnati Health Commissioner who had been arrested on four charges of selling cocaine from his house. The *Post* felt this amount of bond for a physician was unreasonably high.

In 1994, the *Post* blasted Municipal Court Judge Leslie Isaiah Gaines Jr. because he had released Robert Jones from jail after he had been locked up several days on a domestic violence charge, but had failed to foresee that Jones would, immediately upon his release, go to his common-law wife's apartment and beat her into a permanent coma. According to the *Post*'s editorial page writer, Gaines was supposed to know that placing Jones on probation and ordering him to stay away form Christina Best would not work. He was supposed to know, according to the *Post*, that Jones had previously abused Ms. Best in Philadelphia — where they lived together with all of their children prior to her moving to Cincinnati to get away from him. Even though Philadelphia authorities had failed to communicate the history of prior abuse in their city to authorities in Cincinnati, Judge Gaines was supposed to know what Jones would do if the judge released him from custody.

Unfortunately, no judge is given a crystal ball to gaze into when he becomes a jurist. Every judge lives in constant fear that a mistake in judgment may cost someone their life or lead to serious injury or further crime. In each instance when I granted a motion for the restoration of even limited driving privileges on behalf of some person who had been convicted of an offense of driving under the influence of alcohol, I was always concerned that the individual, if granted some driving privileges, might drink again, drive, have an accident and cost some person their life and property. I believed, knowing the attitude of our local print media, that the judge more than likely was going to be held as responsible if not more responsible than the offender. The same holds true for police officers who give someone a break.

It is easy to play the role of Monday morning quarterback and to second-guess the rationale behind any judicial decision. The law is not an exact science. Dealing with people is not an exact science. Often, we are called upon to accept someone's word that they will do or refrain from doing some act, only to learn that they have lied in an effort to obtain leniency from the court — as Richard Gambrell and Patricia Wilson did when they told me that they already had a wedding date set for June 30, 1995.

When I returned to the Courthouse on Monday, November 13, from a trip to Johnson County, Wyoming, I was a lame-duck judge. I had 52 days remaining before my term ended. It was very quiet around my courtroom. The media didn't find me as interesting now that the election had been decided. My friends in the Courthouse, our staff, other office holders and my numerous lawyer friends were very supportive. They expressed disappointment that I would be leaving soon and assured me that they were in my corner. It was comforting to know that the people who worked around me every day still had confidence in my ability and could express their feelings about my impending departure.

My first day back was a bear. The assignment commissioner had put 52 criminal and traffic cases on my docket including a DUI jury trial. It was not until 3 p.m. that we were able to send Ron Flammer down to the jury commissioner's office to collect a panel of prospective jurors to start the DUI case.

On November 20, I was supposed to preside over what I anticipated might be my last criminal jury trial. It was a domestic violence case in which the defendant was a woman who was accused of abusing her boyfriend. I thought to myself, what an irony this was, that my last jury trial as a judge might not only be a domestic violence criminal case but one in which the alleged victim was a man and his abuser was a woman. Well, the case never teed up. The victim didn't bother to come to court, and the prosecutor asked me to dismiss the case. I thought as I signed the dismissal, "Where is Kristen Delguzzi at a time like this?"

December was not much better than November. On December 10, my wife's 48-year-old sister, the family health nut and aerobics teacher, died suddenly of a massive cerebral aneurysm. The day after we buried Donna, I learned from Doctor Charles Abbottsmith at Christ Hospital that

I had suffered a heart attack, probably on August 2, and that the left ventricle of my heart had incurred significant damage. Despite the cardiologist's concern and caution, I told him that I intended to finish my term of office, which, by then, was down to 20 days.

The day after Christmas, my chest pains were so bad that Doctor Abbottsmith scheduled me for an angiogram, which he performed at Christ Hospital on December 27. The results of the test confirmed that I had suffered a heart attack and, in addition, had three blocked arteries, two being 80 percent or higher and the third one 60 percent. The physician feared that I could have a second and more serious heart attack at any moment. Again, I informed him that I intended to finish my term. I told him not to expect to see me until after January 4, 1996.

As usual, we spent New Year's Eve with our close friends Set and Sheila Shahbabian. On New Year's Day, I completed the last of the local swearing-in ceremonies that, for me, had become an annual event. On that day, I administered the oaths of office first to the mayor and the newly elected council members for the village of Cleves and then North Bend. Next, I went to the Township Hall and swore in as trustee Jack Rininger, a great old friend who is a Pearl Harbor survivor, and the Miami Township clerk, Rebecca Prem Groppe, the daughter of Calvin W. Prem, my old mentor in the prosecutor's office.

At noon, I drove with Judy to the Cheviot City Hall, where I observed the best installation of the day. My son, Mike, had been elected a councilman in Cheviot. I got to see my son sworn in to his first term in elective office. It was a truly a proud moment for me.

On January 2, 1996, I heard 57 cases. On January 3, I heard 53 cases. On each of these two days, many lawyers stopped by and asked permission to approach the bench to shake my hand and say "Goodbye."

For January 4, I planned to finish up my packing after a light trial docket and make the rounds to see the Courthouse regulars who were so important to the operation of the court system. But this never came to pass. My desire to finish out my term was cut short by one day. Unfortunately, everything caught up with me on the afternoon of the 3rd and the result was an early ride to the operating room at Christ Hospital on the 4th. Thanks to the skill of Doctor Donald Mitts, thoracic surgeon, I survived the triple bypass procedure that he claimed was necessary to keep me alive. I did not wake up until around 4 o'clock that afternoon. Ron Flammer and my son, Mike, had stayed with Judy while I was in surgery. My first visitors while I was still in Intensive Care were Set and Sheila

Shahbabian. I had a whole mouthful of tubes and couldn't talk. I also felt as though I had been run down by a truck.

Several days after my open-heart surgery, I was given a copy of an *Enquirer* article that Kristen Delguzzi had written on January 4, in which she reported the unexpected resignation of my colleague, Judge Leslie Isaiah Gaines, and how much his judicial service would be missed. As I read her article, I couldn't help think, "No one in this town's media has written that I'll be missed."

I was sent home on January 9 and by mid-February I was beginning to feel like I wanted to re-engage in something more useful than watching CNN news and going to cardiac rehab to work out three afternoons a week. I had just received a phone call from Dee Dunn of Anderson Publishing Company asking me whether I would be able to continue as co-author of *Anderson's Ohio Criminal Practice and Procedure* handbook. Of course, my answer was "Yes." Remaining part of Anderson's writing team, along with Judge Robert Gorman of the court of appeals; James Perry, noted criminal trial lawyer; and Professor Glen Weissenberger of the University of Cincinnati Law School was extremely important to my mental well-being.

Since I had also taught, first criminal law and then criminal procedure at my alma mater, the Salmon P. Chase College of Law (now affiliated with Northern Kentucky University) from 1971 to 1979, I decided to pursue at least a part-time teaching position with the law school. I contacted my longtime friend and teacher W. Jack Grosse, who had also served at several different times as the dean of the law school. Jack proceeded on my behalf to inquire as to the possibility of my rejoining the teaching faculty of the school. Since I had served in the past as an associate adjunct professor of law, I thought that I might be a good candidate for a teaching position. And, after all, I had also been published. Unfortunately, the attitude toward part-time teaching staff had changed since 1978, and the new dean of the law school had decided that the school's image would be better enhanced if all of the professors were graduates of more widely known institutions of legal education. Thus my efforts to return to a classroom at a law school came to naught.

Then near the end of February I received a call from R. Barry Andrews. Barry is the founder and chief executive officer of the Police Training Institute, a nonprofit corporation that has been certified by the Ohio attorney general as an accredited police training facility. I had known Barry for over 20 years. I had been teaching three courses for him since 1991. Now, Barry wanted me to teach six different subjects at the school. He also requested that I consider developing an eight-hour class dealing with the subject of civil rights suits involving police officers, and how a police officer should prepare to defend this kind of civil action. Barry and I also discussed a subject that we had considered for several years, which was the publication of a search warrant manual.

So it was that after several meetings with Dee Dunn and John Mason, president of Anderson Publishing Company, that I signed a contract to author *The Ohio Search Warrant Manual*, which was released by Anderson on July 9, 1997, and which is now in its fourth edition. This manual — which is designed for use by police officers, lawyers and judges — deals with the subjects of writing legally effective search warrants, orders for electronic surveillance and forfeiture proceedings. It has sold over a thousand copies thus far.

In November 1996, Shirley Smith, longtime friend and mayor of the village of North Bend, the smallest village in Hamilton County, approached me with the request that I agree to be appointed village law director. The lawyer who had held this position was planning to step down, and Mayor Smith wanted me to accept the job.

Since the village had disbanded its police department and dispensed with mayor's court, I would not be required to prosecute misdemeanor offenses committed in the village. My role would be strictly confined to legal advice and drafting ordinances, resolutions and an occasional letter. I accepted Shirley's offer, and in January 1997 was appointed village law director for a small annual retainer — plus $100 per month for attending the monthly council meeting. I am currently in my fourth year as village law director and enjoying the position immensely.

In April 1997, I was reprimanded by the Ohio Supreme Court for ordering couples to marry as part of court-imposed probation and for insulting Edna Ellery. I had pled no contest to these accusations in 1996 because I had made those orders and had certainly made an offensive remark to Edna Ellery. In my mind, to have denied that I made the orders or the statements would be dishonest as well as dishonorable. My "no contest" plea was reviewed, and a recommendation was made by the Commissioners on Grievances and Discipline that I receive a public reprimand. I was, at the same time, humbled and overwhelmed by the outpouring of support represented by more than 100 letters presented to the Ohio Supreme Court on my behalf from fellow jurists, lawyers, friends, acquaintances and even from my former Army commander. The court, in its ultimate ruling, even made mention of these letters. I am eternally grateful to these individuals for their efforts and kind words on my behalf.

Much to Judy's dismay, I was still not busy enough to suit my energies. She believed that I was driven. Nevertheless, I ran for and was elected to parish council for St. Joseph Roman Catholic Church in North Bend. At this time, I am in my fourth and final year as a member of parish council and the president of council. Our pastor, the Reverend Harry Gerdes, and I are working on the future needs of the parish, which may well include a new church — since the parish is continuing to grow as more new families move into our area.

North Bend is a historic Ohio River community. The village was established in 1789 by Judge John Cleves Symmes of New Jersey, who had negoiated the purchase of 1 million acres of land in southwestern Ohio from the federal government. This land purchase became known as the Miami Purchase. Today, it includes Cincinnati and all of Hamilton County. Judge Symmes' daughter Anna married a young Army captain in 1795, a fellow named William Henry Harrison. It was from North Bend that Harrison was elected ninth president of the United States in November 1840, becoming Ohio's first president. Unfortunately, Harrison, then the oldest man elected president and destined to remain such until Ronald Reagan was elected in 1980, died on April 4, 1841, after only 30 days in the White House. On July 14, 1841, the president, a former major general in the United States Army, was interred in a newly constructed mausoleum overlooking the Ohio River at North Bend.

In the early part of the 20th century, the Harrison family deeded the mausoleum and surrounding park-like land to the state of Ohio. The site is maintained by the Ohio Historical Society. In 1922, a handsome monument was constructed above and around the former president's resting place. Unfortunately, thereafter this significant historic place was allowed to deteriorate badly — so that by the early 1990s the roof of the mausoleum leaked and the grounds were overgrown and neglected.

In 1992, a small group of local residents, of which I had become a member, formed the Harrison-Symmes Memorial Foundation Inc., a non-profit corporation that had as its goal the restoration of the Harrison family tomb and monument as well as the Congress Green Pioneer Cemetery located across the road from the monument.

The result of the efforts of our foundation included a grant by the Ohio General Assembly to the Ohio Historical Society of $318,000 in 1996 to completely renovate and restore the mausoleum, the monument and the cemetery. At the present time, we are trying to create a museum to house items of local history — much of which deals with the Harrison and Symmes families, all very relevant to the early days and the settlement of this part of Ohio, Northern Kentucky and eastern Indiana.

In order to keep in touch with the local legal community, I have worked with John Norwine, the executive director of the Cincinnati Bar Association, to conduct several continuing legal education seminars for local attorneys in the area of criminal law. In September 1998, I presented a seminar on search warrants for a group of approximately 75 lawyers and judges. The bar association had this seminar videotaped so that it can be shown to lawyers throughout the state of Ohio as part of the Arm Chair C.L.E. series approved by the Ohio Supreme Court. At the present time, I am putting the finishing touches on a criminal practice and procedure seminar for the bar association, which I will present along with Judge Robert Gorman and Jim Perry.

In April 1993, Judy and I purchased 400 acres of rolling prairie in north central Wyoming, on the eastern slope of the Big Horn Mountains. We both love the West and had spent many vacation days in that part of Wyoming. When the Pradere Ranch of 28,000 acres was broken up into 40-acre tracts, we purchased 10 tracts. I only wish that we could have purchased more of the land. The acreage, which we currently lease to a local rancher, Ellis Elsom, for grazing livestock, has a spectacular view of the Big Horn Mountains to the west. The summits of the mountains are snow-capped almost the entire year. We have nine-tenths of a mile of road frontage on a country road, which was once the route of the old Bozeman Trail.

At least twice each year, Judy and I travel the 1,400 miles to visit the rolling prairie and walk this grassland, looking for bison bones and arrow-heads. Occasionally, we also find an old teepee ring — a ring of small stones used by the Sioux and Cheyenne, who inhabited this region, to hold down the bottom of their tepees when they were following the buffalo herds during their annual migrations.

Our place has only one tree. It is a huge cottonwood that some have said is at least 300 years old. It is in a depression next to a hillside where we have found bleached-out bison bones. I like to look at the old tree, which has five main trunks, and envision a cottonwood seed being carried in caked mud stuck in a cloven buffalo hoof until it fell out in this depression and commenced a long life, which has renewed itself each year to the present time. This old tree is the annual home to a pair of nesting hawks, who raise a new brood of chicks each year and who circle high overhead screeching their high-pitched cry whenever their tree is approached by a human intruder during nesting season.

In 1997, we had a 9,000-cubic-yard earthen dam built across a natural drainage area called Sand Run Draw. Within three months, a nine-acre lake had developed behind the new dam. The lake has become home for frogs, crickets, trout, ducks, geese and even a pair of sand hill cranes. We plan in the near future to start a home on a plateau above the lake, facing the mountains.

I remember certain days on the bench when the aggravation level got close to my limit thinking to myself that, "All I ever really wanted to be was a cowboy." Well, maybe that thought will come true one of these days very soon.

I am a former cigarette smoker who still longs occasionally for a cigarette. Similarity there are times when I miss the arena of the courtroom and the busy world of the Courthouse. But times have changed a great deal. I am now old enough and hopefully wise enough to accept the fact that neither my heart nor my nerves could deal with the stress of trial work on a regular basis, and I have no real desire to do real estate or probate work. I liken my feeling about trial work to being a professional baseball pitcher. There are only so many pitches in a pitcher's arm, just as I believe that there are only so many jury trials in a trial lawyer's career. It all makes me recall the American Express commercial when the older archeologist says that he used to be a lawyer. I used to be a lawyer. Then I used to a judge. The one aspect of the law that I still love is the teaching part. I truly enjoy sharing my experiences with others, who, hopefully, will profit, grow wise and not commit my mistakes. That can be considered my final goal in the field of law.

The Posteal Laskey trial seems to have occurred a long time ago now. Posteal is no longer news. Neither am I. Although, he will no doubt become news once again — when he next becomes eligible for parole consideration, which will probably be in 2002. But for me, by then I will no doubt be repairing fences in Johnson County, Wyoming, looking at those mountains and thinking about the past and Martin Luther's declaration: "There I stood. What else could I do?"

If you <u>don't</u> like what you've heard about
                                    Judge Albert Mestemaker . . .

Judge Mestemaker gives "Addyston man 9 months to marry the woman he punched in the mouth" -- *Cincinnati Enquirer* 7/15/95

Judge Mestemaker "<u>Not Recommended</u> at this time" -- *Cincinnati Bar Association*

On June 2, Mestemaker presided over a domestic violence case of a man who abused his wife of 17 years. He said the man was "legally, technically guilty..." But then, the judge said he had no intention of putting the man in jail and found him not guilty. -- *The Cincinnati Enquirer*, 7/20/95

"Life is too short . . . (They) can assign these domestic violence cases to somebody else." - Judge Mestemaker quoted in *The Cincinnati Enquirer* 7/21/95

. . . then you might like to hear about <u>Jim Kenney</u>

√ Lawyer in private practice for 20 years
√ <u>Recommended</u> by the Cinti. Bar Assn.

√ Husband and father of three

√ Volunteer for St. William School and St. Rita's School for the Deaf
√ Believes domestic violence should be treated as a serious offense

On Nov. 7, you can help make a change. Please vote <u>Jim Kenney</u> for District 7 Municipal Court Judge.

Jim Kenney for Judge
It's Time for a Change

"Kenney for Judge" fliers were received by women voters in the judicial district in the Saturday mail before the Tuesday election. Negative campaign tactics, such as Mestemaker's opponent employed, are much more effective in a two-person race than in a field race.

THE CINCINNATI ENQUIRER   THURSDAY, NOVEMBER 16, 1995.. **A17**

Proud wife defends judge's reputation

TO THE EDITOR: My husband and I were out of town before the recent election, and upon returning to Hamilton County, I was deeply saddened to find a mailer attacking my husband, Judge Albert Mestemaker (Hamilton County Municipal Court). The mailer was sent to our home by judicial candidate James Patrick Kenney. To put it simply, I should vote for him because of *The Enquirer's* attack on my husband and not because of Kenney's qualifications.

My husband is not and has never been soft on domestic violence offenders. A young, ambitious reporter took certain facts and skillfully wrote a story, not the whole story, but a story that would be read and believed by certain people because they read it in *The Enquirer.*

A judge cannot defend himself against the press's ink or a young journalist's belief that she has righted a wrong. I can tell you, as Albert Mestemaker's wife, that domestic violence is a behavior he abhors and he has dealt fairly with it in his courtroom.

I am proud of my husband. He has served this county well and his legal

READERS' VIEWS

knowledge shall be sorely missed. Unlike his opponent's, my husband's campaign was based on his qualifications — he never attacked Kenney. I am disappointed that Kenney felt it necessary to conduct himself in a manner that is unbecoming to a member of the legal profession and the judiciary.

JUDY MESTEMAKER
North Bend

Editor's note: *Kenney defeated Mestemaker for the seat.*

Letter to editor from Judy Mestemaker, Cincinnati Enquirer.

Mike Mestemaker compared book notes with friend Vincent T. Bugliosi, the famed California trial lawyer and author, at a criminal law seminar in Hamilton County in 1998.

Mike enjoys legal writing and teaching, community service, and spending time with old friends and with his wife, Judy, and their children—Sara Enneking, daughter-in-law Lisa Mestemaker and Mike Mestemaker. Daughter Tonya lives in Chicago.

In 1993, the Mestemakers purchased a ranch in Wyoming where they are building a second home. Judy and Mike delight in their almost treeless but beloved "goddamitgotohellandstarvetodeath ranch."

Judy and Mike at home.

Judy Mestemaker during South Dakota bison hunt, January 1988.

Judy Mestemaker in Wyoming high prairie country, October 1996.

Judge Mestemaker and his baliff, Ron Flammer, enjoy a moment together at the 50th anniversary party of Ron and his wife, which coincidentally was the Judge's birthday.

E5 Sergeant Mestemaker on manuvers, United States Army, 1960.

Judge Albert J. Mestemaker at veterans ceremony honoring Pearl Harbor veterans

I have always believed that we are the sum total of our genetics, our upbringing and our life experiences. There are many friends and acquaintances who have influenced my professional life, and perhaps without knowing it, have contributed in a measurable way to this book. They are acknowledged here in tribute and in gratitude for their interest in me and their great friendship.

R. Barry Andrews
Cliff Bell
Anthony W. Brunsman II
Vincent T. Bugliosi
Honorable Joseph T. Deters
Sara J. Enneking
Ron and Dot Flammer
Jeff Garner
Honorable Frank M. Gusweiler
Bill and Gloria Kettler
Leonard Kirchner
Harold Latimer
Honorable Joseph Luebbers
Honorable William A. Mathews
Honorable William R. Matthews
Edward A. and Jean McCafferty
Albert V. Mestemaker
Gerald L. Mestemaker
Michael Mestemaker
Tonya Mestemaker
Donald G. Montfort
Honorable Mark P. Painter
Sue Ann Painter
Calvin W. and Lee Prem
Honorable Melvin A. Rueger
Honorable Raymond E. Shannon
Elizabeth Siegert
Lamprose "Blackie" Touris
Philip Vannatter
Carl W. Vollman
Honorable John A. West